Biblical Interpretation
The Meanings of Scripture – Past and Present

Biblical Interpretation

The Meanings of Scripture – Past and Present

Edited by John M. Court

T & T CLARK INTERNATIONAL
A Continuum imprint
LONDON • NEW YORK

CONTENTS

Abbreviations ix

List of Contributors xi

INTRODUCTION
John M. Court 1

NOT (JUST) THE PLAIN MEANING:
ORIGEN AND ALLEGORICAL INTERPRETATION
John M. Court 10

CHRISTIAN PILGRIMAGE: STRUCTURES OF DEVOTION/
STRICTURES OF OBEDIENCE
Glen Bowman 22

THE PREACHER WITH A GOLDEN TONGUE: JOHN CHRYSOSTOM
John M. Court 41

INTERPRETING SCRIPTURE FOR THE LOVE OF GOD:
HUGH OF ST VICTOR ON READING AND THE SELF
Jeremy Worthen 54

A MENDICANT PERSPECTIVE: SAINT BONAVENTURE
OF BAGNOREGIO
Michael Robson 71

THE WHOLE BIBLE IN ENGLISH
David Daniell 88

GEORGE HERBERT: PRIEST, PASTOR, POET
Tina Leeke 103

JOHN TOLAND: *CHRISTIANITY NOT MYSTERIOUS*
  Kevin Loughton   125

THE THEISM OF JEAN-JACQUES ROUSSEAU:
'THE CREED OF A CURATE OF SAVOY'
  Philip Robinson   140

DIVINE RIGHT THEORY AND ITS CRITICS
IN EIGHTEENTH-CENTURY ENGLAND
  Grayson Ditchfield   156

BLAKE AND THE BIBLE:
BIBLICAL EXEGESIS IN THE WORK OF WILLIAM BLAKE
  Christopher Rowland   168

THE BIBLE IN THE LIFE AND WRITING OF JAMES HOGG,
THE ETTRICK SHEPHERD
  Alison Jack   185

THE RISE OF PREMILLENNIAL DISPENSATIONALISM AS
THE CORNERSTONE OF AMERICAN FUNDAMENTALISM
  Jennifer Martin   202

VICTORIAN PREACHERS AND THE NEW BIBLICAL CRITICISM
  T. Mervyn Willshaw   210

'WE ARE TIED TO THESE TEXTS':
SCRIPTURE IN THE WORK OF KARL BARTH
  Richard Arrandale   233

BIBLICAL STRUCTURALISM AND THE COMPUTER
  Ian Mitchell Lambert   250

RAINBOW HERMENEUTICS AND ST PAUL'S LETTER
TO THE GALATIANS
  G. Daan Cloete   268

THE EPIPHANY OF THE DOVE: HEALING AND PROPHECY IN
MARK'S GOSPEL (NEW APPROACHES IN WOMEN'S STUDIES)
  Julie Hopkins   284

PRAGMATISM, POSTMODERNISM AND THE BIBLE AS A
MEANINGFUL PUBLIC RESOURCE IN A PLURALISTIC AGE
    Philip Knight   310

Index of References   326
Index of Authors   331

ABBREVIATIONS

AFH	*Archivum Franciscanum Historicum*
ANCL	*Ante-Nicene Christian Library* (Edinburgh from 1864)
BibInt	*Biblical Interpretation: A Journal of Contemporary Approaches*
CD	Karl Barth, *Church Dogmatics*
DSSBOO	*Doctoris Seraphici S.Bonaventurae opera omnia*, Quaracchi, Florence, in ten volumes, 1882-1902.
EETS	Early English Text Society (Oxford: Oxford University Press, 1876/1935)
HTR	*Harvard Theological Review*
HUT	*Hermeneutische Untersuchungen zur Theologie* (Tübingen: Mohr Siebeck)
IJED	Journal of Education
JRH	*Journal of Religious History*
JTS	*Journal of Theological Studies*
Neot	*Neotestamentica*
PG	J.-P. Migne (ed.), *Patrologia cursus completa... Series graeca* (166 vols.; Paris: Petit-Montrouge, 1857–83)
PL	J.-P. Migne (ed.), *Patrologia cursus completus Series prima [latina]* (221 vols.; Paris: J.-P. Migne, 1844–65)
SBLDS	SBL Dissertation Series
TynBul	*Tyndale Bulletin*
TZ	*Theologische Zeitschrift*
VT	*Vetus Testamentum*

LIST OF CONTRIBUTORS

John M. Court was Senior Lecturer and Chairman of Theology and Religious Studies at the University of Kent at Canterbury; he is now a freelance teacher, researcher and consultant. Among recent publications are *New Testament Writers and the Old Testament* (London: SPCK, 2002) and *The Book of Revelation and the Johannine Apocalyptic Tradition* (JSNTSup, 190; Sheffield: Sheffield Academic Press, 2000).

Glenn Bowman lectures in Anthropology at the University of Kent, Canterbury. He contributed a chapter on 'Christian Ideology and the Image of a Holy Land' to J. Eade and M.J. Sallnow (eds.), *Contesting the Sacred: The Anthropology of Christian Pilgrimage* (London: Routledge, 1991).

Jeremy Worthen is Vice-Principal and Director of Studies of the South East Institute of Theological Education, and Honorary Lecturer in Theology and Religious Studies at the University of Kent at Canterbury.

Michael Robson is himself a member of the Order of Friars Minor Conventual, and Dean and Fellow of St Edmund's College in Cambridge. His study of the life and legend of St Francis was published by Geoffrey Chapman in 1997.

David Daniell, President of the Tyndale Society and founding editor of the journal *Reformation*, has produced editions of Tyndale's translations as well as writing the biography. His academic career began as a Shakespearean scholar; he is now a fellow of Hertford College, Oxford.

Tina Leeke lives in Shrewsbury and is a teacher of Religious Education.

Philip Robinson is Professor in eighteenth-century French Studies at the University of Kent, and the author of a major study: *Jean-Jacques Rousseau's Doctrine of the Arts* (Bern: Peter Lang, 1984).

Grayson Ditchfield teaches in the School of History at the University of Kent, Canterbury. He is a specialist in eighteenth-century studies, particularly in the relationship between History and Theology.

Christopher Rowland is Dean Ireland's Professor of Biblical Exegesis at the University of Oxford.

Alison Jack is a minister of the Church of Scotland. She holds a PhD from the University of Edinburgh, awarded in 1996, for a thesis on 'Texts Reading Texts, Sacred and Secular: Two Postmodern Perspectives on the Revelation of John and James Hogg's *Confessions*'.

Jennifer Martin was an American student on a one-year exchange at the University of Kent.

Mervyn Willshaw now lives in Harrogate. He retired from the office of Chairman of the London South-East District in the Methodist Church, within which he is a celebrated preacher. His doctorate was awarded by the University of Kent for a thesis on nineteenth-century religious thought.

Richard Arrandale until recently was a Senior Lecturer in Religious Studies at Canterbury Christ Church University College. In this role, his research interests were centred on the religious dimension of modern drama. Rick now lives in Somerset where he is working on books on religion and spirituality in Glastonbury and Grail mythology.

Ian Mitchell Lambert is the UK Director of the Center for the Study of Early Christianity (The University of the Holy Land, Jerusalem).

G. Daan Cloete teaches New Testament at the University of the Western Cape.

Julie Hopkins is a United Reformed Church minister in Wales; previously she taught Feminist Theology in the Free University of Amsterdam, and she holds a doctorate from the University of Bristol, awarded in 1989, for a thesis on 'The Understanding of History in English-speaking Western Christian Feminist Theology'.

Philip Knight currently lives in Canterbury where he studied at Christ Church College and the University of Kent. He was awarded a PhD degree by the University of Durham for a thesis on the work of John Dewey.

INTRODUCTION

The letter kills, but the spirit gives life (2 Cor. 3.6).

Interpretation is itself an act that estranges man from a paradise in which words are serious, unambiguous, and have the force of deeds (Richard K. Fenn).[1]

Many times in the concluding decades of the twentieth century it was claimed that the book, as a means of information storage and retrieval, was in terminal decline; the new technologies of the electronic media were accordingly blamed (or praised) for this situation. A fairly obvious corollary of this in the field of philosophical theology has only rarely achieved a mention, let alone been discussed. If books in the future have only minimal significance, what will be the consequences for the so-called 'People of the Book'? Is the age of religions of the book coming to an end?

This is to pose in starkly final terms a question that is implicit at almost every stage of the present volume. The phenomenon of reading is a key theme in the study of the Humanities; it is equally of critical importance in biblical hermeneutics. How do people read, especially in the format we know as the book? And what are the presuppositions and the factors that condition the ways in which people read the 'Book of Books', the Bible, the Holy Scripture of Christianity? What has been, and is, specific about Christian reading?[2]

One way of assembling the data for an answer to this question is by taking a sequence of historical soundings within the ages of Bible use, up to and including the present day. Without any pretensions towards an exhaustive chronicle, nonetheless this sampling readily demonstrates how

1. *Liturgies and Trials: The Secularization of Religious Language* (Oxford: Basil Blackwell, 1982), p. xii.

2. These questions are discussed in a more technical sense, in terms of a science of writing, by Hermann Timm in *Sage und Schreibe: Inszenierungen religiöser Lesekultur* (Kampen: Kok, 1995).

many methods of interpretation have been employed within the history of the Bible. It is also clear how many different aims and objectives are revealed by analysis of the ways in which the Bible has been used. The present volume can illustrate a broad spectrum of this variety, as well as highlighting some common factors. Within these pages is a symposium or banquet of individual dishes, a menu formed by contributors, each with their own studies of the way the Bible is used and interpreted in a particular time and place.

In seeking our answers to questions about the specifics of Christian reading, it is as well not to lose sight of the anterior question of the phenomenon of reading. This embraces the issue of literacy, and the different modes of oral and written communication; but it also involves the cultural customs and constraints on the practice of reading. One can illustrate the different attitudes towards any book, and by extension the Bible, when reading and writing are select professional skills, or when literacy is widespread and nearly taken for granted, or in the contrasted valuations of a manuscript and a printed book. The private presses that still survive, in the present age of mass production and desktop publishing, can illustrate sharply for us the modern argument from design, focused on the relationship between outward appearance and contents. Well-designed books are triumphs of appropriateness, a large and splendid production representing the grandeur of the Bible in the Authorized Version. But has the valuation of the Bible changed, or been changed, when a copy of the New Testament in paperback can be bought for just less than a pound sterling?

If we go back to the beginnings of the New Testament, some interesting implications arise straight away, if the format of the text is considered. John Riches describes well the situation of the earliest Christians:

> They will leave few archaeological traces of these early years; nor do they feature often in imperial records. What they leave behind are writings: a series of letters, accounts of the spread of the movement and the 'acts' of its leading figures, a strange book of revealed mysteries, and a number of accounts of the life, teaching and death of Jesus Christ. For this purpose they made their own a new form of writing material, the codex, less venerable than the scroll, but more convenient both for small notes and excerpts and even for longer narratives such as the Gospels. These books achieved remarkable distribution throughout the Empire and would, alongside the more venerable scriptures of the Jews, be accepted within less than three hundred years as the official sacred texts of the Empire.
>
> The very form in which they [the Gospels] circulated, the codex, encouraged a kind of portability for the new traditions. At the same time, their very mobility meant that they were vulnerable, open to interpretation out-

side of any established framework, open to reworking and refashioning as other Gospels, suggesting other forms of community and world-view.[3]

What is at issue here is not only the shape of the literary product, or even the intentions of the first Christian authors, but also the larger social implications for the Christian community in the longer term, with the construction and assembly of what is to be a biblical tradition. These ideas are described by Hans-Robert Jauss:

> Texts are not so much world-depicting (*weltabbildend*) as world-building (*weltbildend*). They provide us with the cultural language and symbols to construct a new vision of the world. They create a literary history, in which a community's understanding of reality is forged by its engagement with the text (and its own life-experiences). This is a process which may go through many stages. The view of reality adopted by the community at any time in response to a given text, changes the horizon of expectations with which subsequent generations will approach and interpret the same text, leading to the formation of rather different imaginative reconstructions.[4]

The present symposium can trace its origins to a module taught now for a number of years within the undergraduate degree programme in Theology and Religious Studies at the University of Kent. This course is complementary to the regular studies of modern criticism in Biblical Scholarship, and the practice of exegesis (following a variety of critical methodologies) in the study of selected New Testament texts. Its rationale was once expressed in this way: 'We study the Bible by studying ourselves, or our contemporaries or our predecessors, in the act of studying the Bible.'[5] The aim of the course is to acknowledge the fact of pluralism in approaches to the Bible, now and in the past, and most significantly to include within the scope of academic study a whole variety of ways of using the biblical material that are not usually regarded as academic. So the Bible in worship and meditation, in art and film, is as relevant as the Bible in the scholar's study and the seminar.

A different kind of analogy to this act of taking note of a whole range of active possibilities is suggested by a recent biography of C.M. Doughty,

---

3.   John K. Riches, *Conflicting Mythologies* (Edinburgh: T. & T. Clark, 2000), pp. 2, 306.

4.   The work of Hans-Robert Jauss, translated as 'Literary History as a Challenge to Literary Theory', in Ralph Cohen (ed.), *New Directions in Literary History* (Baltimore: The Johns Hopkins University Press, 1974); quoted in Riches, *Conflicting Mythologies*, p. 15 n. 3.

5.   J.M. Court, 'The Bible and University Study', in D.M. Cohn-Sherbok (ed.), *Using the Bible Today* (London: Bellew, 1991), pp. 11-17.

the pioneer traveller in Arabia in the nineteenth century and the author of
Travels in Arabia Deserta (1888):

> At Medain Salih he had found a grotesquely carved comic mask, grinning
> from a bearded face, its tongue lolling out contemptuously.
>
> 'Seeing this larva [mask] one might murmur again the words of Isaiah,
> "Against whom makest thou a wide mouth and drawest out the tongue?"
> [Isaiah 57.4] I called my companions who mounted after me; and looking
> on the old stony mocker, they scoffed again, and came down with loud
> laughter and wondering.' [*Travels* 1.168]
>
> An archaeologist might have drawn one set of conclusions from the carved
> stone face, an anthropologist another, and a geologist another. They would
> all have looked at the rock and the carving through the lens of their own
> scientific specialization. But Doughty, whom no one could accuse of undue
> levity, sees a centuries-old joke; he sees the link between the verses of the
> Bible and the simple Arabs who are his companions. His view of the stone
> face is imaginative, introspective: like the crudely carved names and slo-
> gans he had already found along the trading routes, it is a silent reminder
> that the present is at one with the past, that he is himself the heir of those
> who have gone before. It is the conclusion of a poet rather than a scientist.[6]

The basic principle of arrangement for these selected historical studies
in biblical interpretation is simply chronological, for ease of reference. It
is clear that many of the main issues, such as the authority of the text, its
inspiration, and the methods of exegesis and practical application, will
recur, but in different relations and in widely differing contexts. A broadly
chronological organization of the chapters then allows the student to draw
general conclusions about any development in attitudes and approaches.

The story begins with two examples from the Patristic period: Origen
and John Chrysostom. As well as representing their own time zones and
regional traditions, Origen introduces the whole concept of allegorical
interpretation of the Bible, a dominant technique for many centuries and
now rediscovered in some modern readings, while John Chrysostom stands
as the founder of a liturgical tradition still celebrated in Eastern Orthodoxy. Such Patristic examples remind us of the importance of the sermon
in biblical interpretation, conceived as extended series or homiletic commentaries. In recognizing the practical requirements of spirituality and
worship, there is a need to recognize the whole range of ideas associated
with literal as well as metaphorical pilgrimage. For this reason a study of

---

6.   Andrew Taylor, *God's Fugitive: The Life of C.M. Doughty* (London: Harper-
Collins, 1999), pp. 231-32.

alternative customs of pilgrimage, where biblical ideas are interpreted in terms of place, is included between the more intellectual traditions of biblical exegesis in the Patristic schools of Alexandria and Antioch.

Two chapters provide a perspective on the Middle Ages, covering in particular the ideas of the twelfth and thirteenth centuries. Both concentrate on single individuals, as striking representatives or innovators of movements of thought, who are therefore symbolic of their generation. Jeremy Worthen's contribution focuses on the work of Hugh of St Victor, who strove to build a bridge between monastic and scholastic approaches to the biblical text. The sequel, by Michael Robson, concentrates on the work of St Bonaventure of Bagnoregio, taking a mendicant perspective which looks to the theological schools established by the followers of St Francis in furtherance of their mission to preach and to teach an orthodox exposition of the Bible; here the bridge is between academic rigour and effective popularization.

Translation is a vital question in biblical interpretation; it can fairly be said that any process of interpretation is a form of translation, out of one thought-world and into another. This was true at the earliest stage of the New Testament in the transition from Palestinian to Graeco-Roman worlds of thought, even if Greek could function as a common denominator of self-expression in both worlds. The study by David Daniell of the work of William Tyndale should be taken as a symbol of this whole process of translation into the local vernacular language of the immediate audience. Tyndale's ambition was to present the whole Bible in English 'in the language people spoke, not as the scholars wrote. At a time when English was struggling to find a form that was neither Latin nor French, Tyndale gave the nation a Bible language that was English in words, order and lilt.' One can see how this is an endeavour of creative originality, with the reciprocal aspect that the Bible in turn influences the language of the people.

The Protestant Reformation saw the text of the Bible in the vernacular firmly established in the centre stage of religious life. Martin Luther's translation of the New Testament into German, made with astonishing speed in just 80 days at the Wartburg, and published in September 1522, is the most well-known example. In turn the linguistic power of Luther's translation shaped the expressive potential of German literature (as Herder, Goethe, Nietzsche and Brecht all acknowledged). George Herbert's devotional poetry in English may well be work on a different scale, but has certainly had an enduring influence on worship and spirituality in the centuries since the seventeenth. Tina Leeke's study looks at the way his poetry echoed biblical language directly, and through the worship patterns of the *Book of Common Prayer*. The relationship between the Bible and worship is a constant theme of this symposium.

The next two chapters provide the basis for an interesting comparison in theological and philosophical reflection on biblical ideas, between John Toland in England and Jean-Jacques Rousseau in France. John Toland's work of 1696, *Christianity not Mysterious* is a classic work of Deist argument (a system of natural religion within the grasp of human reason). Deism, as an English movement, became widely influential in France through the work of Voltaire and Rousseau. The extract from Rousseau's work *Émile*, specially translated by Philip Robinson, is a statement of the bases of 'natural' belief, fictionalized as 'The Creed of a Curate of Savoy'. Such a text gives an opportunity to consider the practical implications of this rational belief, applied to the Bible (where the material is selectively regarded as historical or problematic) and to its corollaries in Christian worship, spirituality and ethics.

The next three chapters all have a focus in the eighteenth century, with glances forward and back. Grayson Ditchfield's study investigates the biblical basis of the idea that a monarch possesses a divinely given right to his royal status and authority. He examines the historical contexts in which this theory originated, and particularly the eighteenth-century debates about it. We then pass from history to the realms of literature and the arts in the next two studies of fascinating (perhaps eccentric) personalites, namely, William Blake and James Hogg. Christopher Rowland is particularly interested in the biblical themes of prophecy and the revelation of God's glory; his study of William Blake concentrates on his use of these two themes and on his creative rereading of the work of John Milton. In conclusion there are reflections on Blake's method of interpreting the Bible, with special reference to the world of the imagination and its challenge to reason. Equally challenging, and actually subversive, was James Hogg's way of using the Bible in his poetry, short stories and novels (such as *The Private Memoirs and Confessions of a Justified Sinner*, 1824). Alison Jack's study sheds light on the status of the Bible in eighteenth-century Scottish Calvinism, as well as its scope as an open text for subversion and abuse.

An American student's contribution to the symposium introduces a trans-Atlantic perspective on the related issues of Fundamentalism, Revivalism, Dispensationalism and Millennialism. In many ways these issues are still with us, as the intensified interest since 11 September 2001 in fundamentalist attitudes in religion makes clear. A literal and anti-intellectual approach to the Bible contrasts with the imaginative creativity of a William Blake, or the rationalism of Rousseau. The Dispensation of God's plan is illustrated in Scripture by schemes of temporal ages, such as those of the book of Daniel. The impact of millenarian expectations takes a variety of forms, principally dependent on whether the Millennial (or Thousand Year) Kingdom described in Revelation 20 precedes, or is the consequence of, the Parousia or Second Coming of Christ. A literal reading still leaves scope for elements of the text to be assembled in different ways.

The impact of the refined processes of Higher Criticism, applied to the Bible in the latter half of the nineteenth century, could be much more shattering still. Historical criticism, perhaps associated with the newly Darwinian approaches to science, and literary and source criticism, in a quest for the original form of the text like the explorer's quest for the source of the Nile, had a profound effect on the way the scholar viewed the text. In turn, when the wider public was introduced to these ideas by popularizing texts and translations (such as George Eliot's translation of the work of D.F. Strauss in 1846), the impact on the Christian believer could be devastating. Mervyn Willshaw's study looks at the ways in which three contemporary Victorian preachers (Liddon, Dale and Jowett) responded to these challenges in the sermons they preached.

The closer the chapters of this collection move towards the present day, the more they function as explorations of topical issues for our day and age. All the historical studies in this collection raise issues of relevance to an understanding of how the Bible is used; that is why they have been included. But the studies from the twentieth century offer that extra immediacy, of open-ended issues where there can still be much creative work to be done. The first of these twentieth-century topics is the study of Karl Barth by Richard Arrandale. To assess Barth among the great theologians of modern times is scarcely controversial; but Arrandale's approach is highly original and provocative. He seeks to recapture the shock effect of Barth's message of the priority of Scripture by using a postmodern retrospective and comparison with the late Hans-Georg Gadamer's 'game-theory' and Antonin Artaud's 'theatre of cruelty'.

Information technology is the most generally accepted revolution of our modern age; what is not so widely accepted is the application of computers to the interpretation of texts. Ian Mitchell Lambert's own research project explored the possible parallels between computer programming (computer modelling) and structuralist interpretations of the biblical text (which have been particularly popular in French-speaking circles since the work of Ferdinand de Saussure). His paper is a snapshot from a particular period of the late 1980s and early 1990s of structuralist methodologies and computer work on literature and language.

One of the most peaceful revolutions of modern times is the bloodless transition to a multi-racial society in the Republic of South Africa. In theological terms the corresponding transition for that nation was between the African Nationalist brand of Liberation Theology and the post-Liberation evaluation of multi-religious experience and indigenous theologies. Daan Cloete teaches at the University of the Western Cape and describes an insider's view of these theological changes in the 'Rainbow Nation'. He provides a reading of Paul's letter to the Galatians as a document of exactly this kind of cultural transformation. As well as illustrating a pluralist approach to biblical interpretation ('Rainbow Hermeneutics'), this chapter is a working example of a new kind of literary critical reading, or reader response, essentially a present-day dialogue with the biblical text.

Another related kind of Liberation Theology, much in evidence in the latter part of the twentieth century, is Feminist Theology. This was never monolithic; in fact the term covered a polarized range of alternative responses to gender issues, particularly when the Bible is seen as a prejudiced, patriarchal text. Julie Hopkins's contribution is a creatively positive response to problems of this kind: it shows by a reading of Mark's gospel how the themes of prophecy and healing of suffering can assist in the development of a female paradigm of discipleship. This understanding of early Christian women as role models of discipleship is enhanced by the pluralism of Julie Hopkins's interests in religious experience, ecstatic prophecy and Coptic spirituality.

In the final decades of the twentieth century it was also widely agreed that there was a crisis of authority. In the words of James Barr, writing a report for the World Council of Churches:

> Authority is no longer conceded *a priori* but is accepted only where it actually proves itself as such. Accordingly it becomes increasingly difficult to assert biblical authority in a general way. We no longer suppose that the acceptance of biblical authority is a sure way to rightness in our exegesis, or even that its acceptance is a necessary precondition of right interpretation.

From such observation logically followed Barr's own lifetime campaign against the presuppositions of Fundamentalism. To reflect this twentieth-century crisis in the authority and use of the Bible in the public domain, which has undermined and demoralized much modern biblical interpretation, Philip Knight's substantial contribution to this volume takes what could be called 'a worst-case scenario' but also cautiously indicates where there are grounds for hope. A problem-orientated perspective sees the limitations on public meaning as seriously threatening, while a more neutral or pragmatic approach might interpret this as liberating, with its creative opportunities for the extension of meaning from within the Bible's resources.

NOT (JUST) THE PLAIN MEANING:
ORIGEN AND ALLEGORICAL INTERPRETATION

John M. Court

Editor's Introduction

*To leap ahead, from the Patristic period and the formative work of such
people as Origen, to the running commentaries on biblical texts, as composed in the theological schools of mendicant orders like the Franciscans
in the thirteenth century (see Michael Robson's chapter later in this collection), seems an enormous leap from the perspective of time, but themati-
cally in terms of the methods of Bible study it is a much smaller leap, to a
point where Origen's principles (and those of other Church fathers, such
as John Cassian) have been tidied into a neat and standardized pattern.
For example the 'postilla' of the Franciscan Nicolaus of Lyra in the second
quarter of the fourteenth century begins with a neat rhyme: 'Littera gesta
docet, quid credas allegoria, quid agas tropologia, quo tendas anagogia.'
(The letter teaches events, allegory what you should believe, tropology
what you should do, anagogy where you should aim). To demonstrate the
point, an example is needed. The one most frequently quoted is Jerusalem,
which comes straight from the* Collationes *(or* Conferences *14.8) of John
Cassian. Historically Jerusalem is a city of the Jews; allegorically it stands
for the Christian church; tropologically it is the individual human soul;
and anagogically it is the heavenly city of God. The process of interpretation here is an extrapolation from the literal and an evolution of meaning.
Such a process is not straightforward; in the case of Jerusalem the fourth
sense emerged before the middle two, in a development of prophetic critique and eschatology within the Old Testament tradition.*

*Particularly in ages when allegory was unfashionable, it was customary
to denigrate it as an unscholarly process, or flight of fancy. It is therefore
important when discussing Origen to set out his principles of interpretation
in the wider context of his preparation for biblical study. From this it
emerges that his contribution to biblical scholarship was enormous, and
his methods were at least as well defined and scholarly as those of his
fiercest critics. He has been called 'the supreme pioneer of Christian biblical textual criticism'; such an accolade still applies, despite his mistakes
(such as the assumption of a single authentic Hebrew text which the Dead*

Sea Scrolls have disproved). While nowadays allegory has reclaimed some of its fashionable status, through a curious combination of anti-intellectualism, aesthetic romanticism, and the prioritisation of reader-response in new-style literary criticism.

Origen of Alexandria was a Christian scholar in the early third century CE, committed to Christ, to the study of the Scriptures, and to Neo-Platonic philosophy. In the words of Henry Chadwick:

> Origen…combined a humanist's mastery of classical Greek philosophy with passionate Christian convictions, and consequently wrote millions of words in exposition of scripture (of which only a relatively small proportion survives). On matters left undefined by apostolic tradition he felt free to speculate; in his time there were no conciliar decrees.[1]

As such he is a figure of controversy, admired and fiercely criticized in his own lifetime and up to the present day: should he be regarded as a model of the Christian apologist, presenting the gospel in the cultural terms of his own day, or as an extreme heretic, distorting the truth in an anticipation of Arianism?

There is no doubting the sincerity of his dedication to Christ. During his boyhood in Alexandria, at a point of Christian persecution, it is said that he wanted to rush to become a martyr; it was only because of his mother's deviousness in hiding his clothes and preventing his leaving the house that his desire was thwarted. Much later, according to Eusebius the church historian, he castrated himself in literal obedience to the command of Jesus recorded in Mt. 19.12. Finally, in the year 250, during the violence of the Decian persecution, Origen was imprisoned and tortured so severely that he never recovered, dying in 254 CE.

Origen was probably born in 184/5 CE in Alexandria; his parents were Christian (his father may well have been Leonides, martyred in the persecution of Septimius Severus in 202 CE) and certainly Origen received a double education both in Hellenistic *paideia* and in the Bible. In turn he seems to have become a private tutor, but events were to change dramatically when he took charge of the catechetical school in Alexandria, after a severe Christian persecution had removed the church leadership. This may have been as early as 203 CE (when Origen would only have been 17) but perhaps more likely in 211 CE (when he was 25). In his new role Origen

---

1. Quoted from a review in *The Times Higher*, 28 May 1993, p. 22. See also H. Chadwick, *The Early Church* (Pelican History of the Church; Harmondsworth: Penguin Books, 1967 and reprints), pp. 100-14; *idem, Origen: Contra Celsum* (trans. Henry Chadwick; Cambridge: Cambridge University Press, 1965).

was placed in the forefront of church teaching and exposition of the Bible in the major Christian centre of Alexandria.

In the early third century there was in practice a Christian Bible consisting of Old and New Testaments, although the more theoretical questions about the exact limits of the canon of Scripture were then still under active discussion. Much more highly debated was the whole issue of how the Bible should be interpreted. In Maurice Wiles's words, 'Origen was forced to grapple more deeply than any of his predecessors with the questions, What constitutes the Bible? And How is it to be understood?'[2] Origen used three means of communication in addressing these problems: *Scholia* or brief notes dealing with points of textual difficulty; *Commentaries* written on a number of books of the Old and New Testaments (many of these surviving only as fragments); and *Homilies* or expository sermons (these coming mainly from the period of his life spent in Caesarea. More than 200 sermons survive, recorded by stenographers; they mostly belong to a continuous sequence of expositions, following the three-year lectionary of Bible readings). It would not be accurate to regard these categories of communication as distinct and exclusive, as would be the expectation today. The homilies, with their depths of biblical exposition, are actually more like lectures, while the commentaries are equally concerned with the spiritual applications of the text.

It is entirely appropriate to regard Origen as a biblical scholar, in a way that bears comparison with modern expectations. For the Old Testament he used the Hebrew text in dialogue with the Jews, having learnt the Hebrew language for the purpose. Within the Church tradition he relied on the Septuagint Greek translation of the Old Testament, which also included the extra books often referred to as the Apocrypha. As an illustration of his scholarly method, one can quote from his *Commentary* on Matthew 15.14:

> With the help of God's grace I have tried to repair the disagreements in the copies of the Old Testament, on the basis of the other versions. When I was uncertain of the Septuagint reading because the various copies did not tally, I settled the issue by consulting the other (Greek) versions and retaining what was in agreement with them. Some passages did not appear in the Hebrew; these I marked with an obelus as I did not dare to leave them out altogether. Other passages I marked with an asterisk to show that they were not in the Septuagint but that I had added them from the other versions in agreement with the Hebrew text. Whoever wishes may accept them; anyone who is offended by this procedure may accept or reject them as he chooses.

2.   'Origen as Biblical Scholar', in P.R. Ackroyd and C.F. Evans (eds.), *The Cambridge History of the Bible*, I (Cambridge: Cambridge University Press, 1970), pp. 454-89 (454).

The climax of this scholarly comparison of texts was achieved in the *Hexapla* (a work no longer extant, although it survived in the library at Caesarea until the Moslem conquest in the seventh century).

Eusebius described the *Hexapla* in his *Church History* (6.16);[3] the language lacks precision and the details seem to have been misread by Epiphanius and Jerome. The text of the Old Testament was arranged in parallel columns: alongside the Hebrew text[4], transliterated into Greek characters, were the Greek versions by Aquila (2nd century CE), and by Symmachus (c. 200 CE), a revised version of the Septuagint translation, and the translation by Theodotion (c. 180 CE). Basically the work was a Tetrapla, but with two or sometimes three other versions added for some parts of the Bible. Its purpose was as a tool for interpreters, to assist in the elucidation of the Septuagint translation, regarded in the Christian tradition as sacrosanct. The text critical marks mentioned by Origen (such as the asterisk and the obelus, had been adopted from classical grammarians, and had been particularly used by scholars of Homer). It is possible that the Jewish tradition possessed a synopsis of the translations of Aquila and Symmachus that could have been adopted by Origen as a basis for his own work; Aquila's translation was very close to the Hebrew, while Symmachus's was noted for the purity of its Greek and the absence of Semitisms.

Origen used this resource of text material to make critical comparisons that he was then able to deploy in preaching, as well as in Christian apologetic and dialogue with the Jews. Whereas in the modern day to identify a mistranslation of a Hebrew phrase in the Greek of the Septuagint would lead to the rejection and discarding of that meaning, for Origen it was quite the reverse. He could preach about the Greek mistranslation as well as the Hebrew: '...even mistranslation can be of spiritual profit in the providence of God.'

In the New Testament Origen's main emphasis is on the Gospels. The Epistles, which clearly contain some explicitly personal and human judgments (see, e.g., 1 Cor. 7.12), are accordingly regarded as being at a somewhat lower level of inspiration. Origen is also happy to use other early Christian texts on the fringes of the New Testament—such works as the Gospel of the Hebrews and the Epistles of Clement and Barnabas, which were ultimately excluded from the canon of Scripture. In the New Testa-

3. See J. Stevenson (ed.), *A New Eusebius* (London: SPCK, 1963), pp. 181, 210-11.

4. Pierre Nautin argued that the Hexapla would not have contained a column in Hebrew. On the debate about how much Hebrew Origen would have known see Chapter 11 of Eugene Urlich, *The Dead Sea Scrolls and the Origins of the Bible* (Grand Rapids: Eerdmans; Leiden: E.J. Brill, 1999).

ment, as in the Old, Origen was significantly concerned with textual variations and the task of determining the original text. But in the course of his
preaching he is equally happy to suggest ways of interpreting the alternative
readings as well.

Origen is fundamentally convinced firstly that Scripture is written by the
inspiration of the Holy Spirit. The fact of inspiration, rather than its method,
is what matters, although the process is certainly regarded as rational, an
activity of the *Logos* as Reason (in accordance with the ideas of Neo-
Platonism). A second major conviction is that Scripture contains a deeper
meaning than is apparent on the surface. The surface meaning of so much
of the Bible was regarded as essentially unattractive. The laws of Moses as
human laws compared unfavourably with the laws of Rome, Athens or
Sparta. The surface meaning of a book like the Song of Songs (the Song of
Solomon) was acutely embarrassing, and palpably unworthy of God. The
God of the Old Testament, who appears to command massacres, seems, on
the surface, to be acting unjustifiably. Discrepant accounts of events that
seem historically implausible (such as the divergence between the Synoptic
Gospels and John's Gospel over the timing of the cleansing of the Temple)
might seriously undermine faith. But Origen's perception was that 'spiritual
truth can be preserved in material falsehood'. The existence of differing,
but apparently factual accounts, may be designed by God to provide a range
of spiritual meaning. The hidden meaning is then of primary importance,
and ultimately may be the only one that has any claim to truth.

The rationale for such interpretation is that God's revelation is accom-
modated to human capacity for understanding. To put it negatively, God
does not cast pearls before swine, not only to preserve the value of the
pearls, but also to save the swine from committing blasphemy out of ignorance. Expressing the point positively, one can say that God starts from
where we are and Scripture is provided as part of a process in the education of human-kind. We could not take the full truth all at once; it is argued
that a student values more highly the knowledge that takes the most effort
to acquire. So Scripture offers stages in a process towards deeper truths,
and Christians are classified by ability (or attainment) as *simpliciores/
incipientes*; *progredientes*; and *perfecti*.

Origen's views on inspiration and interpretation are fused together in an
early work of New Testament exegesis, his *Commentary on John* (1.10):[5]

> We have now to transform the gospel known to sense perception into one
> intellectual and spiritual. For what would the narrative of the gospel known

5.   Edited by A.E. Brooke (2 vols.; Cambridge: Cambridge University Press, 1896).

to sense-perception amount to, if it were not developed into a spiritual one? It would be of little account or none. Anyone can read it and assure himself of the facts it tells—nothing more. But our whole energy is now to be directed to the effort to penetrate to the depths of the meaning of the gospel and to search out the truth when it is divested of its prefigurations.

What this means is that we should treat the gospel text not primarily as a literal record of history; we are to 'lift up and allegorize' (1.26) expressions that on the surface appear to be meant literally. In the words of Frances M.Young,

> Origen required that each detailed verse or problem be understood in the light of the Bible's overarching thrust or meaning, which he took to be Christological... Holy scripture is one book, he affirms...written about Christ, for Christ is written of in the Pentateuch, the prophets, the Psalms, indeed in all the scriptures.[6]

The inherent unity of the Bible ('Holy Scripture is one book') was a widespread assumption among patristic authors. This readily led to intra-textual links between biblical books, as the concepts of historical time were easily merged when considering a divine text. A significant example of this practice is in Origen's *Commentary on the Song of Songs*, where he considers the three books attributed to Solomon and their order in the Old Testament. In Origen's view these represent Morality (the book of Proverbs); the Natural Discipline (Ecclesiastes); and the Contemplative (Song of Songs). This can be seen to be connected indirectly with the traditional divisions of Greek philosophy: moral, natural and contemplative. The connection is permeative rather than explicit. It highlights Origen's interaction with his cultural environment, rather than a conscious desire to 'paganize' Christianity or 'Christianize' paganism. The elements are Christianized in an almost subconscious way, rather than feeling the need to rationalize Christianity through the introduction of Greek themes. Therefore the very organization within the Bible is considered allegorically, connecting textual material across historical and authorial boundaries, in order to demonstrate the inherent principles of Christianity.

As a sample of Origen's practice of allegory we could look at one of his 226 extant homilies, that is Homily 13[7] on the text of Num. 21.27: 'Therefore they say enigmatically, "Come to Heshbon that it may be built." '

---

6. Frances M. Young, *Biblical Exegesis and the Formation of Christian Culture* (Cambridge: Cambridge University Press, 1997), p. 21; cf. Origen, *Commentary on John, ANCL*, add. vol., pp. 346ff.

7. Origen, *Homélies sur les Nombres*, II (ed. and trans. Louis Doutreleau; Sources Chrétiennes, 442; Paris: Cerf, 1999).

(This and other homilies on Numbers survive in a fourth century Latin translation by Rufinus or Jerome.) Origen followed putative Hebrew etymologies in order to identify the name Heshbon as meaning 'intentions', and Sihon, king of the Amorites, as Satan, because his name means either 'barren tree' or 'full of pride'. These etymologies provided a stepping-stone to this theologically favourable reading of a text that might otherwise have been regarded as an episode of ethnic cleansing:

> The first Heshbon fell, or rather, was overthrown and burnt, and another is to be rebuilt. How does this happen? We shall use an example to show. If you see a pagan living a dishonourable life, or erring in religion, do not hesitate to call him 'a city of Heshbon in the Kingdom of Sihon', for a king who is barren and proud reigns in that person's thoughts. If 'Israel', that is, a son of the Church, comes up to this person, and throws at him the spears of God's word, and attacks him with the sword of the Spirit, he thus destroys in that person all the defensive works of pagan belief, and burns away the haughtiness of his arguments with the fire of truth. Let him say that, in that person's case, Heshbon, a city of Sihon, has been destroyed. But the one, in whom pagan beliefs have been destroyed, is not left deserted and desolate. It was not the Israelites' custom to leave devastated the cities they destroyed, but after they had undermined and overthrown someone's bad thoughts and impious interpretations, they constructed in that person's heart a replacement for what they had destroyed; they brought in good thoughts, pious interpretations and true doctrines; transmitted rites of true worship; taught a way of life involving upright morals and demonstrated what statutes were to be observed.

A regular feature of Origen's allegorical exegesis is that the Bible itself should be concerned, to a very large extent, with its own self-interpretation and exposition; in other words that in its rhetorical structure and details it should speak about its own meaning. So, for example, in Numbers Homily 12, as in *Commentary on John* XII, the actions of digging a well, or coming to draw water from a well, refer to this process of interpreting Scripture. The kings who excavate wells in the rock symbolize the Apostles and their successors who are charged with opening up the deeper meaning of the otherwise impenetrable, literal sense of the text. Likewise, Num. 23.24b ('they shall not rest until they have eaten prey and shall drink the blood of the wounded') is interpreted in Christian mode as a prophecy of the sacrament of the Eucharist, which is regarded as the occasion for the assimilation of good, sound doctrine. And in terms of the Christian life, Num. 24.5 ('how fair are your tents, O Jacob, your encampments, O Israel') is interpreted by Origen in Homily 17 as the infinite spiritual progress referred to as 'straining forward' by Paul in Phil. 3.13 (anticipating a similar interpretation by Gregory of Nyssa).

The modern reader, influenced by structuralism, rhetorical criticism, and other new literary critical methods, may be much more sympathetic to Origen's quest for deeper, spiritual meanings, than would the student of the Bible of a century ago. The attraction of allegorical reading has a long history in Christendom.[8] In eighth-century Northumbria the Venerable Bede assembled some powerful images to characterize favourably the relationship between the spiritual and literal senses of Scripture:

> The literal is a veil which has to be drawn aside to reveal the spiritual sense; it is the bark one must strip off to come to the pith; it is the shadow of the allegorical truth. When one translates the literal sense into the spiritual it is like the change of water into wine, like rolling the stone away from our uncomprehending hearts. Or again: a honeycomb is wax containing honey; but the honey in the wax is the spiritual sense of the divine words in the letter, which is properly described as a dripping honeycomb. The honeycomb is dripping indeed since it has more honey than its waxen cells can contain.[9]

Five centuries earlier, Origen was equally confident about the theological necessity of the search for deeper meanings, in a quotation from Homily 11 on Numbers:

> We have shown, I think, with the authority of Holy Scripture, that *some of the things* which are written in the Law [the Old Testament] are certainly to be cautiously avoided, lest they should be literally observed by students of the Gospel; but that *other things* are at all costs to be retained as written. In the case of *certain other passages*, it is useful and necessary for us to accept them in an allegorical sense, in addition to accepting their literal truth.

Origen, and Clement (a predecessor of Origen's at Alexandria), had both evolved the principles of allegorical reading from the example of the Jewish philosopher Philo (also associated with Alexandria, much earlier, c. 20 BCE–50 CE). Philo was an approximate contemporary of St Paul, and it often seems that Christian interpretation of Scripture at Alexandria owes more to Philo than to Paul. For example, Clement of Alexandria used Philo's interpretation of the story of Hagar and Sarah (ctr. Galatians 4.21-31).[10] Similarly Origen frequently echoes Philo in his homilies on the Pentateuch. But Origen often used the allegorical reading in addition to literal exegesis, rather than as a substitute for it (see the third category

8. On the general issues see my *Reading the New Testament* (London: Routledge, 1997), Chapter 8.

9. Quoted from Donald Nicholl, *The Beatitude of Truth* (London: Darton, Longman & Todd, 1997), pp. 18-19.

10. Clement, *Stromateis* 1.5.30, see R.P.C. Hanson, *Allegory and Event*, p. 118.

indicated in the quotation above from Homily 11 on Numbers). Origen
was aware of the danger in treating apparent historical events merely as
allegories, and he himself protested strongly against the Gnostic treatment
of the physical miracles of Jesus as simply allegories of spiritual cures. In
this example from his *Commentary on John* 4.22, Origen gives the verse
its literal interpretation, before proceeding to discuss the deeper levels of
meaning he claimed to have discovered:

> 'Ye worship that which ye know not, we worship that which we know; for
> salvation is from the Jews.' The 'Ye', taken literally, refers to the Samari-
> tans; in a deeper sense, it refers to those who have heterodox views about
> the Scriptures. The 'We' taken literally, refers to the Jews; taken allegori-
> cally, it means 'I', the Logos, and those who are formed after me, who have
> salvation from the Jewish Scriptures.

Origen does not despise the literal interpretation as a matter of principle;
he only dispenses with it, if he finds the plain sense of a passage problematic or repulsive.

The application of figurative interpretations is a requirement at virtually
every point in Scripture, irrespective of whether a passage is judged to be
historical or improbable. Origen generalizes a principle, for the final reference of scriptural interpretation to heavenly realities, at the close of a discussion about the meaning of Passover in his *Commentary on John* (10.18):

> We ought not to suppose that historical events are types of other historical
> events and material things of other material things; rather material things
> are types of spiritual things and historical events of intelligible [reasoned]
> realities.

Maurice Wiles describes this exegetical process in these terms:

> Sometimes the figurative meaning of some part of the New Testament is
> itself developed in historical terms. As the Old Testament points forward to
> the dispensation of the New, so the New may point forward to the dispen-
> sation of the Church. When Jesus withdrew to a desert place on hearing of
> the death of John the Baptist (Matthew 14.13) the mystical meaning of his
> action was a 'withdrawal, from the place in which prophecy was attacked
> and condemned, to the place which had been barren of God among the Gen-
> tiles, in order that the Word of God might be among the Gentiles' (*Commen-
> tary on Matthew* 10.23). But much more often and much more importantly
> the whole drama of New Testament history is seen as a type of the eternal
> truth, which may be expounded either in terms of present spiritual experi-
> ence, or more fully in terms of that heavenly Jerusalem already existing and
> one day to be entered into and enjoyed by the believer. What the Law is to
> the recorded Gospel, that the recorded Gospel is to the Eternal Gospel.[11]

---

11. 'Origen as Biblical Scholar', pp. 484-85.

According to his own statement of the theory, in *De Principiis* 4.2.4, Origen separates out three levels of meaning—the literal, the moral and the spiritual—in his exegesis of Scripture. This formal structure is developed on analogy with beliefs about human psychology, corresponding to the body, the soul and the spirit in the human being. Given the importance of the authority of Scripture, the procedure is also supported by scriptural proof-texts, such as the Septuagint reading of Prov. 22.20 ('Describe these things in a threefold way'). A reading of Jn 2.6 suggests an option of taking three or two levels, on analogy with the water-pots at the Cana marriage, which contain 'two or three firkins apiece'. If one takes this reduced option, this would probably mean, for Origen, the discounting of the literal level of meaning. Should we look for an alternative analogy within communication theory, one probably more acceptable within the conventions of modern thinking, this might be achieved by applying to Origen's exegetical process the comment of the newspaper columnist Janet Daley, when writing in *The Times* on 16 March 1995: 'Every conversation has three levels of meaning—what you say, what you mean, and what you wish to be understood as meaning.'

Even in Origen's own work, it is not easy to sustain a clear distinction between the higher levels of moral and spiritual senses that he identified. Sometimes Origen distinguishes them as differing levels of spiritual attainment in the journey towards Christian maturity. Elsewhere the distinction Origen makes may be more a matter of theological content than of exegetical method, when 'the spiritual interpretation is that which relates to Christ and the great truths of God's saving dispensation, whereas the moral interpretation is one which relates to human experience'. One can see how Origen's exposition of the Bible establishes a relevance both for the individual and for the community, as the text is freed for these kinds of application. The importance of the Scriptures rests in their application, their spiritual meaning, as this engages the reader personally and the Christian church communally. So, for example, in the *Commentary on the Song of Songs*, 'The dramatic situation is extrapolated from the needs of the text, the teachings on the church are drawn from the details of the dramatic situation, the church is the model for the soul, and the soul is the model for the reader.'[12]

Towards the end of the fourth century CE, a youthful Jerome and his schoolfriend Rufinus of Aquileia endeavoured to introduce some of the

---

12. Karen Jo Torjesen, *Hermeneutical Procedure and Theological Method in Origen's Exegesis* (Berlin: W. de Gruyter, 1986), p. 56.

good theology of Eastern Christianity into the Latin West, by means of translating some of Origen's sermons and commentaries from the Greek. The process was interrupted by outraged complaints about Origen's orthodoxy from the Cypriot bishop Epiphanius. Rufinus then concluded that Origen's works must have been doctored by heretics, and he consequently produced an expurgated version of Origen's work of speculative theory, *De Principiis*. Unfortunately Rufinus destroyed his friendship with Jerome by quoting, in the preface to this new version, Jerome's panegyric on the unsurpassed achievements of Origen, thus representing Jerome as a dedicated Origenist. The consequence was a bitter war of words, between Jerome in his monastery in Bethlehem, supported by Theophilus archbishop of Alexandria, and Rufinus on the Mount of Olives, which split their supporters into rival parties. Moderating influences, such as Paulinus of Nola and Augustine of Hippo, tried in vain to reconcile the factions.

Jerome himself left a huge legacy of careful biblical scholarship, which is pervaded by the influence of Origen (whether he liked it or not); this is not only an influence in erudite learning in text-critical matters, but also in allegorical interpretation. So Jerome becomes one of the principal purveyors of this spiritual exegesis of Origen to the West, where his influence as a biblical interpreter came to prevail. Western saints like Gregory the Great and Bernard, who read the Song of Songs as a love affair between the soul and its Saviour, had learnt their spirituality through the commentary by Origen that Jerome had made available.

BIBLIOGRAPHY

Balthasar, Hans Urs von (ed.), *Spirit and Fire: A Thematic Anthology of the Writings of Origen* (Edinburgh: T. & T. Clark, new edn, 2001).
Caspary, Gerard E., *Politics and Exegesis: Origen and the Two Swords* (Berkeley: University of California Press, 1979).
Chadwick, Henry, *Early Christian Thought and the Classical Tradition: Studies in Justin, Clement and Origen* (Oxford: Clarendon Press, 1966).
—*Origen: Contra Celsum—Translated with an Introduction and Notes* (Cambridge: Cambridge University Press, 1965 [pb. 1980]).
Clark, Elizabeth A., *The Origenist Controversy: The Cultural Construction of an Early Christian Debate* (Princeton, NJ: Princeton University Press, 1992).
Crouzel, Henri, *Origen* (Edinburgh: T. & T. Clark, 1989).
Gallagher, Eugene V., *Divine Man or Magician? Celsus and Origen on Jesus* (SBLDS, 64; Chico, CA: Scholars Press, 1981).
Greer, Rowan A., *Origen: An Exhortation to Martyrdom, Prayer and Selected Works—Translation and Introduction* (London: SPCK, 1979).
Lange, Nicholas de, *Origen and the Jews: Studies in Jewish–Christian Relations in Third Century Palestine* (Cambridge: Cambridge Oriental Publications, 1976).

Lawson, R.P., *Origen: The Song of Songs—Commentary and Homilies (Translation and Annotation)* (Ancient Christian Writers; London: Longmans, Green; Westminster, MD: Newman Press, 1957).

Layton, Richard A., 'Recovering Origen's Pauline Exegesis: Exegesis and Eschatology in the *Commentary on Ephesians*', *Journal of Early Christian Studies* 8.3 (2000), pp. 373-411.

Nautin, P., *Origéne: Sa vie et son oeuvre* (Paris: Beauchesne, 1977).

Rist, John M., *Eros and Psyche: Studies in Plato, Plotinus and Origen* (Toronto: University of Toronto Press, 1964).

Runia, David D., *Philo in Early Christian Literature* (Philadelphia: Fortress Press, 1993).

Scott, Alan, *Origen and the Life of the Stars: A History of an Idea* (Oxford: Clarendon Press, 1991 [pb. 1994]).

Simonetti, Manlio, *Biblical Interpretation in the Early Church: An Historical Introduction to Patristic Exegesis* (Edinburgh: T. & T. Clark, 1994 [pb. 2001]).

Torjesen, Karen Jo, *Hermeneutical Procedure and Theological Method in Origen's Exegesis* (Berlin: W. de Gruyter, 1986).

Trigg, Joseph W., *Origen* (ed. Carol Harrison; The Early Church Fathers; London: Routledge, 1998).

—*Origen: The Bible and Philosophy in the Third Century Church* (Atlanta: John Knox Press, 1983; London: SCM Press, 1985).

CHRISTIAN PILGRIMAGE:
STRUCTURES OF DEVOTION/STRICTURES OF OBEDIENCE

Glenn Bowman

Editor's Introduction

Biblical interpretation in the Christian tradition is not always a matter of being face to face with a text (or even ear to mouth with the gospel message). Factors of place and time may well be involved, as well as the echo of a scriptural text. In this way the words of a text interact with the popular imagination of a religious group in a particular location or at a certain period. The ideas of the text then become real for them where they are, or in relation to a journey they are undertaking. So celebrations in the form of local festivals or pilgrimages become satisfying ways of interpreting the text 'on the ground'. These celebrations may be influenced by political considerations or sponsorship, at the command of the Emperor Constantine, the Empress Helena, or their successors.

The present collection of essays seeks to embrace traditions of popular spirituality as well as scholarly interpretation of the text. Glenn Bowman's chapter provides an example of the former category, encouraging us to include the fact of Christian pilgrimage traditions within our evidence. Pilgrimage literature exists comparatively early in Christianity, at least as early as the account of Egeria's travels in the Holy Land. While the traditions are ancient, of course it does not necessarily mean that the identifications of biblical sites are authentic, although the traditional association may sometimes be reckoned as quite a powerful argument for authenticity. It is also possible to encounter and experience these long-standing traditions in the present day. This is what Glenn Bowman did, and his narrative provides an instructive comparison between a very localized and popular shrine to the Virgin Mary on Cyprus, and the idea of Holy Land pilgrimage (widespread throughout the Christian world) here focused on the observances on the Via Dolorosa in Jerusalem. Glenn describes his experiences and analyzes them both as a theologian and as a social anthropologist who has researched the ideas and practice of pilgrimage.

In the following paper I would like to draw upon some observations of Mediterranean holy places I carried out in the course of field research on

Christian pilgrimage. The first set of observations were made in the vicinity of Greek Cyprus's central holy place, Kykko Monastery, in the course of a short visit I made to that island in 1984; the second were gathered in the Old City of Jerusalem where I had the fortune to live for twenty-two months between 1983 and 1985. Although in the paper I in large part abjure the use of footnotes and references in an attempt to keep the argument clear and disencumbered, I close the paper with a list of texts that the enthusiastic reader might want to explore in pursuit both of verification and of further insights.

I'd climbed up from the monastery to the *Throni*, or Virgin's Throne, where there is both a shrine commemorating the Virgin Mary's mythical visit to Cyprus and the tomb of Bishop Makarios, the first president of Cyprus and one of the leaders of the liberation struggle against Britain. Both shrine and tomb are pilgrimage sites of sorts; the latter buried in wreaths that Cypriots, to this day, bring to mark their allegiance to Makarios and the independent Cyprus he represents, the former filled with lit candles and litre bottles of olive oil that Greek Orthodox Christians bring to the mother of Cypriot Christianity. There was a constant flow of both natives and foreign tourists past Makarios's tomb and through the shrine of the Virgin, and the site was well enough marked in the international guide books to have its own tourist guides.

What I wanted to know about, however, the guides wouldn't discuss. On a small bush next to the shrine were hung dozens of white strips of cloth, tied in loops and draped over the branches. A nearby guide, when I asked about these objects, answered the way most 'enlightened' natives do when they feel a foreigner's image of their country is threatened by the 'primitive' ways of less progressive countrymen; he snapped 'It is just something the local people do' and quickly shepherded his following towards Makarios's tomb where he could talk about liberation struggles against colonialists rather than about superstitions. While I'd been trying to get the guide to talk a Cypriot had approached and was listening. He had come from Limassol (about 30 miles away) with his wife and daughters 'to see the monastery and pray to the Virgin Mary'. When the guide was out of earshot, he told me that people, after praying to the virgin, hung strips of cloth—which they had first tied round their heads like headbands—on the bush closest to the shrine. They did this, he said, so the Virgin would remember their prayers and take away their headaches. He left as another guide approached us, but in leaving said, 'If you are interested in this—if you want to see something about how we approach the Virgin—go back up the road three kilometres, park your car, ignore the metal sign in English that points to the picnic area, look for the wooden hand-painted one in Greek, and follow that path in. You'll be surprised.'

I wasn't in any rush—I was prevented from returning to Haifa for another couple of days by waiting for a ferry and I felt I could learn something about how Greek Orthodox persons worshipped in the Holy Land by seeing how they worshipped at home—and so I drove the three kilometres, parked the car, and walked down a tiny but well-worn trail into the depths of a valley. It was a bright day, the thyme smelled strongly and the path led me through woods, into gorges and across small meadows, but after about three miles of walking I began to feel I'd either wandered from the right path or that I'd been tricked. I was about to turn around when things grew strange. The path pulled into the shadow of a cliff and twisted around a bend to reveal, along the high cliff's base, a cluster of trees and bushes across which were scattered fragments of cloth. Further on the green of the foliage disappeared beneath what seemed a carefully arranged profusion of rubbish; unlike on the *Throni* the branches were not here bedecked with uniform strips of white cloth but socks, shoes (men's, women's and children's), trousers, skirts, blouses, shirts, bras, underpants (male and female), hanks of hair, eyeglasses, necklaces, walking sticks and all sorts of other things with which the human body comes into frequent contact. The aura was grotesque—evocative more of *vodoun* shrines in Haiti or a Hollywood fantasy of deepest African savagery than of a holy place dedicated by European Christians to the Virgin Mary. This was, nonetheless, clearly a shrine to the Mother of Christ, as one could see by examining the box, rather like a pressed metal bird house, standing in the midst of the forest of clothing. Within it were a pair of small commercially produced icons of Mary, dozens of candle stubs (two burning), several tiny and rudimentary oil lamps (no more than wicks floating in a pot of olive oil), and a couple of packs of matches. The base of this makeshift altar was surrounded by a number of bottles of deep-green olive oil—obviously of the first pressing. Behind it, bolted to the wall of the cliff, was another small box, filled and surrounded with similar paraphernalia. Next to that was what I eventually discovered was the reason for the site—a small cavity, approximately four inches in diameter and extending between twelve and eighteen inches into the rock face, filled with a sludgy and mosquito-infested pool of water.

I later collected the pertinent story from a local man. After Christ's ascension the Virgin Mary travelled to Cyprus and, one extremely hot afternoon, was carried up the valley towards the *Throni* by several men. The men were thirsty and pained by the weight of their load, but there was no water to be found. According to my informant, the Virgin, aware of their discomfort,

> reached her arm *through the glass* and plunged it into the solid stone of the cliff they were walking by, and when she withdrew her arm the hole it left filled with water. The men drank the water and were marvellously refreshed; they not only were no longer thirsty, but their tiredness was gone along with whatever illnesses they had previously had. That water has never since gone away—you can drink as much of it as you like, at any time of the year, and it will always replenish itself.

People, knowing the Virgin Mary had been there (although the description of her as reaching *through the glass* suggests that she had been carried there in the form of an icon *through* which she had performed the miracle) and seeing in the self-replenishing pool of water evidence that her power still resides there, bring her gifts of olive oil and candles. They drink some water and take some home with them (to sprinkle around the house, to put in jars in the icon corner and to feed to sick children). The water is, however, less important than opening of communication with the Virgin through giving her a gift. She is then more or less obliged to return gift for gift, and the objects left behind indicate precisely the cure the visitors desire in return by metonymically representing illnesses or dysfunctions in those parts of the body they customarily contact.

The audience for this sort of shrine is largely local, and those who know of it know of it solely through the media of the oral traditions generated by and around it. Those who approach it do so either individually or in small family groups, and their appeals to its powers are direct and physical. The audience for Christian Jerusalem is international to the extent—as we shall see later—that local people are forced out, the traditions referring to it are widely disseminated through texts, images, liturgies and songs, it is the focus of highly structured group visits, and the power it holds is so abstract as to appear almost immaterial. I will here describe the Friday afternoon Catholic procession along the Via Dolorosa, because this seems to concentrate many of those traits characteristic of Holy Land pilgrimage in general.

On Friday afternoons, between half past two and three o'clock, a large crowd gathers in the forecourt of a school on the north-eastern side of the Muslim Quarter of Jerusalem's Old City. The school is a religious school —for Muslims—but the tradition is so ancient that it is also the 'Praetorium', the place where Pilate condemned Christ to crucifixion, so the Muslims grudgingly make way one day a week for an influx of Catholic priests, pilgrims and tourists. It is at first hard to tell what is going on; there are so many people and none of them is doing anything that seems particularly religious. There is just a great milling about and snapping of cameras until, precisely at three, a single line of 20 or so brown-robed, rope-belted officiants enters the courtyard. It is clear that these men (and they are all men) are the focus of activity, and they will remain that until the whole entourage disbands an hour or so later. The priests group together around four of their members who share a megaphone, and wait until the crowd (as many as 300 at times) goes silent and focuses its attention on them. One of the Franciscans then reads, in a sing-song voice, a long passage of a text in a language (Latin) that virtually no one in the crowd understands. Despite this, many in the crowd mutter along with the words with relative ease, not because they know the language but because they have spent much of their life hearing and repeating those same words in different places. The other three priests then take turns reading translations of the original Latin phrases into the megaphone; they read in French, Italian and English (no one reads in Arabic, the language of the local Christians, but then there are virtually no local Christians present). After these readings— recited ritualistically, not in an explanatory tone—the priests process out of the courtyard and the people crush together in their haste to follow. Following, and staying within hearing distance, is easier said than done however; the streets are narrow and crowded, and the pilgrims and tourists end up trailing along in a narrow queue often as far as a hundred yards behind the priestly phalanx. This is unfortunate for those not brutal enough to hold their place at the head of the procession, because for the next hour what will happen is that the priests will stop at 13 sites—each representing the location of a moment in Christ's passion—read at each of them appropriate passages in each of the four languages, and quickly pass on to the next. Those who are forced out of hearing distance—a bit more than half of the people processing—experience the Via Dolorosa merely as a series of stops and starts in the midst of the shouting and heckling of a heavily touristed Middle Eastern bazaar. Nonetheless, those who are pilgrims (the tourists, after the first ten minutes or so, start to look bored and wander off into shops or start taking pictures of the other people in the procession) do their best not to be distracted, and walk slowly with their heads down and their lips moving all the way to the procession's end at the Holy Sepulchre —the alleged place of the Crucifixion and Resurrection. They don't look at the holy sites they pass; they might not even know when they are passing the places where tradition says Veronica wiped Christ's face with her veil and Simon was forced to take up the cross, because without the priests stopping in front of those places and marking them and what they signify by reading from their booklets the sites are not particularly noticeable. The pilgrims try to ignore the shopkeepers who shout at them and the children who push at them while attempting to get through the crowd with carts or goats, and they do their best not to take offence at the fact that their fellow country persons have decided that they too are tourist sites worth photographing. In fact, what they are trying to do is *not* to be where they are (in Jerusalem) in order more effectively to be exactly where they are (in Jerusalem). The real city, the city of Israeli machine guns, cheap imported tourist goods and constant sexual come-ons distracts from and, in a very real sense, destroys the city they revere and which they have come on pilgrimage to visit. Their pilgrimage is focused on a Jerusalem that has been constructed in their imaginations throughout their lives by liturgies, sermons, religious readings and the like—and that city is not, except in a painfully realistic sense, the city they walk through on the Via Dolorosa. They have come to Jerusalem to 'walk in the footsteps of Christ' and the procession along the Via Dolorosa is the fulfilment of that desire. What they are thinking of with their heads turned down and their ears closed to the cacophony of the street is the sequence of events leading up to Christ's death on the cross, and the pilgrim does this so that, as the official Franciscan guidebook on the Via Dolorosa says, he or she 'becomes a companion of Christ…become[s] his imitator' and in order to remember 'how high a price was paid for salvation' (Storme 1976: 4). The pilgrim, in other words, abstracts himself or herself from the real city in which he or she walks in order to imagine himself or herself partaking in a series of events that happened nearly 2,000 years ago. Success in doing so is effectively a miracle—although it may not be manifest in cured limbs or renewed sight; what the pilgrim gains from walking the 'Way of the Cross' is an abrogation of his or her individuality that fosters a closer awareness of absolute dependence on the Messiah, whose crucifixion enabled his or her salvation. Such an awareness, such a self-abnegation, can only bring the pilgrim closer to Christ and therefore closer to following Christ from this life into the redemption of the next. The Via Dolorosa, by taking the pilgrim to the place from which the body of Jesus was resurrected, takes him or her spiritually to a moment of resurrection after which the pilgrim will—or should—follow Christ's way through this world and into heaven. The pilgrim comes to Jerusalem to cancel individuality, abrogate the centuries that have passed since Christ ascended, and to become one with that man/god at the moment of his glory.

These two forms of pilgrimage may seem very different, but there are certain characteristics that they share with pilgrimages throughout the

world. I will talk briefly of what they have in common before talking
about the differences. The differences, however, are what are enlighten-
ing, because it is when we look at what distorts something out of its typical form that we understand the important things about even the normal
type.

The unnamed pilgrimage to the local shrine of Mary, like the world
famous Via Dolorosa leading to the Holy Sepulchre, offers access to a
place where divine power is somehow more manifest in the world than at
other places. Power, of course, is a hard thing to define since it takes different forms in different contexts. The power manifest in Cyprus is the
power to straighten twisted or broken limbs, restore potency or fertility,
cure sick children, stop hair from falling out or going grey, and so on. Jerusalem doesn't have that sort of miracle; in the two years that I was there
the only time I saw healing miracles being acted out was in a modern
theatre in West Jerusalem during a conference of Christian fundamentalists, and they don't consider Jerusalem to be particularly holy. In Jerusalem
bodies may not be reformed, but souls are saved. The surface manifestation
of such a miracle may not be as dramatic as a healing, but for Christians,
for whom eternal salvation is far more important than temporal comfort,
the miracle of being brought into God's grace is of ultimate importance.
In either case, however, as with all other pilgrimages throughout the religions of the world, a pilgrimage brings one closer to or into contact with
divine powers. By praying before a shrine, slaughtering an animal and
pouring its blood over the shrine's monument, crawling under an altar,
falling into a trance near a holy man's tomb, drinking water mixed with
dust from the ground around the shrine or with stone powder scraped from
its walls, or simply circumambulating the holy place, pilgrims announce
their presence before the powers that rule their lives and ask them for
grace. The powers show themselves in different ways, depending in part
on the forms of secular power that dominate the society and in part on the
sorts of religious groups that control the shrines.

A local shrine, like the one in Cyprus, will perform miracles of local
interest; some serve to bring the rains and keep off locusts, others cure
bodies and minds, some enable feuding groups to work out their problems
and recreate their alliances before the god or gods, and certain types serve
to invest the authority of ancestral gods into living persons. A local shrine
thus brings the power of divinity (often through intermediate powers like
saints or holy men—dead or alive) into contact with the limited domain of
familial relations, regional powers, group interactions, and so on.

The priesthoods of such shrines, if there are any (there was no priest at the holy place in Cyprus), are usually made up of single holy men or small brotherhoods or sisterhoods. They are often not well educated in anything beyond the rites and traditions of their shrine; they sometimes are not even integrated into the wider networks of the hierophants of their religions. They live off the shrine and its offerings, and very much depend on the popularity of the shrine for their well-being. Thus, in many cases the officiants are the greatest perpetrators and recorders of miracles; a knowing look at the holy men around Hindu shrines in India or Islamic shrines in Northern Africa, with their feats of petty magic, like glass eating and self-mutilation, tends to transform the whole thing into an impressive, but nonetheless quite purposive, commercial for the power of the shrine and its divinity. Such self-advertising is not surprising; local shrines, unlike universal ones like those of Jerusalem and the Holy Land, have only a local press, and are not popularized by massive systems of pilgrimage promotion.

Universal shrines tend, unlike local ones, to deal with universal issues; Jerusalem, like Kandy, Lhasa, Ankhor Thom and Rome, has served to bolster imperial rule as well as to legitimate the ideological hegemony of its religions over national and international populations. Kings and emperors build churches and monuments in pilgrimage centres and bequeath the orders that run them great gifts in order to guarantee that the power of their rule is linked with that of the rule of God. Priests, patriarchs and popes, through pilgrimage and the constant reiteration of the names of the holy places, stress the links of their church and its hierarchy with the religions that were founded or somehow marked in the pilgrimage centres.

Curiously, central shrines like Jerusalem are as important to the individual as they are to those concerned with universal control systems like empires and religions. The universal and the individual are brought together by their common dependence on the central holy places. This is because, just as the universal escapes particular local structures by transcending them, the individual escapes the constraints of regional powers and social constructs because of the ease with which they can fall through their nets. In Huxley's words:

> the moment we start resolutely thinking about our world in terms of individual persons we find our selves at the same time thinking in terms of universality... The reason of this connection between universality and solitude is that universality is a disconnection from immediate surroundings (Huxley, 1959).

The individual might go to a local shrine to ask for divine help with something that effects his or her relations to the normal course of life—sickness, infertility, conflicts with others, and so on—but when he or she is concerned with that which affects him or her regardless of location, the devotee goes to the same universal pilgrimage shrine as that a king or emperor calls upon when trying to legitimate a rule that disavows regional limits.

The dependence of the small shrine's priesthood on the population of the local region should be contrasted with the support given the hiero-phants of a universal shrine by the entire institutional structure of the religion that the shrine serves. This support is manifested in several ways. A universal shrine usually has a complex hierarchy of religious organizations functionally divided to deal with different facets of running the pilgrimage centre. Thus there are schools for training future priests, religious courts for dealing with infractions of proper deportment, groups of priests to deal with parish duties and others for particular services at the shrines themselves, hostelries and guide groups to take care of the pilgrims, and so on. These people are well trained and closely in touch with the wider networks of the religion. Furthermore, they have no need to promote the place because the pilgrims who come to a universal shrine do so because they already know about it, and just want to see what they have heard of—the Holy Sepulchre, the Kabala, the Wailing Wall, the Potala, the Bo Tree, or whatever. Thus, there is little need for spectacular miracles and there is no system of elaborate records relating to the miracles enacted at the place. Furthermore, the religious organizations tend to resent their power being infringed upon by people outside their group, and therefore do their best to prevent the colourful intrusion of the miracle makers and holy men one tends to see at certain medium-sized shrines. There tends to be a rather stultifying sense of orthodoxy around the big central shrines; no dervishes driving swords through their cheeks, no fakirs hanging from hooks, no groups of people in trance dancing rhythmically through crowds of onlookers.

It was interesting in Jerusalem to watch what happened when local people tried to treat the high shrines of Christianity like local shrines. One Palestinian tradition holds that a child conceived in the Holy Sepulchre on Holy Saturday eve, the night before Easter Sunday, will be particularly blessed. Priests on that night are extremely vigilant, and you can watch them through the night examining shadowed corners with flashlights, attempting to catch a pair of copulating commoners. Furthermore, the tradition of a first fruit offering has been standardized in liturgical tradition to the point that it is hard to tell that the ritual has anything at all to do with fertility and harvest. The local people, however, know it does, and they attempt, during the ceremony, to bring in grapes and other fruits to lay on the altars. I have watched Greek Orthodox priests pick up these offerings—the literal versions of what they themselves have been symbolically offering up to God—with looks of profound disgust, and listened to them shouting—in Greek—at the Arabs who'd left them there. The miracles of a major holy place have all been performed in the past, and they are to be celebrated—quietly and decorously—only in the processions, in the legendry, on the wall paintings and the icons.

There are good reasons for seeing miracles as advertisements, and advertisements become unnecessary once the place is known (consider Canterbury Cathedral, with its basements full of ancient tomes of carefully recounted miracles and its present-day air of a museum). A major religious shrine becomes a site wherein religion is stated in its pure form; as much as possible the irreligious or merely secular is shoved aside while the symbols and rituals of devotion are amplified and endlessly reiterated. Alan Morinis, writing of Hindu pilgrimage shrines, describes what could be any major shrine throughout the world:

> a pilgrim entering the sacred zone enters an environment filled with a large number of objects and edifices of a limited range, in keeping with the type of sacred zone. The pilgrim sees temples and shrines, which will be outstanding for their classical temple architecture. The outside walls of these are usually decorated with symbolic imagery depicting motifs relevant to the shrine deity and his associated mythology. The symbols are found repeatedly by the pilgrim in all corners of the sacred zone—in the shops of the pilgrimage souvenir sellers, on the walls of houses, lodges and eating places, in the words of the temple priests and the pleading cries of the beggars (who invoke the local deity as they beg), in the pamphlets for sale in the temple area itself, in the songs sung by other pilgrims. The air and the visual space of the sacred zone is filled with the presence of this deity and associated mythology, portrayed in rich symbolism through many media. The pilgrim takes in an intensely concentrated infusion of messages from this densely packed field of overlapping symbols. Whatever information about the deity the pilgrim possessed before making his pilgrimage is here reinforced as his mind receives a vivid imprint of the history, glories, powers, etc. of the shrine deity. The sacred centre is therefore a perceptual field of a limited range of stimuli in which the pilgrim is freed from the distractions of ordinary social life to concentrate upon and interact with the symbolic environment he has entered (Morinis 1984: 210).

The pilgrim no longer sees a world into which the miraculous intrudes; he enters into a world that is, in itself, a miracle.

Both the Cypriot shrine and the Via Dolorosa are located with reference to particular places; the former on the site of a small spring that neither overflows nor goes dry and the latter along a path between places where a series of historical events are said to have taken place. The establishment of a holy site at a place where something occurs that appears anomalous with reference to the natural course of things is a universal religious phenomenon; the fact that nature has in some way been diverted from its normal course is enough to signify that there is an entity active at that place with supernatural power. Robertson Smith, in his early study of Semitic religions (Smith 1907: 118), pointed out how any outstanding rock formation or unusual tree in the landscape would be marked out as a holy place. With the shrine in the Cypriot woods the anomaly, the spring, has been overlaid with the story of its creation by the Virgin Mary, but it nonetheless physically remains the centre point of the site. In Jerusalem there is as well a physical anomaly at the centre of the web of narratives. The central holy place for both Jews and Muslims there is the massive rock beneath the dome of the Mosque of Omar, otherwise known as the Dome of the Rock. The Muslims built their shrine over that rock because they believed that it had previously been the foundation stone of Solomon's Temple and, according to the Bible, Solomon built there because it was already a Canaanite holy place. Thus there was an original natural marker, a round protrusion on the top of a hill in the midst of a bowl-like valley, which was made a holy place by the Canaanites or whoever came before them. When the Israelites took the city of Jerusalem their king purchased the site and called it holy to his god. Later his son built over it a massive temple. That temple was destroyed by other conquerors, but by that time it had been memorialized as the site of Abraham's attempted sacrifice of Isaac and as the centre of God's mission to the world in the texts we now call the Old Testament. When the Christian religion was chosen by the ruling elites of Rome, Christianity took over from those texts the tradition of a stone that was the centre of the world and of the divine mission, but they denied that the Jews had the stone right and instead located the biblical mountaintop on the shaft of an old quarry cutting, Golgotha. Around this stone they built their central shrine—the complex that would become known as the Holy Sepulchre. When the Muslims came, they, like the Christians before them, could not accept the traditions of the previous dominant religion and denied the veracity of the Christian link of Golgotha with the site of Abraham's sacrifice. They moved the referent back to the stone that the Jews claimed the Temple had been built upon. They then spun out a whole series of narratives to cover the stone and its site, and thereby made it a central holy site for Islam. Thus we can see how a natural site, which draws the attention of local peoples, becomes a holy place, and then becomes a subject of literary discourse that itself becomes more real than the original object itself. The original site is not quite forgotten, but it is buried beneath the traditions and the monuments that accrete around it.

The first stage of such a process can be seen occurring with the spring in Cyprus—the spring has already become a mere embellishment on the story of Mary's coming to Cyprus—but it is unlikely that the process will go much further. Pilgrimage shrines become important or fail to become important because of the functions they fulfill and the populations they serve. Jerusalem became significant because, first, it was the seat of an Israelite kingdom and then, after its fall, the focus of Jewish messianic prophecies. The early Christians, who were Jews, used those prophecies to sanctify their devotion to the man they called Messiah, Jesus, and through that process of sanctification the idea of Jerusalem as a holy and royal city entered into the traditions of the West. When Constantine and his successors legitimated their rule by linking it with the rule of Christ they welded that bond by building massive memorials and churches in the city. Some of these still stand and memorialize the traditional sites. In the meantime, in the deserts of the Arabian peninsula, a charismatic leader was attempting to forge a following out of a mixed population of Jews, pagans and Christians, and to do so claimed to be speaking the words of God—a god that had spoken first to the Jewish patriarchs and Moses, then to Jesus, and finally to him— Mohammed. He used the Bible to try to bring Christians and Jews together under his religio-political leadership, and thus brought into his message traditions pertaining to Jerusalem or *al'Uds* (the holy). Thus Jerusalem and its holy rock played a major role in the formation of a state and a religion and, because of that, was enshrined in a text, the Bible, that was later used to forge two great missionizing religions. It would be unlikely, considering Jerusalem's place in world history, for it to ever be anything but a major religious shrine or, as it is now, three major religious shrines.

The people who worship at the shrine in Cyprus are, on the other hand, a diverse mix of farmers, herders and urbanized peasants. Their worship of the holy spring can probably be traced back as far as the origins of human life on Cyprus—long before the coming of Christianity. The fact, however, that these people have been and remain historically inconsequential means that their shrine gets appropriated, assimilated, taken over every time a new set of conquerors takes their land and imposes a religion on it. The same spring that may at one time have attested to the miraculous power of Demeter, Ceres or 'Al-Khadr' (the Green One), now speaks for the power of the relatively new Christian pantheon. It may in the future speak for another god.

In a sense, the name does not matter much; the shrine serves the local population by convincing it that in its vicinity there is a benevolent force that fights against the daily decay of its members' lives and instils into the implacable course of nature a touch of grace. Such shrines do not go away—in Africa they have even survived (under different names and slightly different rites) the depopulation and repopulation of areas, while in South America the Jesuits could only drag the Indians away from the worship of Oxtotoetheotl by taking over his shrines and putting statues of Jesus on their altars in place of those of the Aztec god.

A local shrine sits on the edge of the community that uses it—or, if several use it, on the borders between them—and serves as a place where people can go for succour away from the communities' constant squabbles. Such shrines perch on the borders because the power they bring into their communities comes from beyond them—both in a spatial sense and in the sense that the power is much more than human. Divine power cannot be owned by any member of the community, symbolically because no person can own god, and practically because the exercise of that power must appear to be non-partisan. It will only be trusted so long as it is seen to act according to motives and principles that transcend the desires and designs of individual peoples and groups. Even Jerusalem, after the fall of Israel, reigned in spiritual supremacy from the border areas of Byzantine and European power. Later, after the rise of Islam, Jerusalem remained the spiritual centre of Christianity even while it was outside the European and Christian world altogether. With the central shrine as well as the local one, the worshipper goes away from immediate surroundings to gain a sense of transcendence, since it is only in a state of transcendence that a power greater than the world can be located. Pilgrimage shrines that are in the centres of the political world—places like Jerusalem for the Israelites or Rome for the Catholics—are the palaces of demi-gods and they, as such, are marked off from their surroundings by boundaries that signal a qualitative shift to crossers. The Vatican City belongs to God and to his spokesman, the Pope, and David's Jerusalem was his city—not part of either Israel or Judaea (he distinctly established it as his own by capturing it with his own mercenaries and keeping it juridically separate from the areas of the 12 tribes). Where the palace and the shrine coincide resides a ruler who speaks with an authority that comes from a realm outside the social world. David was God's adopted son and the Pope inherits the mantle of Peter; both claimed their authority devolved from heaven. The 'Heavenly Cities' of the Chinese emperors, known as 'the pivots of the four worlds', were microcosms of heaven, and one walked through their corridors and approached their inhabitants with the same reverence one would accord to God and his angels. Pilgrimage shrines and centres don't have to be on the edge of human society; they do have to be beyond or outside of it.

It is clear that the character of a pilgrimage shrine and of the miracles enacted at it have a lot to do with that shrine's influence and the influence of its audience—in other words with power. God may act through a pilgrimage site, yet, though it may be the same god acting through each site whatever the mediators, an adaptation of Orwell's adage is apropos—'All revelations are equal but some revelations are more equal than others'. Some sites, like some people, have big gods and some have little gods, even when the priests say that the big ones and the little ones are the same. The gods of major shrines perform different functions from those of minor shrines, or perhaps it would be more accurate to say that the different gods perform different tasks in a single process of enculturation. I would like, in closing, to talk once again of our two pilgrimages—one to the peasant shrine in Cyprus and the other along the Via Dolorosa—and to relate them to miracles. Miracles, as Augustine points out in the 8th chapter of the 22nd book of his *Civitas Dei* (St Augustine 1945: 366-375), exist not to make people happier or healthier but to prove to people that God exists and that Christ did ascend to heaven to sit at his right hand. The argument is elaborate, but essentially it is this: Christ is one with God, and the saints, through their faith and their martyrdom, made themselves one with Christ; the fact that the relics of Christ and the mementoes of the saints are able to perform miracles, even after the death of Christ and of his martyrs, is proof that despite worldly appearance, these persons are not dead but still alive and active; therefore Christ has been resurrected and has ascended; therefore his followers have risen with him; and (unspoken) therefore those who sacrifice their own selves and desires to Christ will, like him and the saints, dwell after death in heaven. Thus miracles are signs of the possibility of salvation through God and his son; the fact that they cure is extraneous. People who hang their old clothes on bushes in Cyprus are, one might suspect, not terribly interested in the semiotic function of the magic of their shrine. They cross themselves, they burn candles and dedicate some oil to the Virgin, and they say their prayers, but in large part—at least in the context of the shrine—they do these things because these activities are necessary parts of the mechanisms one must set in motion to cure one's maladies. Nonetheless, despite the appearance of rank superstition, what they are doing does effectively strengthen the hold of the church and its officiants on them. Every time a cure is effected, or, more to the point, every time people say a cure has been effected, that cure will be chalked up to the account of the Virgin Mary. What happens at that little shrine, isolated from any church or priest, will later be connected in church with the great ideological system of orthodox religion, and the recipient of the cure (or the person who heard that someone did receive a cure) will acknowledge that there is power behind the Virgin, her son, the saints and their modern-day representatives. That connection may not be particularly significant; the impact of that sort of thing depends on much more than what is going on in the religious field. Perhaps, though, the peasant will give the local priest a bit more of his crops or his money, perhaps he or she will take the priest's word and vote against the communists, or perhaps she will simply listen a bit more closely at the next sermon. Perhaps, eventually, the peasant will become a pilgrim and go to Jerusalem, not to seek a cure, but because he or she has been convinced that in the ultimate sense all things depend on religion and the proper practice of it. There is not a great distance between individuals and small groups who, in pursuit of some very material ends, scuttle through the woods to hang underclothing, spectacles and combs on bushes, and a flock of three hundred persons who shuffle up a Middle Eastern street in close order muttering Latin prayers by rote, conscientiously shut out the world around them and stop too far from their leaders to see what they are pointing at or to hear what they are saying. Both groups think they are serving their own best interests, and both are involved in learning a discipline—the discipline of religious obedience. Miracles teach such people where the power lies and who is to be obeyed to gain the benefits of that power, and the fact that empires, universal religions and a dense network of local and central pilgrimage shrines have always developed in tandem should provoke thought.

BIBLIOGRAPHY

Asali, K. (ed.)
    1989   *Jerusalem in History* (London: Scorpion).
Augustine of Hippo
    1945   *The City of God*, II (ed. Ernest Barker; trans. John Healey; London: J.M. Dent and Sons).
Bagatti, B.
    1971   *The Church from the Circumcision: History and Archaeology of the Judaeo-Christians.* (trans. Eugene Hoade; Studium Biblicum Franciscanum, Collectio Minor No. 2; Jerusalem: Franciscan Printing Press).
Barker, M.
    1991   *The Gate of Heaven: The History and Symbolism of the Temple in Jerusalem* (London: SPCK).

Ben-Arieh, Y.
    1984   *Jerusalem in the Nineteenth Century: The Old City* (New York: St. Martin's Press).

Bowman, G.
    1991   'Christian Ideology and the Image of a Holy Land: The Place of Jerusalem Pilgrimage in the Various Christianities', in J. Eade and M. Sallnow (eds.), *Contesting the Sacred: The Anthropology of Christian Pilgrimage* (London: Routledge): 98-121.
    1992   'Pilgrim Narratives of Jerusalem and the Holy Land: A Study in Ideological distortion', in Alan Morinis (ed.), *Sacred Journeys: The Anthropology of Pilgrimage* (London: Greenwood Press): 149-68.
    1993   'Nationalising the Sacred: Shrines and Shifting Identities in the Israeli-Occupied Territories', *Man: The Journal of the Royal Anthropological Institute* 28.3: 431-60.
    1998   'Mapping History's Redemption: Eschatology and Topography in the Itinerarium Burdigalense', in Lee Levine (ed.), *Jerusalem: Its Sanctity and Centrality to Judaism, Christianity and Islam* (New York: Continuum Press).

Brown, P.
    1981   *The Cult of the Saints: Its Rise and Function in Latin Christianity* (London: SCM Press).

Campbell, J.
    1964   *Honour, Family and Patronage: A Study of Institutions and Moral Values in a Greek Mountain Community* (Oxford: Clarendon Press).

Canaan, T.
    1927   *Mohammedan Saints and Sanctuaries in Palestine* (London: Luzac).

Christian, W.
    1972   *Person and God in a Spanish Valley* (New York: Seminar Press).

Davies, W.D.
    1974   *The Gospel and the Land: Early Christianity and Jewish Territorial Doctrine* (Berkeley: University of California Press).

Dillon, M.
    1997   *Pilgrims and Pilgrimages in Ancient Greece* (London: Routledge).

Dubisch, J.
    1995   *In a Different Place: Pilgrimage, Gender and Politics at a Greek Island Shrine* (Princeton Modern Greek Studies; Princeton, NJ: Princeton University Press).

Dumper, M.
    2001   *The Politics of Sacred Space: The Old City of Jerusalem in the Middle East Conflict* (London: Lynne Rienner).

Eade, J., and M. Sallnow (eds.)
    1991   *Contesting the Sacred: The Anthropology of Christian Pilgrimage* (London: Routledge).

Galavaris, G.
    1981   'The Icon in the Life of the Church', *Iconography of Religions* 24.8: 1-21.

Gauthier, M.
    1983   *Highways of the Faith: Relics and Reliquaries from Jerusalem to Compostella* (trans. J.A. Underwood; Secausus: Wellfleet Press).

Geanakopolos, D.J.
  1966   'Church Building and "Caesaropapism", A.D. 312–565', *Greek, Roman and Byzantine Studies* 7: 167-86.
Gibson, S., and J. Taylor
  1994   *Beneath the Church of the Holy Sepulchre Jerusalem: The Archaeology and Early History of Traditional Golgotha* (Palestine Exploration Fund Monograph Series Major; London: Palestine Exploration Fund).
Goitein, S.
  1966   'The Sanctity of Jerusalem and Palestine in Early Islam', in *Studies in Islamic History and Institutions* (Leiden: E.J. Brill): 135-48.
Hart, L.
  1992   *Time, Religion and Social Experience in Rural Greece* (Greek Studies: Interdisciplinary Approaches; Lanham, MD: Rowman & Littlefield).
Hertz, R.
  1983   'Saint Besse: A Study of an Alpine Cult', in S. Wilson (ed.), *Saints and their Cults: Sudies in Religious Sociology, Folklore and History* (Cambridge: Cambridge University Press): 55-100.
Hunt, E.D.
  1982   *Holy Land Pilgrimage in the Later Roman Empire A.D. 312–460* (Oxford: Clarendon Press).
Huxley, A.
  1959   'Words and Behavior', *Collected Essays* (New York: Harper & Brothers, 1959).
Idinopulos, T.
  1996   'Sacred Space and Profane Power: Victor Turner and the Perspective of Holy Land Pilgrimage', in Bryan F. Le Beau and Menachem Mor (eds.), *Pilgrims and Travellers to the Holy Land* (Studies in Jewish Civilization, 7; Omaha, NE: Creighton University Press): 9-19.
Just, R.
  2000   *A Greek Island Cosmos* (World Anthropology; Oxford: James Currey; Santa Fe: School of American Research Press).
Kuhnel, B.
  1987   *From the Earthly to the Heavenly Jerusalem: Representations of the Holy City in Christian Art of the First Millennium* (Rome: Freiburg and Vienna).
MacCormack, S.
  1990   'Loca Sancta: The Organization of Sacred Topography in Late Antiquity'. in Robert Ousterhout (ed.), *The Blessings of Pilgrimage* (Illinois Byzantine Studies, 1; Urbana: University of Illinois Press): 7-40.
Mauss, M.
  1969   *The Gift: Forms and Functions of Exchange in Archaic Societies* (trans. Ian Cunnison; London: Routledge & Kegan Paul).
Morinis, A.
  1984   *Pilgrimage in the Hindu Tradition: A Case Study in West Bengal* (Oxford University South Asian Studies Series; Delhi: Oxford University Press).
Nolan, M., and S. Nolan
  1989   *Christian Pilgrimage in Modern Western Europe* (Studies in Religion; Chapel Hill: University of North Carolina Press).
Ouspensky, L.
  1978   *Theology of the Icon* (New York: St Vladimir's Seminary Press).

Peters, F.E.

    1985   *Jerusalem: The Holy City in the Eyes of Chroniclers, Visitors, Pilgrims and Prophets from the Days of Abraham to the Beginnings of Modern Times* (Princeton, NJ: Princeton University Press).

    1986   *Jerusalem and Mecca: The Typology of the Holy City in the Near East* (New York University Studies in Near Eastern Civilization, 11; New York: New York University Press).

Prawer, J.

    1980   'Jerusalem in the Jewish and Christian Perspective of the Early Middle Ages', *Settimane* 26: 739-812.

Pullan, W.

    1993   'Mapping Time and Salvation: Early Christian Pilgrimage to Jerusalem', in Gavin Flood (ed.), *Mapping Invisible Worlds* (Edinburgh: Edinburgh University Press): 23-40.

Ranger, T.

    1987   '"Taking Hold of the Land": Holy places and Pilgrimages in Twentieth Century Zimbabwe', *Past and Present* 117: 158-94.

Reader, I., and T. Walter (eds.)

    1993   *Pilgrimage in Popular Culture* (Basingstoke: Macmillan).

Safrai, S.

    1969   'Pilgrimage to Jerusalem at the End of the Second Temple Period', in *Studies on the Jewish Background of the New Testament* (Assen: Van Gorcum): 12-21.

    1980   'Pilgrimage to Jerusalem after the Destruction of the Second Temple', in A. Oppenheimer *et al.* (eds.), *Jerusalem in the Second Temple Period* (Jerusalem).

Sallnow, M.

    1987   *Pilgrims of the Andes: Regional Cults in Cusco* (Smithsonian Series in Ethnographic Inquiry; Washington, DC: Smithsonian Institution Press).

Scully, V.

    1962   *The Earth, the Temple and the Gods: Greek Sacred Architecture* (New Haven: Yale University Press).

Smith, W.R.

    1907   *Lectures on the Religion of the Semites* (London: A. & C. Black).

Spitzer, L.

    1949   'The Epic Style of the Pilgrim Aetheria', *Comparative Literature* 1.3: 225-58.

Stewart, C.

    1988   'The Role of Personal Names on Naxos, Greece', *Journal of the Anthropological Society of Oxford* 19: 2.

    1991   *Demons and the Devil: Moral Imagination in Modern Greek Culture* (Princeton, NJ: Princeton University Press).

Stopford, J.

    1994   'Some Approaches to the Archaeology of Christian Pilgrimage', *World Archaeology* 26.1: 57-72.

Storme, A.

    1976   *The Way of the Cross: A Historical Sketch* (trans. Kieran Dunlop; Jerusalem: Franciscan Printing Press).

Sumption, J.
    1975   *Pilgrimage*: *An Image of Medieval Religion* (London: Faber & Faber).
Telfer, W.
    1957   'Constantine's Holy Land Plan', in *Studia Patristica: Papers Presented to
                the International Conference on Patristic Studies* (Berlin: Akademie Verlag):
                696-700.
Turner, V.
    1974   'Pilgrimages as Social Processes', in *Dramas; Fields and Metaphors*
                (Ithaca, NY: Cornell University Press): 167-230.
    1975   'Death and the dead in the pilgrimage process', in Michael Whisson and
                Martin West (eds.), *Religion and Social Change in Southern Africa* (London:
                Rex Collings): 107-27.
Turner, V., and E. Turner
    1978   *Image and Pilgrimage in Christian Culture*: *Anthropological Perspectives*
                (Oxford: Basil Blackwell).
Walker, P.
    1990   *Holy City, Holy Places: Christian Attitudes to Jerusalem and the Holy Land
                in the Fourth Century* (Oxford: Clarendon Press).
    1995   'Jerusalem and the Holy Land in the Fourth Century', in Anthony O'Mahony
                (ed.), *The Christian Heritage in the Holy Land* (London: Scorpion Caven-
                dish): 22-34.
Werbner, R. (ed.),
    1977   *Regional Cults* (ASA Monograph, 16; London: Academic Press).
Wharton, A.
    1992   'The Baptistry of the Holy Sepulchre in Jerusalem and the Politics of Sacred
                Landscape', *Dumbarton Oaks Papers* 46: 313-25.
Wheatley, P.
    1971   *The Pivot of the Four Quarters: A Preliminary Enquiry into the Origins
                and Character of the Ancient Chinese City* (Chicago: University of Chicago
                Press).
Wilken, R.
    1992   *The Land Called Holy: Palestine in Christian History and Thought* (New
                Haven: Yale University Press).
Wilkinson, John
    1971   *Egeria's Travels* (London: SPCK).
    1977   *Jerusalem Pilgrims before the Crusades* (Warminster: Aris & Phillips).
    1989   'Jerusalem under Rome and Byzantium 63 BC–637 AD', in K.J. Asali (ed.),
                Jerusalem in History (London: Scorpion): 75-104.
    1990   'Jewish Holy Places and the Origins of Christian Pilgrimage', in Robert
                Ousterhout (ed.), *The Blessings of Pilgrimage* (Illinois Byzantine Studies, I;
                Urbana: University of Illinois Press): 41-53.

The Preacher with a Golden Tongue: John Chrysostom

John M. Court

Editor's Introduction

History is frequently written as a record of places and personalities; such a procedure may be pragmatic, but it can scarcely be entirely accurate, because of all the other features that emerge from a close scrutiny of any period. It is more useful as a technique for highlighting the main contrasts in a retrospective approach, for example, in the recent surge of 'histories' of one or two millennia, such as the Channel Four television series Millennium Minds. *In addition it is important to balance the impact of great personalities with the continuing influence of schools of thought, traditions that are often focused in particular places. So in the world of biblical interpretation it is appropriate to contrast a figure like Origen (in that first chapter) with that of John Chrysostom. And as major representatives they should be seen to stand within two rival schools of exegesis, associated with the ancient church centres of Alexandria and Antioch respectively. Antioch attacked Alexandria for 'perverting the plain sense of Scripture and robbing its contents to manufacture stupid fables'. For Antioch the practice of the apostle Paul was regulative; they claimed that what he meant by 'allegory' was strictly typology (the juxtaposition and comparison of Old and New Testament events in an historical perspective). Perhaps the Alexandrians were unfairly maligned, because they actually employed allegory only as one among several levels of meaning.*

But it is not only as a working example of Antiochene exegesis that John Chrysostom justifies his place in this volume. We are already noticing that biblical interpretation is not only the business of intellectual research into the meaning of the text. There are also many other ways in which the Bible text is applied (and thereby interpreted): in popular spirituality; in formal worship and the development of the liturgy; and in the broad field that could be labelled aesthetics, containing all kinds of artistic media, not least the architecture of church buildings as places of worship. John Chrysostom recalls for us many of these aspects, not least with his awesome reputation as a preacher on scriptural texts, but also as the inspiration for one of the principal traditions of Greek Orthodox liturgy, and a theologian with a vision of the ultimate purpose of Christian worship.

According to S. Alfonso de' Ligouri (1696–1787, the founder of the Redemptorist Order) St John Chrysostom 'should be styled a martyr' in the
original New Testament sense of the term, which includes 'those who
have sanctified themselves in the world by suffering a continual martyrdom', being constant in their witness to Christ.

His epithet (literally 'golden mouthed') was given in the sixth century
CE, but reflects his preaching skills, which were admired and celebrated in
his lifetime; it is unlikely that it merely referred to a beautiful dulcet voice,
as was the case with Antiochus of Ptolemais, also called Chrysostom. In
the West John was included among the pre-eminent 'Greek Doctors of the
Church' with Saints Athanasius, Basil and Gregory Nazianzen, while in
the East he is regarded as one of the Three Holy Hierarchs and Universal
Teachers. Born c. 347 CE, he died in 407; from 398 he reluctantly became
Bishop (Patriarch) of Constantinople. His frequent representation in icons
is of course stylized, but may contain authentic details in the receding hair,
sparse beard and emaciated ascetic face.

Many Christian authorities in the Patristic and Byzantine periods denounced the moral degeneracy of Constantinople. In this respect John Chrysostom was no exception. He pointed the finger of blame particularly at
Constantinople's notoriously lascivious theatre:

> When you seat yourself in a theatre and feast your eyes on the naked limbs
> of women, you are pleased for a time, but then, what a violent fever you
> have generated! Once your head is filled with such sights and the songs that
> go with them, you think about them even in your dreams. You would not
> choose to see a naked woman in the marketplace, yet you eagerly attend the
> theatre. What difference does it make if the stripper is a whore? It would be
> better to smear our faces with mud than to behold such spectacles.

At an earlier stage John had been equally vocal as a moral watchdog
while he was bishop in Antioch, denouncing lax practices there. He was
critical of what were termed 'spiritual partnerships' between monks and
nuns, and he had also accused Antioch's upper-class women of being in
the habit of exposing themselves in front of their servants, 'their softly
nurtured flesh draped only in heavy jewellry'. The significance of Antioch
as a primary centre of Christianity was particularly important to John. He
repeatedly called attention to Acts 11.26 as evidence that 'it was in Antioch
that the disciples were first called "Christians" '. In another homily[1] John
warns newly-baptized Christians against belief in omens and the wearing
of amulets; such was the attraction of magic, including magical papyri

---

1.   *PG*, XLIX, pp. 223-40.

with texts culled from the Bible (e.g. Ps. 90, the Lord's Prayer, St Matthew's Gospel and the book of Proverbs).

Another target for John's crusading zeal was the Jews; in this respect also he conformed to Christian thinking of the early centuries, but his eloquence added significantly to the stock of anti-Jewish invective, as this sermon example indicates:

> If [the Jews] are ignorant of the Father, if they crucified the Son, and spurned the aid of the Spirit, cannot one declare with confidence that the synagogue is a dwelling place of demons? God is not worshipped there. Far from it! Rather the synagogue is a temple of idolatry… A synagogue is less honourable than any inn. For it is not simply a gathering place for thieves and hucksters, but also of demons. Indeed, not only the synagogue, but the souls of Jews are also the dwelling places of demons.

John had been well trained in Greek culture and rhetoric by the pagan orator Libanius (314–393), although he subsequently reacted strongly against his teacher's beliefs. Among his criticisms was a condemnation of 'empty rhetoric', but, given John's own oratory, this should be taken as a critique, not a total rejection of the rhetorical techniques of the ancient world. Among Libanius's critical attitude to Christian institutions was a description of monks as 'that black-robed tribe who eat more than elephants, sweeping across the country like a river in spate, ravaging the temples and the great estates'. Nor was this by any means an atypical attitude in Antioch, to judge from another of John's sermons:

> Wherever the people gathered to gossip you could find one man boasting that he was the first to beat up a monk, another that he had been the first to track down his hut, a third that he had spurred the magistrate into action against the Holy Men, a fourth that he had dragged them through the streets and seen them locked up in jail.

The other major dimension of John's education was the study of Scripture in the School of Antioch under Melitius of Antioch and Diodore of Tarsus. They were early representatives of a major tradition of biblical exegesis and theology that developed in the fourth century at Antioch, in rivalry with the allegorical tradition of exegesis in the School of Alexandria (see the chapter above on Origen). Antioch's approach to Scripture was more literal, concerned principally with the historical sense of the text. An example given by Theodore is to regard the Song of Songs as a straightforward marriage hymn, not to be allegorically interpreted (as in the Alexandrian and medieval traditions) of the church or the Christian soul in union with Christ; as a result the Song of Solomon was deemed suitable for domestic use, but not for public reading, in Antioch. It has been suggested that this exegetical approach may have been influenced by Antiochene Judaism, as well as reflecting the theological emphasis by Antioch on both the human and the divine natures of Christ. As it happened, because of the condemnation for heresy of two of the leading figures of the School of Antioch, the firebrand/ heretic Nestorius in 431 CE, and the major commentator and theologian Theodore of Mopsuestia in 553 CE, the tradition of Antioch diminished substantially in importance and the significance of its legacy has only been rediscovered in modern times.

The Alexandrian, or Monist, tradition in Christology always had the tendency to underplay the humanity of Christ, according it less significance, and in its most extreme form actually truncating the humanity, compared with the divinity of Christ. What was important to them was a revelation of the Word (the Logos), to which manhood was added as an extra and appropriated mode of self-expression, a channel of divine communication. Humanity was a means to the end of revelation, and it could be limited and rudimentary, so long as it served the theological purpose. The rival (Dualist) tradition of Antioch, in terms of Word and Man, rather than Word and Flesh, operated with a much fuller conception of the manhood of Christ, and strove to maintain an equilibrium between Christ's humanity and his divinity. They were concerned with the realism of the human life, emotions and experiences of Jesus, and focused on the theological significance of the fact that Christ possessed a human soul. But the problem for Antioch was how to preserve the unity of the person of Christ. To emphasize the importance of humanity and divinity, they were forced to ascribe the human and divine attributes to two distinct personal 'subjects'. Only by these means did they think they could preserve the balance between the two equally vital aspects, and prevent the divine nature becoming confused with, or changed by, the human nature.

Redemption comes by intervention from God, but by means of a perfectly obedient man. A key biblical text for the Antiochenes was Phil. 2.5-11. The 'form of a servant' that the Logos has assumed is unique among men, because he alone has endured human trials and sufferings without flinching from his obedience to the divine purpose. Such obedience was essential if he was to be the Second Adam, through whom the restoration of humanity was to be accomplished. This man is the 'man of God's own choosing', foreordained as the recipient of God's special election and grace, and yet he is a perfectly free moral agent; at any stage prior to his glorification at the resurrection he could have repudiated the Logos. It was inadequate, from the Antiochene perspective, to make do with the concept, or the physical shell, of humanity. An ethical situation entailed the risk of a conflict of wills (divine and human); this was essential, given the importance of the ethical element of obedience in the Dualist understanding of redemption. John Chrysostom, later preaching on the text of 1 Cor. 6.20 ('You are not your own; you are bought with a price'), points out that the first half of his text, with its important moral implications, is a view that is shared by Christians and Greek philosophers; but the latter part of the text is a distinctively Christian insight, because it bases this moral claim on the fact of Christ's redemptive sacrifice.

To return to the life of John Chrysostom: the earliest biography we have is in the *Dialogue of Palladius*, which speaks of early recognition and encouragement within the church at Antioch:

> He was gifted with unusual ability, and was carefully trained in letters, for the ministry of the oracles of God. At the age of eighteen, a boy in years, he revolted against the professors of verbosities [rhetoric]; and a man in intellect, he delighted in divine learning. At that time the blessed Meletius the Confessor, an Armenian by race, was ruling the Church of Antioch; he noticed the bright lad, and was so much attracted by the beauty of his character, that he allowed him to be continually in his company. His prophetic eye foresaw the boy's future. He was admitted to the mystery of the washing of regeneration [baptism], and after three years of attendance on the Bishop, advanced to be reader [ἀναγνώστης, member of a minor order in the church]. But as his conscience would not allow him to be satisfied with work in the city, for youth was hot within him, though his mind was sound, he turned to the neighbouring mountains; here he fell in with an old man named Syrus, living in self-discipline, whose hard life he resolved to share.[2]

Between 373 and 381 CE, before ordination, John had lived as a hermit under the Pachomian Rule. The Egyptian Pachomius (who died from the plague in 346 CE) is traditionally credited with the development of cenobitic monasticism (perhaps influenced by the example of early Manichaean groups in Egypt), whereby monks lived within the same complex under a common rule that regulated their meals, work and patterns of prayer; previously the practice (exemplified by St Anthony) was that of anchorites living as solitaries. The common rule did not prevent individual acts of asceticism, and John's own excessive asceticism, coupled with the damp conditions of his cave hermitage, are thought to have undermined his health. To stand up all the time was one form of self-discipline commonly practised; John once pursued this uninterruptedly for two years.

---

2. *The Dialogue of Palladius* (trans. H. Moore; 1921), pp. 37-39.

John Chrysostom's writing includes a significant early work, *On the Priesthood* (*De sacerdotio*/περὶ ἱερωσύνης), the content of which is principally focused on the work of bishops, and several series of his celebrated sermons: *On the Statues* (occasioned by civic violence, breaking the statues of the Emperor and his family, in protest against imperial taxes); *On the Incomprehensibility of God* (against Arian Christians); and *Against Judaizing Christians* (on the dangers for Christians of participating in Jewish festivals—a series with anti-Semitic potential). Interestingly the topic of preaching is given extensive (it might be said disproportionate) attention in Books 4 and 5 of *On the Priesthood*. The effective comparison here might be between the emphasis on Christian preaching in the fourth and nineteenth centuries (see the later chapter in this symposium by Mervyn Willshaw). John's discussion 'reveals the man who was first trained in secular oratory, who was to make his name at Antioch as a preacher, and who made his enemies and brought about his own downfall at Constantinople to a large extent by his preaching'.[3]

The treatise *On the Priesthood* was probably written around 390 CE. It is presented as a dialogue between himself and his boyhood comrade Basil, and it includes some autobiographical material designed to explain that his original refusal to be forced into ordination was based on his sense of unworthiness for the priestly office. From the historians' perspective the curiosity about this work is that such a forced ordination for John is not mentioned in the early biography, the *Dialogue of Palladius*, although it appears to have happened to Basil; the work resembles, and is certainly strongly influenced by, Gregory Nazianzen's discourse *De fuga* on the same topic. J.N.D. Kelly summarizes the description of priesthood in John's discourse in these words:

> the awesome dignity and terrifying responsibilities of a priest or bishop, privileged as he is (for example) to baptise, to absolve sinners, even to make Christ present on the altar, but also liable to be held to account in the life to come for the misdeeds any of his charges may have committed.[4]

There is a clear coordination in terms of sacrifice between past and present: 'the Lord being sacrificed and laid upon the altar, and the priest standing and praying over the victim'.[5] 'We do not offer another sacrifice,

---

3.   Graham Neville in the Introduction to his translation of *Six Books on the Priesthood* (New York: St Vladimir's Seminary Press, 1984), p. 29.

4.   J.N.D. Kelly, *Golden Mouth: The Story of John Chrysostom, Ascetic, Preacher, Bishop* (London: Gerald Duckworth), p. 84.

5.   *De sacerdotio* 3.4.177.

as the high priests of old, but we ever offer the same, or rather we make the memorial of, the sacrifice.'

Chrysostom's other major works are exegetical homilies on the Bible, expounding Genesis, Matthew, John, Acts of the Apostles, Romans, Galatians, 1 and 2 Corinthians, Ephesians, Philippians, Colossians, Thessalonians, Timothy, Titus and Philemon. Many of these commentaries resemble sermons, as, for example, that on Romans (*PG* LX); in contrast the commentary on Galatians (*PG* LXI), written at Antioch c. 395 CE, is an almost uninterrupted explanation of the biblical text. It might have seemed significant that there is no exposition of apocalyptic texts, such as the book of Revelation, but the most likely explanation for this fact is that Chrysostom worked with the Syrian list of books of the New Testament, as found in the Peshitta version, which did not include 2 Peter, 2 and 3 John, Jude and Revelation. While Chrysostom was predictably opposed to allegorical exegesis, his exposition combines spiritual insights with practical applications. A quotation will demonstrate how his great zeal for social righteousness finds expression here too:

> You honour the altar in church, because the Body of Christ rests upon it, but those who are themselves the very Body of Christ you treat with contempt, and you remain indifferent when you see them perishing. This living altar you can see everywhere, lying in the streets and market places, and at any hour you can offer sacrifice upon it.

He argues that the reason for the weak state of the Church is that it has abandoned the 'angelic life of Pentecost', the life of sharing and common ownership, and has fallen back on private property. If wealth was shared, Chrysostom claimed, it would lead to a 'universal upheaval' and to the conversion of the world. It is in his sermons on Matthew's Gospel that we see the most passionate critique of wealth, and the insistence on the need to see and serve Christ in the oppressed. Chrysostom speaks thus of the sacrament of the brother.

A difficulty presented to exegetes from the Antiochene School, in their controversy with the allegorical exegesis of Alexandria, was the fact that St Paul himself had used the word ἀλληγορέω (to speak allegorically) in Gal. 4.24. Theodore of Mopsuestia, commenting on this text, had taken the opportunity of attacking the allegorists of Alexandria who perverted the plain sense of Scripture and robbed its contents to manufacture stupid fables. What St Paul had meant by allegorism was the juxtaposition and comparison of events in the past (of the Old Testament) with events in the present. Nowadays we would regularly label this interpretative method as

Typology rather than Allegory and demonstrate from the context of Galatians 4 that a typological comparison is what Paul intended.

Theodoret of Cyrus insisted even more strongly than Theodore on the historical character of Pauline allegorism: 'When the Apostle said "these things contain an allegory" he meant that they had an additional meaning; for he did not discard the historical narrative, but taught what was foreshadowed in it.' It was actually John Chrysostom who added the further comment that Paul was using this Greek term in Gal. 4.24 in an unusual sense, since what he called an allegory was in fact a type. So, following this example, John insists that the stories of Noah's Ark and of Abraham's sacrifice of Isaac are records of actual historical events, but in addition they are able to prefigure (respectively) Christ and the Church, and the Crucifixion.[6] In the same way Aaron and Eli are Old Testament examples and warnings for the priesthood of the Christian church.[7] But Chrysostom emphasizes that students of the Bible are not to act as if they are the lords of Scripture. Their task is not to adapt such passages as Isa. 5.1-7 to suit their own preconceived ideas of what the allegory meant, but rather to follow the guidance of the context and accept the interpretation given there. For whatever allegories occur in the Bible, they are invariably accompanied by their interpretations.[8] In short, the plain meaning of the text may be conveyed by a figure of speech (*ek metaphorias*).

The Antiochene Fathers regarded the principles of Pauline exegesis as regulative. But they had no special predilection for Paul's allegorism and usually avoided it as a method in their own exegesis. References to 'allegory' could thus be taken to mean a mode of expression using figurative language, rather than a particular method of scriptural exegesis. Where Chrysostom incorporates a piece of allegorism into a homily, as he does occasionally, he makes plain that he is borrowing it from another source.

There are ten folios of John Chrysostom's sermon-commentaries, which, in J.N.D. Kelly's words 'form the most impressive, and also most readable, collection of patristic expositions of scripture'.[9] But there is no uniformity in the presentation of the texts of these sermon-commentaries; some are just as they might have been taken down by secretaries as John Chrysostom preached, while others show signs of varying degrees of re-editing. A sermon series, such as *On the Statues*, has been carefully edited and polished to a final version by John himself, and the commentary on

---

6.   *Hom. de Lazaro* 6.7; *in Ps.* 46 (*PG* XLVIII, p. 1037; LV, p. 209).
7.   *De sacerdotio* 4.1.357.
8.   *Isa. interpr.* 5.3.
9.   Kelly, *Golden Mouth*, p. 94.

Galatians has been so thoroughly revised as to lose almost all signs that it was originally preached.

Even granted the historical concerns of Antiochene method, the approach in scriptural exposition is clearly different from modern critical exegesis. John shared with all other Patristic commentators a belief in the direct authorship of Scripture by the Holy Spirit. As with Origen, the human writer's involvement provided some explanation of errors, such as 'the discrepancy between the evangelists in small matters'.[10] But again in comparison, or rather contrast, with Origen, and perhaps because of John's own strong instincts for Christian education and pastoral care, he seems to have felt an empathy with the apostle Paul and was therefore able to relate to the Pauline letters as actual correspondence.

John Chrysostom's interest in Paul was particularly directed to the moral and devotional aspects of his writing. The doctrine of justification by faith in Paul's writings, so important for Luther and the Protestant Reformation, was not a central argument for John Chrysostom. So much the contrary that Pelagius was able to cite John as his authority in the debate with Augustine of Hippo. John's emphasis on the moral and devotional in the Bible also explains his selection of favourite preaching topics, such as the suffering of Job, the injunctions of the Sermon on the Mount, the parable of Dives and Lazarus, and the examples of the apostolic church. In the judgment of Hans von Campenhausen, John's sermons 'reflect something of the authentic life of the New Testament, just because they are so ethical, so simple, and so clear-headed'.

The case of Pelagius, just mentioned, was by no means the last of such instances when John Chrysostom would be cited as authority for a doctrine, and regarded as bringing with him the full weight of orthodox, Patristic teaching. Another instance was when Martin Luther cited Chrysostom's exegesis of Jn 6.63 ('the flesh is useless') in support of his argument against Zwingli over the nature of Christ's presence in the Eucharist. Chrysostom, commenting on this verse, had interpreted 'the flesh' as the weakness of human understanding, and urged upon his hearers a spiritual understanding that would allow them to perceive Christ's divine nature (as represented in John's gospel) despite his human form. Luther transposed this into the context of his argument on the Eucharist, and in a very precise application asserted that Chrysostom was saying, 'Just because humans cannot understand the concept of spiritual eating, it does not follow that

10. *In Matt. hom.* 1.1 (*PG*, LVII, p. 16).

Christ's flesh, being spiritual, cannot be present in the Eucharist.'[11] So Chrysostom is made to support Luther's view of eucharistic presence over against Zwingli's view of an entirely symbolic presence.

To return to the religious politics of Chrysostom's life from those of a much later age: at the beginning of the fifth century John launched a crusade against the paganism of Ba'albek and the Lebanon, by sending a task force of monks to destroy the pagan temples in the area. According to Theodoret's account:

> Hearing that some of the inhabitants of Phoenicia were addicted to the worship of demons, John selected some ascetics who were filled with fervent zeal and sent them to destroy the idolatrous temples, inducing some ladies of great opulence to defray the monks' expenses; and the temples of the demons were thrown down from their very foundations.

It does not seem that John was particularly impressed by the growing interest in Christian pilgrimage to Palestine, apparently in danger of becoming a mass phenomenon (at least in the view of Jerome). John's comment in a sermon is frequently quoted in studies of pilgrimage: 'the whole world runs to see the tomb which has no body'.[12]

Chrysostom's career as a bishop was coloured by political rivalry with Theophilus archbishop of Alexandria, who sought to use the continuing controversies in the Church over the theology of Origen and his successors, in order to unseat John Chrysostom from Constantinople, after John had granted asylum to Origenist refugees from Theophilus's repressive rule. There were also dissensions with the Empress Eudoxia, no doubt fostered by John's tactlessness, or concern for free speech. After he was recalled from a first brief exile, he finally alienated Eudoxia by a sermon that could only be construed as a deliberate public challenge to her. This may have been the occasion when he compared Eudoxia with Jezebel (in 1 Kgs 21), on the grounds of depriving a widow of her possessions, while it may only be an apocryphal story that he compared her with Herodias, demanding the head of John (the Baptist). In 403, at the Synod of the Oak (Chalcedon), Chrysostom had been condemned and removed from his see, subjected to two exiles and hastened to death (14 September 407).

In his lifetime he was noted for liturgical reforms, redefining the boundaries of sacred and profane. The liturgy which bears his name is now in

---

11. Cf. Irena Backus, 'The Early Church in the Renaissance and Reformation', in Ian Hazlett, *Early Christianity* (London: SPCK, 1991), pp. 294-95.

12. *Hom in Ps.* 109.5 (110.5) (*PG*, LV, p. 274a). Compare this attitude with the views reflected in Glen Bowman's contribution to this Symposium.

general use in the Eastern Orthodox Churches, except for the few days on which the Liturgy of St Basil is appointed. In its present form the liturgy is of course much later than Chrysostom's time, and it is debatable how closely it should be connected with him. Although Robert Taft[13] has recently presented an interesting argument: he identifies the Anaphora of St John Chrysostom as a redaction of a now-lost original. This original has another developed form in the Syriac Anaphora of the Apostles. Taft sought to demonstrate by a computer comparison of these two existing texts that Chrysostom himself may have been responsible for much of the redaction of the original. Presumably the whole liturgy of St John Chrysostom was so influential because it was the liturgy of Constantinople; it assimilated and superseded the older liturgies of St James (Jerusalem and Antioch) and St Mark (Alexandria). Archbishop Cranmer also drew the Prayer of St Chrysostom in the Anglican Book of Common Prayer from this Liturgy. Cranmer's version first appeared in the liturgy of 1544; it is a translation of the prayer of the Third Antiphon.

John's series of sermons provided another extensive legacy, although one suspects that they were not always read aloud in later generations with the same zeal and rhetorical skill that their author would have used. The nineteenth-century travel writer Robert Curzon, for example, records in *Visits to Monasteries in the Levant*[14] how

> I have been quietly dining in a monastery when shouts have been heard, and shots have been fired against the stout bulwarks of the outer walls, which, thanks to their protection, had but little effect in altering the monotonous cadence in which one of the brotherhood read a homily of St. Chrysostom from the pulpit provided for that purpose in the refectory.

St John Chrysostom's vision of heaven on earth, realized in liturgical form, is however one of the main inspirations of Orthodoxy: 'The church is the place of the angels, of the archangels, the kingdom of God, heaven itself.' Today Greek Orthodox believers would readily say that when they stand within an Orthodox church—the walls and iconostasis dense with icons, and the ceilings painted with stars and pictures of the Pantocrator—they stand in Paradise in the presence of God, the Virgin Mary and all the saints. The entry into the holy space serves, in effect, to presage their entry at death into eternity. A special event, such as a group pilgrimage to the Holy Land, would represent a preparation for death, both by individual

---

13. In P.F. Bradshaw (ed.), *Essays on Early Christian Eucharistic Prayers* (Collegeville, MN: Liturgical Press, 1997).

14. London: George Newnes, 1897.

self-purification and by collective participation in eternity, as represented by the churches on the sacred sites where Christ had worked. The essential process of metastoicheiosis, or trans-elementation, is symbolized by the icons of Christ and his mother in such pilgrimage churches. The redemptive potential of Christ is cosmological, and hence eventually universal, as summarized in the words of St Gregory of Nyssa in his *Catechetical Oration*:

> As the principle of death took its rise in one person and passed on in succession through the whole of the human nature, so the principle of the Resurrection extends from one person to the whole of humanity… This is the mystery of God's plan with regard to His death and His resurrection from the dead.

The way that St John Chrysostom symbolizes in his own person the noblest vision of Orthodoxy and the greatest powers of the Byzantine Empire is well illustrated by a Pontic folk-song, composed five hundred years ago, when the news of the fall of Constantinople reached Trebizond, a translation of which is included by Neal Ascherson in his book *Black Sea—The Birthplace of Civilisation and Barbarism*:[15]

> A bird, a good bird, left the City [Constantinople],
> it settled neither in vineyards nor in orchards,
> it came to settle on the castle of the Sun.
> It shook one wing, drenched in blood,
> it shook the other wing, it had a written paper.
> Now it reads, now it cries, now it beats its breast.
> 'Woe is us, woe is us, Romania [Byzantium] is taken.'
> The churches lament, the monasteries weep,
> and St. John Chrysostom weeps, he beats his breast.
> Weep not, weep not, St. John, and beat not your breast.
> Romania has passed away, Romania is taken.
> Even if Romania has passed away, it will flower and bear fruit again.

BIBLIOGRAPHY

Attwater, Donald, *St John Chrysostom: Pastor and Preacher* (London: Harvill Press, 1959).
Bradshaw, Paul, *Search for the Origins of Christian Worship* (London: SPCK, 2002).
Broadus, J., 'St Chrysostom as a homilist', in Ph. Schaff (ed.), *The Writings of the Nicene and Post-Nicene Fathers*, I.13 (Grand Rapids: Eerdmans, 1956), pp. v-vii.
Campenhausen, H. von, *The Fathers of the Greek Church* (London: A. & C. Black, 1963), Chapter XI.

15. London: Vintage, 1996, p. 182.

Carter, R.E., *The Chronology of Saint John Chrysostom's Early Life* (Traditio, 18; New York: Fordham University Press, 1962).

Field, F. (ed.), *Chrysostomi Homiliae in Epist. II ad Corinth* (30 sermons) (Cambridge: Cambridge University Press, 1845).

Kelly, J.N.D., *Golden Mouth: The Story of John Chrysostom, Ascetic, Preacher, Bishop* (London: Gerald Duckworth, 1995)

Kinzig, W., 'The Greek Christian Writers', in Stanley Porter (ed.), *Handbook of Classical Rhetoric in the Hellenistic Period 330 BC–AD 400* (Leiden: E.J. Brill, 1997), pp. 633-70.

Mitchell, Margaret M., *The Heavenly Trumpet: John Chrysostom and the Art of Pauline Interpretation* (HUT, 40; Tübingen: Mohr Siebeck, 2000).

—' "A Variable and Many-sorted Man": John Chrysostom's Treatment of Pauline Inconsistency', *Journal of Early Christian Studies* 6.1 (1998), pp. 93-111.

Moore, H. (trans.), *The Dialogue of Palladius* (1921).

Nairn, J.A. (ed.), *De Sacerdotio of St. John Chrysostom* (Cambridge, 1906).

Neville, G. (ed.), *Six Books on the Priesthood* (New York: St. Vladimir's Seminary Press, 1984).

O'Keefe, John J., ' "A Letter That Killeth": Toward a Reassessment of Antiochene Exegesis, or Diodore, Theodore and Theodoret on the Psalms', *Journal of Early Christian Studies* 8.1 (2000), pp. 83-104.

Staats, R., 'Chrysostomus über die Rhetorik des Apostels Paulus. Makarianische Kontexte zu 'De Sacerdotio' IV,5-6', *Vigiliae Christianae* 46, pp. 225-40.

Thurén, Lauri, 'John Chrysostom as a Rhetorical Critic: the Hermeneutics of an Early Father', *BibInt* 9.2 (2001), pp. 180-218.

Wilken, R., *John Chrysostom and the Jews: Rhetoric and Reality in the Late Fourth Century* (Berkeley: University of California Press, 1983).

Interpreting Scripture for the Love of God: Hugh of St Victor on Reading and the Self

Jeremy Worthen

Editor's Introduction

*The focus of this chapter is the work of Hugh of St Victor (c. 1096–1141) and it discusses several treatises by him, one in particular being little known. These particular texts are especially significant, within the present context of studies in biblical tradition and interpretation, because they can be used to illustrate the various strategies for the reading of Scripture that were prevalent in this period of the Middle Ages. As well as fitting into the whole tradition of monastic reading (*lectio divina *and the concepts of* cogitatio, meditatio *and* contemplatio), *Hugh relates to contemporary and earlier instances of 'philosophical' allegorical reading (such as that of Macrobius). So this chapter visits the landscape of mediaeval culture and theology, introducing and commenting upon various different traditions of thought, including philosophical allegory, Augustinian theological history, monastic ascesis and mysticism. Perhaps the most surprising and exciting thing is that it is possible at the same time to suggest relationships between Hugh's hermeneutics and modern methods, such as those of Paul Ricoeur and Frank Kermode.*

The divide in interpretation between historical meaning and contemporary application, anticipated as it was in Scholasticism, has been largely taken for granted in modern hermeneutics, although called into question just recently. Hugh of St Victor is worth revisiting simply because he strove to bridge the divide between monastic and scholastic approaches (and classic writers on the Middle Ages therefore differ in their estimate of him!). He saw interpretation as an ethical and spiritual discipline, not an exercise in academic neutrality but an experience of conversion to share in the history of God's people on the road to salvation. The function of allegory within this system is carefully defined, not as a matter of opposition between narrative and meaning, fiction and truth, but as a deepening experience of the historical and the work of interpretation.

1. *Introduction*

Western mediaeval culture was devoted to the activity of interpretation. In part, this reflected the common legacy of late antiquity shared with the Eastern Christian empire, Talmudic Judaism and subsequently the Islamic world, where sacred texts from the past were identified as the definitive source of truth and therefore their decipherment and application became the supreme goal of all cultural activity. Yet Western mediaeval culture also became devoted to the activity of interpretation in more specific and far-reaching ways. The initial Western response in the eighth century to the second council of Nicea, which had attempted to settle the question of the place of images within Christian spirituality, already demonstrated a relentless attention to the book as the focus for theology and devotion, one that would not be balanced or supplemented by the visual image in the same way as was becoming customary in Eastern Christianity.[1] The great artefacts of the seventh and eighth centuries in the West, intricately and lavishly decorated illuminated manuscripts of Scripture in whole or part testify to this emerging cult of the book. At Charlemagne's court, reforming theology and church had to begin with attempts to produce an agreed correct text of the Bible and the production of biblical commentaries in great profusion, many of them summarizing or anthologizing the exegetical labours of earlier times. Indeed, the sheer volume of biblical exegesis generated throughout the Middle Ages needs to be properly weighed in any understanding of Western mediaeval Christianity, despite the fact that so much of it still remains untranslated and that it has been too often neglected in studies of the period's religious and theological literature.[2]

While this devotion to the interpretation of Scripture remained constant, it was also subjected to shifting configurations through the millennium conventionally bracketed as the mediaeval period. As with many other aspects

---

1.   Peter Brown, *The Rise of Western Christendom: Triumph and Diversity AD 200–1000* (Oxford: Basil Blackwell, 1996), pp. 293-98.

2.   One of the foundational works of modern scholarship in this area, Henri de Lubac, *Exégèse médiévale: Les quatres sens de l'Écriture* (4 vols.; Paris: Aubier, 1959–64), has only recently begun to be translated into English; first two volumes have now appeared, as *Medieval Exegesis: The Four Senses of Scripture* (trans. Mark Sebanc; 2 vols.; Edinburgh: T. & T. Clark, 1998, 2000), while there are also some extracts from all four volumes included in Henri de Lubac, *The Sources of Revelation* (trans. Luke O'Neill; New York: Herder & Herder, 1968). Unfortunately, much writing in English over the last 40 years on mediaeval biblical interpretation does not engage with de Lubac's research and therefore needs to be treated with some caution.

of Western mediaeval culture and society, the twelfth century tends to be identified as the site of some of the most far-reaching changes, a time when long-practised approaches to interpretation were able to flourish but also began to be both complemented and supplanted by new tendencies related in part to the economic growth and increasing urbanization in contemporary Western European society. Two classic works of modern scholarship, with quite different perspectives, both share this orientation towards the twelfth century as the decisive period for the history of mediaeval interpretation of the bible. Jean Leclercq, in *The Love of Learning and the Desire for God*, develops the concept of contrasting 'monastic' and 'scholastic' theologies in the Middle Ages, with the twelfth century representing the finest flowering of the former yet also marking the beginning of the ascendancy of the latter.[3] 'Monastic' theology as he defines it is driven by the love of God and the pursuit of union with God, and the interpretation of Scripture as practised within the monastery is supremely an expression of this desire. One of the most famous outlines of the process of monastic reading, the so-called *lectio divina*, comes from Guigo II, a Carthusian monk.[4] For him, the bare 'reading' of a particular text should serve to lead on to a more ruminative 'meditation' that explores the sense and searches for parallels and illumination from other biblical passages. Such meditation incites a further movement to 'prayer' as the reader recognizes the distance between the fullness of truth glimpsed through the page and his or her own life that is darkened by sin and limited by creatureliness. This prayer is then answered by the gift of 'contemplation', silence and peace within which the meaning of the text is known and owned—for a moment, for the cycle of these distinct movements within the one act of interpretation requires continual recapitulation. At what point one is in the cycle is of less significance than that one keeps moving through it within a form of life framed by monastic discipline and dedicated to living constantly within and before the book of the Scriptures.

Biblical interpretation for such a style of monastic reading can only be understood as belonging within a complete way of life; it is one element, and a critical one, in the training (*ascesis*) and preparation for the kingdom of heaven. While the practice of such interpretation may draw on the resources of biblical scholarship and doctrinal formulations, it remains at

---

3. Jean Leclercq, *The Love of Learning and the Desire for God: A Study of Monastic Culture* (trans. Catharine Misrahi; New York: Fordham University Press, 1961).

4. Guigo II, *Scala claustralium*, in *The Ladder of Monks: A Letter on the Contemplative Life and Twelve Meditations* (trans. Edmund Colledge and James Walsh; London: Mowbrays).

root an ethical and spiritual exercise whose origin and goal is the transformation of the self of the reader. There is an attempt to balance, it would seem, within this model what to borrow terms from Paul Ricoeur we might call distanciation and appropriation, explanation and understanding.[5] For Leclercq (and he is not alone among mediaeval historians), beyond the achievements of the twelfth century this balance became lost: the new scholastic theology, taught in cathedral schools and the emerging universities to all comers in a competitive educational market, no longer within the enclosure of the monastery to those united by the common desire for God, seized hold of the pole of 'explanation' and wrenched it away from its beginning and end in appropriation, from its place within the overarching task of transforming the reader for union with God. Biblical interpretation became instead an autonomous sphere of intellectual activity, as teachers like Peter Abelard offered to use their exegetical prowess to explain the obscurities of Scripture to anyone who cared to pay, regardless of ethical or spiritual commitment.[6]

We might contrast with Leclercq's book another classic work of mediaeval scholarship, Beryl Smalley's *The Study of the Bible in the Middle Ages*.[7] While sharing with Leclercq a view of the twelfth century as the period of decisive change in mediaeval approaches to biblical interpretation, Smalley has a far more positive view of the coming of scholasticism and its impact on the reading of Scripture. Far from disrupting a delicate balance, for her the new scholastic interpreters represented a necessary and decisive turning away from the arbitrary procedures of allegorical reading that had dominated earlier mediaeval hermeneutics towards a clear focus on the literal meaning, deriving ultimately from the author's intention, as the only reliable foundation for Christian theology. The monastic pattern of isolating individual texts and allowing them to strike sparks from an imagination soaked in the memorization of the Bible may have been a valuable path for personal devotion, but if theology was to be placed on a properly rigorous footing, able to respond to the new intellectual and social challenges of the twelfth and thirteenth centuries, it needed to be rooted in a more disciplined hermeneutics. Discovering the literal meaning, bound up with the historical meaning for pre-Enlightenment hermeneutics, was gradually

---

5.   Cf. Paul Ricoeur, *Interpretation Theory: Discourse and the Surplus of Meaning* (Fort Worth: Texas Christian University Press, 1976).

6.   Jacques Le Goff, *Intellectuals in the Middle Ages* (trans. Teresa Lavender Fagan; Oxford: Basil Blackwell, 1993), pp. 5-64.

7.   Beryl Smalley, *The Study of the Bible in the Middle Ages* (Oxford: Basil Blackwell, 3rd edn, 1983).

recognized in the twelfth century as the overriding priority for biblical exegesis, with further levels of understanding (tropological, allegorical, anagogical) not ruled out but accountable to and derivative from this baseline, 'foundational' level of interpretation.

It is noteworthy that on Smalley's analysis, the scholastic approach as thus defined anticipated just the kind of split between historical meaning and contemporary application that has been viewed as virtually self-evident orthodoxy within modern theological hermeneutics. This 'two-stage' approach to biblical interpretation, with the 'historical' meaning providing the supposedly objective foundation and starting point, has, however, been increasingly questioned during the past couple of decades through such diverse though intersecting influences as liberation theology, hermeneutical philosophy and literary theory.[8] If the analyses of Leclercq and Smalley both retain some validity, then twelfth-century biblical interpretation may be worth revisiting as a place where questions about the relationship between inherent literal meaning, shared presuppositions and individual reader responses were being worked out with an intensity comparable to our own time. And if within biblical interpretation today it is sometimes felt that some of the apparent dichotomies that exist with regard to these questions could or should be resisted, then there may be particular reasons for considering Hugh of St Victor; for in his own life and writings, Hugh strove to bridge the growing hermeneutical divide between older monastic and newer scholastic approaches to biblical interpretation, confident that they could enrich one another.

2. *Hugh of St Victor: Across the Divide*

Hugh of St Victor is something of an anomaly for Leclercq and a ground-breaking thinker for Smalley. His writings show an encyclopaedic mind, passionately devoted to the task of interpreting Scripture as the greatest work of the human intellect, willing to engage with the new insights and methods of scholasticism yet bringing it all within a form of spirituality that remains in clear continuity with older monastic ideals. The community at the abbey of St Victor in Paris to which he belonged, founded in 1110, was comprised of Regular Canons: priests who lived, under the Rule of St Augustine, in a strict form of religious community, yet who also recognized a calling to preach and teach in the wider church. Hugh arrived there

---

8.   See, for instance, Francis Watson, *Text, Church and World: Biblical Interpretation in Theological Perspective* (Edinburgh: T. & T. Clark, 1994).

around 1118 and stayed until his death in 1142. The community produced some notable figures after Hugh for the history of biblical interpretation, including Andrew, who drew on contemporary Jewish learning in his commentaries on the Old Testament, and Richard, who read scriptural texts through the glass of his own profound mystical vision. By the beginning of the thirteenth century, however, the Victorines were no longer a significant force, and scholastic theology, while still sometimes referring to Hugh's voluminous works, was more influenced by its more immediate predecessors. We need to look to the friars and in particular to such figures as Bonaventure for later attempts to realize Hugh's ideal of bringing together all learning, ancient and contemporary, within an explicitly theological framework that would sustain and inspire people in search not so much of worldly advancement or the stimulation of new ideas but rather of the kingdom of heaven.

While he did not succeed in establishing a lasting theological tradition that could hold together the new scholastic thinking with the values of monastic culture, Hugh in fact spent much of his life seeking to provide foundations and frameworks for an ambitious theological programme where scriptural interpretation represented the summit of all achievement. His *Didascalicon: De studio legendi* was an introduction to the study of theology as an interpretative discipline, a discipline of 'reading', that could embrace inherited wisdom of various pedigrees together with contemporary developments in the liberal arts and the use of dialectical forms of argument in theology, yet harness these things to the end of a self-transforming engagement with Scripture.[9] He begins by urging his students, who had come to the 'open school' of the abbey, to familiarize themselves with the range of intellectual activity going on around them in the schools of twelfth-century Paris, its arts and sciences, which he categorizes according to his own distinctive scheme. In explaining later on in the work how all this can be placed in the service of the monastic ideal of *lectio divina*, Hugh employs the traditional division of the three senses of Scripture in its formulation by Gregory the Great: literal, allegorical and tropological.[10] The student must begin with the literal sense, which requires careful reading of the 'historical' books in Old and New Testaments and memorization of relevant information about events, people and places; Hugh himself prepared chronicles and maps to help students at this stage, as well as a

---

9.   *The Didascalicon of Hugh of St Victor: A Medieval Guide to the Arts* (trans. Jerome Taylor; New York: Columbia University Press, 1961).

10.   Hugh of St Victor, *Didascalicon*, pp. 135-45.

treatise on the ancient art of memory with which he expected his students to be familiar.[11] Tedious all this may be, but Hugh is scathing about those who think their brilliance allows them to neglect it and press impatiently on to the dazzling secrets of the deeper meaning; such people cite Paul's text 'The letter killeth', thinking that they can thereby dispense with Hugh's requirement that 'we should follow the letter in such a way as not to prefer our own sense to the divine authors', something he clearly regarded as a persistent danger.[12] Context and authorial intention need to regulate continually the interpretative work undertaken at this stage to which in turn all other stages remain accountable. Only with this historical framework firmly established can the student then safely pass to the higher stage of allegory, where the letter is read so as to reveal the deep truths of faith. It is important to stress that Hugh belongs in this respect within the mainstream of the patristic and mediaeval tradition of biblical interpretation, for which allegory was not a matter of something aside from or even against the letter but rather of a deeper and more synthetic appreciation of the central doctrinal themes glimpsed across the diverse historical accounts of the Scriptures as focused in the (itself historical) paschal mystery.[13] The fact that allegory *can* refer to a mode of reading in which the outer 'shell' of the literal meaning and the inner sense of spiritual truth are only contingently related should not be allowed to determine our understanding of the meaning of allegory for pre-modern Christian exegetes, as this remains for them only a secondary use of the term. Since allegory in Hugh's sense presupposes a grasp of the whole sweep of God's dealings with the world and the truths made known through historical revelation, Hugh also provided his own 'text-book' on doctrine for his students, in a work to be discussed in a moment. Finally, the *Didascalicon* explains that the mature student will move on from allegory to the tropological sense, the sense that speaks of virtue rather than knowledge, the point where the text tells us not just how things are but how we should be; where it makes concrete demands on us, changes us, re-forms us.

At the very end of the treatise, Hugh notes that his exposition of reading is not in this book complemented by an exposition of meditation, which he had coupled with reading in the preface as the principal means given humanity by which it might advance in knowledge. As he notes in passing

11. Ivan Illich, *In the Vineyard of the Text: A Commentary to Hugh's Didascalicon* (Chicago: University of Chicago Press, 1993), pp. 35-38.

12. Hugh of St Victor, *Didascalicon*, pp. 143-44.

13. De Lubac has long since sought to establish this important distinction which continues to be too often ignored; see, e.g., *Sources of Revelation*, pp. 11-13.

later on in the text, meditation serves as the hinge between reading-as-study and the pursuit of God through prayer, practice (*operatio*, translated as 'performance' by Taylor) and their fruit, contemplation;[14] thus Hugh envisages the 'technical' disciplines of the arts and of biblical interpretation all feeding into the continuing practice of *lectio divina*. This is no self-sufficient treatise, then, but a stage along the way of wisdom, which is to be sought above all things, according to the very first sentence of the book. The treatise tells us clearly, however, that the way of wisdom begins with the discipline of reading.

The structure of the *Didascalicon*, therefore, embraces Hugh's clear commitment to scholarly study as essential for biblical interpretation, as celebrated by Smalley, and also his maintenance of the same fundamental balance and tension between distanciation and appropriation, explanation and understanding that was noted in the traditional 'monastic' approaches to reading described by Leclercq, where biblical interpretation remains essentially an ethical and spiritual discipline, not the expression of what was then often denigrated as the vice of curiosity (and we might call academic neutrality). It is Hugh's doctrine of the fall that makes such disinterested investigation appear worse than trivial: while the eye of the flesh remains sound, humanity's two other eyes, the eye of reason and the eye of contemplation, have become darkened outside of Eden, and it is a matter of absolute urgency that we begin to repair the damage.[15] As the damage to the eye of reason, though serious, is less complete than the blinding of the eye of contemplation, the strenuous pursuit of knowledge is a possible path towards the restoration of the second eye and thence of the whole creature; and for Hugh, here standing squarely in the Western mediaeval tradition sketched out in the introduction, the beginning of knowledge is reading. The *Didascalicon*, therefore, is just as much offering a remedy for the effects of the fall as an up-to-date introduction to mid-twelfth-century biblical studies. Disciplined, intelligent reading of Scripture marks the road to salvation, and it would be unpardonable frivolity, from Hugh's point of view, to engage in it from any other motivation or for any lesser end.

It is important to note that in the *Didascalicon*, allegory is the pivot that enables us to move between scholarly exegesis of the literal meaning and the life-changing response of the heart to God's word (tropology). De

---

14. Hugh of St Victor, *Didascalicon*, pp. 132-33.

15. On the 'three eyes' of humanity, see Hugh of St Victor, *De sacramentis* 1.10.2 (*PL*, CLXXVI, pp. 329C-30A).

Lubac would argue that this is true to the consensus of the pre-modern
Catholic tradition of biblical interpretation, although anagogy, that which
leads the soul to union with God, came to be recognized by later exegetes
as the other 'pole' of the spiritual reader's response to the invitation of the
text alongside tropology. While the function of allegory is thus in one
respect relativized, it also becomes critical to the entire interpretative enterprise. In his own *summa* of Christian doctrine, the *De sacramentis*, Hugh
attempted to provide not just the outlines of a doctrinal system that would
keep students' allegorizing within the limits of ecclesiastical truth but a
narrative theology that was structured by a hermeneutics accountable to
history rather than by any *a priori* or systematic requirements. The *De
sacramentis* lays out the shape of doctrine by telling and explaining the
story of redemption and its 'sacraments' (which for Hugh are scattered
right across the history of the world, mysteries disclosed already within
the patterns of creation), not by formulating a sequence of questions in the
manner of Aquinas and other subsequent scholastic theologians. And just
as doctrine is inseparable from exegesis, so both are inseparable from
Church history: 'Holy Church began to exist in her faithful at the beginning, and shall last to the end,' Hugh writes; 'from the beginning to the
end, no period lacks its faithful to Christ'.[16] Doctrine, which for Hugh is
ultimately coextensive with allegorical reading of the Scriptures, cannot
help but explain by narrating and then reflecting on this narration, and the
story it thereby tells is always at one level the history of a people, the city
of God. And we, Hugh's imagined readers and students, are (we hope) that
people; and therefore we are ourselves both agents and objects of such an
interpretive programme, we are inside the narrative patterns that doctrine
reveals, and we cannot actually begin the life of interpretative study set
out in the *Didascalicon* unless we recognize that we too have our being
within the work of scriptural interpretation and construct our inner life out
of its dynamics. Interpretation, then, requires conversion, a decision and
desire to share in the history of God's people that is coextensive with the
history of the world in creation and restoration. While texts like the *Didascalicon* and the *De sacramentis* map the external shape of the interpretative programme that Hugh's students would follow, the interior drama of
conversion that it presupposes is sketched out in a less well known but
still fascinating text, the *De vanitate rerum mundanarum*, 'On the Vanity
of Worldly Things'.[17]

16. Quoted in Smalley, *Study of the Bible*, p. 90.
17. There is no English translation of this work in its entirety. The complete Latin

3. *Conversion, History and the Love of God*

For Hugh, the work of interpreting Scripture required the reader to have not just an adequate grasp of the contemporary arts and sciences, inherited doctrinal frameworks and multiple hermeneutical levels; it also needed a particular 'shape' for the reader's inner life, a shape of conversion to the way of the people of God, and to understand this we now turn to the *De vanitate*. The work is written in a literary genre, not uncommon in the Middle Ages, that could be called the interior dialogue, in which different elements of the self were named and their conversation with one another represented in the text. Augustine's *Soliloquies*, in which the convalescing writer is interrogated by Reason (*ratio*), was an important precedent here. In Hugh's *De vanitate*, Reason is again the one who sets the agenda for discussion and leads the other element of the self towards truth, but whereas in the earlier text the 'other' element of the self addressed by reason is very definitely the writer Augustine, albeit in literary guise, in Hugh's interior dialogues this 'other' is universalized simply as 'Soul' (*anima*). This dialogue is, therefore, on one level, about anyone and (potentially) everyone. More specifically, however, it is about the person who reads it, and who thereby takes on the personae of the interior drama within her/himself—so long as this reader is prepared to 'perform' the script of the self's conversion that they are reading or to allow it to rehearse and define whatever conversions may have preceded it. It is a text that defines the student of theology as a convert to the pursuit of wisdom whose interiority remains marked by a basic polarity of reason and not-reason, but one which is nevertheless on the way to being overcome through the labour of biblical interpretation.

The four books of the *De vanitate* begin with Soul overhearing Reason's lament over the folly of love for this world. Soul asks for an explanation, so Reason paints a series of colourful scenes: sailors on the sea, merchants crossing the lands, a man of great wealth, a happy couple getting married, bright young men beginning their study of the arts and sciences. In each

text of the four books is printed in *PL* CLXXVI, pp. 703-40; the greater part of books I and II is translated in Hugh of St Victor, *Selected Spiritual Writings* (trans. A Religious of CMSV; London: Faber, 1962), pp. 157-82, which also includes extracts from another of Hugh's treatises referred to in this chapter, the *De arca Noe morali*. I have used this translation where possible, indicating where I have felt obliged to make alterations; otherwise, translations in the text are my own. Various different versions of the *De vanitate* in fact circulated during the Middle Ages prompting a variety of hypotheses among modern scholars; I have argued in some detail for the approach taken here in 'The Self in the Text: Guigo I the Carthusian, William of St Thierry and Hugh of St Victor' (Dissertation, University of Toronto, 1992), pp. 385-404.

case, apparent human success is shown to anticipate catastrophe, waste and loss, forcing Soul to acknowledge, over and over again, of everything that seems most deserving of admiration and most able to confer happiness, 'It is vanity, and vanity of vanities'.[18] Language from the biblical book of Ecclesiastes, on which Hugh wrote a series of homilies, is here illuminated through the categories of Platonic metaphysics as reflection on the chasm between eternal being and transient becoming. Indeed, Soul, through Reason's compelling analysis of the things of the world, is brought, like the participant in one of Plato's Socratic dialogues, to a point of *aporia*, of perplexity: for if all the glories of the world amount only to vanity and folly, what else can there be, what possible means of escape?

So ends book I, but at the beginning of book II Reason suggests an image to Soul to help her imagine a resolution.[19] The world is a flood, and its lovers victims of shipwreck drowning in its waves. God remains above and beyond this ocean of sorrowful flux, but there is, according to Reason, a third term with the potential to span the divide between these two:

> Now, consider the human soul situated so to speak in between. By a certain native excellence it rises above the mutability below it, but it has not yet attained to that true changelessness that is above it with God.[20]

Positioned on the boundary between the unchanging God above and the ever-changing world below, Soul, Reason's interlocutor in the interior dialogue, can attend to the world and suffer *distractio* ('distraction', taking apart), or raise herself towards God and experience *collectio* ('collection', drawing together). It is Soul who then introduces the key metaphor of the text by comparing herself to an ark, as the one hope for deliverance from the chaotic waters of the world. The answer to her *aporia* is now clear—she is her own solution, and once this is grasped, conversion to wisdom and the way of God can begin:

> To ascend to God means, therefore, to enter into oneself, and not only to enter into oneself, but in some ineffable way in the inmost parts of the self even to pass beyond oneself [*seipsum transire*]. Therefore that person who by so to speak entering internally and penetrating inwardly transcends himself truly ascends to God.[21]

---

18. Hugh of St Victor, *Selected Spiritual Writings*, pp. 161, 163, 165, 167, 170.

19. Both Reason and Soul are feminine nouns in Latin, so it has seemed sensible to use feminine pronouns in English when discussing the text.

20. Hugh of St Victor, *Selected Spiritual Writings*, p. 175 (translation altered); *PL*, CLXXVI, p. 713C-D.

21. Hugh of St Victor, *Selected Spiritual Writings*, p. 176 (translation altered); *PL*, CLXXVI, p. 715B.

Entering and penetrating the self must be here at least to some extent metaphors for knowing the self, but the notion that self-knowledge is the pivotal element in transition from the visible to the invisible and in the conversion to wisdom is not something that originates with Hugh. It is almost as old as the Western intellectual tradition itself. In the *Alcibiades*, a dialogue either by Plato or one of his followers, and considered by the Greek Neo-Platonists to be the basis of all philosophical knowledge, Socrates seeks to convert Alcibiades to the philosophical life. He begins by persuading Alcibiades of the importance of taking care of oneself. But, asks Socrates, how can one care for oneself if one does not know oneself (128e-129a)? Discussion of what constitutes the self concludes that the self is the soul (130c-e), and knowing the soul, Socrates argues, involves also knowing the divine (133b-c). Now, Hugh of St Victor had no direct access to the *Alcibiades*. But the principal ideas within it reached him through numerous intermediaries, especially from late antiquity, both pagan and Christian. The progression in these texts from a concern with the self to a knowledge of the soul, which in turn opens up the horizon of the eternal and the divine, is essentially the same progression that we find in the *De vanitate*. What is quite different from Plato and ancient philosophy here, however, and so indicative of the quite different shape of the emerging culture of Western Europe, is that coming to know the self (and thereby reaching out towards the divine) is a work of reading, of narrating history as recorded in texts, of becoming a scriptural interpreter.

Reason and Soul have agreed that Soul is herself like an ark by which humanity may pass from the waters of the world towards the unchanging God. Yet how is such an ark to be entered, what are the steps Soul must take? Initially, Reason again echoes the conventional rhetoric of Platonism: entering the self involves rejection of the transitory and desire for the eternal. Yet then she glosses that rhetoric with another, rather different sort of language: 'Then the self indeed returns to itself when it meditates on those things that pertain to its salvation.'[22] Moving into the self and up towards God, rather than out and down towards the world, is not simply a matter of attending to the immaterial rather than the material, at least not directly. The movement into the self, like the movement out of it, is effected by consideration and love of what is accessible to the senses. But there are two kinds of things in the world to which we may give our attention and affection: the *opera conditionis* and the *opera restaurationis*,

---

22. *PL*, CLXXVI, p. 716B. The whole of this critical section is actually omitted in *Selected Spiritual Writings*, so this and the following translation in the text are my own.

the works of creation and the works of restoration. Reason explains the distinction:

> the works of creation are the elements of this world which were made so that they might serve man while he was still standing [i.e. prior to the fall]. The works of restoration are the sacraments of the incarnate Word which were given for a remedy so that they might raise him up once he had fallen.[23]

Whether we ascend or descend, then, are gathered or scattered, hinges on which of these we choose to love. Entanglement in the good works of creation actually continues to mire the fallen self in the vanity of the world. But attention to the works of redemption raises the self towards God; and here, once again, we encounter the theme of interpretative study as a means of reversing the fall and restoring humanity to God. Soul has to understand, with Reason's help, that escape from the temporal world comes only, paradoxically, through the redemption of the world in time. Interior conversion proceeds, in the subsequent sections of the *De vanitate*, not through some ineffable experience that blanks out the present order but via a meticulous and wide-ranging history lesson that is itself a map and model for the work of interpretation to which the converted soul is now called. The *opera restaurationis*, works within the world that restore the soul to life with God, extend across the whole history of creation and are known principally through the pages of Scripture; hence their contemplation requires from us the disciplines of reading, memorization and hermeneutics. The supremacy of incarnation for Hugh's theology is matched by the supremacy of interpretation within his understanding of conversion as a summons to a text-framed wisdom.

It is not, therefore, perhaps surprising that already in the latter part of book II of the *De vanitate*, the image of the ark shifts away from Soul herself to become identified with the works of redemption. To escape the false and destructive illusion of the world as all, as all there is, we must know ourselves as not reducible to the world; and to know ourselves, we must study the history of saving revelation, from its beginning to its end, for we can only know ourselves in relation to the God of revelation. This is the project that Reason proposes to Soul at the conclusion of book II, which is then sketched out in books III and IV (a good half of the entire text) as Reason takes Soul through the elementary landmarks of this narrative, from the fall of Adam to the pontificate of Gregory the Great, from the tragedy of Israel to the triumph of the Christian church. And Hugh makes it quite clear that the study of history as it appears in books III and

---

23. *PL*, CLXXVI, p. 716B-C.

IV of the *De vanitate* is inseparable from the study of Scripture, the study of the book, so that the metaphor of the ark, which was originally attached to the soul and then was used for the *opera restaurationis* becomes finally an image of reading: the ark's length is God's works, studied through Scripture's historical sense, its breadth God's mysteries, discerned through the allegorical sense, and its height the virtues, elaborated through the tropological sense.[24] We are back with the schema of history–allegory–tropology that we have already commented on in connection with the *Didascalicon*. To connect the self so closely with history is not only to connect it with narrative, but to connect it with interpretative activity, working on texts. The drama of conversion represented in the dialogue of the *De vanitate* becomes, through the pivotal conception of self-knowledge developed in book II, a process of interpretation. We enter the self through the reading of history; we come thence to the eternal God by way of the meticulous decipherment of biblical texts. The guiding image of the ark holds together in related tension the self, history and disciplined reading: there is no escape, no solution and no real conversion that avoids their careful interleaving.

For there is, according to Hugh, a kind of reading that remains unconverted and outside the kind of biblical interpretation as spiritual discipline that he is seeking to develop. In another treatise, in which the ark appears from the outset as the focal image, the *De arca Noe morali*, Hugh explains that God is always both revealing and hiding at the same time because faith must be tested and deserving of merit (hence revelation is never wholly transparent) while lack of faith must be condemned as wilful refusal (hence revelation is never wholly absent or inaccessible either).[25] Such divine concealment is a mechanism for judgment, for separating the insiders from the outsiders in interpretation, where the insiders are not those who successfully find the hidden meaning, but those who are provoked by its very hiddenness to seek it, awoken to their own ignorance and exclusion, and aroused by its persisting hiddenness to seek it with ever greater intensity:

> But when He speaks, He always withdraws Himself, as if He wished to hide; (and this He does) so that He may reprove man's heart by the fact that He speaks of Himself, and draw it to Himself by the fact that He escapes to hide. For He arouses our desire that He may increase it, quickening the love of Him in us by speaking, and goading us to follow him by running away.[26]

24. Hugh of St Victor, *Selected Spiritual Writings*, p. 171; *PL*, CLXXVI, p. 717C-D.
25. Hugh of St Victor, *Selected Spiritual Writings*, p. 130 (*PL*, CLXXVI, p. 668B).
26. Hugh of St Victor, *Selected Spiritual Writings*, p. 132 (*PL*, CLXXVI, p. 669B).

Such patently erotic imagery may seem beside the point when considering
the sober subject of biblical interpretation, but for Hugh this is not something sober at all but something truly intoxicating for those who have been
fired by the love of God. God's 'strategy' of judgment in revelation, furthermore, is reflected directly in the interpretative strategies required
by the 'converted' reader of Scripture, and the effect of its words on the
unconverted:

> As in the law and prophets, so in the gospel also He spoke by parables and
> riddles. For it is fitting that the secrets of the mystical sense should be hid-
> den beneath figures of speech; for were they open to all, they would be
> quickly cheapened. In this way truth keeps the faithful busy in searching it
> out, and at the same time continues hidden, lest it be found by unbelievers.
> When it is hard to find, it fires the former with yet greater longing, but it
> blinds the latter when it cannot be found at all.[27]

The conclusion to the *De arca Noe morali* contains some remarkable
observations on the unlimited nature of the interpretative process for converted readers of the Bible. The treatise itself is an exposition of a single
scriptural image, the ark of Noah, also deployed, as we have seen, in the
De vanitate, which Hugh here elaborates through a dazzling series of
exegeses in order to present to his hearers a complex mental image that
can help them hold the many truths of theology within the memory. Hugh
ends by defending his own methodology, his attempt to connect so much
theology and spiritual instruction to a single motif:

> So what is this ark, about which we have said so many things, and in which
> so many different paths of knowledge are contained? Surely you do not
> think it is a labyrinth? Not a labyrinth, nor labour within [*non labyrinthus,*
> *nec labor intus*], but rest within.[28]

Hugh admits that the ark that he has described in the treatise may seem
like a labyrinth, with its endlessly proliferating interpretations of the most
apparently arbitrary scriptural details, yet he also claims that the ark is not
labor but *requies*, not work but rest. Hugh introduces another image to
make his point:

> This ark is like a storehouse filled with all manner of delightful things. You
> will look for nothing in it that you will not find, and when you have found
> one thing, you will see many spread before your eyes.[29]

---

27. Hugh of St Victor, *Selected Spiritual Writings*, p. 134 (*PL* CLXXVI, p. 670B).
28. Hugh of St Victor, *Selected Spiritual Writings*, p. 151 (translation altered; *PL*,
CLXXVI, p. 679D).
29. Hugh of St Victor, *Selected Spiritual Writings*, p. 151 (*PL*, CLXXVI, p. 680A).

The object of interpretation is still inexhaustible, but with the richness of a storehouse rather than the barren confusion of a labyrinth; a place where one is nourished and enriched, and there is always more to come.

4. *Conclusion*

The devotion to the book and the pervasiveness of textual models and metaphors that characterize Western mediaeval conceptuality as it develops after the eighth century are well demonstrated by Hugh's own deployment of the book at various points as a metaphor for the second person of the Holy Trinity, written inwardly in the eternal nature of the divine wisdom and then inscribed and expressed outwardly twice, first through the creation and then again decisively through the incarnation.[30] Yet passages like this also relativize the pages in one's hand as fragmentary and precious allusions to, rather than the absolute fixation of, the eternal book of holy wisdom; as witness to God's Word, in Barthian idiom, rather than the Word made black-and-white text. We have tried to trace the interweaving of history, interiority and interpretation that underpins his distinctive approach to reading that book in the hand out of love for the book of the Word through some of his major works and more particularly through one of the less well known, the *De vanitate*.

Augustine had long before taught that in the Bible not only words but also things have meaning: and it is that same sense that the text is fraught with the meanings of history, and history to be read through the forms of the text, that leads Hugh to bind his whole enterprise to the historical 'sense' of the Scriptures and therefore, as Smalley rightly emphasizes, to push forward the disciplined investigation of literal/historical meaning with all the scholarly resources at his disposal. Yet the reason for this intellectual activity is equally clear: so that we might know ourselves and know God—it is Hugh's way of responding to Augustine's old prayer, *Noverim me, noverim te*: 'I would know me, I would know you.' God is not to be known simply through doctrines and teachings presented in isolation from the labours of exegesis and the vector of historical narrative, hence the narrative structure of the *De sacramentis*, Hugh's 'doctrinal' *summa*; and in a parallel fashion the spiritual search and the reading activity that fosters it cannot afford to sit light, in his view, to the given internal structures of biblical writings, grammatical, poetic, narrative, nor

30. See in particular the discussion at *De sacramentis* 1.4.5 (*PL*, CLXXVI, pp. 266D-67B).

to their opening onto a historical reality of creation and redemption behind the world of the text. Reading Scripture requires a twofold attention, to the patterns within the texts and to their ties to the world before God, the greater book of eternal wisdom, which is seen both through them and beyond them. In his attempt to hold together many of the most vital strands of mediaeval biblical interpretation at a critical juncture in its development, but still more for his commitment to hearing the truth through the study of Scripture, Hugh deserves our continuing attention.

BIBLIOGRAPHY

Brown, P., *The Rise of Western Christendom: Triumph and Diversity AD 200–1000* (Oxford: Basil Blackwell, 1996).

Evans, G.R., *The Language and Logic of the Bible: The Earlier Middle Ages* (Cambridge: Cambridge University Press, 1984).

Goff, J. Le, *Intellectuals in the Middle Ages* (trans. Teresa Lavender Fagan; Oxford: Basil Blackwell, 1993).

Henri de Lubac, *Medieval Exegesis: The Four Senses of Scripture* (trans. Mark Sebanc; 2 vols.; Edinburgh: T. & T. Clark, 1998, 2000).

Hugh of St Victor, *The Didascalicon of Hugh of St Victor: A Medieval Guide to the Arts* (trans. Jerome Taylor; New York: Columbia University Press, 1961).

—*Selected Spiritual Writings* (trans. A Religious of CMSV; London: Faber, 1962).

Illich, I., *In the Vineyard of the Text: A Commentary to Hugh's Didascalicon* (Chicago: University of Chicago Press, 1993).

Leclercq, Jean, *The Love of Learning and the Desire for God: A Study of Monastic Culture* (trans. Catharine Misrahi; New York: Fordham University Press, 1961).

Ricoeur, P., *Interpretation Theory: Discourse and the Surplus of Meaning* (Fort Worth: Texas Christian University Press, 1976).

Smalley, Beryl, *The Study of the Bible in the Middle Ages* (Oxford: basil Blackwell, 3rd edn, 1983).

Southern, R.W., 'Beryl Smalley and the Place of the Bible in Medieval Studies', in Katherine Walsh and Diana Wood (eds.), *The Bible in the Medieval World: Essays in Memory of Beryl Smalley* (Oxford: Basil Blackwell, 1985), pp. 1-16.

Watson, F., *Text, Church and World: Biblical Interpretation in Theological Perspective* (Edinburgh: T. & T. Clark, 1994).

A Mendicant Perspective: Saint Bonaventure of Bagnoregio[*]

Michael Robson

Editor's Introduction

This chapter provides an historical sequel to the previous one, focusing as it does on the work of the Friars Minor, the followers of St Francis of Assisi (1181/2–1226). They were rapidly drawn into the mission of preaching and teaching, in response to the urgent need for zealous and theologically articulate preachers to combat the malaise and heresy in the Church of the first half of the thirteenth century. Some (like John of Wales whose work was used in turn by Chaucer in Canterbury Tales*) were highly effective popularizers. This enterprise demanded that the friars should be steeped in the teaching of the Bible and its orthodox exposition. Even before their founder's death the Franciscans had moved to the new university centres of Paris, Oxford and Cambridge, where they opened schools that were soon integrated into the faculty of theology. Biblical studies were central to the theological instruction by Robert Grosseteste at Oxford in the early 1230s, and at Paris by Alexander of Hales in the 1230s and 1240s. These masters, who were the founders of the school of Friars Minor, produced their own biblical commentaries as well as more speculative theological writings. Scriptural commentaries became a major vehicle for debating theological questions; the early masters produced numerous glosses and expositions of the books of Old and New Testaments. Throughout this century friars were given Bibles, sometimes with commentaries; the glossed Bible was a feature of their manuscript collections and a tool employed by lectors in their teaching.*

This study illustrates the friars' approach to biblical studies through the example of one of the leading theologians of the mendicant movement, St Bonaventure. The chapter is in two parts: first, a discussion of themes illustrating the scriptural foundation of theological studies; and secondly, the work of a biblical commentator on the Gospel of St Luke, demonstrating how this mastery of the text is applied to the lives of clergy, laity and friars.

[*] I am indebted to the Revd Dr Gerald Gleeson of the Catholic Institute of Sydney and a Visiting Scholar of St Edmund's College, Cambridge, for his valuable comments and suggestions. Abbreviations: AFH = *Archivum Franciscanum Historicum*;

Saint Bonaventure of Bagnoregio was one of the leading theologians of the mendicant movement, which dominated theology in the thirteenth century. The early masters of the Franciscan school in the University of Paris, including Alexander of Hales, John de la Rochelle and William of Melitona, produced several biblical commentaries in the 1230s and 1240s.[1] One of Bonaventure's favourite authors was Hugh of Saint Cher,[2] the Dominican master, whose pupil he may have been before entering the community of the Cordeliers at Paris in 1243.[3] Bonaventure served as the fifth regent master of the friars' school between 1254 and 1257. His theological studies were firmly rooted in the detailed examination of the Scriptures and he spent four years attending the cursory and ordinary lectures on all the biblical books, that is, the introductory reading of the full text followed by a more detailed exploration of it.[4] His lectures formed the basis of his Commentaries on Ecclesiastes and the Gospel of Saints John and Luke. He exemplifies the friars' biblical studies in the middle of the thirteenth century. This study samples themes from the prologue of his *Breviloquium*[5] and his *Commentary on the Gospel of Saint Luke*.[6]

1. *The Scriptural Foundation of Theological Studies, the* Breviloquium

The *Breviloquium* offered new students in the faculty of theology a distillation of Bonaventure's experience as a master about 1256/7. The manual's

DSSBOO = *Doctoris Seraphici S. Bonaventurae opera omnia* (10 vols.; Florence; Quaracchi, 1882–1902).

1. I. Brady, 'Sacred Scripture in the Early Franciscan School', in *La sacra scrittura e i Francescani* (Rome: Pontificium Athenaeum Antonianum, 1960), pp. 65-82, F.M. Delorme, 'Deux leçons d'ouverture de Cours Bibliques données par Jean de la Rochelle', *La France Franciscaine* 16 (1933), pp. 345-60; B. Smalley, 'The Gospels in the Paris Schools in the Late 12th and Early 13th Centuries', *Franciscan Studies* 39 (1979), pp. 230-54, and 40 (1980), pp. 298-369; *idem, The Gospels in the Schools c.1100–c.1280* (London: Hambledon Press, 1985), pp. 118-43.

2. Cf. C. Van Den Borne, 'De fontibus commentarii S. Bonaventurae in Ecclesiasten', *AFH* 10 (1917), pp. 257-70; R.J. Karris, 'A Comparison of the *Glossa Ordinaria*, Hugh of St. Cher, and St. Bonaventure on Luke 8.26-39', *Franciscan Studies* 58 (2000), pp. 121-236.

3. B. Smalley, *The Study of the Bible in the Middle Ages* (Oxford: Basil Blackwell, 1952), p. 273.

4. J.G. Bougerol, *Introduction a l'étude de S. Bonaventure* (Bibliothèque de Théologie, Série 1; Théologie Dogmatique, 2; Paris: Desclee and Co., 1961), pp. 134-35.

5. *Breviloquium*, DSSBOO, V, pp. 199-291.

6. *Commentarius in evangelium S. Lucae*, DSSBOO, VII.

prologue is described by M.D.Chenu as *très belles pages, le plus beau programme d'herméneutique sacrée* of the thirteenth century[7] and it supplies a programme for the study of the Scripture, *quae theologia dicitur*;[8] the terms of Scripture and theology are sometimes used interchangeably.[9] Among various themes addressed are Bonaventure's thoughts on the initial difficulties experienced by new members of the faculty of theology, the unrivalled authority enjoyed by the sacred text and the primacy of faith to direct the work of the expositor.

a. *Teething Troubles for New Students in Biblical Studies*
This manual was written for the benefit of beginners who felt overwhelmed by the transition from the faculty of arts to the faculty of theology. The students' frustrations are acknowledged and the image of the forest, that uncharted territory beyond the safety and security of the mediaeval city, is twice evoked. Bonaventure, who associated order with the work of creation[10] and redemption,[11] accepted that those beginning their studies often dreaded the Scriptures, feeling them to be confusing, disordered and as uncharted as an impenetrable forest. He readily conceded that the patristic exposition of these themes lay embedded in a large number of treatises and commentaries, which could not be explored by the uninitiated, even if sufficient time were available. Drawing upon his own experience in the schools, he compiled a brief guide to the principal questions of theology, from God to the last judgement.[12]

A thorough grounding in philosophy formed the background to theological studies in the new universities of Paris and Oxford.[13] Newly enrolled students were encouraged to develop another set of scholastic criteria for their biblical studies. The different functions of philosophy and theology are underlined. While philosophy studies things as they exist in their nature, theology, a science based on faith and revealed by the Holy Spirit, focuses on grace, glory and eternal wisdom. Philosophical knowledge, borrowing from the natural order what it needs to make a mirror for the representation of the divine, is subservient to theology, which erects a ladder whose

7.   M.D. Chenu, *La théologie comme science au XIIIe siècle* (Bibliothèque Thomiste, 33; Paris: J. Vrin, 1957), p. 54.
8.   Bonaventure, *Breviloquium*, prol., no. 1, p. 201.
9.   Bonaventure, *Breviloquium*, p. 1, c. 1, no. 2, p. 210.
10.   Bonaventure, *Breviloquium*, p. 2, c. 5, no. 1, p. 222.
11.   Bonaventure, *Breviloquium*, p. 4, c. 9, no. 2, p. 249.
12.   Bonaventure, *Breviloquium*, prol., VI, nos. 4-5, p. 208.
13.   E.g. J. Marenbon, *Later Medieval Philosophy (1150–1350): An Introduction* (London: Routledge & Kegan Paul, 1987), pp. 20-22.

foot rests upon the earth but whose apex reaches heaven.[14] The philosophical errors circulating in the faculty of arts in the 1250s[15] and 1260s demonstrate that the subject cannot be considered without reference to revelation.[16]

The Scriptures are unlike the other fields of knowledge, which are circumscribed by the rules of reasoning, defining and dividing.[17] While philosophy is divided into theoretical and practical branches, the Scriptures are arranged in the Old and New Testaments. The Scriptures constitute knowledge stemming from faith, which is the motive power and foundation of morals, justice and right living; there cannot be in the Scriptures any dissociation between knowledge pertaining to faith and morals.[18] The charge that theology lacks both unity and order is rebutted by the conviction that it is the only perfect science (*scientia perfecta*),[19] an organized science.[20]

The second half of the prologue addresses the exposition of the Scriptures, whose meanings are profound. In addition to the literal text of the Bible there are three other modes of interpretation.[21] First, the allegorical sense whereby one thing represents another in the realm of faith; secondly, moral teaching or tropology, which shows what must be accomplished; thirdly, the anagogical, which offers instruction on what must be sought or desired.[22] Expositors, however, are exhorted to be sparing in their recourse to allegories or mystical interpretations.[23] They are to draw upon their knowledge of the Scriptures to explain various passages,[24] and

14. Bonaventure, *Breviloquium*, prol., III, no. 2, p. 205.

15. Bonaventure, *Breviloquium*, p. 2 c. 1, no. 1, p. 219.

16. Bonaventure, *De decem pracepetis*, II, nos. 24-25, in DSSBOO, V, p. 514.

17. Bonaventure, *Breviloquium*, prol., no. 3, p. 201.

18. Bonaventure, *Breviloquium*, prol., I, no. 2, p. 203. *Idem, De reductione artium ad theologiam*, no. 1, DSSBOO, V, p. 319, where philosophy, the *lumen interius*, was subordinate to the *lumen superius*, the *lumen gratiae et sacrae Scripturae*.

19. Bonaventure, *Breviloquium*, I, c. 1, no. 2, p. 210.

20. Bonaventure, *Breviloquium*, prol., VI, no. 6, p. 208.

21. Bonaventure, *De reductione artium ad theologiam*, no. 5, p. 321. The first sense teaches Christians what they should believe concerning the divinity and humanity of Jesus Christ; the second instructs them on how they should regulate their lives; and the third guides them towards unity with God

22. Bonaventure, *Breviloquium*, prol., IV, nos. 1, 4, pp. 205, 206.

23. Bonaventure, *Breviloquium*, prol., VI, nos. 2-3, pp. 207-208.

24. Bonaventure, *In Hexaemeron*, XIX, no. 7, in DSSBOO, V, p. 421, where he explains that any single passage of the Bible depends upon another, or, rather, any single passage is related to a thousand others.

this is exemplified by Bonaventure's interpretation of Ps. 34.2. Students are left in no doubt that such skills are the fruit of constant reading of the Scriptures, which is to be fixed in the memory, and this is exemplified by Bonaventure's own biblical commentaries. Employing an analogy from linguistics, he maintains that just as those who neglect to study the rudiments of language could never understand the exact meaning of words or the rules of composition, so also those who disregard the literal text of the Scriptures would never rise to the understanding of their spiritual content.[25]

b. *The Authority of the Scriptures*
The mendicant movement, whose first fruits were the Dominicans and Franciscans, was rooted in the articulation of evangelical values and their application to daily life. The Bible supplied the mendicant friars with materials for their teaching and preachers were required to be fully immersed in the knowledge of the sacred text and its orthodox exposition. A profound reverence for the Scriptures and an acknowledgment of their supremacy informs the teaching of Bonaventure, who counsels students and masters not to stray too far from the safety and security of the Scriptures.[26]

While God communicated directly with Adam and Eve,[27] their insubordination called for a display of divine mercy and a fitting remedy.[28] The Scriptures supply pilgrim humanity with healing[29] and sufficient knowledge for salvation.[30] They play a sacramental role in restoring harmony between Creator and creatures and are transmitted to shape the thoughts and deeds of individuals towards salvation.[31] God emerges as the redemptive principle in the Scriptures,[32] as Bonaventure affirms: '…the subject of the Scrip-

25. Bonaventure, *Breviloquium*, prol., VI, no. 1, p. 207. Cf. *idem*, *Collationes in Hexaemeron*, XIX, no. 7, p. 421, where Bonaventure affirms that students must concentrate on the Scriptures, just as children learn their ABC.

26. Bonaventure, *Collationes*, XVII, no. 25, p. 413, where the dangers of withdrawing from the house of the Scriptures are underlined.

27. Bonaventure, *Breviloquium*, p. 3, c. 2, nos. 1-5, pp. 231-32.

28. Bonaventure, *Breviloquium*, p. 3, c. 11, no. 5, p. 241.

29. Bonaventure, *Commentarius in evangelium S. Lucae*, prol., no. 15, p. 5.

30. Bonaventure, *Breviloquium*, prol., no. 3, p. 201. Cf. *Quaestiones disputatae de mysterio Trinitatis*, q. 1, a. 2, conc., V, p. 55, where Bonaventure expatiates upon the Scriptures in redemptive terms. Adam and Eve were endowed with sufficient guidance to interpret the *liber creaturae*. The Scriptures are presented as part of the divine response to the Fall and they are ordained for the restoration of the universe.

31. Bonaventure, *Breviloquium*, prol., IV, no. 5, p. 206.

32. Bonaventure, *Breviloquium*, p. 2, c. 5, no. 2, p. 222.

tures is doctrine concerned with God, with [Jesus] Christ, with the works of salvation and with what should be believed.'[33] Unlike philosophical study, with its demand for proof, the Scriptures, which are received from God,[34] require an act of faith as a starting point and students are advised to begin with a prayer for a true knowledge of Jesus Christ.[35] The authority of the sacred text is summed up thus: 'God has given the Scriptures the certitude of authority; so great as to surpass any attainable by the human ingenuity.'[36] Beliefs which exceed the powers of reason are to be accepted in faith. As a general rule, Christians must believe everything that is contained and expressed in the canon of the Scriptures,[37] which are invested with the highest authority in matters of faith. The sacred Scriptures are inspired by the Holy Spirit to guide the Catholic faith. There is no disagreement between revelation and the true faith.[38]

The integrity and orderliness of the Scriptures are vigorously defended by Bonaventure,[39] whose respect for the divine origins of the sacred text leads him to affirm that no passage is to be regarded as valueless, rejected as false or repudiated as evil.[40] The breadth of the Scriptures is emphasized and their progression, beginning with the legal books of the Old Testament and ending with the book of Revelation. Parallels between the two testaments are drawn with appropriate symbols for them.[41] The Scriptures are handed down through divine revelation rather than human research,[42] a conviction that is reiterated elsewhere in the prologue.[43] They resemble a great river, into which tributaries flow,[44] and a poem of immense beauty.[45]

33. Bonaventure, *Breviloquium*, prol., IV, no. 2, p. 205.

34. Bonaventure, *Breviloquium*, prol., V, no. 4, p. 207.

35. Bonaventure, *Breviloquium*, prol., nos. 2, 5, pp. 201-202.

36. Bonaventure, *Breviloquium*, prol., V, no. 3, p. 207.

37. Bonaventure, *Breviloquium*, p. 5, c. 7, no. 2, p. 260.

38. Bonaventure, *Breviloquium*, p. 5, c. 7, no. 5, pp. 260-61.

39. Bonaventure, *Collationes in Hexaemeron*, XIV, no. 5, p. 393. Some claimed that the Scriptures were so composed *ut homo ponit sententiam post sententiam, qui litteras fecit.*

40. Bonaventure, *Breviloquium*, prol., V, no. 4, p. 207.

41. Bonaventure, *Breviloquium*, prol., I, no. 1, pp. 202-203; cf. p. 5, c. 9, no. 1, p. 262, where the ten commandments were said to be inscribed upon the two tablets (Exod. 31.18) by God's own finger.

42. Bonaventure, *Breviloquium*, prol. V, no. 3, p. 207.

43. Bonaventure, *Breviloquium*, prol., no. 2, p. 201.

44. Bonaventure, *Breviloquium*, prol. I, no. 4, p. 203.

45. Bonaventure, *Breviloquium*, prol. II, no. 4, p. 204. Just as no one can appreciate a poem unless he sees it in its entirety, no one discern the orderly beauty of creation without seeing it as a whole.

Similarly, the whole of Scripture is compared to a single zither, and the lesser string does not produce harmony by itself, but only in combination with the others.[46]

c. *Faith as a Key to the Scriptures*

A quotation from Eph. 3.14-19 forms the opening words of the *Breviloquium* and other treatises by Bonaventure. Saint Paul shows that the Scriptures originated under the influence of the Holy Trinity and that their development is proportioned to the individual's capacity to understand.[47] The starting point of this enterprise is faith, without which no one can penetrate the meaning of the sacred text.[48] Distinguishing the study of the Bible from the other sciences, Bonaventure reflects that 'the end or fruit of Holy Scripture is not something restricted, but the fullness of eternal happiness'.[49]

The Scriptures contain the words of eternal life (Jn 6.69) and are composed so that Christians might not only believe, but also possess eternal life. The life-giving nature of the sacred text must be uppermost in the minds of both masters and students in the faculty of theology. Bonaventure presents this as the necessary goal and intention of both the master and the student: '...with this purpose and intention, therefore, the sacred Scripture must be studied, taught and also heard.'[50] Students are advised to reach out to God in pure faith for an understanding of the sacred texts,[51] which unfold by supernatural inspiration and their language is literal sometimes and figurative at other times. The Scriptures sum up the content of the entire universe and display the glory of those finally to be saved.[52] The Bible must be interpreted properly, however, and a defective understanding is demonstrated by the Sadducees' rejection of the resurrection; the *carnalis intellectus* and the *spiritualis intellectus* are contrasted.[53]

A spiritual disposition is required by the theologian, who is required to clothe himself in the appropriate virtues. In contrast, the vices, especially

---

46. Bonaventure, *In Hexaemeron*, XIX, no. 7, p. 421.
47. Bonaventure, *Breviloquium*, prol., nos. 1, 3, p. 201.
48. Bonaventure, *Breviloquium*, prol., no. 3, p. 201.
49. Bonaventure, *Breviloquium*, prol., no. 4, p. 202.
50. Bonaventure, *Breviloquium*, prol., no. 4, p. 202.
51. Bonaventure, *Breviloquium*, prol., nos.2, 5, pp. 201-202.
52. Bonaventure, *Breviloquium*, prol., no. 3, pp. 201-202.
53. Bonaventure, *Commentarius in evangelium S. Lucae*, c. 20, no. 39, v. 33, p. 514.

presumption and an undue curiosity, are identified as obstacles;[54] *curiositas* was shunned by Francis of Assisi in his progress towards communion with God.[55] The cultivation of virtues is appropriate because a mysterious and profound signification is hidden under the shell of the obvious meaning of the sacred text as a deterrent to pride. Echoing the admonitions of patristic authorities, Bonaventure informs students that the very depth that lies beneath the humble word of the Bible reproves the proud, casts out the unclean, drives away the insincere and awakens the slothful to search the mysteries. The Scriptures are addressed to every kind of hearer and those in search of salvation must know something about their teaching.[56] They constitute a science drawing the individual away from evil and impelling him towards goodness by appealing to both fear and love, which symbolize the Old and New Testaments.[57]

The friars' philosophy of education leads Bonaventure to distinguish theology from the other sciences. The purpose of biblical studies is that theologians might advance in virtue and attain salvation; this is achieved by a disposition of the will rather than by mere speculation.[58] Moreover, theology is styled as the only perfect wisdom (*sola est sapientia perfecta*), because it begins with God, the principle of all things made and considers the divine remedy of sin, the reward of merit and the goal of desire. All Christians must burn with longing to attain this knowledge that brings taste, life, and salvation.[59] Just as bishops in the patristic period combined theological accomplishments with personal holiness, the friars were challenged to treat theology as an occasion of spiritual growth.

2. *The Biblical Commentator:*
The Commentary on the Gospel of Saint Luke

Bonaventure delivered his lectures on the Gospel of Saint Luke as a *bachelarius biblicus*;[60] the present form of the commentary was compiled about

---

54. Bonaventure, *Christus unus omnium magister*, nos. 22, 28, in DSSBOO, V, pp. 573, 574.

55. Bonaventure, 'Legenda maior S. Francisci', in *Legendae S. Francisci Assisiensis saeculis XIII et XIV conscriptae* (Analecta Franciscana, 10; Florence: Quaracchi, 1926–41), c. 13, no. 1, p. 616.

56. Bonaventure, *Breviloquium*, prol., IV, no. 3, p. 206.

57. Bonaventure, *Breviloquium*, prol., I, no. 2, p. 203.

58. Bonaventure, *Breviloquium*, prol., V, no. 2, p. 206.

59. Bonaventure, *Breviloquium*, p. 1, c.1, no. 3, p. 210.

60. G. Scalia (ed.), *Cronica Salimbene de Adam* (Scrittori d'Italia, 232; Bari: Laterza, 1966), p. 435.

1256.[61] Dr Beryl Smalley comments that what distinguishes Bonaventure from his mendicant predecessors is the way in which he blends Franciscan themes with his biblical lectures.[62] Francis of Assisi is quoted regarding penance[63] and Giles of Assisi, one of his first disciples, on evangelical poverty.[64] An illustration of Bonaventure's use of the Bible emerges from his views of the dispositions of both master and student, the implications of the Incarnation, and the profile of the preacher.

a. *Biblical Scholarship and Virtue*
Francis of Assisi had wished to apply the principles of the gospel to every human activity and the sole condition which he imposed upon Saint Anthony of Padua, the first lector of the order at Bologna in 1223, was that theological study among the friars was to be dovetailed with the spirit of prayer.[65] From the outset the friars' studies were perceived as a thorough preparation for the pastoral ministry of preaching and hearing confessions.

Jesus' declaration at the beginning of his public ministry (Lk. 4.18), quoting Isa. 61.1, supplies the opening words of Bonaventure's commentary and his protracted discourse on the duties of both theologians and their pupils. Masters are to be anointed with God's grace, instituted according to obedience and aglow with fraternal compassion.[66] The master must be duly commissioned and respond in obedience. The Old Testament supplies examples of the prophets, who were divinely appointed, as was Moses (Exod. 3.10). Moses, who brought the Law and led the sons of Israel from Egypt, is a symbol of the exponent of the divine law who liberates the people of God from the darkness of ignorance. Articulating the evolving legislation in his fraternity,[67] Bonaventure forbids friars from

61. T. Reist, *Saint Bonaventure as a Biblical Commentator: A Translation and Analysis of his Commentary on Luke, XVIII, 34–XIX, 42* (New York: Lanham, 1985), pp. 68-70.

62. Smalley, *Gospels in the Schools*, p. 211.

63. Bonaventure, *Commentarius in evangelium S. Lucae*, c. 9, no. 38, p. 228.

64. Bonaventure, *Commentarius in evangelium S. Lucae*, c. 9, no. 48, p. 231.

65. C. Esser (ed.), *Opuscula Sancti Patris Francisci Assisiensis* (Bibliothea Franciscana Ascetica Medii Aevi, 12; Rome: Grottaferrata, 1978), p. 95; E. Menestò *et al.* (eds.), *Fontes Franciscani* (Medioevo Francescano, Collana diretta da Ernrico Menestò, Testi, 2; Assisi: Edizioni Porziuncula, 1995), p. 55.

66. Bonaventure, *Commentarius in evangelium S. Lucae*, prol., no. 3, p. 3.

67. M. Bihl, 'Statuta generalia Ordinis edita in Capitulis generalibus celebratis Narbonae an. 1260, Assisii an. 1279 atque Parisiis an. 1292 (Editio critica et synoptica)', VI, no. 17, *AFH* 34 (1941), pp. 13-94, 284-358 (72); cf. C. Cenci, 'De Fratrum Minorum Constitutionibus Praenarbonensisbus', *AFH* 83 (1990), pp. 50-95.

arrogating to themselves the office of teaching or seeking it through the intervention of others.[68] Fraternal benevolence is to guide masters, just as the preacher or prelate must show himself to be benign in sign, word and deed.[69] The example of Saint Paul is invoked (1 Thess. 2.7-8) in the nurturing of disciples. The dignity and responsibility of the exponent of the Scriptures is that he preach the divine word: '…the exposition and teaching of the Gospel is to preach the word of God: and, therefore, the doctor must be aflame with fraternal benevolence.'[70] Preachers must seek their own perfection before attempting to edify others[71] and by implication the same obligation rests upon theologians.

Students are admonished to imitate the discipleship expounded in the Gospels. The general constitutions of the fraternity, promulgated at the chapter of Narbonne in 1260 under the presidency of Bonaventure as the minister general (1257–73), considered the conduct and bearing of friars sent to the *studium generale:* they were to be in good health, eloquent, meek, edifying in conversation and peace-loving rather than contentious.[72] The claim that only the gentle (*mansueti*) rightly grasp the divine word is corroborated by the interpretation of Eccl. 5.13, Ps. 25.9 and Jas 1.21. The teaching of the gospel offers instruction on the humility required of disciples (Mt. 11.29). Hence, the prevailing norms of the faculty of arts are to be swapped for new dispositions: '…contentiousness and dispute are the method of the Aristotelians, but they do not provide the way for the disciples of the Gospel.'

This injunction was followed by a quotation from 2 Tim. 2.24, which counsels the disciple to have no truck with quarrelling. Instead, he was required to be kindly towards all and persuasive.[73] Similarly, a contrite spirit is the more advantageous because it produces a humble disposition (Prov. 12.25) and is more disposed to study the divine ways. Students ought to give a faithful assent by surrendering their minds in faith to the supreme teacher (*doctor summus*).[74] The influence of Francis of Assisi is discernible in the exhortation that theologians should seek sanctity and

---

68. Bonaventure, *Commentarius in evangelium S. Lucae*, prol., no. 4, p. 3.

69. Bonaventure, *Commentarius in evangelium S. Lucae*, c. 9, no. 19, p. 222.

70. Bonaventure, *Commentarius in evangelium S. Lucae*, prol., no. 5, p. 4.

71. Bonaventure, *Commentarius in evangelium S. Lucae*, c. 1, no. 144, p. 43.

72. Bihl, 'Statuta', VI, nos. 14-15, p. 72.

73. Bonaventure, *Commentarius in evangelium S. Lucae*, prol., no. 6, p. 4.

74. Bonaventure, *Commentarius in evangelium S. Lucae*, prol., nos. 8, 12, pp. 4-5; cf. c. 2, no. 101, v. 46, p. 67, for similar advice.

wisdom rather than knowledge[75] and in the emphasis on prayer and the discernment of the truth in the Scriptures:

> this must be understood spiritually, that Christ teaches us and that we must learn before we teach... He wished to be found among the doctors in the Temple because in the reading of the Scriptures and in prayer truth is found.[76]

b. *The Incarnation*

The mystery of the Incarnation, which paved the way for the restoration of humanity, was a central feature of the friars' preaching. Just as a fallen angel was instrumental in Adam's fault, the archangel Gabriel was the herald of redemption (Lk. 1.26). The process of the redemption reverses the Fall, even to the extent of positing that the universe was created in March, the month in which the redeemer was conceived[77]—*ut sic respondeat reparatio lapsui.*[78] The account of Mary's response to the archangel owes much to the writings of Saint Bernard, abbot of Clairvaux,[79] the outstanding preacher of the Middle Ages[80] and promoter of Marian piety (*praecipuus Virginis amator et honoris eius zelator*).[81] Mary's modest demeanour in the presence of the archangel, with the emphasis on hearing and obedience rather than speaking, is instructive. Her humble bearing prepared her for the grace bestowed upon her.[82]

The friars' focus on evangelical poverty, a recurring theme in the commentary, is applied to the nativity, although it is largely absent from the corresponding section of the *Breviloquium*. At the time of her delivery Mary was in need of the items customarily associated with childbirth—clothes, a bed, medical assistance; the swaddling clothes in which the Son of God was wrapped are contrasted with the normal clothing of the newborn. This emphasis is bolstered by quotations from 1 Tim. 6.8, Zech. 3.3 and Bernard of Clairvaux. The fact that Jesus was laid in a manger presages two aspects of his ministry: his poverty (Mt. 8.20) and his role as the

---

75. Bonaventure, *Collationes in Hexaemeron*, XIX, no. 3, p. 420.

76. Bonaventure, *Commentarius in evangelium S. Lucae*, c. 2, no. 102, p. 67.

77. Bonaventure, *Commentarius in evangelium S. Lucae*, c. 1, no. 41, v. 26, p. 20.

78. Bonaventure, *Commentarius in evangelium S. Lucae*, c. 1, no. 42, p. 21.

79. J.G. Bougerol, 'Saint Bonaventure et saint Bernard', *Antonianum* 46 (1971), pp. 3-79.

80. Bonaventure, *De reductione artium ad theologiam*, no. 5, p. 321.

81. Bonaventure, *Commentaria in quatuor libros Sententiarum Magistri Petri Lombardi*, III, d. 3, p. 1, a. 1, q. 1, conc. ad ob. 4, DSSBOO, III, p. 63.

82. Bonaventure, *Commentarius in evengelium S. Lucae,* c. 1, nos. 50-70, vv. 29-38, pp. 23-27.

living bread from heaven (Jn 6.41). The mystical and moral applications
follow with the rebuke of those who have dainty beds and enlarged houses
(*aedificiorum amplitudo*), which may allude to the building of controversial towers in the cities of Italy:[83]

> the poor little mother brought forth the poor Christ to invite us to a life of
> voluntary poverty and to enrich us with his need,[84] according to II Corin-
> thians: '*you know the grace of our Lord Jesus Christ, who was rich was
> made poor for us*'... (8.9).[85]

Such poverty castigates those who love fine clothes, elegant furniture
and avaricious opulence. The didactic nature of the circumstances are
explained by Bonaventure:

> having a vile, humble and poor bed, the Saviour of the world was already
> beginning to declare that the values of the secular world (*mundus*)[86] must be
> rejected for three reasons. His own example was already beginning to show
> the state of perfection, which consists in humility, austerity and poverty.[87]

The image of the shepherds provides ample scope for instruction on the
vigilance to be exercised by prelates. The spiritual interpretation of Luke
2.8 dwells upon the watchfulness to be shown by those called to the
pastoral office. They are to be alert to the wiles of the spiritual enemy and
give themselves to contemplation.[88] Similarly, the shepherds' poverty was
ripe for exploitation by the mendicant: '...note that the angel appears to
the shepherds rather than to any other category of humanity because
Christ was coming on account of the poor.' Bonaventure then moves from
the shepherds' poverty to the vigilance required in those who await the
divine visitation.[89] The Saviour assumes humanity to liberate the children
of Adam and Eve from their frailty and impoverishment of spirit. The fact
that there is no other name under heaven by which the human race can be
redeemed (Acts 4.12) occasions immense joy: the means of reversing

---

83. Bonaventure, *Commentarius in evengelium S. Lucae,* c. 2, nos. 11-4, pp. 46-
47; cf. D. Waley, *The Italian City-Republics* (London: Longman, 3rd edn, 1988), pp.
120-30.

84. Bonaventure, *Collationes in Hexaemeron*, I, no. 27, p. 334, where he teaches
that it was necessary that humanity should pass from need to opulence in Jesus Christ.

85. Bonaventure, *Commentarius in evengelium S. Lucae*, c. 2, no. 15, pp. 46-47.

86. Bonaventure, *Breviloquium*, p. 3, c.2, no. 5, p. 232, where the roots of sin are
identified as *mundus, caro et diabolus*.

87. Bonaventure, *Commentarius in evengelium S. Lucae*, c.2, no. 16, p. 48.

88. Bonaventure, *Commentarius in evengelium S. Lucae*, c. 2, nos. 18-21, vv. 8-9,
pp. 48-49.

89. Bonaventure, *Commentarius in evengelium S. Lucae*, c. 2, no. 22, p. 49.

Adam's fall are at hand.[90] The birth of Jesus, *pauper et mendicus*, in a crib serves as a sign both for the shepherds (Lk. 2.12) and humanity, that is, the poor, whom he came to set free; his humility and poverty prefigure his triumphal entry into Jerusalem on an ass (Zech. 9.9). The shepherds were poor, simple and of no account and they were not afraid to approach the infant, the sign of poverty and humility.[91] The theme of poverty pervades the remainder of the commentary on the second chapter of Saint Luke, even down to the offering (*oblatio pauperum*) made after Jesus' circumcision. The poverty of Mary and Joseph is underlined by the fact that they could not even offer a lamb (Lk. 2.24).[92]

c. *The Apostles' Mission*

The friars' ministry was located within the tradition of the 12 apostles, whose life and preaching they imitated;[93] contemporaries accepted this claim.[94] The ninth chapter of Saint Luke's Gospel offers an opportunity for an exposition of the mission and duties of the apostles. The apostles gathered by Jesus denote the principal prelates, who foster unity within the Church. Echoing the concerns of some of his contemporaries, Bonaventure declares that authority is essential to the divine commission. The Twelve were dispatched to preach the kingdom of God, that is, true doctrine, divine grace and eternal glory.[95]

The sacred nature of the apostles' office is linked with the injunction to heal the sick. Just as sickness, symbolized by leprosy,[96] was deemed to be one of the consequences of original sin,[97] so the process of healing belonged to Jesus, the *medicus*.[98] The apostles' capacity to heal was

90. Bonaventure, *Commentarius in evangelium S. Lucae*, c. 2, nos. 23-4, vv. 10-11, pp. 49-50.

91. Bonaventure, *Commentarius in evangelium S. Lucae*, c. 2, nos. 26-7, p. 50.

92. Bonaventure, *Commentarius in evangelium S. Lucae*, c. 2, no. 54, v. 24, pp. 56-57.

93. A. Wachtel (ed.), *Alexander Minorita, Expositio in Apocalypsim* (Monumenta Germaniae Historica, Quellen zur Geistesgeschichte des Mittelalters, 1; Weimar: Nachfolger, 1955), p. 454.

94. N. Bériou (ed.), *Les sermons et la visite pastorale de Federico Visconti archevêque de Pise (1253–1277)* (Sources et documents d'histoire du moyen âge, 3; Rome: École française de Rome, 2001), no. 2, p. 776, which expressly identifies the friars as the apostles' sons by their preaching.

95. Bonaventure, *Commentarius in evangelium S. Lucae*, c. 9, nos. 1-3, vv. 1-2, pp. 216-17.

96. Bonaventure, *Commentarius in evangelium S. Lucae*, c. 17, no. 24, v. 12, p. 434.

97. Bonaventure, *Breviloquium*, p. 4, c. 1, no. 3, p. 241.

98. Bonaventure, *Breviloquium*, p. 6, c. 1, no. 3, p. 265.

viewed as divine confirmation of their mandate: '…whence the sign of the spiritual mission of preaching is the healing of those present from the infirmities of the vices.'[99]

Healing is identified as one of the elements of the ministry of preaching.[100] There are three signs of authenticity: the jurisdiction of the prelate who issues the commission, that is, the episcopal mandate; zeal for souls whereby the preacher seeks the honour of God and the salvation of souls above everything else; the proclamation of the gospel which is to bear fruit in the conversion and spiritual healing of those present.[101]

Evangelical poverty reappears in the advice dispensed to the apostles, who were exhorted to be unencumbered on their travels, living as pilgrims. The disciples are instructed not to have a second tunic because of the counsel to share with those in need; they are admonished to go without staves, scrip, bread, money and a second coat. An implication of such advice is that the preacher exemplifies one whose trust is in providence rather than material things; Francis of Assisi, too, embodies Jesus' teaching by sending out the friars to preach, exhorting them to commit their cares to God. The literal interpretation of the divine precept belongs to perfect preachers who leave everything for Jesus (Mt. 19.27). The spiritual interpretation, however, extends itself to everyone so that the preacher of truth ought to be detached from concern for materials things. Those who combine the proclamation of the gospel with the desire for material rewards are reproved;[102] they are not genuine disciples and earn the rebuke of 2 Pet. 2.14-15. Above all, the preachers of the truth must avoid the vice of cupidity.[103]

The instructions imparted to the 12 disciples (Lk. 10.1-2) are supplemented by the advice given to the 72 disciples, who were prefigured by Moses (Exod. 15.27). The disciples were sent into every city and place (*omnis civitas et locus*), reflecting the friars' own itinerant ministry of preaching not only in cities, but also in towns and villages. This mandate reflects the office laid on the shoulders of contemporary priests, who assist prelates and preach with divine authority. They were dispatched two by two like heralds (*praecones*), reflecting the friars' own practice, to assist each other charitably and to prepare the path for Jesus, making his ways

99. Bonaventure, *Commentarius in evangelium S. Lucae*, c. 9, no. 3, v. 2, p. 217.

100. Bonaventure, *Commentarius in evangelium S. Lucae*, prol., no. 15, p. 5.

101. Bonaventure, *Commentarius in evangelium S. Lucae*, c. 9, no. 4, pp. 217-18.

102. Bonaventure, *De praeparatione ad missam*, c. 1, no. 14, DSSBOO, VIII, p. 104.

103. Bonaventure, *Commentarius in evangelium S. Lucae*, c. 9, nos. 5-7, v. 3, pp. 218-19.

straight (Isa. 40.3).[104] Jesus' image of the harvest (Lk. 10.2) has a particular application to the ministry of preaching, as has the dearth of labourers: '…because there are indeed few good reapers he [Jesus] adds "*the workers are few*"; he calls them workers because the sickle of preaching collects a good harvest…'

Such preachers implement the advice which they dispense to others. The priority which the friars gave to the ministry of preaching[105] and their awareness that heresy was making inroads[106] moves Bonaventure to lament the paucity of zealous preachers and the greater number mired in malice. With a sense of urgency the friar bemoans the fact that the harvest is lost when good workers are lacking. Jesus exhorts his followers to pray for labourers to be sent to the harvest; good preachers ought to carry the sword of the Word of God both on their lips and in their hands. Preaching is a sword that does not perturb the enemy unless it is held in the hand, that is, it is accompanied by appropriate conduct.[107] This protracted meditation on the role of the disciples prompts Bonaventure to emphasize the authority and responsibility of preachers, who are the mouth of God, whose words they proclaim.[108] The preachers are advised to seek their own perfection and then the edification of others;[109] they are to combine the ministry with the pursuit of spiritual gifts.[110]

3. *Conclusion*

The scriptural basis of the friars' studies is reflected in the glosses on the Bible donated to the Greyfriars of Canterbury,[111] Lincoln[112] and Oxford[113]

---

104. Bonaventure, *Commentarius in evangelium S. Lucae*, c. 10, nos. 1-3, pp. 252-53.

105. B. Roest, *A History of Franciscan Education (c.1210–1517)* (Education and Society in the Middle Ages and Renaissance, 11; Leiden: E.J. Brill, 2000), pp. 272-324.

106. Bonaventure, *Commentarius in evangelium S. Lucae*, c. 21, no. 14, p. 525, where various heretics are identified.

107. Bonaventure, *Commentarius in evangelium S. Lucae*, c. 10, no. 4, v. 2, pp. 253-54; cf. c. 9, no. 93, p. 246.

108. Bonaventure, *Commentarius in evangelium S. Lucae*, c. 10, no. 27, p. 261.

109. Bonaventure, *Commentarius in evangelium S. Lucae*, c. 1, no. 144, p. 43.

110. Bonaventure, *Commentarius in evangelium S. Lucae*, c. 4, no. 27, v. 14, p. 96.

111. British Library, MS. Royal 3 C.xi, glosses on the Gospels donated by Ralph of Maidstone, bishop of Hereford (1234–39), who became a friar.

112. Lambeth Palace Library, MS. 57, a gloss on the Pauline letters, was donated by Ralph of Corbridge, who lectured at the universities of Paris and Oxford.

113. British Library, MS. Harley 3249. The glosses on the Pauline letters were donated by Ralph of Maidstone.

by those clothed as friars between 1239 and 1249. Similar texts were bequeathed to several friaries and individual friars by Richard of Wych, bishop of Chichester (1240–53),[114] and Martin de Sancta Cruce, master of the hospital of Sherburn in Durham, in November 1259.[115] Dr Smalley, who points to the enduring popularity of Bonaventure's biblical commentaries,[116] observes that the friars re-established the custom of lecturing on the whole Bible or substantial parts of it.[117] Bonaventure's theological outlook was permeated by the centrality of the Scriptures.[118] The prologue to the *Breviloquium* offers an introduction to the appropriate use of the Bible, identifying areas to be developed elsewhere in his corpus. The *Commentary on the Gospel of Saint Luke* demonstrates his mastery of the Bible and its application to the lives of the clergy, laity and the friars. It consists of a mosaic of quotations from scriptural and patristic texts and Bonaventure nimbly picks his way through a collection of extracts that are arranged to confer the halo of authority on his teaching.

BIBLIOGRAPHY

Bériou, N. (ed.), *Les sermons et la visite pastorale de Federico Visconti archevêque de Pise (1253–1277)* (Sources et documents d'histoire du moyen âge, 3; Rome: École française de Rome, 2001).

Bihl, M., 'Statuta generalia Ordinis edita in Capitulis generalibus celebratis Narbonae an. 1260, Assisii an. 1279 atque Parisiis an. 1292 (Editio critica et synoptica)', VI, no. 17, *AFH* 34 (1941).

Bonaventure, *De reductione artium ad theologiam.*

Bonaventure, *Collationes in Hexaemeron.*

Bonaventure, *Breviloquium.*

Bonaventure, *Commentaria in quatuor libros Sententiarum Magistri Petri Lombardi.*

Bonaventure, *Commentarius in evangelium S. Lucae.*

Bonaventure, 'Legenda maior S. Francisci', in *Legendae S. Francisci Assisiensis saeculis XIII et XIV conscriptae* (Analecta Franciscana, 10; Florence: Quaracchi, 1926–41).

Bougerol, J.G., *Introduction a l'étude de S. Bonaventure* (Bibliothèque de Théologie, Série 1; Théologie Dogmatique, 2; Paris: Desclee and Co., 1961).

—'Saint Bonaventure et saint Bernard', *Antonianum* 46 (1971).

Brady, I., 'Sacred Scripture in the Early Franciscan School', in *La sacra scrittura e i Francescani* (Rome: Pontificium Athenaeum Antonianum, 1960).

114. D. Jones, *Saint Richard of Chichester: The Sources for his Life* (Sussex Record Society, 79; Lewes: Sussex Record Society, 1995), pp. 67-69.

115. J. Raine (ed.), *Wills and Inventories Illustrative of the Northern Counties of England*, I (London: Surtees Society, 1835), p. 11.

116. Smalley, *Study of the Bible*, p. 275.

117. Smalley, *Study of the Bible*, p. 269.

118. Bonaventure, *Commentarius in evangelium S. Lucae*, c. 4, no. 10, v. 4, p. 91.

Cenci, C., 'De Fratrum Minorum Constitutionibus Praenarbonensisbus', *AFH* 83 (1990).

Chenu, M.D., *La théologie comme science au XIIIe siècle* (Bibliothèque Thomiste, 33; Paris: J. Vrin, 1957).

Delorme, F.M., 'Deux leçons d'ouverture de Cours Bibliques données par Jean de la Rochelle', *La France Franciscaine* 16 (1933).

Esser, C. (ed.), *Opuscula Sancti Patris Francisci Assisiensis* (Bibliothea Franciscana Ascetica Medii Aevi, 12; Rome: Grottaferrata, 1978).

Jones, D., *Saint Richard of Chichester: The Sources for his Life* (Sussex Record Society, 79; Lewes: Sussex Record Society, 1995).

Karris, R.J., 'A Comparison of the *Glossa Ordinaria*, Hugh of St. Cher, and St. Bonaventure on Luke 8.26-39', *Franciscan Studies* 58 (2000).

Marenbon, J., *Later Medieval Philosophy (1150–1350): An Introduction* (London: Routledge & Kegan Paul, 1987).

Menestò E., *et al.* (eds.), *Fontes Franciscani* (Medioevo Francescano, Collana diretta da Ernrico Menestò, Testi, 2; Assisi: Edizioni Porziuncula, 1995.

Raine, J. (ed.), *Wills and Inventories Illustrative of the Northern Counties of England*, I (London: Surtees Society, 1835).

Reist, T., *Saint Bonaventure as a Biblical Commentator: A Translation and Analysis of his Commentary on Luke, XVIII, 34–XIX, 42* (New York: Lanham, 1985).

Roest, B., *A History of Franciscan Education (c.1210–1517)* (Education and Society in the Middle Ages and Renaissance, 11; Leiden: E.J. Brill, 2000).

Scalia, G. (ed.), *Cronica Salimbene de Adam* (Scrittori d'Italia, 232; Bari: Laterza, 1966).

Smalley, B., *The Study of the Bible in the Middle Ages* (Oxford: Basil Blackwell, 1952).

—'The Gospels in the Paris Schools in the Late 12th and Early 13th Centuries', *Franciscan Studies* 39 (1979).

— *The Gospels in the Schools c.1100–c.1280* (London: Hambledon, 1985).

Van Den Borne, C., 'De fontibus commentarii S. Bonaventurae in Ecclesiasten', *AFH* 10 (1917).

Wachtel, A. (ed.), *Alexander Minorita, Expositio in Apocalypsim* (Monumenta Germaniae Historica, Quellen zur Geistesgeschichte des Mittelalters, 1; Weimar: Nachfolger, 1955).

Waley, D., *The Italian City-Republics* (London: Longman, 3rd edn, 1988).

THE WHOLE BIBLE IN ENGLISH

David Daniell

Editor's Introduction

In 1994, the year which marked the five hundredth anniversary of William Tyndale's birth, the British Library paid just over £1 million for the only complete surviving copy of the 1526 first edition of Tyndale's translation of the New Testament. Apart from an incomplete copy (lacking 71 pages) in the possession of St Paul's Cathedral, this is the only one of three thousand copies printed to escape the book-burning ordered by the bishop of London.

The sixteenth century is regarded as an heroic age of biblical studies and translation, when concerted efforts were made, first, to establish the best text from the myriad of manuscripts in which the Scriptures had been passed down before the invention of printing, and then to produce vernacular translations. A striking feature of Tyndale's English Bible, according to David Daniell, is that it 'was made in the language people spoke, not as the scholars wrote. At a time when English was struggling to find a form that was neither Latin nor French, Tyndale gave the nation a Bible language that was English in words, order and lilt.' In the words of Laurie Lee's caption for the 1951 Festival of Britain, 'the English Bible put the Divine Word into common speech and inspired the native genius for language'.

Anniversary conferences, exhibitions and other celebrations brought Tyndale's name back to public attention. David Daniell's biography of him (New Haven: Yale University Press, 1994) was the first for fifty years. Previous neglect of Tyndale had been all the stranger, as Laurence Marks observed,

> because of his great political as well as literary influence on British and American culture. The English Bible spiritually enfranchised the ordinary man and woman. Private reading of the Scriptures lies at the heart of Protestant individualism and of the civilisation it created.

The present chapter presents Tyndale, as he would himself have wished, 'first of all as a working translator of the scriptures'. His choice of language, and its implications for biblical interpretation, is presented both in its broadest historical context and with the sensitivity to sound of a comparative literary scholar. The emphasis of the title is highly significant, as representing Tyndale's objective, although he personally did not live to achieve it.

The teaching of the Protestant Reformation can be, and often is, summed up in six words: *sola fide, sola gratia, sola scriptura*—by faith alone, the doctrine of justification by faith, the essential heart of New Testament doctrine, especially Paul's Epistle to the Romans; by grace alone, expressing the sovereignty and priority of divine grace in salvation (over, for example, works); and 'only the Scriptures'—that all Christian teaching on faith and morals is to be based on the truth of the Bible, and any other source is secondary—countering, for example, the Church's teaching at the time, dominant since Basil a thousand years before, that the Bible was itself secondary to the current interpretation of the Church, especially through a secret tradition, never written down, 'unwritten verities' handed down from Jesus himself in ritual and practice, from the disciples to the bishops, and thus absolutely unchallengeable.[1]

But if the ultimate authority was now only the Scriptures, certain things had to follow. The books of the Bible carry God's authority; they contain all that is necessary for salvation and Christian living, all that God requires us to believe; they contain the record of God's unique saving activity in human history, especially in Israel and in Jesus; they are to be interpreted by believers, in faith; and they are to be translated from the original Hebrew and Greek into all the languages of the world, so that all the world may have the truth.

There had been no significant dispute about what books made up the Scriptures since the late fourth century—the New Testament contained 27 books, the Old Testament 39: occasionally the names of Old Testament books were different, according to whether you took the Hebrew, Greek or Latin titles. The Latin Bible as used by the Roman Catholic Church gave weight to 15 shortish books found in the early Greek version of the Hebrew Scriptures, the Septuagint, but not included in the Hebrew Bible itself, not accepted as canonical by Jews or Protestants, and usually printed by the latter as the Apocrypha. The dispute that flared up in Europe early in the sixteenth century—a verb that recalls the flames in which so many perished—was about the necessity for all believers to have access to Scriptures. This, to change metaphor but not the heat, boiled down to two vital and essential matters—that the Bible should be in the language of the people, and that those people should have in front of them the whole Bible, all 66 books, all the Old and all the New Testaments.

To say this was of course heresy in William Tyndale's England in the 1520s and 1530s. Tyndale translated the New Testament into English, twice,

1.   See, for example, *The English Works of John Fisher*, Part I (ed. John E.B. Mayor; EETS; Oxford: Oxford University Press, 1935 [1876]), p. 352.

in 1526 and 1534, from the original Greek, the first to do so (only Luther in German was ahead of him). He translated half the Old Testament from the original Hebrew, again for the first time.[2] This work, done in exile, contravened the Constitutions of Oxford of 1408, whereby it was forbidden to translate the Bible into English (or to possess or even to read it), a selective lever against Lollards and their 'Wyclif' manuscript Bibles of the 1380s. A will to translate the whole Bible suggested that the Church was in error, in denying it to the people, keeping a stranglehold in insisting that only a few lines of the Bible in English should be allowed, and that only to 'the religious' for a service-book in private.

The motivation, so noticeably powerful, of the English reformers in exile to translate and print the whole Bible, with no part omitted, needs further examination, more than is possible here. Tyndale did not know that he was not going to finish the whole Bible, though he may have had a premonition. Miles Coverdale printed his own complete Bible in English, in Antwerp (as we now know)[3] in 1535 while Tyndale was in prison in Vilvoorde. Coverdale worked not from the original languages but from 'five sundry interpreters':[4] Tyndale (whom he may have assisted for a while in Antwerp), Luther, the Vulgate, the Zurich Bible and Pagninus's Latin translation of the Hebrew. It was an enormous achievement, done in a very short time. His Old Testament poetic and prophetic books were taken into John Rogers's complete 'Matthews's Bible' in 1537, the true transmitter of Tyndale's work, and the first licensed Bible in English—freely available within months of Tyndale being burned.

Independently, George Joye was printing English translations of Old Testament books that Tyndale did not live to reach, though only from the Latin—the Psalms in 1530, Isaiah in 1531, Jeremiah in 1534, Proverbs and Ecclesiastes in 1535, Daniel in 1545. They are not very good translations, though not downright bad, and they need much more study.[5] It is odd to find Joye filling in Tyndale's gaps with five books ahead of time, as it were, as if the Spirit was moving everyone towards the whole Bible. There may have been something here more than natural, indeed.

---

2.   See my *William Tyndale; A Biography* (New Haven: Yale University Press, 1994): *Tyndale's New Testament* (New Haven: Yale University Press, 1989) and *Tyndale's Old Testament* (New Haven: Yale University Press, 1992).

3.   See G. Latre, 'The 1535 Coverdale Bible and its Antwerp Origins', in Orlaith O'Sullivan (ed.), *The Bible as Book: The Reformation* (London: British Library, 2000), pp. 89-102.

4.   The phrase is on the title page of his 1535 Bible.

5.   The standard work is still Charles C. Butterworth and Allan G. Chester, *George Joye, 1495?–1553* (Philadelphia: University of Pennsylvania Press, 1962).

It is also curious that in striving to reinstitute the entire Scripture in the vernacular, as something that had to have greater authority than the Church, the English reformers were behaving, regarding Scripture, exactly in the pattern of religions world-wide as recorded throughout history. Common factors in all the major religions over the world at any period include the essential relation of the Scripture to a community, and especially that community's history: its prime authority in organizing public ritual and language; and its necessary inspiration. Always of great antiquity, it is a heavenly book, giving divine authority and decrees, and thus sacred and not to be altered. It achieves its function aurally, being recited or read aloud. It has a tendency to be regarded as magic in some parts of the community. It produces traditions of enormous scholarly volumes of interpretation, and has generated divinely inspired, even miraculous, translations (one thinks of the legend of the origin of the Greek translation of the Hebrew Scriptures, where 70 translators locked up in separate cells produced identical versions—hence the name 'Septuagint'. Perhaps linked with that is the worship, in some parts of its recent history, of the 1611 English version under King James[6]). Such Scripture has a larger cultural effect through its language, especially on later literature. But above all it is the giver of authority to its worshipping followers.

For over a thousand years the Church—uniquely in world religions, as far as I can discover—had reversed that common model, claiming that it was the followers (i.e. the Church) who gave the authority to the Scripture. The reformers, in establishing the primacy of Scripture, were bringing the religion of Christianity back into line with religions everywhere and at all times. (There is an urgent need of further work here, about how those reformers, making Scripture whole and supreme again, were fulfilling some profound global human experience of religion.) If there are such primal forces in the essential nature of Scripture, it is no wonder that the idea of the complete Bible in English produced such horror in the Church—so much so that the humanist scholar Thomas More, dedicated to ancient learning and its dissemination, could seriously find the only solution to the unmistakeable popular clamour for Bibles in English in the 1530s in his curious plan to give parts of selected Bible books in English to individual senior men in a village or town, to be held until their death, and other selected books to others similarly, so that never could the whole thing come together as whole.[7]

6.   Commonly referred to by the ignorant, or merely bigoted, as the 'Saint James Bible'. In English history there may have been monarchs close to sainthood, but James VI and I was not one of them.

7.   More, arch-enemy of Tyndale and his 'heresy' of giving the Scriptures to the people, suggested that a translation under the Church's authority could be made by 'some

The pioneering Luther came to *sola scriptura* as the third of the three *sola*s, finding that Scripture had to be the sole source of authority for the individual Christian and for the Church, as he defended *sola fide* and *sola gratia*. Most importantly, for Luther, *sola scriptura* was Christo-centric. Scripture is the Word of God because in it *the* Word, Christ, is revealed— and at this point the uniqueness of Christianity in world religions in relation to its Scripture might begin to appear. Scripture for Luther is 'the crib where Christ lieth'.[8] The Bible is to be read in order to find Christ, using reason and prayer for the Holy Spirit's guidance. In this sense the Bible will be its own interpreter and will direct the Church, and not vice versa.

Luther understood that the relationship of law and gospel provided the key to the understanding of Scripture. God revealed himself as both a de-manding and a giving God. Luther, we might roughly summarize, assigned the first to the Old Testament and the second to the New Testament, but also found grace in the Old Testament and law in the New.

Now, it is that interlinking that is so vital to *sola scriptura*, and it is one of the main points I want to make. The Old and New Testaments cross-refer all the time: to Christians, the one is not comprehensible without the other. The New Testament frequently says 'that it might be fulfilled…', directly quot-ing the Old: the Old Testament as frequently, Christians say, gives a type of what will be in the New Testament—as Jesus himself explained that Jonah in the whale gives a type of his death and resurrection (Mt. 12; Lk. 11). Clearly that principle cannot work unless you have the whole Bible available —the double emphasis being on you, and on the whole Bible: not the priests alone, and not bits.

The self-interpreting quality of the English reformers' Bible is deeply important. While it is flawed by omissions it cannot function properly. Unlike Luther, the English reformers, especially Tyndale, did not follow Luther into a two-tier Bible, reducing, for example, the epistles of James and Jude, and Hebrews and Revelation to secondary status. True, the *sola scriptura* principle ran into difficulties in Germany in the last seven years of Tyndale's life, most strikingly in the inability of Luther and Zwingli to agree the meaning of 'This is my body', a vital, and costly, clash. But the general idea remained valid. With a complete vernacular Bible, the interpretation was, under the guidance of reason and the Holy Spirit, not in mountains of

good catholic and well learned man'. Copies would be bought by the bishops and broken up and doled out in small pieces to trusted men, on whose death the bishops would reclaim them (*The Yale Edition of the Complete Works of St. Thomas More*. VI. *A Dialogue Con-cerning Heresies* [T.M.C. Lawlor, G. Marc'hadour and R.C. Marius (eds.)], i, p. 341).

    8.   Luther, *Werke*, X (Weimar, 1883–), i, pp. 576.12ff.

learned commentary in Latin piled up for a thousand years and only available to especially learned clergy, but in the hand of every Christian. This releasing of the shackles brought the possibility of reinterpretation of the Bible in every generation, surely a particularly healthy thing, and something that has happened since Tyndale's work.

Using his various printed dissertations, like *The Parable of the Wicked Mammon* or *The Obedience of a Christian Man* (both of 1528) William Tyndale is today, rather perversely, most frequently written about as polemicist, propagandist, political reformer, moralist, theologian, historian, enemy of the institutions of the Church, and often, in less sensitive Catholic circles, as a rather nasty little man who got up the nose of the great Saint Thomas More. Yet in the very first printed words that we have, the opening of the Prologue to the Cologne fragment,[9] Tyndale presents himself first of all as a working translator of the Scriptures. This, his own view of himself, must be the correct one, and it cannot be right to see him as being anything more important than that. He translated two-thirds of the Bible from two relatively unknown ancient languages so well that his translations have not only endured until today (the revered 'Authorised', or 'King James', Version of 1611 is 83 per cent pure Tyndale in the New Testament).[10] This was a labour so great that that list of secondary definitions must surely dwindle by comparison. Tyndale was a worker at the coal-face—and a very dangerous coal-face in several ways—who was never seduced away to a more comfortable surface job. His greatest achievement is the 1534 New Testament, and the opening words of the first Prologue to that give technical details of the work of translation, a scientific explanation of changes from his earlier 1526 version, and from what might have been expected by those who knew the Latin, arising from his research—his (as far as I know) then unique discovery of the strength of the Hebrew forms underlying so much Greek of the New Testament. The third sentence—

> ...consider the Hebrew phrase or manner of speech left in the Greek words. Whose preterperfect tense and present tense is oft both one, and the future tense is the optative mode also, and the future tense is oft the imperative mode in the active voice, and in the passive ever. Likewise person for person, number for number, and an interrogation for a conditional, and such like is with the Hebrews a common usage.[11]

9.   Tyndale began to print an English New Testament in Cologne in 1525, before he was denounced to the authorities and had to flee up the Rhine. The one copy of the sheets that survived, of a Prologue and Matthew as far as ch. 22, is in the British Library.

10.   See John Nielson and Royal Skousen, 'How Much of the King James Bible Is William Tyndale's ?', *Reformation* 3 (1998), pp. 49-74.

11.   *Tyndale's New Testament*, p. 3.

His work had two principles. One was to understand the Greek and the Hebrew as well as possible. The other was to be clear at all times, to write something in English that made sense. To keep both principles alive for every syllable is very skilled work indeed.

It is Tyndale as translator of something approaching the whole Bible that I want to open up now, and in one particular, and almost totally neglected, way. Let me put it baldly, and then refine. Every book is different—different Hebrew, different Greek, so much so that knowledge of Hebrew and Greek means that passages lifted out can easily be put back into place. Even different parts of each book are different, as most obviously with Genesis, Isaiah, Matthew, Acts and Revelation—and one can take that much further. A bad translation eradicates those differences, something all too common, producing a text that is all the same, written in the one language of one translator or, worse, of a committee. The whole Bible does not have a single style of writing. Modern references to later writers using 'biblical English' are misleading, and tend to come from the distancing Latin syntax and vocabulary imported into the King James version after Tyndale, from the conservative Bishops' Bible and the Catholic Rheims New Testament (as in Mt. 6, 'Sufficient unto the day is the evil thereof', which is pure Latin-in-English, overriding Tyndale's 'For the day present hath ever enough of his own trouble').[12] So-called 'biblical English' also comes from use of a 'the+noun+of+the +noun' mannerism (basically a Hebrew form for genitives) with old-fashioned abstract nouns ('the tread of the valiant', 'the might of the righteous') and often to make a sentimental sense of vague uplift ('The kiss of the sun for pardon /The song of the birds for mirth…') which is whole continents away from the New Testament. Technically, there can be no such thing as a 'biblical' style. A good translator is sensitive to all the differences, and for the 66 books of the Bible produces 66 kinds of English—though of course it doesn't quite work as strictly as that, as the Gospel and three Epistles of 'John' share a Greek style, for example.

To illustrate: I once came upon an academic colleague, in a Geology Department, examining a PhD thesis, and the subject of it was the geology of a high mountain in a range at the bottom of the Atlantic Ocean. I offer that image here, of the sea-bed of the Atlantic Ocean, a landscape of towering heights and deep valleys and plains and plateaus, the very interior formations of which must be known. A translator has to give a sense in English of that hidden topography of Greek and Hebrew. The English must not offer a flat watery surface, but be very variable, able to reproduce the quite remark-

---

12. *Tyndale's New Testament*, p. 28.

able differences in the original—in Genesis alone between ch. 3, for example, the tragi-comic story of the Fall, and ch. 22, the bleak, stark story of Abraham and Isaac, and again the short novel about Joseph that makes up the last 14 chapters. Now, obviously, I am going to point out that Tyndale did this in everything he translated. But I am going to stress even more the remarkable way he did it with the material he had to hand, the English language of the 1530s. To know the Bible only in Jerome's fourth-century Latin, the Vulgate as it came to be known, is to know, I find, too smooth a surface, too uniform a language (perhaps it might look a little different if I were myself a fourth-century Latin, as it were, though I doubt it). Tyndale produced a *range* of language-effects in English that was extraordinary for the time, beyond anyone else writing then. Though he was translating and not making poetic drama, it is right to call his range Shakespearean, I feel, for reasons that will I hope become apparent. The measure of this achievement does not become clear until we can map the whole continent, as it were, and see Tyndale working to produce the whole Bible in English. It is all still virtually uncharted territory.

There are vivid variations of style in the doctrinal treatises, particularly in the *Obedience of a Christian Man*, published in Penguin Classics in 2000. Many people are startled, discovering a neglected, most powerful, writer, both unexpectedly organized and again with a remarkable range. But in that book, and his others, he is singing his own song: in the Bible work he is speaking for many different writers in Greek and Hebrew.

In the Pentateuch, he can make clear the apparently endless pages of laws and rituals of all kinds, and even makes some sense of the fittings of the Tabernacle—and let me remind us that Hebrew is not like Greek, with a vast literature and widespread culture: it exists only in the Scriptures, and when baffling words appear they remain baffling (a glance at the definitive solutions to famous Hebrew problems by modern scholars will show this— all definitive, and all different). In the historical books of the Old Testament he can catch the tone of one of the oldest war-songs in the world, in Judg. 5, the Song of Deborah, 'Up up Deborah, up up and sing a song, up Barak, and take thy prey, thou son of Abinoam...'[13] (A very recent translation has 'Rouse yourself, rouse yourself Deborah, rouse yourself, break into song...' which to me has unhappy and comic associations with an elderly aunt rallying a public schoolgirl.) Tyndale can express personal relation to God, as in the Hebrew poetry of the psalms and prophets. Though he was murdered before he reached the great poetic books of the Old Testament—Job,

---

13. *Tyndale's Old Testament*, p. 348.

Psalms, Song of Solomon, the greater and lesser prophets—we have enough from poems embedded elsewhere to warrant a study of Tyndale's translations of Hebrew poetry, something not yet attempted.

How different in Hebrew narrative that human rawness of the Fall at the start of Genesis is from this, towards the end:

> When Joseph came home, they brought the present into the house to him, which they had in their hands, and fell flat on the ground before him. And he welcomed them courteously saying: is your father that old man that ye told me of, in good health ? and is he yet alive ?[14]

The longer reach of those sentences, the social niceties, the physical locations, the adverb 'courteously', the delicacy of Joseph's enquiry about his father, with its qualification lest he should appear too eager—'that old man that ye told me of'—all these come over in a different kind of English, which is not at all 'biblical'—it belongs to the social novel, and could easily be Defoe. More like an Elizabethan writer like Thomas Nashe or George Chapman is the handling of sudden detail and verbal colour in moments of violence in the historical books—indeed, this could be from Chapman's Homer:

> And Joab took Amasa by the chin with the right hand, as though he would have kissed him. And Amasa took no heed to the knife that was in Joab's hand, with which Joab smote him in the short ribs, and shed out his bowels to the ground and smote him but one stroke, and he died.[15]

The effect of the following is wholly different, of Eliah (Elijah) on Horeb, with something baroque in its strangeness:

> And he said come out and stand before the Lord. And behold, the Lord went by and a mighty strong wind that rent the mountains and brake the rocks before him. But the Lord was not in the wind. And after the wind came an earthquake. But the Lord was not in the earthquake. And after the earthquake, came fire: but the Lord was not in the fire. And after the fire, came a small still voice. And when Eliah heard it, he covered his face with his mantle, and went out and stood in the mouth of the cave.[16]

The long court narratives of Samuel and Kings have different ranges of story-telling again: the brightness and excitement of the rhythms of the voice of the Queen of Saba (Sheba) in the following are beautifully done:

> And when the queen of Saba had seen all Salomon's wisdom and the house that he had built, and the meat of his table, and the sitting of his servants,

---

14. Gen. 43; *Tyndale's Old Testament*, p. 70.
15. 2 Sam. 20; *Tyndale's Old Testament*, p. 452.
16. 1 Kgs 19; *Tyndale's Old Testament*, p. 494.

and the standing of his servitors and their apparel, and his butlers and his
sacrifice that he offered in the house of the Lord, she was astonished. Then
said she to the king: the word I heard in my own land of thy deeds and
wisdom, is true. Howbeit I believed it not till I came and saw it with mine
eyes. And see, the one half was not told me: for thy wisdom and goodness
exceedeth the fame which I heard. Happy are thy men: and happy are these
thy servants which stand ever before thee and hear thy wisdom...[17]

Even in Second Chronicles, Tyndale does his best to hold a reader, with
variation in the formulae, and the usual sudden shaft on every page, as in ch.
21—'And after all that, the Lord smote him in his bowels with an incurable
disease.' How modern can you get?

The common business Greek in which the New Testament is written, the
koine, at first blush gives rather less scope for different kinds of English. But
when you look, you find that this is not so. The same aim at clarity, at making sense above all, has to cope with, in the Gospels, the lapidary concise-
ness of the Christmas stories and the parables, the organization of straight
narrative of the deeds of Jesus, the expression of his varied teaching, the
mounting tensions and horror of the Crucifixion stories, the unexpectedness
of the resurrection accounts. The Acts of the Apostles has a dozen different
kinds of narrative and spoken English, including that splendid shipwreck in
ch. 27. The Hebrew-mind-writing-in-Greek to express the discovery of the
meaning of Christ that is Paul (and Peter and John) jumps from the outer
reaches of what a mind can express to the utterly ordinary ('The cloak that
I left at Troas with Carpus, when thou comest, bring with thee, and the
books...'[18]). The surreal events and scenes of Revelation need, and receive
in Tyndale, a language of their own: 'And I saw when the lamb opened one
of the seals, and I heard one of the four beasts say, as it were the noise of
thunder, come and see'.[19] The weirdness of both picture and sound-track is
heightened by the understatement. The 1611 King James Bible put the
thunder earlier, losing the fairy-tale strangeness of 'noise of thunder / come
and see'—so different from Eliah on Horeb.

And all this is just the start of a study of Tyndale's *range* as a translator. I
think what has happened is that the English Bible has for so long been
thought only as a seventeenth-century creation, published in 1611 while
Shakespeare was working, that it has not been thought so remarkable that
the English of the whole Bible should have so phenomenal a range, as that
was the 'golden period' of the language, when it seemed that English could

17. 1 Kgs 10; *Tyndale's Old Testament*, p. 478.
18. 2 Tim. 4; *Tyndale's New Testament*, p. 318.
19. Rev. 6; *Tyndale's New Testament*, p. 375.

do anything. On the one hand, that is a false judgment of the King James Version, which in its Latinate tendency does reduce the original mountain ranges quite a lot, and produce more of a uniform surface: an example is its general tendency to make a Latin participle ('And he answering said') where Tyndale has two finite verbs ('And he answered and said'); or to make a Latin participle clause, in the Latin position, do the work of a single plain subordinate clause: 'and bruising him, hardly departeth from him' replaces Tyndale's 'with much pain departeth from him, when he hath rent him'.[20] On the other, concentration on the King James Version has concealed the fact that that range of language was being made 80 years before, at a time, in Tyndale's 1520s and 1530s, when English was, officially, primitive, severely limited, and not worth attention. It is not fanciful to see an elitist programme to direct attention away from what English might achieve: the English humanists, Thomas More and the rest, saw only things Greek in Italian sunshine— Italian and Greek ideas and literature, and only the very best Latin, were the official models for the century.[21] Our first major work of criticism, Philip Sidney's *Apology for Poetry* (about 1583) says that we should despise the earlier native stuff—even Chaucer except for the *Troilus*—and look wholly to Italy.[22] It was all extremely persuasive, and of course the Italian influence was wonderfully beneficial—12 of Shakespeare's plays, a third of the total, are set in the Italian peninsula. But there was distortion, and it has helped to create a climate in which it has been very difficult to recognize how extraordinary for 1530 was the stylistic and linguistic richness of Tyndale.

After all, who else in the half century before the reign of Elizabeth I was showing Tyndale's ability to be scholarly (and his discovery of Hebrew in the Greek of the New Testament was pioneering work indeed) as well as popular in the best sense, over such large ground—in English? That is not a rhetorical question, by the way. The chroniclers, like Edward Hall in 1548, show some variation, but are marred by slack construction. Even the later great translators under Elizabeth and James, like Golding (Ovid, 1567), North (Plutarch, 1579), Chapman (Homer, 1598) and Florio (Montaigne, 1603) do not have such a need to be so various, and each of them has limitations, like Golding's unhappy choice of metre, or Chapman's excited elaborations of the original, or Florio's excessive freedom. For that mixture of accuracy, range of effect, clarity and sureness of grasp, Tyndale stands above.

20. Lk. 9; *Tyndale's New Testament*, p. 106.

21. The travellers to More's 1516 Utopia take only Greek books. More refused to permit an English translation of his famous book as that would demean it: the first English version was Ralph Robinson's in 1551.

22. *An Apology for Poetry* (ed. Geoffrey Shepherd; 1965), p. 133 and *passim*.

Those others were translating languages with by then a long history of knowledge in England: Tyndale's Pentateuch of 1530 was the first translation ever from Hebrew into English.

I want to go a little closer into detail, and take three examples, of the hundreds that might be taken, of Tyndale at work, in three quite different styles. The first is about a birth, and is from Lk. 2. The shepherds had visited Mary and Joseph and the babe in the manger, and told their story of the angel of the lord speaking to them.

> And all that heard it, wondered at those things which were told them of the shepherds. But Mary kept all those sayings, and pondered them in her heart.[23]

The Greek has, for Mary's 'pondered', *sunballousa* (thrown together) taken by the Vulgate to *conferens* (brought together). Luther has *bewegt* (weighed). The two 'Wyclif' versions of the 1380s (taken from the later Latin, not the original Greek) have, modernised, in the earlier version, 'And his mother kept together all these words, bearing together in her heart,' and in the later, the same except 'and bear them in her heart'. Tyndale's 'pondered' is his own. It matches and extends 'wondered', and does something original and important. It makes the best sense for ordinary English readers, as well as making a rhythmically unforgettable phrase: 'But Mary kept all those sayings, and pondered them in her heart.' (The King James translators altered 'sayings' to 'things'.) Tyndale knew that it did not need explaining what it is for a woman to ponder sayings in her heart.

My second example tells of a death, and shows the skill of Tyndale with both characterization and story-telling. At the end of 2 Sam. 18, a sweep of narrative over six chapters about David's beloved son Absalom, who, misled by a crafty counsellor, Ahithophel, led a rebellion against his father, comes to climax in the death of Absalom and the breaking of the news to his father:

> And the king said to Chusi: is the lad Absalom safe? And Chusi answered: the enemies of my lord the king and all that rise against thee, to have thee, be as thy lad is. And the king was moved and went up to a chamber over the gate and wept. And as he went thus he said: my son Absalom, my son, my son, my son Absalom, would to God I had died for thee, Absalom my son, my son.[24]

Tyndale possibly noted Luther at that point giving eight words to the expression of the idea of doing the king hurt, and simply used three—'to have

23. *Tyndale's New Testament*, p. 91.
24. *Tyndale's Old Testament*, p. 448.

thee'. He also avoided the Septuagint's making the first three cries 'my child Absalom, my child, my child'—he understands the cumulative force of the word 'son'. The repeated double stress around 'he' ('As he went, thus he said') Tyndale miraculously follows with something of his own, found in no other version, an additional 'my son' to balance. The force of that further double repetition, of 'Absalom' and now 'my son' twice, is painful enough for a father in sudden and desperately pointed grief. But between the pairs he puts the anguished cry of David, and makes it entirely in monosyllables, and in two triplets and a doublet, so that it runs 'Would to God / I had died / for thee'. It is the end of the long story, they are the last words, something surely Shakespearean in its linguistic power.

My third example is brief. The Gospel of John calls for a special sureness of touch, conveying the sense of both timeless theological meditation, in a narrative with an inevitable pace up to and through the Crucifixion, all in syntax and vocabulary that can be understood by a child. The combination must give a sense of spiritual experience of the very highest order, available to everyone. Tyndale was fully aware of this. He was so successful that uniquely large amounts of his translation of this gospel went forward untouched into the 1611 version and far beyond. He seems to have gone for model to a native English tradition of devotional writing several centuries old, in which a harmony and balance of short phrases is created with great skill and beauty. This form is most familiar to us in the wonderfully effective short prayers, the 'collects', in Cranmer's *Book of Common Prayer* of several decades later. So in Jn 14 Tyndale has Jesus's words as

> Let not your hearts be troubled. Believe in God and believe in me… I go to prepare a place for you. And if I go to prepare a place for you, I will come again, and receive you even unto myself, that where I am, there may you be also.[25]

The rhythms and the repetitions are peculiarly English. Particularly they are linked with English proverbs. If there is a unifying quality across Tyndale's range, it is that ability to catch the proverbial form. It is ringingly clear in 'Ask and it shall be given you. Seek and ye shall find. Knock, and it shall be opened unto you' of Mt. 7.[26] But it comes everywhere. Again, there is a considerable study of this waiting to be done. Proverbs made a large part of spoken wisdom, and many thousands from the period have been collected— indeed, a surprisingly large number. A dictionary of proverbs in use at this

---

25. *Tyndale's New Testament*, p. 154.
26. *Tyndale's New Testament*, p. 29.

period contains 20,000 proverbs.[27] It is one of the ways in which Tyndale achieves his unusual timelessness, the way his Gloucestershire speech-forms of the time seem to guide him towards proverbial forms. Now proverbs are strange, being apparently quite free from redundancy of expression. They mean what they do, and that is that. I should be glad to know of any recent study that explains why they are so clear: why 'out of sight, out of mind', for example, immediately means what it does, and not what, famously, an early computer was said to make of it, 'invisible idiot'. Modern attempts to be 100 per cent clear can still have fuzzy edges, as shown in the London Underground notice, 'Dogs must be carried on the escalator'. Tyndale not only can't afford fuzziness: he so strongly avoids it, even when dealing with such impossible technical terms as the Tabernacle and Temple fixtures.[28] Shakespeare is doing something different, of course, but the comparison is interesting when dealing with verbal skills across a great range. Sometimes Shakespeare's technicalities can bring comprehension to a sudden halt, as in *Hamlet* the Ghost's despairing cry that he died without having received the sacrament, unprepared and without extreme unction '…unhousel'd, disappointed, unanel'd'.[29] Or take the opening words of *Cymbeline*—the opening words, mind, while the audience is still settling in and thinking it's paid too much for the progamme;

> *1. Gent.* You do not meet a man but frowns; our bloods
> No more obey the heavens than our courtiers
> Still seem as does the King's.

To which the only response is 'eh ?' (And the interesting thing about that passage is that it defies explication: editors and commentators since Samuel Johnson have been happy to come up with paraphrase of what it seems to say, without ever quite getting to what Shakespeare's words amount to.) I know nothing in Tyndale so profoundly unfathomable, though there are for a translator temptations to escape into careless obscurity where Paul is at his densest.

At the heart of Shakespeare's *King Lear* is an opposition of two of the greatest Renaissance matters, Nature and Art, both explored almost too profoundly to experience, and taking on board the manipulation of both concepts by villainy, of which there is a great deal in the play. So it is striking that the first words of the chief villain, Edmund are 'Thou, Nature, art my

---

27. B.J. Whiting and H.W. Whiting, *Proverbs, Sentences and Proverbial Phrases from English Writings Mainly before 1500* (Cambridge, MS, 1968).

28. See the later chapters of Exodus, 1 Kgs 6 and 7, 2 Chron. 3 and 4: *Tyndale's Old Testament*, pp. 121-27, 469-72, 583-85.

29. *Hamlet* 1.5.77.

goddess', where the second and third words are 'Nature' and 'art'. That is rhetorical skill on Shakespeare's part, a careful device all the more effective in that it is largely concealed. Shakespeare, as we are slowly beginning to grasp again, is a master of those skills, so much developed in the sixteenth century in England under the influence of Erasmus two generations before Shakespeare. The wreck of rhetoric, as it has been described, in the sea of Enlightenment self-consciousness and post-Romantic self-expression is gradually now being lifted from the sea-bed. Shakespeare, for the eighteenth century a rural clod animated by a shaft of divine lightning, is now more and more seen as the working artist that he was, well educated, creatively developing as artists do, always alert to syllable, word, phrase, sentence, dialogue, event, with the conscious skill of a maker of computer programs.

And so was Tyndale, two generations before Shakespeare, at the beginning of the educational revolution in England. This point has been extremely unfashionable. In, for example, the construction of a few sentences of one of his doctrinal treatises, we find his rhetorical skills with *admiratio, deflexio, enallage, repetitio, hyperbole, catachresis, auxesis, deflexio* and *epanalepsis.*[30]

Analysis of Tyndale's Bible translations will show more sharply the entire topography of a range and expertise of language skills so far unimagined, and all of it two generations before such a range and skills were thought possible in English. Leading the English reformers, William Tyndale began to give the English people the whole Bible, with all that that meant, at the highest level of accuracy and clarity.

BIBLIOGRAPHY

Alter, Robert and Frank Kermode (eds.), *The Literary Guide to the Bible* (London: Collins, 1987).
Daniell, David, *William Tyndale: A Life* (New Haven: Yale University Press, 1994).
—*Tyndale's New Testament* (New Haven: Yale University Press, 1989).
—*Tyndale's Old Testament* (New Haven: Yale University Press, 1992).
Greenslade, S.L. (ed.), *The Cambridge History of the Bible: The West from the Reformation to the Present Day* (Cambridge: Cambridge University Press, 1963).
Hammond, Gerald, *The Making of the English Bible* (Manchester: Carcanet, 1982).
Norton, David, *A History of the English Bible as Literature* (Cambridge: Cambridge University Press, 2000).
O'Sullivan, Orlaith (ed.), *The Bible as Book: The Reformation* (London: British Library, 2000).
Porter, Stanley E. (ed.), *Religious Language: A Colloquium* (Sheffield: Sheffield Academic Press, 1996).
Schwarz, W., *Principles and Problems of Biblical Translation: Some Reformation Controversies and their Background* (Cambridge: Cambridge University Press, 1955).

---

30. For a faint beginning of such analysis, see Daniell, *William Tyndale*, pp. 248-49.

George Herbert: Priest, Pastor, Poet

Tina Leeke

Editor's Introduction

George Herbert was born on 3 April 1593 in Montgomery in Wales, the fifth son of an aristocratic family. After his father died three years later, the head of the family was the elder brother Edward, who was later to become Lord Herbert of Cherbury, the philosopher and poet. After a highly successful career at Cambridge University, George Herbert represented Montgomery in Parliament for two years and then was ordained deacon in 1626. He was appointed prebendary of Leighton Bromswold in Huntingdonshire, near his friend Nicholas Ferrar's religious community at Little Gidding, and he refurbished Leighton church according to his ideal of how worship should be conducted. In 1630 he moved to Bemerton, near Salisbury. He died of consumption in 1633, just before his fortieth birthday.

The first poems by George Herbert to be published, in 1612, were two memorial poems in Latin, on the death of Prince Henry, the eldest son of James I. Nearly all his surviving poems in English were published posthumously in a collection called The Temple *that appeared in the year of his death, with a preface from Nicholas Ferrar. In D.J. Enright's words: 'George Herbert is undeniably a devotional poet, devoted to Christ and to the Church as Christ's representative on earth, yet his poetry has an energy, inventiveness and intellectual depth and edge usually missing from what we think of as devotional verse.' The present study focuses on George Herbert's poetry from the perspective of its echoes of biblical language (seen through the Protestant Reformation), and its reflection of the concerns of liturgy and spirituality (principally in the biblical tradition of* The Book of Common Prayer*). This context of worship provides the opportunity for echoes of other chapters in this symposium, for example, John Chrysostom, or the mediaeval and Victorian techniques of the sermon, or the emphasis on spirituality in Women's Studies (see the Chapters by John M. Court, Jeremy Worthen, Mervyn Willshaw and Julie Hopkins). Herbert's thinking on the pattern of the pastoral ministry is to be found in* The Country Parson, *written while he was at Bemerton.*

1. *Introduction*

In this chapter I intend to explore George Herbert's central and continuing role in devotional literature, and his broad appeal to people of different churchmanship (or none) throughout the centuries. Although it is difficult to separate Herbert's religious beliefs from his poetry, it is not necessary to adhere to those beliefs to appreciate his work and gain benefit from it. His poetry can be 'valued for the piety, but that piety was not related to any specific political settlement or religious form: it was the communicated record of recognizable religious experience'.[1] Herbert, in a letter to Nicholas Ferrar that accompanied the manuscript of *The Temple*, describes his work as 'as a picture of the many spiritual conflicts that have passed betwixt God and my soul';[2] but it is also possible to find, mirrored in Herbert's poems, the personal struggles that are experienced by everyone in life. By putting pen to paper, Herbert works out his inner conflicts in a way that people from any period can relate to, and see their own experiences in his struggles. Of course, for those who share his religious beliefs, Herbert can be of great assistance along the spiritual journey, and even without consciously picking up a book of his poetry, his words speak to us through hymns like 'Teach me My God and King' taken from his poem 'The Elixir', or 'Let all the World in Every Corner Sing' from 'Antiphon (I)' and 'King of Glory, King of Peace', which is the poem 'Praise (II)'. How many people have sung these hymns without any idea that George Herbert, the seventeenth-century poet and priest wrote them? Words and phrases are often quoted without thought of where they come from as happens with Shakespeare; 'heart in pilgrimage' and 'Heaven in ordinarie' are taken from Herbert's poem 'Prayer (I)'.

The early seventeenth century was a time of religious turmoil; the Church of England had to face problems concerning church government, ritual, theology and the proper conduct of personal life.[3] Within the broad spectrum of the Church, there were both extreme Puritans and Anglo-Catholics, and a wide range of belief was tolerated. The Puritans fought against any formal rites, believed in justification by faith, predestination, election and looked to the Church to suppress any idle recreation or sport. The Anglo-Catholics considered the episcopacy to be the correct form of church gov-

---

1. J.H. Summers, *George Herbert: His Religion and Art* (Medieval and Renaissance Texts and Studies; New York: W.W. Norton , 1981, p. 16.

2. Mario Di Cesare, *George Herbert and the Seventeenth-Century Religious Poets* (New York: W.W .Norton, 1978), p. 242.

3. Summers, *George Herbert*, p. 50.

ernment, and accepted a certain amount of ritual in worship for the edification of the laity; although they considered that the Church of Rome was misguided, it was still part of the true church, unlike the church of Geneva.

Between these two poles, many sought a middle way, a *via media*. This alternative path was 'no marked highway but a vaguely defined area: the paths which conscientious searchers for the truth found through it were rarely identical'.[4] To be an Anglican required the affirmation of the 39 articles, regular church attendance and good conduct; beyond these, the options were vast. In order to chart Herbert's middle way, it is necessary to examine his writings. Using *The Temple* and *The Country Parson* I hope to investigate Herbert's use of the Bible, the influence of the Book of Common Prayer on his work, and his Anglican *via media*.

Through Herbert's poetry, it is possible to chart the process of spiritual development through the various stages of conflict to an acceptance and conclusion, and it is perhaps this process that appeals to Christians and non-Christians alike. L.C. Knights suggests:

> The poems in which the fluctuating stages of this progress are recorded are important human documents because they handle with honesty and insight questions that, in one form or another, we all have to meet if we wish to come to terms with life.[5]

Humanity's fragility, weakness and failure are captured in Herbert's words, and the constant vacillation that is experienced in life can be easily identified with, and the reader can find solace in realizing that these experiences are universal. We are never alone on the path through life; people have trod this way before and will continue to do so while the world is in existence.

Herbert's theology is very firmly based on the twin pillars of Scripture and tradition, and this solid foundation may explain why he has managed to escape passing vagaries and retain his broad appeal. For these pillars have supported the Christian faith from the earliest time of the New Testament and reach further back into the Old Testament tradition. Rather as St Augustine invented a biblical Latin style in his writing, so too does Herbert create a poetical biblical style. All his poems are saturated with biblical references, allusions and images. Chana Bloch sums this up succinctly in her book *Spelling the Word*: 'There is scarcely a poem in Her-

---

4.   Summers, *George Herbert*, p. 53.

5.   L.C. Knights, 'George Herbert: Resolution and Conflict', in M.A. Di Cesare (ed.), *George Herbert and the Seventeenth-Century Religious Poets* (New York: W.W. Norton, 1978), pp. 249.

bert's *Temple*—one might say scarcely a line—that does not refer us to the Bible...'[6]

2. *Biblical Influence*

The Authorized Version or 'King James' version of the Bible was published in 1611 while Herbert was studying at Trinity College, Cambridge, and it was this translation that Herbert would have used throughout his life. The preface to the Authorized Version sums up what the Bible meant to Herbert and his contemporaries:

> It is onely an armour, but also a whole armorie of weapons, both offensive, and defensive; whereby we may save our selves and put the enemie to flight. It is not an herbe but a tree, or rather a whole paradise of trees of life, which bring foorth fruit every moneth, and the fruit thereof is for meate, and the leaves for medicine. It is not a pot of *Manna*, or a cruse of oyle, which were for memorie only, or for a meales meate or two, but as it were a showre of heavenly bread sufficient for a whole host, be it never so great; and as it were a cellar full of oyle vessels; whereby all our necessities may be provided for, and our debts discharged.

It was quite simply the living word of God and in the preface to the 1633 edition of *The Temple*, Nicholas Ferrar informs the reader of what the Bible meant personally to Herbert:

> Next God, he loved that which God himself hath magnified above all things, that is, his Word: so as he hath been heard to make solemne protestation, that he would not part with one leaf thereof for the whole world, if it were offered him in exchange.[7]

In his poems 'H. Scripture I and II', Herbert talks of the Bible as having healing powers; he calls it a medicinal cure for any pain, 'a hony'. Here is an example of Herbert using a biblical image directly from Scripture; this image of 'honey' is taken from Ps. 119.103—'How sweet are thy words unto my taste! *yea, sweeter* than honey to my mouth!' By words alone, Herbert believes Scripture to be capable of inducing an inner transformation in which the believer takes no active role. He also asserts in the second stanza of 'H. Scripture II' that Scripture is the best interpreter of Scripture. This is sometimes called 'the analogy of faith',[8]

6.   C. Bloch, *Spelling the Word: George Herbert and the Bible* (Berkeley: University of California Press, 1985), p. 1.

7.   C.A. Patrides (ed.), *The English Poems of George Herbert* (London: Dent, 1974), p. 31.

8.   J.S. Orrick, 'George Herbert's Debt to the Bible' (Dissertation, Ohio University, 1996), p. 75.

and although this doctrine is not to be found in the Bible, certain passages would seem to support it, such as Mt. 4.5-7 and 12.1-7. This was a typically Protestant view, and for Herbert, the understanding of Scripture is inextricably bound up with self-understanding. The third stanza of 'H. Scripture II' demonstrates the process of reciprocal illumination that Calvin writes about in his commentary on the Psalms, where God's word searches out the reader and acts as a mirror to reveal the true person. For Calvin, 'the mirror of Scripture shows him who he is: "yit did it greatly availe mee to beholde as it were in a Glasse, bothe the beginnings of my vocation, and also the continuall race of my ministerie".'[9] In this way, Herbert sees himself as a living 'commentary' that helps to illuminate the sacred text—one of the great communal enterprises of the Reformation.[10] In Chapter 4 of *The Country Parson* he writes:

> For all truth being consonant to it self, and all being penn'd by one and the self-same Spirit, it cannot be, but that an industrious and judicious comparing of place with place must be a singular help for the right understanding of Scriptures.

The Protestant Reformers considered the Bible to be ultimate truth, the final authority and the perfect guide to leading a Christian way of life. Herbert conforms to this ideal when he writes in his handbook designed to assist the country Parson:

> But the chief and top of knowledge consists in the book of books, the storehouse and magazine of life and comfort, the holy Scriptures. There he sucks and lives. In the Scriptures he finds four things: Precepts for life, Doctrines for knowledge, Examples for illustration, and Promises of comfort.[11]

His poetry bears this out, and we can see how Herbert has been nourished by the Bible, how he has sucked every letter.

> Oh Book! Infinite sweetnesse! Let my heart
> Suck evr'y letter, and a hony gain,
> Precious for any grief in any part;
> To cleare the breast, to molifie all pain'
> (ll. 1-2 of H. Scripture I).

In the first two stanzas of 'The Sacrifice', Herbert alludes to the Bible in several different ways; the title conjures up images of the Old Testament

---

9. Bloch, *Spelling the Word*, p. 9.

10. C. Bloch, 'Spelling the Word', in C.J. Summers and T.-L. Pebworth (eds.), *Too Rich to Clothe the Sunne* (Pittsburgh: Pittsburgh University Press, 1980), p. 16.

11. J.N. Wall, Jr, *George Herbert: The Country Parson, the Temple* (London: SPCK, 1981), p. 58.

and temple sacrifice but also, the sacrificial nature of Christ's death on the cross as a sacrifice once for all (Heb. 9.26; 10.10). Next, there is an almost exact quotation from Lam. 1.12: 'Is it nothing to you, all ye that pass by?' and it is this desperate pleading tone that pervades the whole poem. It also reminds the reader of a passage from the New Testament, Mt. 24.39: 'And they that passed by reviled him, wagging their heads.' The haunting phrase that recurs at the end of every verse, 'Was ever grief like mine?' is reminiscent of the latter part of Lam. 1.12: '...see if there be any sorrow like unto my sorrow...'

In Herbert's first verse, Jesus is suggesting that those who pass him by do not see his agony as their eyes and minds are turned to worldly matters; this idea can be found in Jas 4.4: '...know ye not that the friendship of the world is enmity with God? Whosoever therefore will be a friend of the world is the enemy of God.' The idea that things of this world are contaminated with sin, and are thus incompatible with the ultimate truth of God and Christ, is a recurring theme in the New Testament. Herbert captures this theme with the utmost simplicity but with a hidden strength. The understatement continues with a beautiful description of the Incarnation in only two words, 'took eyes'. Christ becomes immediately so very human, and the reader feels real emotion, responsibility and guilt that Christ came in search of each individual, suffered pain, humiliation and death for each and every one of us.

The second stanza commences with a reference to the Sanhedrin, which was made up of members of the priestly class, scribes and Pharisees, the very people who sought to kill Jesus (Jn 11.47, 53). These two verses are an example of how intricately and almost unconsciously Herbert employs Scripture; it is possible to see why some scholars insist that a working knowledge of the Bible is necessary fully to appreciate and understand Herbert as priest and poet.

> *Oh all ye who pass by*, whose eyes and mind
> To worldly things are sharp, but to me blind;
> To me, who took eyes that I might you find;
>   Was ever grief like mine?
>
> The Princes of my people make a head
> Against their Maker; they do wish me dead,
> Who cannot wish, except I give them bread;
>   Was ever grief like mine?

Biblical references pervade his poetry to such an extent that 'it will not do to call it an "influence", certainly not just a "literary" influence'.[12] Her-

---

12. Bloch, *Spelling the Word*, p. 1.

bert's collection of poems, *The Temple*, uses Scripture in a typological way, just as the Old Testament can be seen to interpret the New. In order to oppose the Roman Catholic Church, the Protestant Reformers appealed to scripture as a more ancient and purer truth. As a result, Protestantism was heavily dependent upon Scripture. This is shown in the words of John Jewel:

> We receive and embrace all the canonical Scriptures, both of the Old and New Testament…whereunto all ecclesiastical doctrine ought to be called to account; and that against these Scriptures neither law, nor ordinance, nor any custom ought to heard; no, though Paul himself, or an angel from heaven, should come and teach the contrary.[13]

Herbert's debt to the Bible is obvious, but in recent years, scholars have been examining whether it is possible that Herbert is more indebted to another source with which he was equally familiar, the *Book of Common Prayer*. The language of the liturgy is extremely biblical, and Barbara Lewalski considers it difficult to distinguish when Herbert's imagery is taken from the Bible or the liturgy, and that it is not always profitable to do so.[14] Yet I agree with Rosemary van Wengen-Shute in her view that 'there are numerous instances where the special significance of a biblical reference is seriously diminished, if not entirely lost, if its specifically liturgical context is not recognized'.[15] Herbert went to great lengths to ensure his congregations were instructed in Scripture; he would use his sermons as a vehicle for religious instruction and explain the Bible readings and gospel and their particular relevance. Izaak Walton wrote in his biography of Herbert:

> The texts for all his future sermons (which God knows were not many) were constantly taken out of the Gospel for the day; and he did as constantly declare why the Church did appoint that portion of Scripture to be that day read as refer to the Gospel, or to the Epistle then read to them; and that they might pray with understanding, he did usually take the occasion to explain, not only the Collect for every particular Sunday, but the reasons of all the other Collects and Responses in our Church-Service; and made it appear to them, that the whole Service of the Church, was a reasonable, and therefore an acceptable Sacrifice to God'.[16]

---

13. Quote taken from Bloch, *Spelling the Word*, p. 10.

14. B.K. Lewalski, *Protestant Poetics and the Seventeenth-Century Religious Lyric* (Princeton, NJ: Princeton University Press, 1979), p. 11.

15. R. van Wengen-Shute, *George Herbert and the Liturgy of the Church of England* (Oegstgeest: Drukkerij de Kempenaer, 1981), p. 22.

16. I. Walton, 'Life of Mr George Herbert', in *Lives* (World's Classics; Oxford Oxford University Press, 1927), p. 295.

It is through the liturgy that Scripture is mediated and the tradition of the Church is put into practice.

3. *Liturgy*

Herbert was brought up in a household that daily said morning and evening prayer and regularly attended church services. As a student at Westminster School this routine was to continue, and for Herbert, would remain a constant for the rest of his life. While at Trinity College, Cambridge both public and private devotions were obligatory, as detailed in the *Book of Common Prayer*. In November 1626, Herbert was ordained deacon and from that time on, it was his duty to fulfil the duties prescribed in the *Book of Common Prayer's* preface:

> And all Priests and Deacons are to say daily the Morning and Evening Prayer, either privately or openly, not being let by sicknesse, or some other urgent cause. And the Curate that ministreth in every Parish Church or Chapel...shall say the same'.[17]

Contemporary evidence of Herbert's devotion to the liturgy of the Church of England can be found at the beginning of the 1633 edition of *The Temple*, where Nicholas Ferrar writes in 'The Printers to the Reader:

> His obedience and conformitie to the Church and the discipline thereof was singularly remarkable. Though he abounded in private devotions, yet went he every morning and evening with his familie to the Church; and by his example, exhortations, and encouragements drew the greater part of his parishioners to accompanie him dayly in the publick celebration of Divine Service.[18]

The word 'liturgy' comes from the Greek word λειτουργία which means a public duty or service. In the New Testament it is used for the service or ministry of priests, but it has become the word used to describe the rites of public worship: the Mass and the Office of the Roman Catholic Church, and mainly the Eucharist, Morning Prayer and Evening Prayer in the Anglican Church. The *Book of Common Prayer* was first introduced in 1549 to bring about conformity of liturgical practice in the Anglican Church, and the act of uniformity, passed in the same year, made it the official service book to be used by all Anglican churches. Its aim is stated clearly in the preface:

17. *The Book of Common Prayer* (Glasgow: Wm Collins Sons), p. 11.
18. F.E. Hutchinson, *The Works of George Herbert* (Oxford: Clarendon Press, 1941), p. 4.

> By this order the Curates shall need none other books for their public
> service, but this book and the Bible: By the means whereof the people shall
> not be at so great charges for books, as in times past they have been… And
> whereas heretofore there hath been great diversity in saying and singing in
> Churches within this Realm; some following *Salisbury* Use, some *Hereford*
> Use, some the Use of *Bangor*, some of *York*, some of *Lincoln*; now from
> henceforth all the Realm shall have but one Use.

Cranmer hoped to provide everything needed for the conduct of church
services in one volume, apart from the Bible. The *Book of Common Prayer*
was published in the vernacular in an attempt to make it more accessible;
it synthesized the Roman Catholic missal, breviary, manual and pontifical.
It was Cranmer's aim to distance the Church of England from Rome and
establish a truly national church. The second *Book of Common Prayer* was
published in 1552 with amendments, and further versions appeared in
1559, 1604 and 1662. The alterations were relatively minor and the liturgy
remained essentially the same.

The two books that have been the firm foundation for the Anglican faith
were the Bible (Scripture), and the *Book of Common Prayer* (tradition),
and Herbert's devotion to the former has been previously mentioned, but
it is through the liturgy that Herbert's

> Christian faith found its outward form…its customes were to him no mere
> conventions but a source of comfort and inspiration…and of central impor-
> tance in his poetry. It is in his poetry that his religious experience finds its
> most natural and its most profound expression.[19]

The structure of *The Temple* can be seen to follow the spiritual journey
of the Christian, and also the liturgical framework of the Eucharist as found
in the *Book of Common Prayer*—*The Temple* opens with self-examination,
the Prayer Book Eucharist begins with the Collect for Purity; 'The Altar'
and 'The Sacrifice' are demonstrations of contrition as are the *Kyries*; the
climax of the service is the Eucharist itself, which is beautifully captured
in 'Love (III)': both have the *Gloria* and the final Blessing.

'The Church-porch' provides the entrance into the building and can be
interpreted as a preparation for Christian life. It deals with the seven
deadly sins and their corresponding virtues, and finishes with a summary
of Christ's new commandment. Herbert calls for each person to undergo
self-examination:

---

19. Wengen-Shute, *George Herbert*, p. 14.

Summe up at night, what thou hast done by day;
And in the morning, what thou hast to do.
Dresse and undresse thy soul: mark the decay
And growth of it.

('The Church-porch' ll. 451-54)

This is reminiscent of the Prayer Book exhortation before the Eucharist, 'First to examine your lives and conversation by the rule of God's commandments' (*Book of Common Prayer*, p. 169). The poem also has a subtitle 'Perirrhanterium', which is the instrument for sprinkling holy water in the act of cleansing, as in the ritual of the Asperges particularly used in Lent. So the spiritual journey begins, and in 'Superliminare', the inscription on the lintel of the door calls the Christian to join in the corporate act of thanksgiving in the Eucharist: '…approach and taste / The churches mysticall repast' (ll. 3, 4). In this poem Herbert acknowledges the two sacraments of baptism (…sprinkled and taught, how to behave…) and the Eucharist that the Prayer Book dictates, and he expresses this sacramental theory in Chapter 22 of *The Country Parson*.

The communal nature of the liturgy and its order were important to Anglicans, as it demonstrated how they differed from the Roman Catholics, who were opposed to the use of the vernacular in the liturgy, and the Puritans, who wished to dispense with a formal liturgy. In 'The Church-porch' Herbert says:

Though private prayer be a brave designe,
Yet publick hath more promises, more love:
And love's a weight to hearts, to eies a signe.
We all are but cold suitors; let us move
    Where it is warmest. Leave thy six and seven;
    Pray with the most: for where most pray is heaven.

At the end of both Morning and Evening Prayer, the prayer of St Chrysostom is said, which has much in common with the above stanza:

Almighty God, who hast given us grace at this time with one accord to make our common supplications unto thee; and dost promise, that when two or three are gathered together in thy Name thou wilt grant their requests: Fulfil now, O Lord, the desires and petitions of thy servants, as may be most expedient for them…[20]

The call both of the prayer and of Herbert's words is for members of the Church of England to gather together in worship and demonstrate the 'love'

20. Wall, *Book of Common Prayer*, pp. 50, 57.

and 'promises' that can be attained within the church community. The importance of public prayer in the seventeenth century can be seen through the work of others from the period. Richard Hooker refers to the liturgy as 'the public prayer of the people of God', and Lancelot Andrewes distinguishes between 'the liturgy and the public service of God in the church and the private prayers and devotions of individual believers'.[21]

Once inside the body of the church, the focal point is 'The Altar', where the community remembers the ultimate sacrifice of Christ and where they re-enact the events of the Last Supper. Herbert uses the form of the pattern poem visually to represent the architectural features of the altar so it becomes a physical reality to the reader, not just a cerebral experience. The poem's mood and tone can be likened to the Collect for Purity that is found at the beginning of the communion service: 'Almighty God, unto whom all hearts are open… Cleanse the thoughts of our hearts by the inspiration of thy Holy Spirit.' Herbert's altar is broken, made of a heart and cemented with tears of contrition. There are further echoes of this Collect when Herbert writes 'To praise thy name' (l. 12); the Collects words are 'that we may perfectly love you and worthily magnify thy holy name'.

> A   broken ALTAR, Lord, thy servant reares
> Made of a heart, and cemented with teares
>   Whose parts are as thy hand did frame;
>   No workmans tool hath touch'd the same
>   A HEART   alone
>   Is   such   a   stone,
>   As   nothing   but
>   Thy pow'r doth cut.
>   Wherefore each part
>   Of my hard heart
>   Meets in this frame,
>   To praise thy name.
>   That if I chance to hold my peace
>   These stones to praise thee may not cease.
> O   let thy blessed   SACRIFICE   be mine,
> And   sanctifie   this   ALTAR   to   be   mine.

'The Altar' suggests the approach in contrition necessary before one can take part in the Church's banquet. Herbert also includes six biblical references: Ps. 51.17, 'The sacrifice of God is a troubled spirit: a broken and contrite heart' (l. 2); Exod. 20.25, 'And if thou wilt make me an altar of stone, thou shalt not build it of hewn stone: for if thou lift up thy tool upon

---

21. Both quotes taken from Wengen-Shute, *George Herbert*, p. 76.

it, thou hast polluted it' (1. 4); Ezek. 36.26, '...I will take away the stony heart... (Pl. 5.6); Jer. 23.29, 'Is not my word like as a fire? saith the Lord; and like a hammer that breaketh the rock in pieces?' (ll. 7-8); Ps. 103.1, 'Bless the Lord O my soul: and all that is within me bless his holy name' (1. 12); Lk. 19.40, 'I tell you that if these should hold their peace, the stones would immediately cry out' (1. 14).

Next in the sequence comes 'The Sacrifice', perhaps the most famous liturgical poem in *The Temple*. Mario di Cesare, in his article 'Sacred Rhythms and Sacred Contradictions', considers it imperative to recognize the liturgical context of the biblical references used together with any typological elements[22] and van Wengen-Shute[23] suggests using Herbert's comparative approach to reveal the source of his imagery (see above on the 'analogy of faith'). By examining the Scripture readings for the Monday and Tuesday of Holy Week (Epistle: Isa. 63 and 50; Gospel Mk 14 and 15.1-39) it is possible to see how they are intended to emphasize the fulfilment in the New Testament of what was foretold in the Old. The Epistles for the Wednesday and Friday (Heb. 9.16-28; 10) bring out the relationship between certain types or figures in the Old Testament that find their fulfilment in Christ. Rosemond Tuve, in her book *A Reading of George Herbert*, poignantly remarks that the Christ of 'The Sacrifice' is not the 'Christ we know in Luke's or Matthew's straightforward narrative —but he *is* the Christ of the liturgy of Holy Week'.[24]

Looking though the index of titles in *The Temple*, it is possible to see many references to the Offices, other services and the church year. 'Mattens', 'Even-song', 'Christmas', 'Easter', 'H. Baptisme' and 'H. Communion' are a few examples. In Herbert's poems dealing with the sacraments of baptism and the Eucharist, the *Book of Common Prayer* is much in evidence. In 'H. Baptisme (I)' the sinner remembers his baptism as a unique transformation that lasts for life. Cleansed by the water that flowed from Christ's side at his Crucifixion and forgiven by his sacrifice, the Christian has begun a new life with Christ. It is a poem of praise and thanksgiving that incorporates the teaching of the Protestant Reformers. Liturgical references from the service of baptism can be found. The prayer that precedes the baptism states: 'Almighty, everliving God, whose most dearly beloved

---

22. M.A. Di Cesare, 'Sacred Rhythms and Sacred Contradictions', in Helen Wilcox and Richard Todd (eds.), *George Herbert: Sacred and Profane* (New York: W.W. Norton, 1978), p. 8.

23. Wengen-Shute, *George Herbert*, p. 23.

24. R. Tuve, *A Reading of George Herbert* (Chicago: University of Chicago Press, 1952), p. 47.

Son Jesus Christ, for the forgiveness of our sins, did shed out of his most precious side both water and blood...' The poem emphasizes the remission of sin and regeneration with Christ, and both can be found in the Prayer Book: '...coming to the holy Baptism, may receive remission of *his* sins by spiritual regeneration...' (p. 182).

In 'H. Baptisme (II)' Herbert talks of infant baptism, highly advocated by the Protestant Reformers who appealed to Mk 10.14 as support for this practice; it is this portion of Scripture that is read as the gospel during the *Book of Common Prayer* service of baptism. Herbert's understanding of baptism corresponds to that of the Prayer Book and that of Richard Hooker, who wrote about baptism and holy communion as 'morall instruments of salvation, duties of service and worship' (V.57.4).[25] Herbert uses the image of the river Jordan to signify baptism, and Rosemond Tuve sees this symbol as a 'public' one, signifying, among other things, 'regeneration, cleansing, dedication, redemptive salvation'[26] and that the iconographical connections are 'too commonplace to need illustration', and considers that Herbert has taken this image from 'texts so popular that they served as iconographical handbooks: the *Biblia Pauperum*, the *Speculum humanae salvationis*, the *Horae*'.[27] Rosemary van Wengen-Shute challenges this and suggests that the most probable 'commonplace' that people would recognize was the opening prayer of the Baptism Service, and C.A. Patrides[28] considers this the most likely source of the image:

> Almighty and everlasting God, who of thy great mercy didst save Noah and his family in the ark from perishing by water; and also didst safely lead the children of Israel thy people through the Red Sea, figuring thereby thy holy Baptism; and by the Baptism of thy well-beloved Son Jesus Christ in the River Jordan, didst sanctify Water to the mystical washing away of sin; We beseech thee, for thine infinite mercies, that thou wilt mercifully look upon *this Child*; wash *him* and sanctify *him* with the holy Ghost; that *he*, being delivered from thy wrath, may be received into the ark of Christ's Church; and being steadfast in faith, joyful through hope, and rooted in charity, may so pass the waves of this troublesome world, that finally *he* may come to the land of everlasting life, there to reign with thee world without end; through Jesus Christ our Lord.

25. W. Speed Hill, *The Folger Library Edition of the Works of Richard Hooker* (Cambridge, MA: Harvard University Press, 1977), p. 246.

26. Tuve, *Reading of George Herbert*, p. 197.

27. Tuve, *Reading of George Herbert*, p. 197.

28. C.A. Patrides (ed.), *The English Poems of George Herbert* (London: Dent, 1974), p. 75.

I am in agreement with this suggestion as the association would be easily made by anyone who had brought their children to baptism or attended the service; it also sums up Herbert's understanding of the effect of joining the body of Christ.

The Eucharist has been described as 'the marrow of Herbert's sensibility',[29] taking precedence over baptism. In his two poems titled 'H. Communion' (one of them not included in *The Temple*), Herbert deals with the reciprocal nature of the relationship between Christ and the communicant. 'The H. Communion' included in *The Temple* talks of Christ entering into the Christian through the bread and wine, bringing 'nourishment and strength' (l. 7), yet it is only through God's grace that these gifts can be effective. This sentiment is to be found in a combination of the Collect for Purity ('Cleanse the thoughts of our hearts by the inspiration of thy holy Spirit...') and the Prayer of Humble Access ('Grant us...so to eat the flesh of thy dear Son Jesus Christ, and to drink his blood, that our sinful bodies may be made clean by his body, and our souls washed through his most precious blood').

The second poem titled 'H. Communion' found in the Williams manuscript and not included in *The Temple* deals with the problem of transubstantiation; something over which there had been much disagreement since the Reformation. The Calvinists claimed that Christ was present in the Eucharist only through faith; the Catholic belief was that the substance of the bread and wine changes into that of the body and blood of Jesus Christ (only the accidence remain); and the Anglicans adopted a more flexible approach and considered that 'the Body and Blood of Christ are really and actually and substantially present and taken in the Eucharist, but in a way that the human mind cannot understand and much more beyond the power of man to express'.[30]

The Litany, a service of supplication that is penitential in nature, 'to be sung or said after Morning Prayer upon Sundays, Wednesdays and Fridays, and at other times when it shall be commanded by the Ordinary',[31] is the inspiration of several poems. The title of 'Sighs and Grones' recalls one of the petitions of the Litany: 'O God, merciful father, that despisest not the sighing of a contrite heart...' The poem opens with 'O do not use me / After my sinnes...' which is an almost exact quotation found after the Lord's Prayer in the Litany:

29. Patrides (ed.), *English Poems of George Herbert*, p. 17.
30. William Forbes, 'Anglicanism: The Thought and Practice of the Church of England' (ed. P.E. More and F.L. Cross; London: SPCK, 1935), p. 471.
31. *Book of Common Prayer*, p. 60.

Priest: O, Lord, deal not with us after our sins.
Answer: Neither reward us after our iniquities.

The structure of the poem reflects the structure of the service. Each stanza beginning and ending with 'O' reflects the opening sentences and responses of the beginning of the Litany:

O God the Father of heaven:
have mercy upon us miserable sinners.
O God the Father of heaven:
have mercy upon us miserable sinners.

Herbert transforms the public nature of the liturgy into a personal experience; he uses the liturgical language to express his own internal conflicts, and the communal public act of worship becomes also a private act of devotion, an expression of personal emotion. The relationship between God and the penitent becomes highly individual. God's gift of grace, the power of the Word and the sacraments are expressed in both the *Book of Common Prayer* and *The Temple*, both attempt to establish a proper code of conduct for the Christian: one in public affirmation, the other in highly personal terms.

The last poem to examine in this section is 'Aaron'. It expresses the human and liturgical function of *The Temple*. It demonstrates the transforming power of the Christian faith. The Roman rite contained vesting prayers, 'the tradition of specified and prescribed prayers during vesting, by way of a definition of the priestly vestments in terms of the symbolism of virtues and graces',[32] where the liturgical vestments comprise part of a complex pattern of communication.[33] The amice, a square piece of linen first worn on the head, then round the neck, represents the helmet of salvation that the good soldier of Christ wears, and also the linen rag with which the Jews blindfolded Jesus; the alb is symbolic of purity and innocence, but also in the Vulgate translation of the Bible, in Lk. 23.10, Herod clothes Jesus in a white robe, which in other versions is translated as 'gorgeous' or 'elegant'; the girdle stands for purity; the chasuble, which represents Christ's seamless garment and is emblematic of charity; and the stole stands for the yoke of Christ.

In the poem, Herbert stresses his unworthiness to be a priest, he is but a

32. M.A. Di Cesare, 'Sacred Rhythms and Sacred Contradictions', in Helen Wilcox and Richard Todd (eds.), *George Herbert: Sacred and Profane*, p. 12.

33. Grisbroke W. Jardine, 'Vestments', in Cheslyn Jones, Geoffrey Wainwright, Edward Yarnold SJ and Paul Bradshaw (eds.), *The Study of Liturgy* (London: SPCK, 1992), pp. 000-000 (544).

sinful man: Aaron is the epitome of the priesthood, holy and perfect, but Herbert is full of profane thoughts, defective and dark. Yet alongside this imperfect head and breast, there is Christ, who has the power to transform the imperfect to perfect. As the priest puts on his garments, their symbolic nature transforms him inwardly and outwardly. The liturgical event has a visible effect on the individual, he is robed as a priest, but there is also an inner transformation and the final conclusion is the 'consumption of the self'.[34] John E. Booty suggests that this poem is

> related to the Book of Common Prayer on the deepest level and is a liturgy in itself. In reading it, the Christian, grounded in common human experience and fed by the church's formal liturgy, is led toward that final joy expressed when the poet exclaims: 'Come people; Aaron's drest'.[35]

Herbert was also profoundly influenced by the Psalms, and they would have been most familiar to him. As a clergyman, Herbert would have heard them recited daily at Mattins and Evensong, and they were read through each month in church. The version that Herbert would have been most familiar with was Coverdale's translation from the Great Bible that was used in the *Book of Common Prayer*; although the Authorized Version of the Bible opted for a different translation, the Prayer Book retained the Coverdale version for liturgical use. Patrides considers that echoes of the Psalter 'reverberate across Herbert's poetry to an extent unmatched by any other poet in English Literature'.[36]

From the earliest times, psalms have been integral to worship, Jewish and Christian; they voice the concerns and joys of God's people, and emphasize shared experience. In a liturgical context, this shared experience transcends the ages, as God does, and is timeless. In Anglican worship, the Doxology is always said or sung after the psalms, and this highlights the omnipresence of God in all time:

> Glory be to the Father and to the Son
> And to the holy Ghost;
> As it was in the beginning,
> is now and ever shall be, world without end. Amen.

In the refrain of 'The Quip', Herbert uses a direct quotation from Ps. 38.15: 'But thou shalt answer, Lord, for me.' Here he clearly associates

---

34. J.H. Summers, *George Herbert: His Religion and Art* (Medieval and Renaissance Texts and Studies, ; New York: W.W. Norton, 1981), p. 137.

35. J.E. Booty, 'George Herbert: The Temple and The Book of Common Prayer', *Mosaic* 12 (Winter 1979), pp. 75-88.

36. Patrides (ed.), *English Poems of George Herbert*, p. 10.

himself with the author of the Psalms; the Psalmist knows that by trusting in God, he will be delivered from his enemies. Herbert personifies his 'enemies', the worldly ambition that distances him from God: Money, Glorie, Wit and conversation. The sentiment is the same in both the psalm and the poem, and the solution to both, is to put one's trust in God, who alone knows all our needs. Chana Bloch writes:

> What we have in 'The Quip' is not simply a literary echo of the Psalter. The rhetorical strategy of the poem reflects a genuine situation from life: the believer in distress repeating verses from the Psalm to invoke their saving power.[37]

4. *The Via Media*

Herbert was writing in the early part of the seventeenth century, between a recent Reformation and a forthcoming civil war. It was a time when a distinctively Anglican position emerged. The Anglican Church stressed the importance of public worship, education through the Bible and through preaching, and the necessity of behaving charitably towards others. The aim was to reform society socially, politically and religiously; 'the official documents of the Tudor Reformation proclaimed all of English society as the proper context for living out the Christian life, and service to the crown as the chief means of doing God's will in this world'.[38] Through baptism, the Christian not only became a member of the body of Christ, but also became a citizen of the body politic.[39]

The Elizabethan Settlement, combining Evangelical and Catholic elements, was precariously balanced. It accepted the importance of scripture, Protestant doctrine, preaching and increased lay participation, but also adhered to a reformed Catholic liturgy, the ecclesiastical government administered through the episcopacy and a supreme, if not absolute monarch. Herbert's 'middle way' expressed this combination, but not in concrete terms in his poetry. In only one poem does he enter into any discussion of the relative virtues of his own and other Churches. 'The British Church' makes the traditional Anglican claim that the Church of England represents the *via media*, avoiding what Herbert considers to be the excessive ornateness of the Roman Catholic Church, 'She on the hill' who is 'painted (l. 13), and the bareness of the 'low' Nonconformist Churches, 'She in the valley' who is 'undrest' (l. 19). The style of 'The British Church' is a beau-

---

37. Patrides (ed.), *English Poems of George Herbert*, p. 19.
38. Wall, *George Herbert*, p. 20.
39. Wall, *George Herbert*, p. 11.

tiful plainness, in both its language and liturgy; it is a beauty that comes from within, and nothing must be allowed to detract from it. It is the internal beauty of the soul, but also the internal beauty of the church building and the liturgy.

Herbert's 'middle way' is further emphasized by its placing exactly in the middle of the Church section of *The Temple*. For Herbert, the Church of England is 'his dearest Mother', the 'mean' that the other Churches miss, and he makes the claim that God chose the Church of England to 'double-moat', in other words, to protect it from either extreme. Even though Herbert loved his Church, he believed that only in heaven would his goals be realized. Things of this world are transient and subject to decay; 'Herbert would not set his heart on the institutional church that he loved, any more than he would on any other earthly institution or thing'.[40] The goal for the Christian must be to reach heaven; all of human life must be lived with this in mind. While on earth, it is important to conduct one's life decently and in an ordered fashion. In Chapter 13 of *The Country Parson*, 'The Parson's Church', Herbert instructs priests to keep their churches well maintained, not just in the fabric of the building, but ensuring that the Bible, the Book of Homilies and the Prayer Book are available and in good condition. He also stipulates that the priest 'takes order…that there be fit, and proper texts of Scripture every where painted, and that all the painting be grave, and reverend, not with light colours, or foolish anticks'.[41] The church building must direct the congregation to heaven, but need not be too ostentatious or bare. The 'middle way' is to keep things in perspective; decoration must be capable of edifying, and Herbert stresses that the externals of worship serve this purpose. The priest keeps his church in order, and provides all things that will direct people to God:

> All this he doth, not as out of necessity, or as putting holiness in the things, but as desiring to keep the middle way between superstition and slovenlinesse, and as following the Apostles two great and admirable Rules in things of this nature: The first whereof is, *Let all things be done decently, and in order*; The second, *Let all things be done to edification,* 1 Corinthians 14:22.[42]

Herbert's 'middle way' allows no holiness in outward structures, their holiness is obtained by declaring God's holiness, and by bringing his people to worship him.

---

40. C. Hodgkins, *Authority, Church, and Society in George Herbert* (Duluth: University of Missouri Press, 1993), p. 208.
41. Wall, *George Herbert,*, p. 74.
42. Wall, *George Herbert*, p. 75.

5. *Conclusion*

Having examined Herbert's poetry, it is interesting to note that, although the poems are often full of uncertainty, doubt and fear, Herbert is never plagued by doubts that he has chosen the right way to worship God. The doubts he does express are not related to the possible shortcomings of the Church, but are wholly personal in nature. It is his own inadequacy, weakness and failure that torment him. His poetry is a reflection of his religious experience, religion that was inseparable from the man; it shaped his whole view of life.

It is perhaps Herbert's ability to make concrete the fleeting and elusive elements of experience, that perpetuates his appeal throughout the ages. With the contemporary move towards spirituality, Herbert is being explored for the insight he can give into distinctly Anglican spirituality. L William Countryman writes that 'the Anglican poetic tradition has a language formed in worship and bespeaks both a spirituality concerned with the inner life of the individual and a spirituality that begins and ends in the community'.[43] In his poetry, Herbert explores his own inner life and turns his emotions into words, but perhaps the most important thing he does is to demonstrate how God's grace, freely given, is available to all. This is beautifully demonstrated by the poem 'Love III'. Although the poem is Eucharistic in nature, it is also reminiscent of the Parable of the Prodigal Son. The Guest at Love's table reminds us of the son who followed his own desires and turned away from his father, and who returns acknowledging his unworthiness to be his father's son. We can also put ourselves in the role of the Guest, as we constantly mar God's image in us. The key to this poem is the overwhelming love and freely given grace that comes from God, without any relation to the worthiness of the recipient. Love's hospitality is entirely unconditional and depends only on the willingness of the Guest to accept it.

> Love bade me welcome, yet my soul drew back,
>   Guilty of dust and sin.
> But quick-ey'd Love, observing me grow slack
>   From my first entrance in,
> Drew nearer to me, sweetly questioning,
>   If I lack'd anything.

---

43. L.W. Countryman, *The Poetic Imagination* (London: Darton, Longman & Todd, 1999).

As a devoted priest, Herbert ministered to his flock and led them in their worship and daily lives, but as a poet he has been able to touch the lives of countless generations. The roles of poet and priest have many similarities. The priest teaches, mediates, intercedes and represents the Church of God on earth. He is said to 'speak for and interpret the inarticulate convictions of the race'.[44] In the act of worship the priest is not speaking his own words, but the set words of the liturgical text, and the poet follows a similar discipline by condensing his feelings into manageable lines and stanzas. Liturgy and poetry can be seen to have a similar function in that they both express feelings, which many are capable of experiencing, however vaguely, but which few can put into adequate words. Herbert epitomises the double role of priest and poet; the poet's role to teach and delight complements the preaching of the priest. In 'The Church Porch'

> Heaken unto a Verser, who may chance
> Ryme thee to good, and make a bait of pleasure.
>   A verse may finde him, who a sermon flies,
>   And turn delight into a sacrifice.

Through his poetry Herbert hopes to evangelize and bring people to God. Those who may not hear, or do not listen to sermons may receive instruction through poetry.

His poems not only reflect his own experience, but the experience of all God's people everywhere. They contain references, explicit and implicit, both to the priesthood and to the art of poetry. Herbert tried to make himself a good priest in the way he tried to make himself a good poet. His poetry is known by many who may not know or care about his religion, and his reputation as a priest is familiar to some who know nothing of his poetry. A.M. Allchin offers comment on Herbert's lasting appeal:

> He lived in a time of change and disruption, of rapid expansion of knowledge, not altogether unlike our own. Without evading the complexity of things, without glossing over the fragility and brokenness of man's experience of life in time, he managed to reaffirm the great unities of Christian faith and prayer. These are unities which draw together the separated strands in the Christian heritage, which draw together past and present in a living and creative appropriation of tradition, which bring together creation and redemption, outer life and inner life into a single, complex but fruitful whole.[45]

---

44. E. Underhill, *Worship* (Welwyn: Nisbet, 1936), p. 4.

45. A.M. Allchin, Preface to J.N. Wall Jr, *George Herbert: The Country Parson, The Temple* (London: SPCK, 1981), p. xvi.

BIBLIOGRAPHY

Primary Sources

Hutchinson, F.E., *The Works of George Herbert* (Oxford: Clarendon Press, 1941).

Patrides, C.A. (ed.), *The English Poems of George Herbert* (London: Dent, 1974).

Wall, J.N., Jr, *George Herbert: The Country Parson, The Temple* (London: SPCK, 1981).

—*The Book of Common Prayer* (Glasgow: Wm Collins,).

Secondary Sources

Allchin, A.M., Preface to J.N. Wall Jr, *George Herbert: The Country Parson, The Temple* (London: SPCK, 1981).

Bloch, C., 'Spelling the Word', in C.J. Summers and T.-L. Pebworth (eds.), *Too Rich to Clothe the Sunne* (Pittsburgh: Pittsburgh University Press, 1980).

—*Spelling the Word*: *George Herbert and the Bible* (Berkeley: University of California Press, 1985).

Cesare, Mario Di, *George Herbert and the Seventeenth-Century Religious Poets* (New York: W.W. Norton, 1978).

—'Sacred Rhythms and Sacred Contradictions', in Helen Wilcox and Richard Todd (eds.), *George Herbert: Sacred and Profane* (New York: W.W. Norton, 1978).

Countryman, L.W., *The Poetic Imagination* (London: Darton, Longman & Todd, 1999).

Forbes W., 'Anglicanism: The Thought and Practice of the Church of England' (ed. P.E. More and F.L. Cross; London: SPCK, 1935).

Hodgkins, C, *Authority, Church, and Society in George Herbert* (Duluth: University of Missouri Press, 1993).

Jardine Grisbroke, W., 'Vestments', in Cheslyn Jones, Geoffrey Wainwright, Edward Yarnold SJ and Paul Bradshaw (eds.), *The Study of Liturgy* (London: SPCK, 1992), pp. 488-92.

Jasper, R.C.D., *The Development of the Anglican Liturgy 1662–1980* (London: SPCK, 1989).

Knights, L.C., 'George Herbert: Resolution and Conflict' (ed. M.A. Di Cesare; New York: W.W. Norton, 1978).

Lewalski, B.K, *Protestant Poetics and the Seventeenth-Century Religious Lyric* (Princeton, NJ: Princeton University Press, 1979).

Speed Hill, W., *The Folger Library Edition of the Works of Richard Hooker* (Cambridge, MA: Harvard University Press, 1977).

Summers, J.H., *George Herbert: His Religion and Art* (Medieval and Renaissance Texts and Studies; New York, 1981).

Tuve, R, *A Reading of George Herbert* (Chicago: University of Chicago Press, 1952).

Underhill, E, *Worship* (Welwyn: Nisbet, 1936).

—*The Study of Liturgy* (ed. C. Jones, G. Wainwright, E. Yarnold and P. Bradshaw; London: SPCK, rev. edn, 1992).

Walton, I, 'Life of Mr George Herbert', in *Lives* (The World's Classics; Oxford: Oxford University Press, 1927), pp. .

Wengen-Shute, R. van, *George Herbert and the Liturgy of the Church of England* (Drukkerij de Kempenaer, Oegstgeest, 1981).

Articles

Bell, I., 'Setting Foot into Divinity: George Herbert and the English Reformation', *Modern Language Quarterly* 38.2 (June 1977).

Booty, J.E., 'George Herbert: The Temple and The Book of Common Prayer', *Mosaic* 12 (Winter 1979), pp. 75-88.

Lynch, K., 'George Herbert's Holy "Altar", Name and Thing', *George Herbert Journal* 17.1 (1973).

Mclaughlin, E., and G. Thomas, 'Communion in The Temple', *Studies in English Literature 1500–1900* 15.1 (Winter, 1975).

Dissertations

Bingham, M.E., 'The Bible in George Herbert's Church' (University of North Carolina, 1992).

Orrick, J.S., 'George Herbert's Debt to the Bible' (Dissertation, Ohio University, 1996).

JOHN TOLAND: *CHRISTIANITY NOT MYSTERIOUS*

Kevin Loughton

Editor's Introduction

John Toland's work, published in 1696, is regarded as the classical exposition of Deism (a system of natural religion developed in England in the late seventeenth and eighteenth centuries) in the manner that he advanced arguments critical of certain concepts of divine revelation and the supernatural. Toland claimed that neither God himself nor his revelation should be beyond the comprehension of human reason; where Christianity was being represented as more mysterious than natural reason could grasp, this was due to the influence of paganism or priestly practices. Inevitably such 'free-thinking' as Toland's had implications for the way the Bible was regarded and interpreted; in particular the miracles recorded in Scripture might be open to natural explanation. Toland's Life of Milton, *published in 1698, caused a further furore because of a passage within it which was thought to call into question the authenticity of the New Testament, although Toland subsequently reacted to this criticism and claimed that his reference was to the apocryphal writings.*

Deism, as an English movement that had restricted appeal in this country, became widely influential in France through the work of Voltaire and Rousseau. On the particular contribution of Jean-Jacques Rousseau, see the next chapter. The movement was also widespread in Germany in the eighteenth century, as for example in the fragments of the work of H.S. Reimarus, which were published by G.E. Lessing. In the following century the denial of any historical foundation for the supernatural elements in the Gospels, represented by the influential theory of 'Myth' in D.F. Strauss's Leben Jesu, *was sufficient to lose Strauss his post at the University of Tübingen.*

Kevin Loughton's own interest in this work of John Toland arose when he read, and translated from the Italian, a refutation of Toland and other English Deists by St Alphonsus Liguori, the seventeenth-century founder of the Redemptorists (a Roman Catholic missionary and teaching order). There is no evidence that Alfonso dei Liguori could read these Deist texts in English, so this offers further indication of how widely this movement's ideas had been disseminated. Kevin Loughton is now continuing his postgraduate studies at the University of Cambridge.

John Toland's Christianity not Mysterious: Or, a Treatise Shewing,
That there is nothing in the Gospel contrary to Reason, Nor Above it:
And that no Christian Doctrine can be properly call'd a Mystery[1]

John Toland was an extraordinarily gifted thinker who revelled in the
controversial role of *agent provocateur*. Although his origins are obscure,
it seems that he was probably born on 30 November 1670 in Inishowen,
Londonderry, allegedly the illegitimate son of a Catholic priest.[2] At 14
years of age he, rather conveniently, converted to Protestantism: this
enabled him to be educated at Redcastle School, Londonderry, before
studying divinity at Glasgow and Edinburgh universities with a view to
becoming a Presbyterian minister. Having graduated Master of the Arts
from Edinburgh in 1690, he undertook further studies in divinity at the
universities of Leiden and Utrecht, but then renounced a clerical career
in order to pursue his political ambitions. On returning to England in 1694
he enjoyed the patronage of John Holles, Duke of Newcastle, Robert
Harley, leader of the Country Forces in the House of Commons, and Sir
Robert Clayton, Director of the Bank of England. However, characteristically restless, Toland set off for the court of the Electress Sophia of
Hanover, herself impatiently waiting to be Queen of England, where he
had an ambiguous encounter with the renowned philosopher G.W. Leibniz,
before moving on to the court of Sophie Charlotte, Queen of Prussia. Yet
despite these rather grand social connections, Toland was unsuccessful
in his repeated attempts to gain a position in the British civil service.
This was primarily due to the notorious reputation he had acquired following the publication of *Christianity not Mysterious* in 1696, which
caused an outburst of controversy. In England, although Toland did not

1. R.E. Sullivan makes an important point in relation to the historico-theological
context of Toland's *Christianity not Mysterious*, saying that the title of the book 'suggests that it was meant as a refutation of Robert South's notorious sermon of 29 April
1694, "Christianity Mysterious, and the Wisdome of God in Making It So"'. R.E.
Sullivan, *John Toland and the Deist Controversy: A Study in Adaptations* (Cambridge,
MA: Harvard University Press, 1982), p. 51. For practical purposes I will refer to
Toland's book throughout in abbreviated form as *Christianity not Mysterious*. All
references are to the second, enlarged edition published for Samuel Buckley, Fleetstreet,
London (1696).

2. R.E. Sullivan, *John Toland*, p. 2. I agree with J.V. Price that Sullivan's work is
the best biographical and critical study of Toland published to date. See Price's introduction in *History of British Deism*, IV (8 vols.; London: Routledge; Thoemmes Press,
1995), p. vi n. 2.

receive a personal censure, a formal complaint was lodged about *Christianity not Mysterious* with the grand jury of Middlesex. He sought refuge from the ensuing furore in Ireland, but while he was there the Irish commons condemned his book, 'ordered to be burned by the public hangman', and he was publicly condemned as a 'heretic'. Consequently, in both countries Toland gained the reputation of 'an abandoned freethinker', much to his chagrin. Nonetheless, *Christianity not Mysterious* had, by 1697, already reached its third edition and has been viewed, albeit somewhat anachronistically, as the first act of warfare between Deists and the Orthodox.[3] In fact, the book elicited 17 published responses between 1697 and 1734 and was, according to H.F.G. Swanston, sufficiently influential to draw Leibniz back into the debate between those who claimed to represent orthodox Christianity and proponents of Deist ideas.[4] But why did Toland's *Christianity not Mysterious* evoke such hostile responses from civil and ecclesiastical authorities alike? A brief account of his central thesis will, I hope, provide some indication as to why Toland's book was considered, especially in ecclesiastical quarters, as dangerously heterodox.

Toland begins *Christianity not Mysterious* by clearly stating his two-fold intentions: to show that 'the Use of Reason is not so dangerous in Religion as it is commonly represented', and to demonstrate that he is making a safe Christian claim in saying, 'I hold nothing as an Article of my Religion, but what the highest Evidence forc'd me to embrace.'[5] In his opinion, this rational approach to religion is in stark contrast to that of many Christians, who appear to give more credence to 'Mystery' than to reason. In so doing, he alleges, they make most noise in praise of what they profess least to understand and, encouraged by the clergy, all too readily espouse the maxim that 'we must adore what we cannot comprehend'.[6] For Toland, this simply leads to the so-called 'Mysteries of the Christian Religion' not only attracting praise without being understood, but, more worryingly, becoming the source of violent disagreements among Christians over the ways in which they cannot understand these 'Mysteries'. From the outset of his book, then, it is clear that Toland vehemently opposes those whom he perceives to be the 'mystery men' of Christianity. He means to exclude from Christianity all that he considers to be

---

3. Sir L. Stephen, *History of English Thought in the Eighteenth Century* (London: Smith, Elder & Co., 3rd edn, 1902), I, p. 105.

4. H.F.G. Swanston, *Celebrating Eternity Now: A Study in the Theology of St. Alphonsus de Ligouri* (Chawton, Hants: Redemptorist Publications, 1995), pp. 201-202.

5. Toland, *Christianity not Mysterious*, pp. vii, viii.

6. Toland, *Christianity not Mysterious*, p. 1.

irrational superstition, unnecessary speculation and, above all, the concept of 'mystery' as traditionally understood by theologians. He is aware that, in undertaking such an enterprise, he will undoubtedly encounter opposition from well-meaning Christians who prefer to rely on ecclesiastical tradition and authority as the means of attaining Christian truth, rather than on reason. However, he declares that he will not bow to opposition of this kind, since the arguments thus presented rest solely on appeals to 'Venerable Names' and 'pompous citations'. On the contrary, against these he holds that *reason* is the only foundation of all certitude and that nothing divinely revealed can be excluded from rational inquiry.[7] Hence, Toland proposes that by relying solely on reason as the 'natural method' of attaining certitude, he will be able to prove that (1) true religion must necessarily be reasonable and intelligible, (2) Christianity is such a religion, and (3) Christianity was not 'framed by men', but divinely revealed from heaven. Before commencing these proofs, however, he provides a detailed explanation of what he understands by the term 'reason', which, quite clearly, is of critical importance to his entire thesis.

Toland's exposition of this 'reason' suggests, as he evidently intended, that he had been greatly influenced by the philosophy of his English contemporary, John Locke.[8] He starts from Locke's definition of reason as a

> Power or Faculty of forming various Ideas or Perceptions of Things: Of affirming or denying, according as he sees them to agree or disagree: And so of loving and desiring what seems good unto him; and of hating and

---

7.   Toland, *Christianity not Mysterious*, pp. 2-5.

8.   This is particularly evident in Toland's appropriation of Locke's description of the role of experience and reason in the attainment of knowledge as the epistemological platform for his argument. However, although the relationship between Toland and Locke (and their respective epistemologies) has been the subject of much scholarly interest, it remains something of an open question. According to Sir L. Stephen, 'following the publication of *Christianity not Mysterious* Locke publicly renounced any association with Toland, whose personal acquaintance with him was slight, and whose theories he altogether disavowed'. By contrast, R.E. Sullivan claims that Locke and Toland were initially close acquaintances, sharing drafts of their respective works. Due to Toland's public notoriety, however, Locke felt impelled to distance himself from Toland. He concludes that Toland and Locke were 'probably much closer than Locke was ever willing to acknowledge'. Similarly, J.C. Biddle suggests that Toland and Locke were 'close acquaintances' and that 'it was Toland who immediately influenced Locke and assisted him in tightening his thesis'. For more detail, see: Stephen, *History*, vol. I, pp. 93-119; Sullivan, *John Toland*, pp. 6-8, 12, 74-77, 109, 120; J.C. Biddle, 'Locke's Critique of Innate Principles and Toland's Deism', *Journal of the History of Ideas* 37 (1976), pp. 412-18.

avoiding what he thinks evil. The right Use of all these Faculties is what we call Common Sense, or Reason in general.[9]

As his account of reason unfolds it becomes apparent that Toland, like Locke, views reason as an active process involving comparison of the agreement or disagreement between our ideas or perceptions and their objects. The end to which this process is ordered is the attainment of exact conformity between our ideas or perceptions and their objects.[10] On this understanding, Toland makes a distinction between 'self-evident' knowledge and knowledge acquired through 'reason or demonstration', but insists that, although self-evident knowledge, by definition, excludes reason or demonstration, all reason or demonstration becomes at length self-evident.[11] For him, it follows from this description of the nature and function of reason that when we have no notion or idea of a thing, we cannot reason about it at all. Moreover, when we have what he calls 'intermediate ideas', we can never go beyond probability.[12] Nonetheless, he is convinced that our God-given faculty of reason enables us to perceive and form ideas of things, to make judgments of them, and, if necessary, to suspend judgement. Therefore, when used correctly, our faculty of reason ensures that we never assent but to clear and true propositions.[13] Toland concludes that, on the proviso of correct use, our reason makes it impossible for us to err in our search for truth since 'what is evidently repugnant to clear and distinct ideas, or to our common notions, is contrary to reason' and, as such, is clearly a falsehood.[14]

Having described what he understands by reason, and knowledge attained by this reason, Toland illustrates how this understanding affects his theological beliefs and his view of Christianity. He agrees with Locke that, through experience and the proper exercise of reason, it becomes evident that the primary indubitable proposition, to which all reasonable people

---

9.   Toland, *Christianity not Mysterious*, p. 9. Cf. J. Locke, *An Essay Concerning Human Understanding* (ed. J.W. Yolton; New York: Everyman Library, 1965), Bk 1, Ch. IV, i, ii.

10.   Toland, *Christianity not Mysterious*, pp. 10, 14.

11.   Toland, *Christianity not Mysterious*, pp. 14-15. Interestingly, Toland qualifies 'at length', suggesting that it can be merely theoretical, for 'in matters of common practice we must, of necessity, sometimes admit probability to supply the defect of demonstration'.

12.   Toland, *Christianity not Mysterious*, p. 15.

13.   Toland, *Christianity not Mysterious*, p. 23.

14.   Toland, *Christianity not Mysterious*, p. 25.

assent, is 'God exists'.[15] Given his preceding account of reason, Toland
seems to be suggesting that the truth of the proposition 'God exists' should
be as luminously self-evident to right-reasoning people as that of mathe-
matical propositions, since its self-evidence is equal to that of mathemati-
cal certainty. Furthermore, he claims that the idea or perception of God is
the unchanging entity of true religion, universally accessible to all through
the faculty of reason.[16] Therefore, any religion claiming to come from
God, who made us convincible by clear ideas and perceptions, must be
entirely free from contradiction with what we have come to know by the
exercise of reason.[17] On this understanding, Toland then aims to show that
'there is nothing in the Gospel contrary to reason'.

While he admits that Christians do not view reason as running contrary to
the gospel, Toland finds them frequently affirming that 'tho the Doctrines of
the latter cannot in themselves be contrary to the Principles of the former,
as proceeding both from God; yet, that according to our Conceptions of
them, they may seem directly to clash'.[18] When Christians of different de-
nominations cannot reconcile reason with the gospel, they then invariably
assume that this is due to their corrupt and limited understandings. Consequently, they make diverse appeals to ecclesiastical tradition and authority:
to 'Scripture', which Toland interprets as 'the Scriptures conformed to their
bulky systems and formularies'; to 'the Fathers' or some 'Doctor of the
Church'; to 'the Councils', or to one of 'the Popes', whom he unflatteringly
describes as 'chimerical supreme Headships and Monsters of infallibility'.[19]
Moreover, Toland finds many Christians simply declaring that they adhere
to the teaching of the Church Fathers and blindly worshipping what, by
their own admission, they cannot comprehend. He finds this particular
tendency most objectionable, describing it as 'the undoubted Source of all
the Absurdities that ever were seriously vented among Christians'.[20] In this
regard, he is scathingly critical of the clergy, who, in his eyes, have been
guilty of acquiescing in, and worse still, actively perpetuating these irrational 'absurdities'. He says of them, 'So desiring to be Teachers of the
Law, and understanding neither what they say, nor those things which they

15. Toland, *Christianity not Mysterious*, p. 42.
16. Toland, *Christianity not Mysterious*, p. 42.
17. Toland, *Christianity not Mysterious*, p. 46.
18. Toland, *Christianity not Mysterious*, p. 26.
19. Toland, *Christianity not Mysterious*, pp. 2-6.
20. Toland, *Christianity not Mysterious*, p. 26.

affirm, they obtrude upon us for Doctrines the Commandments of Men.'[21] In so doing, they have been responsible for making the plainest and most trifling things in the world 'mysterious' in order to ensure that the laity remain completely reliant on their explanations in matters of faith. So, Toland claims, in the clergy's hands Christianity has become an increasingly mysterious and superstitious religion rather than what it ought to be, the religion of reasonable people, whose defining characteristic is its inherent reasonableness as revelation. Contrasting his approach to that of the clergy, Toland repeatedly insists that the authority of the gospel must rest on its reasonableness as revelation. If any doctrine of the Gospel is contrary to reason, he says, he has never come across it, nor has any idea of what it might be.[22] Rather, Toland affirms the primacy of reason in discerning the truth of gospel revelation:

> as tis by Reason [that] we arrive at the Certainty of God's own Existence, so we cannot otherwise discern his Revelations but by their Conformity with our natural Notices of him, which is in so many words, to agree with our common Notions.[23]

In attempting to demonstrate the reasonableness of the gospel as revelation, Toland starts from the principle that the gospel must be read in the same way as any other text. He maintains that, if the gospel is read in this way, with the equity and attention that is paid to more humane works, all reasonable people will come to accept its truth, since they cannot not fail to recognize the inherently rational content of the teachings contained therein.[24] Interestingly, he also argues that, when interpreting gospel texts, 'history', 'language', 'figurative and literal senses', 'genus of speech' and the 'scope' and 'context' of the author must all be taken into account in order to ascertain their proper meaning.[25] In this regard, Toland certainly seems to have been before his time in his employment of the 'historical method' of scriptural exegesis and in his perception of *koine*. He then suggests that this rational approach to the gospel is nothing new, finding the prophets and the people of Israel using reason as their yardstick for assessing the truth of prophetic calls and visions, and in interpreting prophecy and the like.[26] Moreover, he says that at the Annunciation,

21. Toland, *Christianity not Mysterious*, p. 28.
22. Toland, *Christianity not Mysterious*, pp. 28-29.
23. Toland, *Christianity not Mysterious*, p. 31.
24. Toland, *Christianity not Mysterious*, p. 49.
25. Toland, *Christianity not Mysterious*, pp. 34-35.
26. Toland, *Christianity not Mysterious*, pp. 43-44.

> The Virgin Mary, even tho of that Sex that's least proof against Flattery
> and Superstition, did not implicitly believe she should bear a Child that was
> to be call'd the Son of the Most High…till the Angel gave her a satisfac-
> tory Answer to the strongest Objection that could be made.[27]

These examples are, for Toland, illustrative of the fact that it has always
been from clear and weighty reasons, both as to fact and matter, and not by
blind obedience, that the 'people of God' have embraced revelation.[28] He
recommends the same rational approach, asserting that unless our reason
has somehow been distorted or we have wilfully developed a defect in our
understanding, we should be able to apprehend the intrinsic reasonableness
of Gospel revelation. Thus, to believe in the gospel as divine revelation or
the sense of any Gospel passage without rational proofs is, to Toland's way
of thinking, 'a blameable credulity, and a temerarious opinion'.[29] For him,
all the doctrines and precepts of the gospel must, of necessity, agree with
natural reason and our ordinary, common-sense notions.

Toland then sets himself to prove that there is nothing 'mysterious' or
'above reason' in the gospel. He begins by asserting that the terms 'mysterious' and 'above reason' are synonymous and, in common and specifically
Christian usage, denote one of two things. First, they can mean 'a thing
intelligible of itself, but so cover'd by figurative Words, Types and Ceremonies, that Reason cannot penetrate the Vail, nor see under it till it be
remov'd'.[30] Secondly, they can mean 'a thing of its own Nature inconceivable, and not to be judg'd of by our ordinary Faculties and Ideas, tho it be
never so clearly reveal'd'.[31] Understood in the first sense, he says, 'mystery'
has its origins in the superstitious practices of Gentile and pagan cults,
especially the 'ridiculous, obscene, or inhumane Rites' of cultic priests.[32]
Having shared in priestly cultic ceremonies, the 'initiated' were instructed
by their priests not to reveal the secrets or mysteries of the cult on pain of
death. As a result, it was cultic priests who ensured that a veneer of incomprehensibility surrounded Gentile and pagan rites and rituals. Nonetheless,

---

27. Toland, *Christianity not Mysterious*, p. 44.
28. Toland, *Christianity not Mysterious*, p. 45.
29. Toland, *Christianity not Mysterious*, p. 37.
30. Toland, *Christianity not Mysterious*, p. 66.
31. Toland, *Christianity not Mysterious*, p. 66.
32. Toland, *Christianity not Mysterious*, p. 68. Toland provides a detailed etymol-
ogy of the term 'mystery', noting that in Gentile and pagan cults, *Mysterion* signified a
mystery into which people were initiated by cultic priests and that *Mystes* was the
name given to these priests. For more detail, see pp. 69-72.

Toland argues that within these cults the word 'mystery' was clearly understood as relating to things perfectly intelligible of themselves, but so veiled by (priestly) secrecy that they could not be known without some kind of special revelation. Furthermore, he is convinced that 'mystery' was always understood and employed in this sense in Greek and Roman literature and that, in contemporary times, this is still its commonly accepted meaning. Hence, 'when we cannot see clearly into a Business, we say it is a Mystery to us'.[33] Yet Toland insists that this common acceptation of 'mystery', despite its extended lineage, is neither worth knowing nor merits any place within Christianity, the religion of reasonable people. For him, it is and always has been a purely linguistic device, established and still employed by priests, to keep the laity in fear and ignorance by making things that are perfectly intelligible in themselves seem incomprehensible and 'above reason'. What Toland finds even more astounding and deeply disconcerting than this priestly subterfuge is the fact that many Christians, of their own volition, affirm that 'Christian doctrines' are 'mysterious' in the second sense of the word, that is, inconceivable in themselves, however clearly revealed. By contrast, he is adamant that in the New Testament the word 'mystery' is, without exception, used only in the first sense.[34] What is more, in this first sense, the so-called 'veil of mystery' has been definitively removed by the fullness of revelation in Jesus Christ. For Toland, it necessarily follows, and should be abundantly clear to all reasonable people, that the 'Christian doctrines' so revealed cannot therefore be properly called 'mysterious'.

In seeking support for this understanding of 'mystery', Toland examines the various ways in which the word 'mystery' is employed in the gospel, identifying three distinct categories. First, he says, 'mystery' refers to the gospel or Christian religion in general, as a future dispensation totally hidden from the Gentiles and only very imperfectly known by the Jews.[35]

33. Toland, *Christianity not Mysterious*, p. 72.

34. Toland, *Christianity not Mysterious*, p. 73.

35. Toland, *Christianity not Mysterious*, pp. 95-99. Toland cites as examples 1 Cor. 2.7; 1 Cor. 4.1; Eph. 6.9; Rom. 16.25-26; Col. 2.2; 4.3-4; 1 Tim. 3.8-9, 16. He argues from these passages that the 'Mystery of Faith', 'Mystery of God', 'Mystery of Christ', 'Mystery of Godliness' and 'Mystery of the Gospel' are all synonymous and that no doctrine of the gospel can therefore be deemed a 'mystery'. Rather, it is the gospel itself that was, prior to Christ's revelation, a mystery, but that it cannot properly deserve that appellation thereafter.

Secondly, 'mystery' is used for certain doctrines revealed by the Apostles that, before Christ's revelation, were previously undisclosed and so unknowable.[36] Thirdly, 'mystery' denotes anything that is veiled by parables or enigmatic forms of speech.[37] As Toland sees it, none of these instances of 'mystery' in the gospel refer to things inconceivable in themselves: rather, they are used for things that were only unknowable before the new revelation in Jesus Christ. This 'new revelation in Christ' removed the incomprehensible, 'mysterious veil' obscuring these things from reason so that thereafter 'the Mysteries of the Gospel...cannot properly deserve the name of Mysteries'.[38] So, he asserts, in the whole gospel 'mystery' is never put for anything inconceivable in itself, or for anything that we are incapable of judging by our ordinary rational faculties, no matter how clearly revealed.[39] On this line of reasoning, Toland is convinced he has shown that there is nothing in the gospel that can be called a 'mystery' in either sense of the word. Hence, he insists that 'mystery', as traditionally and commonly understood, should be excluded from authentic, reasonable Christianity.

Toland next traces the development of what he perceives to be the authentically Christian idea and language of 'mystery' to the early Church Fathers in attempting to show that they, like the New Testament writers, understood 'mystery' in the same way as he does. Somewhat surprisingly, he finds these early Christian commentators guilty of what appears to be a grave theological error, saying that 'in imitation of the Jews, they turn'd all the Scripture into Allegory'.[40] Worse still, he claims, they went on to transpose events and characters from the Old Testament to the New when they could find the slightest resemblance between names, letters, places and the like. Consequently, various people, places and numbers that appeared in the Old Testament, and were taken to represent something significant in the New Testament, were designated as 'a Type' or 'Mystery'.[41] Nonetheless, Toland contends, although this enabled the early Fathers to find the New Testament in the Old, the Old in the New and, at times, resulted in erroneous explications of the texts, they were of one mind in

36. Toland, *Christianity not Mysterious*, pp. 100-104. Toland's examples are 1 Cor. 15.51-52; Rom. 11.25; Col. 1.25-27; Eph. 1.9-10; 3.1-6, 9; 5.31-32; 2 Thess. 2.3-8.

37. Toland, *Christianity not Mysterious*, pp. 104-106. Here, Toland cites Mt. 13.10-11; Mk. 4.11; Lk. 8.10; 1 Cor. 13.2; 14.2.

38. Toland, *Christianity not Mysterious*, p. 94.

39. Toland, *Christianity not Mysterious*, p. 108.

40. Toland, *Christianity not Mysterious*, p. 115.

41. Toland, *Christianity not Mysterious*, p. 115.

their understanding of 'mystery'. All the Church Fathers of the first three centuries, he asserts, expressly affirm that 'mystery' denotes, not things incomprehensible or inconceivable in themselves, but things that were only unknowable prior to Christ's revelation. However, these things are now perfectly accessible to all through the proper use of reason.[42] Thus, Toland concludes, 'I may justly hope [that] by this time the Cause of Incomprehensible and Inconceivable Mysteries in Religion should be readily given up by all that sincerely respect Fathers, Scripture, or Reason.'[43]

In what appears to be a 'parting shot', aimed at obstinate 'orthodox' opponents who might still remain unconvinced by his argument, Toland formulates a moral justification for his rejection of 'mystery' and his appeal to the plain truth of Scripture and reason. He argues that, in relation to the so-called 'mysteries' contained in the scriptural writings, 'either the Apostles could not write more intelligibly of the reputed Mysteries, or they would not'.[44] If they could not, then no blame can be attached to contemporary believers who cannot be reasonably expected to either understand or believe them, since they are at least as incapable as the scriptural writers in this regard. If they would not write of these 'Mysteries', then all blame must rest with them and not with contemporary believers.[45] From this, Toland reasons, there is no moral purpose in demanding assent to things beyond our comprehension. Why 'puzzle People's Heads with what they could never conceive', he asks, particularly when 'they can scarce find leisure enough for what is on all hands granted to be intelligible'.[46]

On this basis, Toland concludes, with customary self-assurance, that his argument will undoubtedly convince all reasonable people to acknowledge that Christianity is not 'mysterious', that there is nothing in the gospel contrary to reason or above it, and that no Christian doctrine can properly be called a 'mystery'.

Certainly, a number of Toland's fellow 'British Deists' found his argument persuasive, most notably Matthew Tindal who, in his *Christianity as Old as the Creation: Or the Gospel a Republication of the Religion of Nature* (1730), took up Toland's line of reasoning and gave it a moral application. Others, including Locke, were at best ambivalent. Locke certainly seems to have been embarrassed by *Christianity not Mysterious*

---

42. Toland, *Christianity not Mysterious*, pp. 114-19. In particular, Toland cites Clement of Alexandria, Tertullian and Origen in support of his position.

43. Toland, *Christianity not Mysterious*, p. 119.

44. Toland, *Christianity not Mysterious*, p. 137.

45. Toland, *Christianity not Mysterious*, p. 137.

46. Toland, *Christianity not Mysterious*, p. 138.

and clearly distanced himself from Toland following its publication. He expresses his disquiet in a letter to William Molyneux, saying of Toland, 'If his exceeding great value of himself do not deprive the world of that usefulness, that his parts, if rightly conducted, might be of, I shall be very glad.'[47] Locke's attitude towards Toland was, though, more positive than the overwhelming majority of those 'orthodox' contemporaries who published responses to *Christianity not Mysterious*, which were fiercely critical and often openly hostile, both to Toland personally and to his thesis.[48]

One of the most popular replies to Toland's book, for instance, was the scathingly critical *A Letter in Answer to a Book entitled Christianity not Mysterious* (1697) by Peter Browne, Senior Fellow of Trinity College, Dublin. Herein, Browne accuses Toland of trying to 'raise a Notion in the heads of People that Christianity, as it is now generally taught and receiv'd among us, is a Religion made up of dark aenigmatical Allusions, and absurd irrational and unintelligible Notions'.[49] For this Toland has, in Browne's opinion, 'justly become odious and detestable by all Men, who have any concern left for the Christian Religion'.[50] Browne finds it quite remarkable that, despite his widespread notoriety, Toland still holds resolutely to his position, setting 'his Forehead like a Flint' against all that can be said or done against him. Yet he alleges, 'God knows he no more values this ridiculous Nick-name of an Heretick, than [Saint] Paul did before him.'[51] Browne is convinced that Toland's hatred of the established Church and its doctrines and dogmas rather than any genuine scepticism about revelations, miracles and mysteries in Christianity acted as the catalyst for his writing *Christianity not Mysterious*. This, he says, is evidenced by the fact that Toland

> insinuates every where that our Profession is but a Craft…and our Religious Mysteries a Contrivance only to bring us Gain and Credit [and levels the whole Book mainly at the Clergy, and doth all he can to render us odious in the sight of the People.[52]

While Browne is probably correct in this assertion, it seems that in formulating his riposte he allowed himself to be 'side-tracked' by Toland's

---

47. This extract is cited in Sullivan, *John Toland*, pp. 7-8 and in Price, *Deism*, p. v.

48. For a useful survey of published objections to Toland's *Christianity not Mysterious*, see Stephen, *History*, pp. 101-117.

49. P. Browne, *A Letter in Answer to a Book entitled Christianity not Mysterious* (Dublin, 1697), p. 7.

50. Browne, *Letter in Answer*, p. 202.

51. Browne, *Letter in Answer*, p. 202.

52. Browne, *Letter in Answer*, pp. 204, 205.

vitriolic criticism of the clergy, rather than concentrating on the more crucial (and highly controversial) theological components of the latter's argument. Nonetheless, his 'Letter' provides an illustrative example of both the tone and material content of ecclesiastical objections raised against Toland and his book by contemporary, 'orthodox' clergymen.

Interestingly, J.V. Price points out that, while Toland's contemporaries appear to have been unequivocal in their assessments of his character and thought, late twentieth-century commentators have been noticeably divergent in this regard.[53] Thus, B. Willey says, 'The Bible remained a numinous book for Locke, and Toland, and Swift, and Addison, and innumerable polite savants in the eighteenth century.'[54] By contrast, P. Hazard considers Toland a 'born scandal-monger' blighted by a 'morbid mental excitement' that led him to 'uncontrollable rage', 'foaming at the mouth' and 'intoxicated with reason'.[55] Hardly the qualities one would expect from one of Willey's 'polite savants'. P. Gay offers a more measured assessment of Toland's character, commenting that, while he was indeed unwelcome in 'polite society' across Europe, this was primarily due to his controversial opinions rather than any lack of social etiquette.[56] P. Byrne concentrates on Toland's thought rather than his personality, saying, 'A particularly clear statement of the essential characteristic of reason in religion can be found in a work commonly regarded as heavily influenced by Locke— John Toland's *Christianity not Mysterious.*'[57] Here Price points out that Byrne's assessment is very similar to that of J.A.I. Champion, who considers Toland's *Christianity not Mysterious* 'a most articulate and popular history of 'mystery'…In this work he documented in detail the priestly construction of mystery into a self-interested theology.'[58] Yet in a radi-

---

53. Price, *Deism*, p. xi. In what follows I have drawn extensively on Price's survey of late twentieth-century interpretations of Toland, especially pp. xi-xiii of his introduction.

54. B. Willey, *The Seventeenth Century Background* (New York: Doubleday, 1965), p. 226.

55. P. Hazard, *The European Mind: The Critical Years, 1680–1715* (trans. J. Lewis May; London: Hollis & Carter, 1953), p. 264.

56. P. Gay, *The Enlightenment: An Interpretation* (London: Wildwood House, 1973), pp. i, 375.

57. Price, *Deism*, p. xii. Cf. P. Byrne, *Natural Religion and the Nature of Religion: The Legacy of Deism* (London: Routledge, 1989), p. 71. As I have indicated in n. 8, Byrne's view of the relationship between Locke and Toland is by no means uncontested: in fact, current scholarly opinion is clearly divided on this issue.

58. J.A.I. Champion, *The Pillars of Priestcraft Shaken: The Church of England and its Enemies (1660–1730)* (Cambridge: Cambridge University Press, 1992), p. 166.

cally different vein, D. Berman argues that there are specific reasons for believing that Toland, like other so-called 'British Deists', such as Collins, Blount and Tindal, was an atheist and not a deist at all.[59] It seems, then, that within late twentieth-century interpretation of Toland no scholarly consensus has as yet been reached regarding either his personality/character or, more importantly, the value of his theological argument in *Christianity not Mysterious*. Despite, or perhaps inspired by, this lack of consensus, Toland continues to attract much scholarly interest and, more recently, he has received due recognition for his influential contribution to the history of ideas and the history of biblical interpretation.[60] No doubt he would take great delight in this, and in the knowledge that, in his self-appointed role as *agent provocateur* in *Christianity not Mysterious*, he continues to stir theological passions and debate over three hundred years on.

Bibliography

Primary Texts

Toland, J., *Two Essays Sent in a Letter from Oxford (etc.)* (pseudonym L.P.) (London, 1695).
—*An Apology for Mr. Toland (etc.)* (London, 1697).
—*The Life of John Milton (etc.)* (anonymously, London, 1698).
—*Amyntor: or, a Defence of Milton's Life* (anonymously, London, 1699).
—*Vindicius Liberius (etc.)* (London, 1702).
—*Letters to Serena (etc.)* (London, 1704).
—*Socinianism Truly Stated (etc.)* (London, 1705).
—*The Jacobitism, Perjury, and Popery of High-Church Priests (etc.)* (anonymously, London, 1710).
—*Pantheisticon, sive formula celebrandae sodalitatis Socraticae (etc.)* (anonymously, London, 1720).
—*Tetradymus (etc.)* (London, 1720).
—*A Collection of Several Pieces of Mr. John Toland (etc.)* (ed. P. Des Maizeaux; 2 vols.; London, 1726).

Secondary Literature

D. Berman, 'Deism, Immortality, and the Art of Theological Lying', in J.A.L. Lemay (ed.), *Deism, Masonry, and the Enlightenment: Essays Honoring Alfred Owen Aldridge* (London: Associated University Press, 1987), p. 77.

59. D. Berman, 'Deism, Immortality, and the Art of Theological Lying', in J.A.L. Lemay (ed.), *Deism, Masonry, and the Enlightenment: Essays Honoring Alfred Owen Aldridge* (London: Associated University Press, 1987), p. 77.

60. It is widely acknowledged that G. Carabelli's scholarly work, *Tolandiana: Materiali bibliografici per lo studio dell'opera e della fortuna di John Toland (1670-1722)* (Florence: La nuova Italia, 1975) has greatly influenced this renewed interest in Toland.

Biddle, J.C., 'Locke's Critique of Innate Principles and Toland's Deism', *Journal of the History of Ideas* 37 (1976), pp. 412-18.

Carabelli, G., *Tolandiana: Materiali bibliografici per lo studio dell'opera e della fortuna di John Toland (1670–1722)* (Florence: La Nuova Italia, 1972).

Cassirer, E., *The Philosophy of the Enlightenment* (Princeton: Princeton University Press, 1979).

Daniel, S.H., *John Toland: His Methods, Manners and Mind* (Montreal: McGill-Queens University Press, 1987).

De Beer, E.S. (ed.), *The Correspondence of John Locke* (Oxford: Clarendon Press, 1976–89).

Emerson, R.L., 'English Deism, 1670–1755: An Enlightenment Challenge to Orthodoxy' (PhD dissertation, Brandeis University, 1962).

Evans, R.R., 'John Toland's Pantheism: A Revolutionary Ideology and Enlightenment Philosophy' (PhD dissertation, Brandeis University, 1965).

—*Pantheisticon: The Career of John Toland* (New York: Peter Lange, 1991).

Heinemann, F.H., 'John Toland and the Age of Enlightenment', *Review of English Studies* 20 (1944), pp. 125-46.

Leland, J., *A View of the Principal Deistical Writers that have Appeared in England in the last and Present Century* (London: B. Dod, 3rd edn, 1757).

Price, J.V., 'Introduction', *History of British Deism*, IV (London: Routledge; Thoemmes Press, 1995).

Redwood, J., *Reason, Ridicule and Religion: The Age of Enlightenment in England, 1660–1750* (Cambridge, MA: Harvard University Press, 1976).

Reedy, G., 'Socinians, John Toland, and the Anglican Rationalists', *HTR* 70 (1977), pp. 285-304.

Stephen, Sir L., *History of English Thought in the Eighteenth Century* (2 vols.; London: Smith, Elder & Co., 3rd edn, 1902).

Sullivan, R.E., *John Toland and the Deist Controversy: A Study in Adaptations* (Cambridge, MA: Harvard University Press, 1982).

Yolton, J.W., *John Locke and the Way of Ideas* (Oxford: Oxford University Press, 1956).

THE THEISM OF JEAN-JACQUES ROUSSEAU: 'THE CREED OF A CURATE OF SAVOY'

Philip Robinson

Editor's Introduction

This chapter provides an effective sequel to the previous study of the English Deist John Toland, as it offers a fictionalized statement of the bases of 'natural' belief. Rousseau was one of the four great figures of the French Enlightenment (together with Montesquieu, Voltaire and Diderot). In France the Enlightenment took the form of a severe critique of the political and social role of the Roman Catholic church within the monarchy of the Ancien Régime (up to 1789). The aim was to replace authority and dogma with a new scientific approach to the organization of the state and to personal morality. Rousseau firmly believed in God and in the viability of prayer, and so was regarded as a traitor by the other philosophes, *but as a dangerous libertarian by both Catholic and Protestant orthodoxies. 'So now I am alone in the world, with no brother, neighbour or friend, nor any company left me but my own' (*Reveries of the Solitary Walker, *p. 1). Both of his publications in the year 1762,* Social Contract *and* Emile *(from which our extract is taken), were condemned everywhere in Europe except in Britain, and Rousseau was driven from France. The rest of the French Enlightenment tended to argue that questions that were not within the capacity of scientific reason to answer were invalid; but Rousseau regarded ultimate questions as crucial, both existentially and morally, requiring a stance to be taken. Rousseau did not believe in the virtuous atheist. His (admittedly liberal) Calvinist background was important to Rousseau, and so the Bible remained* the *book for him from his childhood. He had read it all through at least three times and it retained a special status in his imagination. He treated the gospel sayings and stories of Jesus as history, with the exception of the miracles. Rousseau's theism (a belief in a living, approachable God) is not in doubt, but even his more sympathetic contemporaries wondered if he was a Christian. Relevant here are the statements towards the end of the extract about the limited special status of Jesus, which provoked Voltaire's question as to whether Rousseau had ever seen a god die.*

Philip Robinson offers an introductory exposition of the extracts from Book IV of Emile, *followed by his own translation of the text.*

1. *Rousseau's Savoyard Curate* (Emile, book IV)[1]

The multiple fictional 'frame' of the extracts that follow is not without its importance and is the first aspect of Rousseau's text to deserve comment. From the hindsight of the condemnation of *Emile* on religious grounds in June 1762, it is tempting for us to interpret this use of fiction as an effort by Rousseau to elude anticipated criticism through the device, as it were, of pushing off responsibility for the views expressed onto a figure different from himself. Those readers who know the author's *Confessions* will support such a view by identifying just this tendency in his autobiography. However, despite being psychologically plausible at one level, such an approach is not especially helpful when considering Rousseau's religious views. Fiction is in fact essential to the entire structure of Rousseau's treatise on education. In order to philosophize about the meaning of education, and this is the unique greatness of *Emile*, Rousseau must imagine, that is, must invent, a situation in which a tutor (the narrator of *Emile*) is faced with the responsibility of bringing up a pupil. Thus Emile is an imaginary orphan of good birth, in a circumstance where there is no problem of resources for funding the education that is to be provided and no question raised about what should be the parental role. In this fictional procedure, Rousseau has the excellent example of Marivaux the dramatist and many other writers for the motif of the 'utopian fiction' that permits philosophizing and that is the instrument for uncovering the essential truth of some human phenomenon or activity.[2] To this extent therefore the Savoyard curate may be seen as one detail of the total fictional structure of *Emile*.

Most crucially, however, the utopian fiction in general and the narrative of the curate in particular, are the sign of the importance that Rousseau lends to the 'correct rhetorical circumstances', not only for the introduction of the subject of religion to the pupil, but also for almost every learning experience that the pupil undergoes as the narrative of his learning process unfolds. The good educator, in Rousseau's view, looks for the favourable moment for every lesson that needs putting across. *Emile* is not a handbook for drafting courses in schools (indeed, schools are objects of contempt for Rousseau), it is rather, as one cannot repeat too often, an exploration of what education

---

1.   The standard English translation of Rousseau's famous text is that of Barbara Foxley (Everyman edition; London: Dent, 1974). The extracts cited here have, however, been newly translated for the purpose.

2.   Thomas More's *Utopia* is of course itself just such a philosophizing fiction.

means, always foregrounding the ethical dimension in the broadest sense of that expression. One of the meanings of education as an art is identifying the right moment and the right circumstances for any lesson one might wish to impart. And lessons, in Rousseau's sense, are almost never verbal and almost always 'object lessons' in one way or another. The young Emile has thus never had to learn his catechism by heart, because, in Rousseau's eyes, to be encouraged to parrot what the mind cannot understand is simply to be taken to a school of lying. Such ideas, one may easily appreciate, are the cause of his condemnation by religious authorities, both Roman Catholic and Protestant.

The fiction of the Savoyard curate is thus, at one important level, an illustration of the kind of circumstances in which it may be opportune to respond to the youth's questionings (and by this time Emile is a youth rather than a child) concerning religion and the meaning of life. One circumstance, considered necessary by Rousseau, is illustrated by the figure of the curate himself. The religious mentor must be both sincere and unbiased. Sincerity in this context implies that the mentor is speaking for himself out of his own most intimate beliefs and experience. Sincerity is impossible unless what the mentor says is unbiased by self-interest or by the objectives of an organization or power structure, such as an established church. The views of the curate are valued in the context of Rousseau's narrative precisely because this figure is the lowliest of creatures within the Roman Catholic hierarchy: he may be relied upon not to put forward implausible dogmas simply because he hopes for advancement within his church or for the favour of his superiors. A crucial characteristic of the curate is that he specifically desires to be out of the ecclesiastical rat race.

A second vital circumstance for the introduction of religious ideas to the pupil is an existing perception of the awesome quality of the observable physical world, or, in religious terms, of created Nature. The heart-to-heart discourse of the curate takes place with the whole spectacle of nature (here, the Po valley) at their feet. Rousseau even describes this spectacle explicitly as a 'text': the youth is now of an age to be able to 'read' Nature as a 'message' that 'speaks' of the power of a creative Deity. Emile's education up to this point has been to gain a direct 'tactile' and practical sensuous knowledge of this same physical world that is now a spectacle before him. Emile is a creature who is completely at ease in the physical world: he is not afraid of the dark; he is not afraid of hard physical toil; he has learned not always to believe the message of a single sense on its own (the 'bent stick' effect created by a branch in clear water is emblematic of the importance of the proper education of the senses by experience); he has now reached an age where his aesthetic sense has begun to develop, where his sensitivity to the 'splendour' of the spectacle of Nature is becoming a reality. This passage is very typical of Rousseau in so far as the aesthetic sense is not readily distinguished from the ethical sense: for Rousseau, in all of his important philosophical texts such as the *Discourse on Inequality* and the *Essay on the Origin of Languages*,[3] the human being begins to acquire an aesthetic sense simultaneously with a sensitivity to the inner life of other human beings. As Rousseau understands matters, Emile is able to appreciate and be moved by the beauty of the scene thanks to the same inner growth that makes him respond to generous friendship as the curate exposes his own personal religious views (as opposed to the theoretical doctrines of the church which he serves). In introducing his Book IV of *Emile,* Rousseau has written of the pupil's 'second birth into life' in order to describe this simultaneous acquisition of the moral and aesthetic sense. It is a 'second birth' that requires no less than a complete revolution in the tutor's strategy of education as the pupil (and this is Rousseau's own analogy) 'navigates' his way through adolescence and its reefs and shoals.

These two aspects of our extracts may therefore be understood as reflecting a quest, in religious education, for a harmony between the outer world of sense experience, on which all the care of Emile's early education has been lavished, and the inner world of personal subjectivity, where the pupil, through his nascent sensitivity to the inner life of fellow creatures, is beginning to become an individual in the proper ethical sense, rather than, as when he was younger, to 'love his sister as he loves his watch'. The religious dimension is thus, in Rousseau's eyes, an inescapable part of ethical education: the human being is a religious being because a social being. And this is so, as we see in the later parts of the curate's confession of faith, because that self-awareness that is also the awareness of other human beings' inner life is understood as being lived as a life of the spirit or the 'soul'. Rousseau inscribes himself in the great Cartesian tradition in so far as consciousness is not only, in this vision, the vital and defining part of our existence, but is also its incorporeal and immortal part.

The French language allows no verbal distinction between consciousness and conscience and it is certain that, in defining the nature of moral conscience, Rousseau exploits this verbal ambiguity. His contribution to, and

3.   *A Discourse on the Origins of Inequality among Men* (trans. with intro. and notes by Maurice Cranston; Harmondsworth: Penguin Books, 1984); *Essay on the Origin of Languages and Writings Related to Music* (trans. and ed. John T. Scott; Hanover, NH: London University Press of New England, 1998).

modification of, the Cartesian tradition, is to conceive of consciousness, or conscience, as moral energy or velleity, rather than as merely the rational ascertainment of ethical truth. He is thus able to persuade himself that the Deity has endowed mankind with an innate moral impulsion towards the good, which may be lost sight of or stifled by our activities in the world, but which is never actually destroyed. Kant takes up this notion, even to the point of considering Rousseau as a kind of Newton of moral philosophy, and re-expresses it as the famous concept of the 'categorical imperative'.[4] Ethical ideas of right and wrong, that is, have about them the quality that they are considered to hold for all human beings categorically. In Rousseau's terms, all human beings have an aspiration towards, or a 'sentiment' for, the moral good. It is only in this sense that Rousseau considers conscience to be a 'feeling' or awareness; he does not consider that conscience is an emotion, as is sometimes claimed by mistranslation of the French *sentiment*.

These, then, are the ideas that are at stake, as the curate articulates, to the youth his interlocutor, the notion of the Inner Light. Rousseau attempts to tune in to the categorical imperative of the conscience and to regard it as the direct voice of God. It is a Law or Authority. In this respect Rousseau shows his considerable debts to traditional thinking about religion. He, too, seeks authority on which to found his faith. Brought up in the (latitudinarian) Calvinism of Geneva, he became familiar with the idea of the Bible as authority. Converting to Catholicism as a result of running away from his native city at the age of 15 and out of need to eat, he is made familiar with the notion of Catholic tradition as an alternative form of authority. In the 'Confession of faith of the Savoyard curate' it is clear that he regards neither of these traditional authorities as reliable. As he exclaims concerning the Biblical authority for miracles: 'how many human beings between me and God!' (p. 6).

Rousseau's certainty of the grounds on which he bases his articles of faith is thus of a similar kind to that of Descartes as he outlines his Method.[5] In the last analysis we have the consciousness that we exist and, for Rousseau, that we exist in a certain mode of being, which he calls free will or the active spiritual principle. This inner conviction or perception is the only valid authority, as far as he is concerned, for religious ideas. This kind of

4.   Kant's extraordinary tribute to Rousseau is reflected in L.W. Beck, *Commentary on Kant's Critique of Practical Reason* (Chicago: University of Chicago Press, 1980), in particular pp. 6 n. 6, 159 n. 68.

5.   See H. Gouhier, *Les méditations métaphysiques de Jean-Jacques Rousseau* (Paris: Vrin, 1970) and the chapter entitled 'Ce que le Vicaire doit à Descartes', pp. 49-83.

view, which has evident affinities with Quakerism (though Rousseau would be highly suspicious of the early pentecostalist quakings of the Society of Friends) and with the Quietist tendency in France, is exceptional in the context of the French Enlightenment. Uniquely among the *philosophes*, Rousseau strives to reconcile the ideals of Reason with the human need for active worship of a Deity. With respect to the Roman Catholic religion, the French Enlightenment takes, almost of necessity, an anti-clerical form, in so far as that church claimed, and legally possessed, sole ethical authority within the absolutist monarchical state. It applied the Mosaic law to individual conduct and its own dogmas were protected by legislation against blasphemy. For such figures as Montesquieu, Voltaire and Diderot, the Roman Church and its power are an important part of the ethical and political darkness that the French Enlightenment makes it its business to dispel by the application of rational and 'philosophical' (in our terms, scientific) thought to human affairs. For the extremists of the Enlightenment, of whom Diderot must count as one, the very idea of God is part of the equipment by which earthly authorities hold ignorant men in thrall. The earlier generation of Montesquieu and Voltaire, on the other hand, is not atheistic and has an approach in which a Deity is still the source of all Reason, and in which the rational order of the physical world (regarded as proved by the cosmology of Newton) is treated as evidence for such a Deity's existence. Where worship is concerned, however, neither of these great figures develops ideas about it: for Montesquieu, such matters should be a private choice outside the domain of legislation for all; and Voltaire famously opines, as a matter of practical politics, that, if God did not exist, he would need to be invented.

Rousseau's effort to reconcile the theistic religious viewpoint, which finds a genuine place for worship of the Deity, with the aspirations of rational French Enlightenment merely incurred the opprobrium of both sides in what, by 1762 through the *Encyclopédie*, had become a bitter ideological war.[6] He was regarded as a traitor to the Enlightenment cause by his former friends the *philosophes*, and as a subverter of Christian beliefs by both Catholic and Protestant authorities all over the European continent. Almost the only country in which his religious views were not officially condemned was the United Kingdom, which may or may not reflect well on that country.

---

6.   The *Encyclopédie, ou dictionnaire des sciences, des arts et des métiers* (1751–65), of which Denis Diderot remained the faithful general editor throughout its chequered publishing history, was one of the most important business projects of the Ancien Régime and used its status as a compendium of human knowledge to promote the free-thinking French Enlightenment viewpoint.

Having to his own satisfaction established, by a Cartesian style of argument, that God exists and that the universal principles of justice and morality manifest themselves directly through the workings of the human conscience, Rousseau addresses himself to two of the major traditional questions concerning the specifically Christian religion. These are the linked issues of the status of the Bible and of the person of Jesus Christ. As far as the Biblical text is concerned, Rousseau, consistently with his attitude to the fundamental question of belief, rejects external proofs of the authority of what the Bible says. In particular, the claims of miracles are treated as fables, since they can only be verified by human testimony, whereas a God who wishes to reveal himself to human beings would surely do so directly through the individual conscience. Rousseau is far more impressed by what the revered holy text contains, by the story that it tells and by the values that it puts forward. In this spirit he writes of the 'majesty' of the *Bible* and of the 'holiness' of the Gospels. That is, the individual conscience is moved to recognize spiritual truth in what these texts tell. The same is true concerning the crucial question of the person of Jesus. Voltaire is particularly scathing of Rousseau's claim to be able, via the perceptions of conscience, to be sure of the divinity of Christ's death, and demands to know if Rousseau has ever seen a god die. It is indeed at points like this that one realizes that Rousseau is overworking the individual conscience in its role as authority.

The orthodox Christian of course demands also to know at this point what is to be made of the claim of Christ's resurrection. And here Rousseau invites condemnation by his omissions: he writes of Christ's death and interprets such self-sacrifice as divine, thus incurring Voltaire's scorn for claiming to know the unknowable. But he leaves us to categorize among the miracles that he will not believe the assertion that Christ rose from the dead, the very tenet without which the historical Christian faith, at least since the Congress of Nicaea, would have no substance.

In the section on worship, the fiction of the Savoyard curate serves Rousseau well again, since through it he is able to 'stage' the important question of how one might practise a particular religious rite, or worship, without necessarily being committed to the precise dogma that the form of worship might imply. What is at stake here, certainly, is the question of how Rousseau himself might take part in the Calvinistic communion, which he certainly did while in the Hohenzollern domain of Neuchâtel (1762–65), while not formally accepting all the dogma that attached itself to that act. His claim, here, that 'the essential worship is that of the heart' was not enough, by 1765, to convince pastor Montmollin of Môtiers that Rousseau was, in any meaningful sense, a Christian. And it was not long before Montmollin's congregation, or some of it, was stoning Rousseau's house and driving him from the principality. The curate, and Rousseau through him, claims the right to distinguish between precisely formulated dogmas, which are seen as merely a function of particular cultures according to time and place, and the true adoration of the timeless God in the sincerity of one's own heart. The problem, of course, is that believers in the dogmas are wont not to regard them as cultural contingencies but rather as the essence of faith itself, to the exclusion of all other forms. The devout Catholic could not but be scandalized by the idea of the Savoyard curate that the forms of the Mass are inessential 'externals' compared with the private adoration of the priest's own individual conscience. One could hardly expect Rousseau's radical idea —that the 'trappings' of religion are largely insignificant compared with essential belief in the Deity and a confidence in the ultimate triumph of Right—to attract the universal assent of the devout.

Rousseau's idea is, in fact, the obverse of one of the principles of Montes-quieu's *Spirit of the Laws* (1748), which links the possible forms of govern-ment systematically with different forms and structures of society itself. Already implicit in Montesquieu's text is a distinction between the social forms that religious ideas may take and the fact of the individual human being's relationship to the Deity. What the Savoyard curate now does, in Rousseau's text, is to treat the socially contingent dimension of religion, its officially established rituals and forms, as inessential and the individual conscience as the real substance. The challenge offered by Rousseau's posi-tion is that it is the dogmatic forms, which so often presented themselves as the bedrock of faith, which are actually contingent on social structures, while true religious vitality is to be found in the communion between the individ-ual soul and God.

This radical individualism in religion becomes a problem in Rousseau's philosophy at the point where, when considering, in the *Social Contract* (a work that seeks to state the principles of the legitimacy of public institu-tions), what form of public worship the state should require of its citizens, he states his conviction that a Civil Religion must of necessity be instituted, on pain of death for those who refuse either to conform to it or to go into exile.[7] It is true, that is, that the forms of religion are contingent upon the other aspects of a given society, but what is not in doubt is that, according to Rousseau, morality is only ultimately sustainable through a belief in the Deity, since the Deity represents the Justice and Right towards which we

---

7. *On the Social Contract* (trans. and ed. Donald A. Cress; intro. Peter Gay; Indi-anapolis: Hackett, 1987).

know, by inner conviction, that our conscience aspires. Considering, now, what the curate says in the light of Rousseau's own rigorous political theory of religion, we may thus assume that, in human affairs, a priest of any official state religion will always of necessity be in a position analogous to that of the curate: there will always be some aspect of public dogma that he may not personally agree with, but that he must of necessity respect because it is a part of the Civil Religion that is essential to the health of the state.

It would thus be hasty and wrong to conclude, as devout Christians did in his time, that Rousseau's individualistic creed implies necessary condemnation of dogmatic public religion. The *Social Contract* indeed makes clear both that the Civil Religion should contain a bare minimum of dogmas and that Christianity, and especially the Roman Catholic form of Christianity, is utterly unsuitable as a Civil Religion, on the grounds that it is wholly orientated towards the after-life. A Civil Religion, on the contrary, must in order to be effective motivate the citizen to fulfil his part of the social contract here and now.

While important aspects of Biblical tradition are thus verified by what the soul's conscience finds convincing in the nature of the central religious stories, the authority of the Civil Religion rests not on any book, but on the idea that if a citizen does not believe in a divine moral law, he can have no credible allegiance to the social and ethical pact into which he enters with his fellow-creatures in founding the social contract of a given legitimate state. And here we touch upon an issue that has preoccupied scholars concerning Rousseau ever since his great philosophical works were first published: Emile's education is conceived both as a response to the conviction that scarcely any legitimate state exists in the modern world and as a preparation for entry to such a legitimate state based on a social contract, should Emile ever be so fortunate as to find one existing in the world. As Rousseau pictures the dichotomy between his two great texts, *Emile* and *The Social Contract*, at the outset of the former work, Emile is the Natural Man developed to his full potential and for his own sake, while the Citizen is a figure committed body and soul to the well-being of his own particular community, indeed knowing no other mode of being apart from that commitment. In his description of the curate's approach to Catholic dogma, Rousseau now seems to pre-figure what may be Émile's own stance, if ever he is to be received as a citizen of a legitimate state: there will be a Civil Religion to which he is required to adhere, but since this will be a bare minimum of belief, such as that there is a Deity which makes the moral Law and that there is public worship in which this Deity is honoured and worshipped, Emile will have no difficulty of conscience in observing that Religion.

2. The Theism of Jean-Jacques Rousseau (1712–78)

Extracts from *Emile* (1762), Book IV (trans. by Philip Robinson), 'The Creed of a Curate of Savoy'.

[Emile's tutor, a persona of Rousseau and narrator of the text of *Emile*, claims in Book IV that he is transcribing the text of someone who, in his vagabond and misspent youth, fell under the salutary influence of a curate from Savoy, whose simple faith and virtue had a lasting effect upon him. We then read the confession of faith that the curate made to this youth. Naturally, the curate (while he may remotely resemble priests Rousseau met in his own life) is the vehicle for Rousseau's mature religious views, whereas the youth is a romanced version of Rousseau himself in his own young days. The multiple fictional 'frame' of the extracts that follow is not without its importance. The 'Creed of a Curate of Savoy' was the main reason for the condemnation of *Emile* by most of the major states of Europe (not the United Kingdom!) and for Rousseau's expulsion from France on 9 June 1762.]

[The character of the curate as recalled by the figure who heard his creed.]

This worthy priest was a curate from Savoy, who, because of some youthful escapade, had been in trouble with his bishop and had crossed the Alps [into Italy] in order to seek the protection denied to him in his own country. He was not without a good mind and some education, and, with his good appearance and demeanour, had found patrons who placed him as tutor to the son of one of the ministers. He preferred to be poor rather than dependent and had little sense of how to succeed amongst powerful people. He was not with the minister long, but in leaving his household did not lose his esteem; as his behaviour was good and as he was well liked by everyone, he hoped to recover the good will of his bishop and to obtain from him some small living in the mountains where he might spend the rest of his days. That was the full extent of his ambition…

What impressed me most was the private life of my worthy master: his virtue without hypocrisy, his lovingkindness without weakness of character and his way of speaking which was always direct and simple and never belied by his conduct. Those whom he helped never heard him ask if they went regularly to vespers or to confession, or whether they fasted on the appropriate days and practised self-denial. He inflicted on them none of those conditions without which, on pain of starving to death, you receive no assistance from the devout and pious.

[The place where the confession of faith is made.]

I showed my impatience to hear what he had to say and the meeting was fixed for no later than the following morning. It was summer and we rose at first light. He led me out of the city to the top of a high hill, at the foot of which flowed the river Po and from which one could see how it meandered on into the distance between its fertile banks; far off, the landscape was crowned by the vast chain of the Alps; the beams of the rising sun were beginning to touch the plains and to cast across the fields long shadows of trees, hillocks and houses, the play of light enriching in a thousand different ways the most beautiful picture which an eye can behold. It was as if Nature were spreading before our eyes all her splendour as a text for our discussions.

[Authority and the need for faith: Reason and the Inner Light.]

My child, expect from me no learned speeches or profound arguments. I am not a great philosopher and have little wish to be one. However, from time to time I show some good sense, and my love of truth is constant. I do not wish to conduct a debate with you or even to convince you: it is sufficient to lay before you what I think, in the simplicity of my heart. All I ask is that you consult your own heart as I speak. If I am mistaken, the error is in good faith and not to be counted against me as a crime. And should you likewise be mistaken, there would be little harm in that. If my thinking is just, then we are both endowed with reason and have the same motive for listening to its voice; why should you not think as I do?...

How in good faith can one be a sceptic on principle? Such an attitude I do not understand. True sceptics are either non-existent or the unhappiest of men. Doubt concerning that which it is vital for us to know is too harsh a state for the human mind: it cannot long remain in such a condition and one way or another takes a decision, preferring to be in error rather than believe in nothing...

I worked on the premise that the inadequacy of the human mind is the first cause of the immense diversity of persuasions among philosophers, and that pride is the second... Although we are only a tiny fragment of a complete whole whose limits are out of our reach, we are arrogant enough to think that we can decide what that whole is in itself and what we are in relation to it...

The first thing I learned from these considerations was to restrict my enquiries to what was of direct concern to me, contenting myself with a profound ignorance about everything else and troubling my mind, even to the point of doubt, only about those things which it was important for me to know.

I also understood that the philosophers of our day, far from ridding me of my futile doubts, would only add many more to those which tormented me and would not resolve any of them. So I chose a different guide and said: 'Let me follow the Inner Light; it will not lead me so far astray as others have done, or if it does the fault will be mine, and I shall be corrupted less by following my own illusions than by trusting their deceits'...

Taking my own inner love of truth as my only philosophy and, as my only method, a clear and simple rule which dispensed with the need for vain and subtle arguments, I went back, with the help of this rule, to the examination of such knowledge as directly concerned myself. I determined to admit as self-evident any article of knowledge that I could not, with sincerity of heart, refuse to believe, and to allow as true everything that might follow necessarily from it. Anything else I resolved to leave undecided, neither accepting nor rejecting it, nor troubling myself to clear up difficulties which did not lead to practical results...

I exist, and I have senses through which I receive impressions. This is the first truth which strikes me and which I am forced to accept. Have I any independent knowledge of my own existence, or am I only aware of it through my sensations?...how can I know if the sense of *self* is something beyond those sensations and maybe independent of them?

My sensations happen within me, since they make me aware of my existence; but their cause is outside me, since they affect me willy-nilly and I am powerless to produce or destroy them. So I clearly perceive that my sensation, which is within me, and its cause or object, which is outside me, are not the same thing.

Thus not only do I exist but also other entities, the objects of my sensations; and even if these objects are only ideas, it is still true that they are not myself.

…Hence all the disputes between idealists and materialists have no significance for me: their distinctions between the appearance and the reality of bodies is entirely fanciful.

I am now as convinced of the existence of the universe as of my own. I next consider the objects of my sensations. Finding that I have the capacity to compare them, I perceive that I am endowed with an active force of which I was not previously aware…

…In my view the distinctive faculty of an intelligent and active being is to be able to make sense of this word 'is'. I search in vain in the purely sensitive entity for that force and intelligence which compares and makes judgments: I find no trace of that force in its nature…

I am thus not merely a sentient and passive entity, I am an active and intelligent one and, whatever the philosophers say, I shall dare to aspire to the honour of thinking. I know only that truth lies in things outside me and not in my mind which judges them, and that the less I put of myself in the judgments I make about them, the more I am sure of getting near the truth. Hence my rule of trusting instinct more than reason is confirmed by reason itself.

[God as Prime Mover or Will: first article of faith.]

The first causes of movement are not within matter itself; matter does not produce movement but only receives or communicates it. The more I observe the action and reaction of the forces of nature playing on each other, the more I see that we must always trace one effect back to another until we find a will, which is the first cause. To assume an infinite succession of causes is to assume no such succession at all. In a word, any movement which is not produced by another can only come from some spontaneous, voluntary act. Inanimate bodies have no activity except by movement and there is no true action without will. This is my first principle. I believe, therefore, that there is a will which sets the universe in motion and gives life to nature. That is my first dogma, or my first article of faith.

[God as Supreme Intelligence: second article of faith.]

If the setting in motion of matter reveals to me a Will, then matter set in motion according to certain laws reveals an Intelligence. This is my second article of faith. To act, to compare, to choose, are the operations of an active and thinking Being: therefore such a Being exists. But where, you may say, do you see Him existing? Not only in the clouds which roll or the sun which gives us light; not only in myself but in the sheep that grazes, the bird that flies, the stone that falls and the leaf blown by the wind.

I judge of the order of the world, although I know nothing of its purpose, because for the sake of making such a judgment it is enough for me to compare the parts of that order one with another, to study their co-operation, their relations and their united action. I do not know why the universe exists, but I see continually how it is changed and how its constituent entities interact closely and lend each other their aid. I am like the man looking at an open watch for the first time: he admires the workmanship, although he does not know what the instrument is for and does not see the face.

[Man has a soul and is free: third article of faith.]

The first principle of all action is in the will of a free being; one can go no further. It is not the word liberty which is meaningless, it is the word necessity. To assume some act, or some effect which does not derive from an active principle, is really to assume effects without a cause: it is to fall into a vicious circle. Either there is no first impetus or every first impetus has no prior cause, and there is no will properly so called without freedom. Therefore Man is free in his actions and, as such, he is animated by a non-material substance. That is my third article of faith. From these first three you will easily deduce all the others without my continuing to enumerate them.

If Man is active and free, he acts of his own accord; what he does as a free being does not enter into the system ordained by Providence, and may not be imputed to it. Providence does not desire the evil which Man does when he abuses the freedom which has been given him; but neither does it stop him doing evil, whether because such evil from a being so insignificant appears as nothing, or because to prevent him would involve the greater evil of inhibiting his freedom and degrading his nature. Providence made him free not that he might do evil but that he might choose the good…

O Man! look no further for the author of evil: you yourself are that author. The only evil is the evil you do or the evil you suffer, and both come from yourself. Evil in general can only spring from disorder, and in the order of the world I perceive an unfailing system. Evil in particular exists simply in the consciousness of the suffering creature: Man was not given this consciousness, he generated it himself. Pain has little hold over someone who thinks hardly at all and has no sense of a past or a future. Take away the fatal progress we have made, take away our errors and our vices, take away Man's handiwork, and all is good.

[Moral conduct and knowing the good: the role of conscience.]

After having thus deduced the principal truths which I needed to know, both from the perception of the objects of sense and from my inner consciousness which leads me to judge of causes by my natural reason, it now remains for me to seek the principles of conduct which may be drawn from these truths and to formulate the rules which I must set for myself in order to fulfil my destiny in this world according to the purposes of my Maker. Still following my method, I do not draw these rules from the principles of some high philosophy, I find them in the depths of my heart, inscribed in indelible letters by the hand of nature. I need only consult myself concerning that which I wish to do: what I feel to be right is right and what I feel to be wrong is wrong: conscience is the best casuist of all, and it is only when we haggle with conscience that we resort to the subtleties of argumentation. Our first concern is for ourselves: yet how often the inner voice tells us that in seeking our own good at the expense of others we are doing evil! We think we are following the impulse of nature and we are actually resisting it; in heeding nature's appeal to our senses, we reject her appeal to our hearts; the active being obeys while the passive being commands. Conscience is the voice of the soul, the passions the voice of the body. Is it surprising if what they say is often in conflict? Which one should we obey? All too often reason deceives us and has more than once given cause to doubt its judgment. But conscience never deceives and is the true guide of Man: it is to the soul what instinct is to the body and whoever follows its voice is obedient to nature and has no fear of being led astray. (Seeing that I was about to interrupt him, my benefactor insisted on this point and sought leave to pursue it further.)

…Let us examine, in abstraction from personal self-interest, which way our inclinations lead us. Which spectacle pleases us most, the suffering or the happiness of others? Do we find more pleasure in a kind action or in an unkind action, and which one leaves behind it the more delightful memory? With which characters do you identify in a play on the stage? Do you take pleasure in the crimes you witness? Do you cry when the evil-doers are punished? We are indifferent, it is said, to everything but our self-interest: on the contrary, we are consoled in our suffering by the sweetness of friendship and the balm of humanity. Even in our pleasures we should be too alone and too miserable if we had no one to share them with us. If there is no morality in the heart of Man, what is the source of his rapturous admiration of noble deeds and of his passionate devotion to great men? What has such enthusiasm for virtue and strength of character to do with our self-interest? Why should I prefer to be Cato stabbing himself in the stomach rather than Caesar in his triumphs? Take away from our hearts this love of moral beauty and you rob us of the joy of life…

…We delight in injustice only so long as it is to our advantage. Otherwise we look to protect the innocent…

There is therefore in the depths of our hearts an innate principle of justice and virtue, by which, despite our own maxims, we judge as good or evil our own actions and those of others. It is to this principle that I give the name of conscience…

Conscience! Conscience! Divine instinct, immortal voice from heaven, thou art the sure guide of a creature who is indeed ignorant and finite but also intelligent and free; thou art an infallible judge of good and evil, giving Man his likeness to God; thou art the excellence of his nature and the morality of his actions; without thee I see nothing in myself to raise me above the beasts, other than the sad privilege of straying from one error to another thanks to an unbridled understanding and a reason which knows no principle.

[No revelation but by Reason.]

I am told that revelation was necessary in order to teach the way in which God wished to be served. The diversity of peculiar cults which men have instituted is taken as a proof: they do not see that this very diversity is due to the fancifulness of revelation itself. As soon as the peoples of the earth made God speak, each did so in its own peculiar way, making Him say what it liked. If what God says to the human heart had been listened to, there would only ever have been one religion among men…

…Let us allow nothing to the privilege of birth or to the authority of the fathers and pastors. Rather let us place before the examination of reason and conscience everything which they have taught us since childhood. In vain they cry: submit your reason. A deceiver might say the same. I require reasons for submitting my reason.

[On scripture and authority.]

God has spoken! A fine phrase indeed. To whom has he spoken? To men. Then why have I heard nothing of it? He has charged other men to relay his word to you. I see! men are going to tell me what God has said: I would rather have heard God himself; it would have been no more difficult for Him and I should have been protected from deception. He guarantees the truth of what is said through the mission of those whom He has sent. How so? By miracles. And where are these miracles? In books. And who wrote the books? Men. And who has seen the miracles? Men who can vouch for them. What! nothing but human testimony? nothing but what is reported to me about what men have reported! How many men between God and me!…

In the three main revelations, the sacred books are written in languages unknown to the peoples who follow them. The Jews understand no Hebrew and the Christians understand neither Hebrew nor ancient Greek; the Turks and Persians understand no Arabic, and modern Arabs themselves no longer speak the language of Mohammed. Is that a simple way of instructing men, always to speak to them in a language they do not understand? These books are translated, you will say. What a splendid reply! And who will guarantee that they are properly translated or that they even can be? And when God takes it upon Himself to speak to men, why should he need interpreters?…

Roman Catholics make great play with the authority of the Church. But what does that profit them, if this authority needs to be established by an elaborate apparatus of proofs comparable to that used by other sects in order to establish their doctrine directly? The Church decides that the Church has the right to decide. What a well-founded authority! Step outside it and you are back to all our discussions…

I confess to you that the majesty of the Bible astounds me and that the holiness of the Gospels speaks to my heart. Consider the works of the philosophers, with all their pomp: how petty they are by comparison! Can it be that such a sublime and simple book is the work of men? Can it be that the one whose history it relates is no more than a mere man himself?

[On the person of Jesus Christ.]

Is his the tone of a fanatic or of an ambitious leader of a sect? What gentleness and purity in his way of life! What touching grace in his teachings! What sublimity in his sayings! What profound wisdom in his sermons! What quickness, what discrimination and what justice in his answers! Where is the man, where is the sage who can live, suffer and die without weakness or ostentation?…What presumption and what blindness there is in the comparison between the son of Sophroniscus and the son of Mary! What a gulf between one and the other! Socrates, dying without pain and ignominy was able to sustain his role right to the end…The death of Socrates, philosophizing peacefully with his friends, is the easiest we could possibly desire; the death of Jesus under torture, insulted, mocked and cursed by an entire people, is the worst our fear might imagine. Socrates, reaching for the poisoned cup blesses the one who holds it out and weeps; Jesus, amidst the most horrible torment, prays for his pitiless executioners. Yes indeed: if the life and death of Socrates are those of a sage, then the life and death of Jesus are those of a God. Shall we say that the Gospel story is pure invention? My friend, such things are not the work of imagination, and the deeds of Socrates, which no one doubts, are attested by less evidence than those of Jesus.

[On worship.]

Such is the scepticism in which I remain despite myself; but this scepticism is not painful to me, because it does not extend to essential points of moral practice, and because I am quite resolute about the principles of all my duties. I serve God in the simplicity of my heart. I seek to know only that which is important to my conduct. As for dogmas which have no influence either on our actions or on our morality and which trouble the minds of so many people, I feel no concern whatever about them. I regard all individual religions as so many useful institutions laying down for each country a uniform manner of honouring God through public worship. they may all be explained by reference to climate, government, spirit of the nation or any other local cause which makes one preferable to the other according to the time and the place. I believe they are all good if they serve God in an appropriate way. The essential worship is that of the heart. Such worship is never rejected by God, whatever form it takes, provided it is sincere. Having been called to the service of the Church within my own religion, I fulfil with absolute scrupulousness the duties which are laid down for me, and my conscience would protest if I wilfully missed out any one of them…I pronounce the words of the sacrament respectfully and I have all the faith which I am capable of summoning in their effectiveness. Whatever may be the truth of that inconceivable mystery, I have no fear that on the Day of Judgment I shall be punished for having profaned it in my heart.

DIVINE RIGHT THEORY AND ITS CRITICS
IN EIGHTEENTH-CENTURY ENGLAND

Grayson Ditchfield

Editor's Introduction

In the historical days of any serious democracy, let alone in more modern times coloured by republican sympathies and a widespread crisis of authority, it might seem impossible that any king, even an hereditary monarch within a line of succession, should possess a divine and indefeasible right to his royal status and authority. It is even more strange to discover that there is a biblical justification for such a divine right, founded in the first instance on Old Testament texts about the kingship in Israel. Such texts were handled less than critically, given the range of evidence in the Old Testament for divergent views on the subject of kingship, between those who saw the king as God's gift to the nation (duly anointed as Saul and David had been), and those who regarded the very idea as a blasphemous usurpation of the power of God himself.

An urgent and practical problem for divine right theory would be posed whenever an actual king proved less than ideal. In such cases active obedience to an evil ruler would seem repugnant and morally impossible. But the theory held that in such cases passive obedience would still be required, so that, in place of rebellious defiance, acquiescence to any punishment incurred as a consequence of non-compliance would still be expected. Here Paul's words in Romans 13 were frequently quoted in support of the theory, without regard to the historic circumstances of Paul's letter and the meaning of his words in context.

This chapter explores the historical contexts in which divine right theory originated, the high and low points in the seventeenth century, and in particular the eighteenth-century debate. It is important to see the theory on the one hand in contrast to the divine right of the Papacy (particularly in the matter of the deposing of monarchs), and on the other hand in contrast to the new rationalism, which saw 'rights' essentially in humanistic terms.

The theory of the divine right of kings may be defined as the belief that the institution of monarchy is divinely sanctioned and that divine approval of monarchy may be amply demonstrated by biblical citation. It is associated with the claim that the succession to monarchy is governed by indefeasible hereditary right through primogeniture and that such a right, acquired through birth, cannot be overridden by usurpation, however durable that usurpation might prove to be. Divine right theory holds that monarchs are answerable not to their subjects but to God. They derive their power solely from God, who alone has the authority to remove them from their thrones. Accordingly, two ramifications of divine right theory were the doctrines of non-resistance and of passive obedience. The former laid down that any act of resistance or rebellion against the king was a sin in the eyes of God. The latter stated that, in the event of a conflict between a command of the king and the law of God, the law of God ought to be obeyed, but that the subject must then passively submit to such punishment as the king might inflict for the act of disobedience. In England during the late seventeenth and the eighteenth centuries these doctrines were popularized by such frequently reprinted and widely read devotional works as *The Whole Duty of Man* (1658) and perhaps even more by the spoken and the printed sermon. The importance of the pulpit as a means of oral communication in a period of severely limited literacy cannot be over-emphasized. Moreover, many thousands of sermons were published in the eighteenth century and it is from their contents that it is possible to derive a firm indication of the biblical passages that were deployed to bolster, or in a few cases to qualify or to undermine, the theory of divine right.

The divine right of kings may be said to have evolved from the mediaeval disputes between the claims of the Papacy and of the Holy Roman Emperors over the sovereignty of Christendom. The divine right of the emperors in the fourteenth century amounted to resistance to papal claims to temporal authority, claims which could lead to the deposition of secular rulers. With the rise of the major European monarchies, particularly those of France, Spain and England, divine right theory served as an ideological defence against the exertion of papal authority over national churches. Pope Pius V's excommunication, and attempted deposition, of Elizabeth I of England in 1570 was a prime example of a papal claim that monarchies found it in their interest to resist. In the previous year a Catholic rebellion against Elizabeth had indeed taken place and it was hardly a coincidence that the Church's *Homily against Wilful Rebellion*, published in that year, stressed the sinfulness of resistance to the Lord's anointed. By 1600, divine right theory clearly postulated 'that unity in a state is only to be obtained by the unquestioned supremacy of some one authority, whose acts are subject to no legal criticism'.[1] That

---

1.   Figgis, p. 49.

single authority was also subject to no kind of external suzerainty. Article 37 of the Church of England gave the king power 'which we see to have been given always to all godly Princes in holy Scriptures by God himself' over 'all estates and degrees committed to their charge by God, whether they be Ecclesiastical or Temporal'.

Divine right theory was repeatedly justified by a series of key biblical texts. Those most frequently cited in eighteenth-century sermons derived mainly, although by no means exclusively, from the New Testament. It was common in this period to seek confirmation for political practices, as well as theological doctrines, from the example of the early Christian Church. Of particular importance was the thirteenth chapter of St Paul's epistle to the Romans, vv. 1-7. This passage begins:

> Let every soul be subject unto the higher powers. For there is no power but of God: the powers that be are ordained of God. Whosoever therefore resisteth the power, resisteth the ordinance of God: and they that resist shall receive to themselves damnation (vv. 1-2).

Here was a biblical endorsement of the doctrine of non-resistance. Similarly, the second chapter of the first epistle general of St Peter, vv. 13-14, enjoined:

> Submit yourselves to every ordinance of man for the Lord's sake: whether it be to the king, as supreme; or unto governors, as unto them that are sent by him for the punishment of evildoers, and for the praise of them that do well.

Verse 17 contains a further specific injunction: 'Honour all men. Love the brotherhood. Fear God. Honour the King.' The two latter phrases were frequently used by John Wesley in the later eighteenth century, partly to prove his own loyalty and partly to express his disapproval of the American rebellion against the rule of George III. 2 Peter 2.9-10 reserves punishment for those 'that walk after the flesh in the lust of uncleanness, and despise government'. Two other epistles of St Paul provided texts that were central to the divine right tradition. The epistle to Titus 3.1 urges its recipient to 'Put them [i.e. his followers] in mind to be subject to principalities and powers, to obey magistrates, to be ready to every good work'. The first epistle to Timothy, 2.1-3, calls for 'supplications, prayers, intercessions, and giving of thanks...for kings, and for all that are in authority; that we may lead a quiet and peaceable life in all godliness and honesty'. The most frequently cited Old Testament text was Prov. 25.2: 'My son, fear thou the Lord and the King: and meddle not with them that are given to change.'

The popularity of these texts with the clergy of the Church of England and with their Dissenting counterparts is evident in John Cooke's elaborate bibliographical compilation *The Preacher's Assistant*, published in 1782–83. Designed to provide inspiration, if not direct plagiarism, to clergymen in search of ideas for their preaching, this work listed, by biblical texts and by author, an immense number of sermons that were published between the restoration of Charles II in 1660 and the end of the War of American Independence in 1783. No text from the Old Testament served more frequently as a text for sermons in Cooke's listings than Prov. 24.21, Rom. 13.1, Tit. 3.1 and 1 Tim. 2.1-2 were among the most common of all the New Testament texts, exceeded in popularity only by Mt. 7.12 and Rev. 14.13.

However, there were many other texts that were relevant to this theme and other, controversial, interpretations of those texts. James I, one of the most articulate of divine right theorists, had cited 1 Sam. 8.18 ('And Ye shall cry out in that day because of your king which ye shall have chosen you; and the Lord will not hear you in that day') to justify non-resistance. But, as Conrad Russell and others have pointed out, divine right theory belonged to a wider context of social understanding, a 'great chain of being', which argued for divine sanction as legitimizing a whole series of social relations that made up a polity. Romans 13.1, could be used to justify the divine right of all lawfully constituted authority, including judges and other inferior magistrates. Divine right could be claimed, for instance, in support of the authority of fathers over their families, a doctrine developed in Robert Filmer's *Patriarcha*, written in the 1630s but not published until 1680, to justify kingly power by the paternal comparison. But if divine rights other than those of the king could be cited, then divine right might be invoked to limit, as well as to defend or enlarge, royal power. Acts chapter 5 verse 29 ('Then Peter and the other apostles answered and said, We ought to obey God rather than men') was widely seen as an instruction to place the law of God above human law when the two came into conflict; this was the manner in which it featured in the Church's *Homily of Obedience*.[2] Hence opponents of Charles I in the 1640s tended not to deny divine right theory as such but to accuse the king of abusing it and of betraying the trust placed in him by God.

The execution of Charles I in 1649, however, provided divine right theorists with a royal martyr and the anniversary of his execution, 30 January, became an official day of fasting and humiliation in the Anglican calendar until its removal from the *Book of Common Prayer* in 1859. Sermons preached on 30 January, and on 29 May, the date of Charles II's return to England in 1660, made heavy use of the texts cited above. Comparisons between Charles I and Christ, although sometimes seen as

2. Russell, pp. 118-20.

bordering on the blasphemous, were common between 1660 and 1800. So too were denunciations of the evils of rebellion. In 1661 John Paradise preached on the text 1 Sam. 24.6, 'The Lord forbid that I should do this thing unto my master, the Lord's anointed, to stretch forth mine hand against him, seeing he is the anointed of the Lord.' Similarly, David's refusal to assassinate Saul, recounted in 1 Sam. 26.9 ('Destroy him not: for who can stretch forth his hand against the Lord's anointed and be guiltless'), was used to excoriate the regicide of 1649. Charles I was also compared to Josiah, the only Jewish king in the Old Testament who was both approved by God and who met a violent death. The texts cited by those drawing this comparison included 2 Chron. 25.25, and Zech. 12.11, and they may be found, for instance, in the anonymously published *The Subjects Sorrow: Or Lamentations upon the Death of Britains Josiah King Charles* (1649). A little over 30 years later the poet laureate John Dryden drew heavily on 2 Sam. 15–18 for his verse epic *Absalom and Achitophel*, which relates the triumph of Charles II over his opponents in the Exclusion Crisis of 1679–81, thinly disguised as David's victory over unlawful rebellion:

> Once more the godlike David was restored,
> And willing nations knew their lawful lord.

Allied to divine right theory was the thaumaturgical power, the belief that divine right manifested itself in the monarch's ability to heal by the royal touch the tubercular condition known as scrofula, or the 'king's evil'. It was an obvious, if limited, imitation of Christ's healing of the sick. The practice in England continued until the death of Queen Anne in 1714; one of those whom she touched, unsuccessfully, for the king's evil, was the two-year-old Samuel Johnson. However, with the Hanoverian succession the ceremony was abandoned, since George I and his heirs were kings by parliamentary designation under the terms of the Act of Settlement (1701), and more than 50 Catholic Stuarts with a stronger claim to the throne had been set aside in their favour. It is noteworthy that the Stuarts in exile after 1688 maintained the royal touch, as a signal to their Jacobite followers of their retention of the status of *de jure* monarchs, and the practice was also continued under the Bourbon monarchy in eighteenth-century France.

The effective deposition of James II in 1688, and the failure of attempts to restore him to his throne, have been depicted as a mortal blow to divine right theory in England. After all, James II had succeeded to his kingdom by hereditary right and the legitimacy of his dynastic succession was unimpeachable. Yet he had been forced to flee from his dominions and his daughter Mary and son-in-law William of Orange were installed in his stead—and during his lifetime. Most clergy of the Church of England, however, were quick to come to terms with these events, arguing plausibly that James II had been laid low not by a rebellion of his subjects—making the crucial contrast with 1649—but by a foreign (Dutch) invasion guided to British shores by a divine wind, in order to save the Protestant English from the horrors of Catholicism. The date of William's landing at Torbay in 1688, 5 November, as well as the anniversary of the Gunpowder Plot of 1605, became a further occasion for commemorative sermons, in this instance for the denunciation of popery. Apologists for divine right theory began to formulate a 'divine right of providence', whereby unjust kings may be punished by God by deprivation and their successors approved by God. In 1691, Bishop William Lloyd published a sermon entitled *God's Ways of disposing of Kingdoms* on the text of Ps. 75.7-8: 'For promotion cometh neither from the east nor from the west, nor from the south. But God is the judge: he putteth down one, and setteth up another.' Gilbert Burnet, a vigorous adherent of the new regime, who soon became bishop of Salisbury, preached a sermon on 23 December 1688 with the text 'This is the Lord's doing; it is marvellous in our eyes' (Ps. 118.23).

The essence of the 'divine right of providence' lay in its denial that an internal rebellion had taken place in 1688 and that any future rebellion could be justified. This argument carried wide appeal. Former supporters of James II, mainly Tory, had been alienated by his pro-Catholic policies and transferred their loyalty, uneasily, to William and Mary and, with more warmth, to Queen Anne. Adherents of William and Mary, mainly Whig, had no wish to undermine a doctrine that, reinforced by biblical sanction and preached to the unlettered, gave them a powerful protection against any subsequent insurrection. In 1714 the Presbyterian minister Samuel Rosewell, in a sermon entitled *The King's True Divine Right*, took as his text Ps. 132.17-18: 'I have ordained a Lamp for mine anointed: his enemies will I clothe with shame: but upon himself shall his Crown flourish.' But Rosewell emphasized that divine providence could, in certain circumstances, override the indefeasible hereditary right embodied in primogeniture: 'God himself did not please to regard it, when He preferred Jacob to Esau, Judah to Reuben, Saul, who descended from Benjamin, the youngest of Jacob's sons; and David and Solomon, to others of their Brethren superior in Age' (p. 8). Moreover, the evidence of the Old Testament showed that on several occasions God inflicted the severest punishment upon those monarchs who infringed his laws. Ahab been delivered to his (Syrian) enemies in battle (1 Kgs 22); Saul strayed from God's law and was consequently rejected by him (1 Sam. 15.26; 16.1); Solomon's pursuit of idolatry resulted in God's decision to 'rend the kingdom' out of his hands (1 Kgs 11.11). Rosewell was expressing a widely held view when he declared that James II, by departing from God's law, had deservedly met a similar, if more merciful, fate.

The accession of George I in 1714 certainly altered perceptions of divine right theory, but did not destroy its credibility or its appeal. It was, for instance, kept alive by the non-jurors, whose consciences prevented them from taking oaths of allegiance to the new regimes in 1688 and 1714, and whose opinions were exemplified in the writings of George Hickes, Charles Leslie, William Law and Thomas Hearne. It was also sustained by the Jacobite movement in the British Isles and in exile. Not until the aftermath of the death of Charles Edward Stuart in 1788 was the Scottish Episcopalian Church, for instance, persuaded to pray for George III rather than for 'Charles III'. The English non-juror Thomas Brett claimed also a divine right of episcopacy in order to justify the independent spiritual authority of bishops, citing Mt. 16.18 ('Thou art Peter and upon this rock I will build my church') and Acts 2.47. Moreover the Hanoverian regime itself had every reason to draw to itself at least some trappings of divine right theory, especially as it faced a serious Jacobite rebellion in 1715–16, before it had time to consolidate its position. Although George I and George II were unmistakably monarchs by parliamentary choice, they too, like William and Mary, were presented by some clergymen as rulers by divine providence. At the coronation of George I, William Talbot, bishop of Oxford, presented the new monarch as a deliverer, with the text 'Blessed be he that cometh in the name of the Lord' (Ps. 118.26). For the coronation of George II in 1727 Handel composed four anthems, including *Zadok the Priest*, based on the story of the anointing of Solomon in 1 Kgs 1. The clear implication was that the choice of God and of the people was the same (1 Kgs 1.39-40) and that the will of God was recognized by the acclamation of the populace.

This argument had already been developed in a series of important sermons by the Presbyterian minister Thomas Bradbury. As a Dissenter and Whig, he was particularly committed to the Hanoverian succession. But in *The Divine Right of Kings enquir'd into* (1718) he rejected non-resistance and passive obedience as unjustified in Scripture and denied that the key biblical texts supported indefeasible hereditary divine right. He continued: 'These are not the doctrines of the Bible: That throws no Loads upon your Liberties. It may teach you how to *bear* them, but it will hath no share in *laying them on*' (pp. 9-10). He observed that when Saul became king in Israel there was no inconsistency between 1 Sam. 10.24 ('See ye him whom the Lord hath chosen') and 1 Sam. 11.15 ('And all the people went to Gilgal; and there they made Saul king'). Similarly, David was chosen by God (1 Sam. 16.12) and was subsequently anointed king by the men of Judah (2 Sam. 2.4). Significantly, Bradbury also denied that the Bible demonstrated that monarchy was the only form of government that was pleasing to God: 'Whilst the Judges governed Israel, the Lord was with the Judge' was his close paraphrase of Judges 2, verse 18. Had not the divine favour smiled upon the (Protestant) United Provinces, with their republican form of government, in their successful revolt against Spanish rule? And the (Protestant) cantons of Switzerland had shown that God 'has given us no Model of a Constitution, nor laid the Bible open to the Charge of Impertinence; as it must have been, had it controul'd the different ways of thinking that Nations have got into for so many Years, and beaten them into one scheme' (pp. 15-16). Divine right was open to libertarian as well as authoritarian interpretations, and the invocation of *vox populi, vox dei* continued to exert a considerable appeal. But Bradbury and others did not extend the right of rebellion to those who might seek to overthrow the monarchy that divine providence had conferred upon Britain. In a sermon preached before the House of Lords on 29 May 1749 Edward Cresset, bishop of Llandaff, chose as his text Ps. 66.7: 'He ruleth by his power for ever; his eyes behold the nations: let not the rebellious exalt themselves.' The allusion to the unsuccessful Jacobite rising of 1745–46 could hardly be missed.

In 1767, Robert Lowth, bishop of Oxford, repeated one aspect of Bradbury's interpretation of divine right theory, albeit in a more conservative form: 'Government in general is the ordinance of God: the particular Form of Government is the ordinance of man'.[3] However, Lowth added that 'It is the duty of every individual to acquiesce in that form of government under which Providence hath placed him.' By the time of the accession of George III in 1760 very few doubted that, although other forms of government were theoretically acceptable in the eyes of God, England had been providentially blessed with a Protestant monarchy, under which liberty and property were protected, wars were generally successful and commerce was expanded. Moreover, with the fading of Jacobitism, George III attracted the allegiance of former Tories who had remained aloof from recognizing either of his two predecessors as anything but *de facto* rulers. The high churchman George Horne, for instance, regularly preached on the familiar texts to elevate the monarchy of George III. At an assize sermon at Oxford

3.   Quoted in Hole, p. 15.

in 1769 he took as his text the first words of Rom. 13.4: 'He is the minister of God to thee for good.' On 25 October 1788, the anniversary of the accession of George III, Horne, by this time dean of Canterbury, preached on 1 Tim. 2.1-2.

By the later eighteenth century, as J.C.D. Clark has convincingly argued, a modified form of divine right theory had evolved, extolling not solely the person of the monarch but the social and political structure of government at all levels, as well as existing distinctions of rank and wealth (Clark, pp. 256-84). It claimed divine sanction for the nature of society as a whole, with the Hanoverian monarchy as its legitimate head. Such texts as Mt. 22.21 ('Render unto Caesar the things which are Caesar's') were cited in its support. It remained very strongly providential, owed much to the 'great chain of being' and drew on biblical notions of a 'chosen people' to emphasize the peculiar blessings divinely conferred upon the English. The king was 'the focus and standard of civic and religious virtue'.[4] When the Tory high churchman Samuel Johnson composed two sermons for his friend the Rev. John Taylor of Ashbourne, he chose as his texts Prov. 29.2 ('When the righteous are in authority, the people rejoice') and Jas 3.16 ('where envying and strife is, there is confusion and every evil work'). The first of these sermons, appropriately, was to be preached on an anniversary of 30 January.

This 'transference' of divine right theory from the royal person to the hierarchy of which the monarch was the head was undoubtedly stimulated by the political circumstances of the years immediately after 1760. New challenges to authority seemed to threaten the religious as well as the secular order. In England, popular agitation associated with the issues raised by John Wilkes, himself a notoriously irreligious individual, directed an insulting antagonism towards king and clergy. In the empire, the prospect, followed by the reality, of rebellion in the North American colonies led to nervous comparisons with the 1640s. The disputes over the right of Britain to tax its colonies led to debates over sovereignty that in turn revived earlier controversies over divine right theory. In the 1770s the sermons preached by Anglican clergymen on 30 January invoked the sinfulness of rebellion with renewed vehemence. The first four verses of Luke 2 were held up as evidence of the appropriateness of paying taxes. In *The Bible and the Sword* (1776) John Fletcher of Madeley, a leading follower of John Wesley, drew upon Judges 20 to vindicate the British policy of coercion towards the colonies and the day of fasting that had been proclaimed by George III

4. Clark, p. 267.

to supplicate for divine assistance in the war. Of the 95 sermons examined by Henry Ippel between 1776 and 1783 that mentioned the war, 79 supported the British government; most did so by citation from the traditional texts beloved of divine right theorists (Ippel 1982–83: 197 n. 37). When in 1775 the Epistle from the Yearly Meeting of the Society of Friends in London restated its pacifist convictions and refused to countenance the American rebellion, it quoted Acts 23.5, in which St Paul, brought before the high priest, reminds his listeners: 'It is written, Thou shalt not speak evil of the ruler of thy people.' The following year James Smith lamented, with Isa. 1.2, that 'I have nourished and brought up children, and they have rebelled against me.' Clergy who deplored what they regarded as the perversion of traditional liberty into licence and anarchy found 1 Pet. 2.16 ('As free and not using your liberty for a cloke of maliciousness') particularly congenial.

Sermons of the 1770s that denounced the War of American Independence as a distressing and unnecessary civil conflict rather than as a sinful rebellion also drew upon biblical inspiration. Most of them were preached either by Dissenters or by low church Anglican clergy. On many occasions the war was directly compared to episodes in the Old Testament, such as the civil war between Israel and the Benjaminites in the book of Judges. As John Duncombe put it in a sermon of 1778, 'Just as Israel went against their brother and was discomfited, so too Britain has been discomfited in its war with its American brethren'.[5] Familiar scriptural parallels with unjust rulers reappeared. In 1781 the Baptist minister Rees David of Norwich compared the British government's treatment of its American colonies with Ahab's seizure of Naboth's vineyard (I Kgs) and likened Ahab's court to the British cabinet. The Presbyterian James Murray of Newcastle upon Tyne went further, quoting Eccl. 10.16, 'Woe to thee, O land, when thy king is a child, and thy princes eat in the morning.' While acknowledging that George III was hardly a child (the king was 43 in 1781) he identified the 'princes who eat in the morning' with the king's ministers, particularly Lord North and the American Secretary Lord George Germain.[6] The British defeat in the war, with its enormous financial cost, was widely attributed to divine punishment for *hubris*, the sin of overweening pride.

A measure of the gradual decline of appeals to divine right theory in the later eighteenth century is seen in the way in which few senior clergy who

---

5.   Quoted in Ippel, 'American Sermon', p. 199.
6.   Ippel, p. 200.

preached the statutory 30 January sermon before the House of Lords and the House of Commons treated Charles I as a martyr. Some of these sermons, such as that of George Pretyman, bishop of Lincoln, in 1789, strongly condemned Charles I for misusing his power in order to establish absolutism and popery. It has been suggested by Robert Hole, moreover, that by the beginning of the nineteenth century arguments that were predominantly religious in nature were yielding to arguments that were broadly secular in the ideological canon of those who sought to justify the existing order. Utilitarianism and political economy, as it were, replaced, or at least reinforced, religious arguments, of which divine right theory had been in the forefront. Louis XVI of France, executed in 1793, never achieved the halo of martyrdom that surrounded Charles I. The speed of this process should not be over-estimated. The French Revolution gave rise to another outpouring of sermons extolling social subordination and their preachers found the key texts of the divine right theorists highly suitable for their purpose. Traditional critics of Catholicism compared the overthrow of the Papacy by French revolutionary armies in 1799–1800 to the apocalyptic events described in the book of Revelation. English society remained one in which Bible reading continued to permeate the culture of the elite and of the populace. Critics of divine right theory characteristically tried to refute or reinterpret it by appealing to, not by repudiating, biblical authority. But it was difficult on moral as well as political grounds to apply divine right theory to the monarchy when it was represented by George IV, either as Regent (1811–20) or as King (1820–30). When George III, blind and mentally incapable, died in January 1820, his reputation for personal conscientiousness and for the promotion of virtue led to comparisons between his funeral rites and the obsequies for Old Testament kings. 2 Chron. 32.33, describing the honours paid to Hezekiah on his death, was used as the text of the sermon preached by William Dealtry at Clapham on the day of George III's funeral. Another preacher chose 1 Chron. 29.28, describing how David 'died in a good old age, full of days, riches and honour'. Sermons such as these naturally embodied a valedictory note; however, they were sounding the knell not only for an old and popular king, but also for the doctrine that had buttressed his and preceding dynasties for so long.

BIBLIOGRAPHY

For the primary texts cited in this essay, the reader is advised to consult the *Eighteenth-Century Short Title Catalogue* and the British Library catalogue. The most helpful secondary works include:

Cooke, John, *The Preacher's Assistant* (2 vols.; Oxford, 1782–83).

Clark, J.C.D., *English Society 1660–1832: Religion, Ideology and Politics during the Ancien Regime* (Cambridge: Cambridge University Press, 2000).

Figgis, Neville J., *The Divine Right of Kings* (Cambridge: Cambridge University Press, 1896).

Hole, Robert, *Pulpits, Politics and Public Order in England 1760–1832* (Cambridge: Cambridge University Press, 1989).

Ippel, Henry P., 'Blow the Trumpet, Sanctify the Fast', *Huntington Library Bulletin*, 44 (1980), pp. 43-60.

—'British Sermons and the American Revolution', *JRH* 12 (1982–83), pp. 191-205.

Russell, Conrad, 'Divine Rights in the Early Seventeenth Century', in John Morrill, Paul Slack and Daniel Woolf (eds.), *Public Duty and Private Conscience in Seventeenth-Century England* (Oxford: Clarendon Press, 1993), pp. 101-120.

Sack, James J., *From Jacobite to Conservative: Reaction and Orthodoxy in Britain, c.1760–1832* (Cambridge: Cambridge University Press, 1993).

Straka, G.M., 'The Final Phase of Divine Right Theory in England, 1688–1702', *English Historical Review* 77 (1962), pp. 638-58.

BLAKE AND THE BIBLE:
BIBLICAL EXEGESIS IN THE WORK OF WILLIAM BLAKE

Christopher Rowland

Editor's Introduction

If we try to polarize fundamentalist responses to the Bible and liberal readings of the text, this would be an oversimplification; although the contrast between the extremes of submission to dictation and independent creativity does frame the field of reference. William Blake clearly belonged to the tradition that made room for the human imagination as part of the divine story: poets and storytellers, inspired by the Bible, plundered its riches seemingly for their own ends, but paid homage to it by constantly creating new meanings around it.

Peter Ackroyd opens his recent biography of Blake *(London: Sinclair-Stevenson, 1995, p. 25) in this way:*

> It has been said that there is nothing in Blake's work which is not first to be found in the Bible; it is an overstatement, but it does emphasise an important truth. His poetry and painting are imbued with biblical motifs and images; the very curve and cadence of his sentences are derived from the Old Testament, while his passages of ritualistic description and denunciation come from the words of the great prophets that were heard in the house in Broad Street [in London where his parents who were Dissenters lived].

It was Blake's dictum that 'the whole Bible is filled with Imagination and Visions'. Divine communication should be seen as closer to the work of poetry or the artistic media. Blake regarded Jesus and the apostles all as artists: a view that might seem, at least to conservative Evangelicals, to make divine revelation rest upon the shifting sands of human subjectivity. In David Scott's words: '...the biblical sources make a kind of contemplative sense, but Blake skews the meaning, and adapts and adds a private language, until the mood is changed to something more sinister, emptied of the accessible, incarnate Christ.'

Like his 1997 Ethel M. Wood Lecture, this study starts from his perspective as commentator on the book of Revelation and writer on radically political interpretations of prophetic texts.

1. *Introduction*

William Blake is an interpreter whose work is not likely to be found among those recommended for study by students of the Bible. Like his great contemporary S.T. Coleridge, however, he stands at the transition to what we know as historical criticism. His method is never systematic and is governed by spontaneity, insight and intuition, not to mention vision. It is captured in a rather dusty response to an enquirer who suggested that Blake offered an explanation of his poetry and illuminated texts. As the following extract from the letter Blake wrote in response indicates, the explanatory is seen by Blake as reductive. What is important about a text is its allusiveness, its capacity to speak afresh in every situation in which the defined and precise cannot do. Texts that allow the 'spirit' to be available rather than confine the reader to the 'letter' are those that stimulate the imagination and open the way to the divine. This the Bible did better than any other book (as Coleridge was to put it a little later, 'in the Bible there is more that finds me than I have experienced in all other books put together'). He challenged the subservience to memory rather than allowing imagination to flourish:

> You say that I want somebody to elucidate my ideas. But you ought to know that what is grand is necessarily obscure to weak men. That which can be made explicit to the idiot is not worth my care. The wisest of the ancients consider'd what is not too explicit as the fittest for instruction, because it rouzes the faculties to act. I name Moses, Solomon, Esop, Homer, Plato... Why is the Bible more Entertaining & Instructive than any other book ? Is it not because they are addressed to the Imagination, which is Spiritual Sensation and but mediately to the understanding or reason... (Letter to Trusler K793-94).

This essay has two parts. In the first I shall examine Blake's use of particular biblical themes and their significance for biblical interpretation. I start with Blake's prophecy and in particular focus on the vision of God enthroned in glory. I shall suggest that Blake's caricature of the enthroned divinity in his *Europe A Prophecy* was part of his challenge to dominant conceptions of God in a way that parallels John's vision of the Lamb and the throne in the book of Revelation. Both John's and Blake's apocalyptic prophecies offer a transformed perspective on divine monarchy. I shall move on to explore Blake's approach to the two testaments and the way in which he sets up a dialectic between old and new revelations in ways similar to that found in the Pauline corpus. I conclude the first part of this essay with a look at the significance of Blake's relationship with Milton's writing, and the way Blake explores the redemptive possibilities which take place through creative rereading of an earlier author. In the second part of the essay I shall offer some reflections on the hermeneutical opportunities and challenges of Blake's reading of Scripture.

2. *'Would to God That All the Lord's People Were Prophets'*

William Blake was a visionary[1]. He communed with angels and even his dead brother regularly. Early biographers report that he saw his first vision when he saw on Peckham Rye a tree filled with angels. Blake was suspicious of memory, by which he meant the mere repetition of that which was received without that enhancement of that which has been received through the creativity of the visionary imagination. Blake thought of himself as standing in a tradition of prophets. In the Preface to *Milton* he quotes Numbers 11.29: 'Would to God that all the Lord's people were prophets.' The sense of prophetic vocation and insight equips Blake to offer the meaning of contemporary events, like the biblical prophecies against the nations. Indeed, he recognizes the prophets of the Bible as kindred spirits (after all in *The Marriage of Heaven and Hell* he dines with Isaiah and Ezekiel). The major hero of his own idiosyncratic myth is Los, a figure whose prophetic role is thoroughly explored. Blake can write in their style and use their images.

Blake's prophecies were not intended to predict exactly what would happen, for they were written after the events that are described, as he puts it succinctly in a marginal note he wrote in 1798:

> Prophets in the modern sense of the word have never existed. Jonah was no prophet, in the modern sense, for his prophecy of Nineveh failed. Every honest man is a prophet; he utters his opinion both of private and public matters. Thus: If you go on So, the result is So. He never says, such a thing shall happen let you do what you will. A Prophet is a Seer, not an Arbitrary Dictator (Annotations Watson K392).

The prophecies lay bare the inner dynamic, of history and revolution, the potential for positive change that exists and the corruption of those impulses. Any revolutionary optimism that Blake may have harboured in the last decade of the eighteenth century is tempered by a need to plumb the complexities of the human personality and its succumbing to the 'dark delusions' of the world in which religion and theology have all too often

---

1. G.E. Bentley, *The Stranger from Paradise: A Biography of William Blake* (New Haven: Yale University Press, 2001).

played their part. Europe, a continent that was to be briefly lit with the flame of revolution, is seen as sleepy and immune to this spirit of change.[2] Europe is entangled in a religion and an ethic that made it impervious to revolutionary change, a dreamy world cut off from reality. Revolution would only produce 'the strife of blood' not the bliss of Paradise. The coming of Christ heralds not only the blissful salvation of the Lamb but the wrath of the 'Tyger', to use Blake's contrasting images in S*ongs of Innocence and Experience*. This parallels the awesome consequences of the exaltation of the Lamb in Revelation 5, which results in the cataclysmic apocalypse described in the following chapters. The prophet must speak, but it is no privileged role, for, as Blake's Isaiah puts it in *The Marriage of Heaven and Hell*, ' "the voice of honest indignation" [which] is the voice of God, who cares "not for consequences but wrote" ', echoing Jeremiah's words in Jer. 20.9.

In the 'Preface to Milton we find some of the recurring themes of Blake's writing: his campaign against an education based solely on memory rather than inspiration and his conviction that the domination of classical culture had quenched the vitality of biblical inspiration'.[3] The New Jerusalem is not something remote or far off but a possibility, something that may be built in England's green and pleasant land. There is not a disjunction between human activity and divine activity in bringing it about. God is involved through the imaginative and creative work of the artist. There is an application of the texts to the writer and his contemporaries. Elijah's chariot is not just part of past history or even future expectation, but something that can be the inspiration of a new Elijah in every generation who is willing to condemn the Baalism of a contemporary culture and politics, which, according to Blake, had led to the capitulation of Christianity to a religion of virtues, rules and the acceptance of war and violence. The spirit and power of Elijah were ever available for those who would exercise their imagination and contemplative thought.[4] Prophecy is

2.   See L. Tannenbaum, *Biblical Tradition in Blake's Early Prophecies: The Great Code of Art* (Princeton, NJ: Princeton University Press, 1982), p. 168; C. Burdon,*The Apocalypse in England: Revelation Unravelling, 1700–1834* (London: Macmillan, 1997), pp. 180-208; and M.J. Tolley 'Europe "to those ychaind in sleep" ', in D. Erdman and J. Grant, *Blake's Visionary Forms Dramatic* (Princeton, NJ: Princeton University Press, 1970), pp. 115-45.

3.   N. Goslee, ' "In England's green & pleasant land": The Building of Vision in Blake's Stanzas from *Milton*', *Studies in Romanticism* 13 (1974), pp. 105-25.

4.   'Los is the spirit of prophecy, the ever apparent Elijah' ('Milton' 24.71; *Jerusalem* 44.31; *Marriage of Heaven and Hell* 24; Byron is hailed as Elijah in 'Ghost of Abel').

not a thing of the past, for it is the vocation of *all* people.[5] The vision of
the new Jerusalem is one that is open to all and the task of building
belongs to all. What is not often noticed in this poem is its context and the
contrasts within it. It is based on a contrast between what is actually the
case and what might be. The contrast between the implied question of the
opening lines becomes explicit at the beginning of the second stanza and
the hope for Jerusalem in this green and pleasant land. What is needed for
that hope to be fulfilled is not just honest endeavour, but 'Mental Fight'.
The use of military imagery here reflects Eph. 6.10, a favourite passage of
Blake that he quotes as a preface to his long poem *The Four Zoas*. 'Mental Fight' is the process of challenging the way in which dominant patterns
of thinking and behaving make it difficult for all God's people to be prophets. The 'satanic Mills' is the grinding logic of the reason of the philosophers, which has to be overcome to allow imagination to flourish in the
spirit of biblical religion.

    In a typically idiosyncratic interpretation of Rev. 14.14-19, Blake's paint-
ing of William Pitt, 'The Spiritual Form of Pitt guiding Behemoth' (Tate
Gallery, London) together with its companion, 'The Spiritual Form of
Nelson guiding Leviathan', Blake sees Pitt as the destroying angel of Rev.
14.14. The war with France is seen as an apocalyptic event. They are seen
to be agents of the divine will, much like Assyria in Isa. 10.1 or Cyrus in
Isa. 45.1-4. Remarkably, given Blake's political inclinations, these figures
are not particularly demonic but are (albeit unknown to themselves) agents
of judgment (this is a theme that runs right the way through the often complicated continental prophecies, 'America' and 'Europe').

3. *The Vision of God*

The Apocalypse of Enoch, brought back from Ethiopia, where it had been
preserved by the Ethiopian Church, was first published at the beginning of
the nineteenth century. It is a book that has fascinated and tantalized biblical scholars ever since because of the many similarities with the passages
in the gospels, particularly the references to the Son of man, and many commentators have suggested that Jesus and the earliest Christians may have
drawn on it . Blake left illustrations for it incomplete at his death in 1827
(though he may have been aware of the book and had access to excerpts of
translations from it years before).[6] One can understand why this enigmatic

5.   Burdon, *The Apocalypse in England*, p. 181.
6.   J. Beer, 'Blake's Changing View of History: The Impact of the Book of Enoch',

work should have fascinated Blake. It is a visionary work full of the mythological approach to the world, which characterizes much of Blake's poetry.
Its doctrine of the origin of human sin, in contrast with that in Genesis,
ascribes the primal sin to the illicit communication of wisdom that cor-
rupts humanity (*1 En.* 6–18 parallel to Gen. 6).[7] Angels teach humanity
charms and spells and the art of warfare. The result is, as *1 Enoch* puts it,
that 'the world was profoundly changed'. In consequence judgment comes
on those who had revealed illicit wisdom and on those who had colluded
with them. Enoch, who is considered a prophet in the New Testament
Letter of Jude, is commissioned to intercede between God and the angels
(*1 En.* 12.1). He appears as a mysterious figure standing on the boundary
between angels and humans with access to divine secrets, a 'steward of
the mysteries of God' (1 Cor. 4.1), a situation not unlike that in which
Blake found himself.

Among the unfinished sketches there is one of *1 En.* 14.8-20, a chapter
that has exercised the minds of students of Second Temple Judaism, because it offers an extended description of the vision of God, the Great
Glory, enthroned in the inmost recesses of the heavenly Temple. *1 Enoch*
14 is full of imagery borrowed from Ezekiel 1, itself a chapter that became
the basis for later visionaries to glimpse again the awesome vision that
had appeared to the prophet by the waters of Babylon. The first chapter of
Ezekiel exercised Blake's imagination and was the inspiration of his poem
The Four Zoas or *Vala*. In addition he captures the vision in visual form in
'Ezekiel's Wheels'. What is striking about this picture is the prominence
of the human figure among the four creatures (man, lion, ox and eagle)
that surround the divine throne-chariot.

The narrative of the transformation of divine monarchy begun in the
vindication of a slaughtered lamb in Revelation 5 in some ways anticipates
Blake's parody of the monarchical law-giver and the need for an understanding of God that is less abstract and remote. Blake ruthlessly parodies
the remote deity in Plate 11 from *Europe*, with his 'brazen Book That
Kings and Priests had copied on Earth, Expanded from North to South'.
Here the grim law-giver appears with his forbidding book of brass. It is
that kind of theology that Blake repeatedly challenges, nowhere better

in S. Clark and D. Worrall, *Historicizing Blake* (Basingstoke: Macmillan, 1994), pp.
159. On the importance of *4 Ezra* or 2 Esdras for the exponents of radical Christianity,
see A. Hamilton, *Apocryphal Apocalypse* (Oxford: Oxford University Press 1999).

7.   M. Barker, *The Older Testament* (London: SPCK, 1987).

demonstrated than in his 'Job' sequence.[8] The one enthroned is the power that holds humanity in thrall through a religion of law. It is the stern words 'Thou shalt not' that determine life rather than mutual forgiveness. This is characteristic of the religion of Europe, dominated by a remote deity too exalted to wipe tears from eyes. For Blake the worship of God involves a recognition of God not as remote divinity, such as he captured so tellingly in his 'Ancient of Days', which forms part of the preface to *Europe a Prophecy*, but in the person of other men and women who embody the divine image: 'The worship of God is Honouring his gifts in other men each according to his genius…' (*The Marriage of Heaven and Hell* 22).

John's apocalyptic vision is a central component of many aspects of Blake's visionary world and also informs his understanding of his own political situation. As he put it in 1798 in his annotations to his copy of Bishop Watson's 'Apology for the Bible', 'To defend the Bible in this year 1798 would cost a man his life. The Beast and the Whore rule without control' (K383). Indeed, Blake explicitly traces a continuity between his own mythical world and the vision seen by John, as he makes clear at the conclusion of the Eighth Night of *The Four Zoas*:

> Rahab triumphs over all; she took Jerusalem Captive a Willing Captive by delusive arts impell'd To worship Urizen's Dragon form, to offer her own Children Upon the bloody Altar. John saw these things Reveal'd in Heaven On Patmos Isle, & heard the souls cry out to be deliver'd. He saw the Harlot of the Kings of Earth, & saw her Cup Of fornication, food of Orc & Satan, pressd from the fruit of Mystery (*Four Zoas* 8.597-603).

Nevertheless, as is evident from the previous quotation, Blake's use of the Apocalypse represents a visionary continuity with the text rather than a commentary or analysis of it. He stands in the prophetic tradition of which John of Patmos also is a part, whose harsh indignation might enable humans to see that 'every Kindness to another is a little death in the Divine Image, nor can man exist but by Brotherhood' (Jerusalem 95.28).

4. *The Old and New Testaments*

Blake described 'the Old and New Testaments as 'the great code of art' (*Laocoön* K775). Yet in his work he offers a radical critique of aspects of Old Testament religion, particularly of law and sacrifice. His is an ambiva-

---

8.   William Blake, *Blake's Illustrations for the Book of Job* (New York: Dover, 1995), cf. *Book of Urizen* 4 where the book of brass concerns 'one King, one God one Law'.

lent relationship with the Old Testament. At first sight his portrayal of the law-giving deity, called in his peculiar mythology Urizen (or Your—Reason) seems to be the Old Testament deity in Satanic guise (as is particularly evident in illustration to Job 7.14), a throwback to some second-century Gnostic theology. Blake, however, uses his stark contrasts between the religion of the Old and New Testament as a heuristic device to illuminate the antinomies in the human personality and the way society exploits a religion of law to deny imagination and mutual forgiveness. With this aim, Blake probes the fissures in the depiction of God within the narrative of Genesis,[9] partly to challenge dominant readings of the Bible of his day, in which appeal to an authoritative book was used to inculcate a particular form of moral virtue. Blake, heir to Protestant radical writing in England of an antinomian kind,[10] considered a religion based on rules, contrary to the religion of Jesus. In *The Marriage of Heaven and Hell* Jesus exemplifies the protest against the religion of rules:

> …did he not mock at the sabbath, and so mock the sabbath's God ?…turn away the law from the woman taken in adultery ? steal the labour of others to support him ? bear false witness when he omitted making a defence before Pilate ? covet when he pray'd for his disciples, and when he bid them shake off the dust from their feet against such as refused to lodge them ? I tell you, no virtue can exist without breaking these ten commandments. Jesus was all virtue, & acted from impulse, not from rules' (*Marriage of Heaven and Hell* 24).

Blake wrote books that parody the Pentateuch, particularly the account of creation. *The Book of Urizen* is the best example. Existing as it does in different versions, Blake wants to deny readers recourse to one authoritative text and, in a manner that has a very postmodern ring to it, challenges the notion of a hegemonic text. Blake subverts the elevation of Scripture into a text that, in a transparent manner, could transmit a list of moral rules demanded of the believer.[11]

The critique of a religion of law, and the pre-eminence of the prophetic and the visionary, both contribute to Blake's remarkable exegesis of the

---

9. Blake exploited the Yahweh/Elohim distinctions long before the source critical solutions of the Pentateuch became fashionable and was probably indebted to the source criticism of Alexander Geddes see J. Mee, *Dangerous Enthusiasm* (Oxford: Oxford University Press, 1990), pp. 165-66.

10. E.P. Thompson, *Witness against the Beast William Blake and the Moral Law* (Cambridge: Cambridge University Press, 1993); C. Hill, *The World Turned Upside Down* (London: Penguin, 1972); and J.F. McGregor and B. Reay, *Radical Religion in the English Revolution* (Oxford: Oxford University Press, 1984).

11. J.L. McGann quoted in Mee, *Dangerous Enthusiasm*, p. 16.

book of Job, a project he completed only shortly before his death. We are assisted in understanding the theological significance of Blake's images of Job by virtue of the fact that, in addition to the watercolours, we have the later engravings in which he comments on what he has portrayed by reference to biblical passages.[12] For Blake Job is like the 'Lutheran Paul' who converts from book religion to the immediacy of vision. The religion of law and sacrifice is diabolical (we may note the contrast between Job sacrificing and praying in 1.5 and 42.8). The remote god of that kind of religion needs to be dethroned thereby enabling the annihilation of 'the selfhood of deceit and false forgiveness' (*Milton* 15). Job's conversion comes about as the result of visionary insight. Elihu bears witness to the importance of the visionary as a means of true understanding of God, anticipating the vision of God to Job, and the function of the Elihu sequence is seen as a precursor of the dramatic revelation to Job. The vision of God in the whirlwind is interpreted christologically as a vision of Jesus Christ (similarly also in the New Testament in Jn 14.8, the latter passage actually being

12.   Passages quoted in the engravings:

1.   1.1,5; Mt. 6.9; 2 Cor. 3.6; 1 Cor. 2.14.
2.   1.6-8; 19.26; Dan. 7.9; The Angel of the Divine Presence (cf 'Laocoön', The Angel of the Divine Presence & Gen. 16.7 & Lev. 20.1; Isa. 64.8; Ps. 17.15; Ps. 89.26 Job 29.5).
3.   1.18-19; 2.2; 1.12; 1.16.
4.   1.14-15; 1.7; 1.15-16.
5.   2.7 cf. 1.12; 2.6; 30.25; Ps. 104.4; Gen. 6.6.
6.   2.7: 1.21.
7.   2.12; 2.10; Jas 5.11.
8.   3.3; 2.13; 3.7.
9.   4.15; 4.17-18.
10.   19.21; 14.1-3; 12.4 c. Ps. 22.7; Job 13.15; 23.10.
11.   7.14; 19.22-27; 20.5; 30.17; 30.30 2 Cor. 11.14; 2 Thess. 2.4.
12.   32.6; 33.14-17; 33.23; 33.29-30; 34.21; 35. 5-7.
13.   38.1-2; 38.28; Ps. 104.3.
14.   38.7; 38.31; Gen. 1.3, 6, 9, 16, 20, 24.
15.   40.15, 19; 36.29; 37.11-12; 41.34.
16.   36.17; 11.7-8; 26.6; Rev. 12.10; Jn 12.31; Lk. 10.17-18; 1 Cor. 1.26-7.
17.   Job 42.5; 1 Sam. 2.6; 1 Jn 3.2; Ps. 8.3-4; Jn 10.30; 14.7, 9, 11, 16, 17, 20, 21, 23, 28.
18.   42.8, 9, 10; Mt. 5.44-5, 48.
19.   42.11; 1 Sam. 2.7; Job 38.41; Ps. 136.23.
20.   42.15; Ps. 139.8, 17; Test Job 46.
21.   42.12, 16, 17; Rev. 15.3; Heb. 10:6 cf Ps. 51.16.

quoted in Blake's engraving). Blake not only reads in his own interpretative agenda into the text of Job but brilliantly exploits the space offered by a text which is 'not too explicit' to read the book of Job as an account of a conversion not, as most modern commentators have done, as a profound disquisition about the problem of evil, a reading that has to ignore significant parts of this enigmatic text.[13] Blake's concern throughout the illustrations is to challenge the monarchical transcendent God of church and state and to stress the prominence that is to be given to the visionary element in religion. Job starts as an adherent of a religion of the letter who is overwhelmed by apocalypse and converted to a religion of the spirit. Meanwhile the prophet had to contest the downgrading of imagination by attention to the 'minute particulars' of existence that could 'rouze the Faculties to act' (K793).

The Paul of Romans cannot bring himself to deny the importance of law (Rom 7.16) and yet he sees the emergence of another law that is at odds with the law of God. Paul cries out at the end of Romans 7 'who will rescue me from the body of death?' The spectre of the other law standing over against what the 'inner person' most desires is the object of Paul's critique, just as the Urizenic religion of repression and moral virtue was for Blake. In *Milton* Blake writes of the annihilation of selfhood (*Jerusalem* 45.13; *Milton* 17.3) that encourages a perverted religion of 'laws of chastity and sacrifice for sin (*Jerusalem* 49.24).[14] In Plate 15 of *Milton* the ancient code is finally fractured[15] as the Urizenic figure is confronted by a man to be redeemed under the caption 'to annihilate the selfhood of deceit and false forgiveness'. It is surrounded with minstrels suggesting rejoicing: 'there is joy among the angels in heaven over one sinner who repents' (Lk. 15.25; Exod. 15.20). Blake rejects sacrificial religion, which involves the denial of prophetic inspiration and the bondage of ceremonial law (*Book*

---

13.   Blake, *Book of Job*; M. Butlin, *The Paintings and Drawings of William Blake* (New Haven: Yale University Press, 1981); B. Lindberg, *William Blake's Illustrations to the Book of Job* (Åbo: Åbo Akademi, 1973); K. Raine, *The Human Face of God: Blake and the Book of Job* (London: Thames & Hudson, 1982); *idem, Golgonooza City of Imagination: Last Studies in William Blake*(Ipswich: Golgonooza, 1991), esp. pp. 121ff on Job; A. Wright, *Blake's Job: A Commentary* (Oxford: Clarendon Press, 1972).

14.   William Blake, *Milton, a Poem* (ed. R.N. Essick and J. Viscomi; Blake's Illuminated Books, 5; London: Blake Society; Tate Gallery, 1993), p. 12.

15.   The Hebrew letters on the tablets of stone makes no sense, apart from *tohu* suggesting chaos. Elsewhere blots and smudges are found in picture of book in Urizen 4 indicating that this book of brass really made no sense.

of Ahania 4 K252).[16] A religion of sacrifice and law, is, in Blake's view, a throwback to Canaanite theology, which contaminated Israel when it entered the promised land. It is sacrificial religion that Blake, by his own inspired rereading of Milton, seeks to expunge from the writing of his predecessor, much as New Testament writers sought to reclaim and redeem their literary ancestors in their formulation of their new redemptive vision.

Blake protests at the 'web of religion', the authoritarian religion of rules and memory, that has enslaved humanity, and so graphically evoked in these words: 'over the doors Thou shalt not; & over the chimneys fear is written' (*Europe* 12). Just as the relationship between Law and Gospel is a refrain in Paul's major letters, so throughout Blake's writing there is a probing of the relationship between the law-giver and the divine mercy, as well as the rational and the imaginative. While *The Marriage of Heaven and Hell* suggests that by temperament Blake sided with the prophetic, the hope expressed in Blake's *Jerusalem* is for an eschatological integration of imagination and reason when with true prophetic religion would be linked with that of Newton, Bacon and Locke, that trinity whose baleful influence, in Blake's view, epitomized the triumph of reason over imagination in the society of his day.

5. *Milton and Blake*

Blake was a creative, imaginative interpreter not a detailed exegete. He took earlier texts, whether biblical or otherwise, and allowed them to become part of his mental furniture and imaginative world. For him any rereading of an authoritative text is a creative process. This is exemplified in Blake's *Milton*. In this poem the living poet (Blake) takes up and reformulates the work of a deceased predecessor,[17] thereby through this second act of creativity to redeem the inadequacies of Milton's writing and life. *Milton* is in part a critique by Blake of the turn taken by the seventeenth-century poet to a religion of rules. But it is also a moment of inspired recapitulation in which the later poet redeems the earlier's work, initiated when Blake sees Milton's spirit enter into his left foot (*Milton* 14.49-50).

In *Milton*, there is confusion of identity between the writer and the ancient poet. The way in which the latter's artistic and personal redemption

---

16. Tannenbaum, *Blake's Early Prophecies*, pp. 233-34.

17. Blake, *Milton, a Poem*, p. 12: 'It is an existence Blake wished to overcome and replace with a more fluid and open concept of being where the gulf between self and other is bridged—indeed, annihilated.'

is effected has overlaps with themes in biblical texts where successors take up, take further, refine or even alter the work of a predecessor. Blake's relationship with Milton is a tandem relationship similar to those scattered throughout the Bible, whereby the persona or charisma of one is carried on and transformed in new situations. One thinks of Elijah and Elisha; John the Baptist and Jesus; and Jesus and the Spirit-Paraclete. Elisha asks Elijah to give him a double portion of his spirit (2 Kgs 2.9). In the case of Blake and Milton, however, the successor is more important than the predecessor and corrects the work of the earlier poet.

In the final section I want to look at the way in which Blake continues to offers readers a means whereby the imagination may itself be stimulated and assumptions challenged.

6. *The World of Imagination*

For Blake the visionary and imaginative is all important. Allowing reason to triumph over imagination denies a wisdom 'Permanent in the Imagination', through which one could be 'open [to] the Eternal Worlds'. Such access would be 'to open the immortal Eyes Of Man inwards into the Worlds of Thought, into Eternity Ever expanding in the Bosom of God, the Human Imagination' (*Jerusalem* 5.18). A 'mental fight' is required to gain access to that other perspective on existence, particularly given the dominant ideology, which militates against at it. This perspective can at once be a refuge and a resource for thinking and doing things differently. It is imperative that this is done, for, as Blake's prophetic hero Los asserts, 'I must Create a System. or be enslav'd by another Mans. I will not Reason and Compare: my Business is to Create' (*Jerusalem* 10.20). It is only by the suspension of what counts for normality that humanity may glimpse how 'the dark Religions might depart and sweet Science reign' (*Four Zoas* End of Night the Ninth).

So Blake invokes the exercise of the imagination. The vocation of the reader of the Bible is to become participants in mental agony which may confound and entices from habit and convention,[18] which stand like a closed door preventing access to that which is eternal. There is need for a hermeneutical conversion reminiscent of Paul's suggestion that what is required is not a preoccupation with the letter that kills (2 Cor. 3.6) but the Spirit who offers freedom and life (3.16). Readers are called like John in

---

18. On this see N. Frye, *Fearful Symmetry* (Princeton, NJ: Princeton University Press, 1947), pp. 3-7.

Revelation 4 to 'come up here, to go through an open door, and I will show you what must take place'. Indeed, the use of the door as an image of insight or incomprehension in several prints, for example *Jerusalem* frontispiece, 'America' Plate 14 *Songs of Experience*, 'London', and *Jerusalem* 84. In London and Jerusalem the old man (a symbol, perhaps, of the ancient deity and a tired culture) is led by a child. Blake's use of the child leading the old man, reminiscent of the use made by Jesus in Matthew 18 and 19, suggests that innate wisdom may need to guide the wisdom of experience and mere rote learning, to new and more wonderful insights. In a letter (Trusler K793-94), Blake suggests that 'a great majority of [children] are on the side of imagination or spiritual sensation' and 'take a greater delight in contemplating my pictures than I ever hoped'.[19]

Reading some of Blake's poems presents formidable problems for interpreters, particularly so with the illuminated books where the process of reading is complicated by the engagement with the visual images (the opening of *Europe A Prophecy* is a good example where text and illustration seem to have nothing to do with one another). Readings of the text must be set in the context of the illuminations. Here the problems start, for text and illumination seem to have little contact. We tend to link what we see with what we read. An early commentator, A. Swinburne,[20] wrote with regard to the opening page of *Europe* that 'the amount of connection between the texts and the designs... [is]...in effect about as small as possible'. As the poem goes on in both writing and illumination there is oscillation between the historical and the mythological with the boundaries between the two remaining constantly vague as Blake exemplifies the abrupt transitions from heaven to earth, so typical of prophetic writings. The readers/ beholder of Blake's illuminated text find themselves disconcerted, without a stable means of interpreting.[21] The indeterminate relationship between writing and illustration demands that readers engage with the text, and their own imagination contributes to making sense of

19. Children also appear in the two 'Holy Thursday' poems in *Songs of Innocence and Experience*, where Blake uses the images of the Apocalypse as a way of viewing contrasting scenes in contemporary London, see C. Rowland, ' "Rouzing the faculties to act": Apocalypse and the "Holy Thursday" Poems', in S. Brent Plate (ed.), *The Apocalyptic Imagination: Aesthetics and Ethics at the End of the World* (Glasgow: Trinity St Mungo Press, 1999), pp. 26-36.

20. A. Swinburne, *William Blake: A Critical Essay* (London: John Camden Hotten, 1868).

21. D.W. Dörrbecker (ed.), *William Blake The Continental Prophecies* (Blake's Illuminated Books, 4; London: Blake Society; Tate Gallery, 1995), p. 153.

the two.[22] There is no escape for the reader who is throughout encouraged to 'rouze the faculties to act' in order to find meaning in what is very deliberately 'not too explicit'. Blake wishes to do all he can to resist the idea that there is an authoritative interpretation offered by authoritative interpreters. His texts are there for all to use and to have their own imaginations stimulated.

There has been intensive investigation of the popular culture of the late eighteenth century[23] which has enabled one to see that Blake was not totally isolated and idiosyncratic.[24] In Blake's works biblical texts have become part of and transmuted into the prophet's visionary world. The Blakean myth, drawing on an array of contemporary ideas, demands of the reader not some explanatory key so much as the imaginative participation to explore the tensions and problems that the text poses, for 'to the eyes of the man of imagination, nature [can be] imagination itself' (K794). With eyes attuned we may perceive 'visions of eternity…[but] we only see as it were the hem of their garments when with our vegetable eyes we view these wondrous visions' (*Milton* 26.10). So the 'Old and New Testaments as the Great Code of Art' (Laocoön K 777) are just the most symptomatic form of art that can, with proper use, open up the way to the eternal and thereby link the divine and humanity, pervaded as it is with divine imagination, however dulled the sense of it might be. Blake writes, 'Why is the Bible more Entertaining & Instructive than any other book ? Is it not because they [sic] are addressed as to the Imagination, which is Spiritual Sensation and but mediately to the understanding or reason' (Letter to Trusler K794).

Blake would have frowned on an exegetical enterprise that meant that imagination was excluded and the way to eternity closed off as a result. The Bible is not to be regarded solely as a history of past events, for 'the Hebrew Bible and the Gospel of Jesus are…Eternal Vision or Imagination of all that exists' (*A Vision of the Last Judgement* K604). The exegetical task involves reading, hearing, appropriating, in whatever way our faculties allow, and with whatever aids we need to break the 'mind forg'd manacles', that discourse in which the conventions and wisdom of the age are passed on without question. Exegesis of the Bible needs must involve a

22. H. Glen, *Vision and Disenchantment* Cambridge: Cambridge University Press, 1983), esp. p. 71.

23. E.g. D.V. Erdman *Blake Prophet against Empire* (Princeton, NJ: Princeton University Press, 1977); Mee, *Dangerous Enthusiasm*, and also on the prophetic context S. Goldsmith, *Unbuilding Jerusalem* (Ithaca, NY: Cornell University Press, 1993).

24. See Erdman, *Blake: Prophet against Empire*.

variety of essays whose aim is to provide ways of rousing the faculties, to offer ever new moments of unveiling, through images, metaphors, additional words or myths. If I look for analogies to Blake's exegesis, I turn to the enigmatic appropriations of Ezekiel's vision or the journeys through the heavenly palaces to the divine *merkabah* in those writings that come from those shadowy figures who stand at the beginning of the Jewish mystical tradition. Or in *The Spiritual Exercises of Ignatius of Loyola*, in which the reader is asked to place herself within the narrative, thereby in effect creating another story through the act of imaginative identification that has been set in train. Or in the typological and contextual appropriations of the basic ecclesial communities meeting in shanty towns in Brazil and other parts of the Third World.[25] All these seem to parallel in different ways Blake's use of the Bible.

The neglect of Blake by biblical exegetes and theologians is to the impoverishment of biblical study and theology. Not only is he a significant epitome of trends in religion at the beginning of the nineteenth century, and is an example of the characteristics of radical Christianity, but he also offers a well-documented source for an understanding of the confluence of the visionary and antinomian currents and the distinctive hermeneutical perspective they offer. His myth-making and creative use of Scripture, filtered through personal experience and social upheaval, represents a unique opportunity for the interpreter to see how the visionary mind appropriates and transforms received traditions within a particular, and well-documented, social context. Blake was a visionary, saturated in the Bible and inventive in the way in which he seeks to liberate the Bible from the dominant patterns of interpretation of his day. His exegesis represents a distinctive reformulation of the text, woven as it is into his own mythical world. His work presents peculiar, and at times formidable, problems of exposition and epitomizes the difficulty of assessing the interplay between tradition and innovation that has always been such a central feature of New Testament exegesis. He is one of the most biblically based, and prophetic, poets yet his poems are often only loosely related to the Bible, and reformulate the Bible in new ways, leaving behind the determining character of their original context.[26] Mere repetition or even deriva-

25. See C. Rowland, *The Cambridge Companion to Liberation Theology* (Cambridge: Cambridge University Press, 1999), esp. pp. 109-52.

26. In this respect Blake's work represents a strong challenge to the work of writers like Richard B. Hays (*Echoes of Scripture in the Letters of Paul* [New Haven: Yale University Press, 1989]; cf. S.P. Moyise, *The Old Testament in the Book of Revelation* [Sheffield: Sheffield Academic Press, 1995]), who argues that biblical context is

tive exegesis of what was in the Bible was unable to wrest the Bible from the hands of those who misunderstood it and forged it into a system that supported the political and economic interests of the rulers of empire. A different perspective was needed to tell the story in language that might subvert a Bible in thraldom to dominant ways of interpreting. Blake's hermeneutical radicalism is, in a sense, already suggested by the Apocalypse itself, which is not a biblical interpretation but itself a reformulation of prophetic predecessors. Blake and John of Revelation present the symbols and myths of Scripture in a new visionary guise, much as Blake accomplished in his mythic writings, which seek to revive their message and challenge the domestication that overcomes metaphorical texts. Blake's resort to Scripture and myth in his illuminated books are a means by which the complexities of life, and the insight into, and response to, the divine mystery could be expounded. They are, to paraphrase Blake's own words, examples of a 'Poetry Unfetter'd' (*Jerusalem* 3); the purpose of both is, for Blake, above all, 'to rouze [our] Faculties to act' (Letter to Trusler K793).

BIBLIOGRAPHY

Bentley, G.E., *The Stranger from Paradise: A Biography of William Blake* (New Haven: Yale University Press, 2001).
Blake, William, *Blake's Illustrations for the Book of Job* (New York: Dover, 1995).
—*William Blake's Illuminated Books* (ed. David Bindman; 6 vols.; London: Tate Gallery Publications; William Blake Trust, 1991–95).
—*Blake: The Complete Writings* (ed. G. Keynes; Oxford, 1972 [K]).
Burdon, C., *The Apocalypse in England: Revelation Unravelling 1700–1834* (London: Macmillan, 1997).
Butlin, M., *The Paintings and Drawings of William Blake* (New Haven: Yale University Press, 1981).
Davies, J.G., *The Theology of William Blake* (Oxford: Clarendon Press, 1948).
Erdman, D.V., *Blake: Prophet against Empire* (Princeton, NJ: Princeton University Press, 1977).
Frye, N., *Fearful Symmetry* (Princeton, NJ: Princeton University Press, 1947).
Glen, H., *Vision and Disenchantment* (Cambridge: Cambridge University Press, 1983).
Lieb, M., *The Visionary Mode* (Ithaca, NY: Cornell University Press, 1991).
Lindberg, B., *William Blake's Illustrations to the Book of Job* (Åbo: Åbo Akademic, 1973).
Mee, J., *Dangerous Enthusiasm* (Oxford, 1990).

carried over into the use of the Old Testament in the New Testament. Blake, I believe, like Paul uses the language but as a vehicle for a new understanding of the divine message that may at times be at odds with the letter of the text (see further C. Rowland, *Revelation* in *New Interpreter's Bible* 12; Nashville: Abingdon Press, 1999).

Raine, K., *The Human Face of God: Blake and the Book of Job* (London: Thames & Hudson, 1982).

—*Golgonooza City of Imagination: Lost Studies in William Blake* (Ipswich: Golgonooza, 1991).

Tannenbaum, L., *Biblical Tradition in Blake's Early Prophecies: The Great Code of Art* (Princeton 1982).

Thompson, E.P., *Witness against the Beast: William Blake and the Moral Law* (Cambridge: Cambridge University Press, 1993).

Tolley, M.J., 'Europe "To those ychain'd in sleep" ', in D. Erdman and J. Grant, *Blake's Visionary Forms Dramatic* (Princeton, 1970), pp. 114-45.

THE BIBLE IN THE LIFE AND WRITING OF JAMES HOGG, THE ETTRICK SHEPHERD

Alison Jack

Editor's Introduction

William Wordsworth acknowledged his debt when he read in the Newcastle paper a notice of the death of James Hogg on 21 November 1835:

> When first, descending from the moorlands,
> I saw the Stream of Yarrow glide
> Along a bare and open valley,
> The Ettrick Shepherd was my guide.

James Hogg was born in 1770 in the Forest of Ettrick and spent most of his working life as a shepherd. But the characterization of the 'Ettrick Shepherd' began as a rather patronizing way of describing him in Blackwood's Magazine, *although Hogg subsequently used it as a literary device in his own writing. Hogg's most celebrated work,* The Private Memoirs and Confessions of a Justified Sinner, *a high point in Scottish literature, was written in 1824, at a time of political and religious controversy. The author combines black humour, mockery and disturbingly Gothic frissons in his account of the degradation of a pious young man who uses the Calvinist doctrine of predestination to justify the murder of his brother.*

This chapter provides an account of how Hogg used the Bible in his poetry and short stories as well as in his novels, setting this against the background of Hogg's own childhood experiences, the status of the Bible in the late eighteenth century and its interpretation in the early nineteenth. Hogg saw the Bible as an open text, available to be abused; he employed the Bible, as to a lesser extent did Scottish contemporaries, such as Thomas Carlyle and Robert Burns, in subtle and subversive ways.

1. *The Ettrick Shepherd*

The Ettrick Shepherd, James Hogg, was profoundly shaped by his childhood experiences. The exposure to the Bible he received as a child was utterly typical of his time and place, although remarkable to us today. The depth of knowledge of the Bible he acquired in his natural home setting is widely demonstrated in his many works, although, it will be argued here, Hogg was more than capable of subverting biblical tradition for his own ends.

James Hogg, the son of a tenant farmer, was born in 1770 in the Ettrick Forest near Selkirk in the Scottish Borders. His mother was a well-known collector of old Scottish songs and poetry, and the whole family was steeped in the oral tradition. After only six months' schooling, Hogg was placed as a cowherd on a neighbour's farm. His parents had lost their money and were turned out of their house. Hogg continued to work on one farm or another until his late thirties. However, he used what free time he had in the reading of a broad range of literature. He claimed he taught himself to read by memorizing the Psalms, and by 17 he was attempting Allan Ramsey's *Gentle Shepherd*. His master's wife, a Mrs Laidlaw, gave him books of a chiefly theological nature to read while tending his flock.[1] His early writings show an indebtedness to Fielding, Pope, Swift, Burns, renaissance drama and classical poetry in translation, as well as an extensive knowledge of the King James Bible, the Scottish metrical Psalms and a wide range of folk tales, songs and poetry.

Hogg was determined to become a poet like Robert Burns, and cultivated a friendship with Walter Scott when Scott's interest in Border Ballads led him to consult Hogg's mother. He had limited success at publishing his poetry while he continued to work in agriculture, but in 1810, on the collapse of his latest farming venture, he travelled to Edinburgh to pursue a literary career. Success finally came to him with the publication of a collection of poetry in 1813, *The Queen's Wake*, and this was followed in 1816 with a collection of satires on Wordsworth, Byron, Scott and others, called *The Poetic Mirror*.

Hogg's first novels appeared in 1818 (*The Brownie of Bodsbeck*), 1822 (*The Three Perils of Man*) and 1823 (*The Three Perils of Woman*). Drawing on folk tradition, and displaying Hogg's characteristic energy, ambiguity and imagination, they failed to succeed among the literati of Edinburgh society. His most famous work today, *The Private Memoirs and Confessions of a Justified Sinner*, appeared anonymously in 1824, and also made little impact beyond provoking the hostility of many of its reviewers. One critic wrote that the novel was an 'experiment' inspired by insolence and

---

1.   J. Hogg, 'Memoir of the Author's Life', in *Memoir of the Author's Life and Familiar Anecdotes of Sir Walter Scott* (ed. Douglas S. Mack; Edinburgh: Scottish Academic Press, 1972), p. 4.

whisky-punch', intended merely 'to ascertain how far the English public will allow itself to be insulted'.[2]

More poetry, prose and a controversial memoir of the late Sir Walter Scott followed until Hogg's death in 1835. Then his reputation as a rough, self-educated Scottish shepherd was enough to ensure that his greatest work would be quickly forgotten.

It was not until 1947 that the *Confessions* came to widespread public notice, when the novel was republished with an Introduction by the French novelist Andre Gide. Since then, it has slowly gained in critical acclaim among modern readers, many of whom find its Gothic darkness, its multiple levels of irony and ambiguity and its satire of hypocrisy appealing to the modern and even postmodern mind. Certainly, as a shrewd study of all levels of nineteenth-century Scottish society it has few equals.

It is hard to do justice to the plot and structure of the novel in summary, and even a first reading of the text usually fails to provide much in the way of comprehensive understanding. In terms of structure, most of the main events are narrated twice, by two opposing narrators with very different perspectives. In the first half of the novel we are offered an 'objective' account by an 'editor', written in 1823, more than a century after the events have occurred. Through this 'editor' we are given an external view of the main character, Robert Wringhim, and some social and historical information about his background, including the religious controversies raging in Scotland at the time. In the second half, the mood changes completely and we are offered the view from Robert's perspective. His childhood suffering and loneliness are charted in such a way that the reader is given an explanation for his acceptance of the predestinarian doctrines of his parents, and an understanding about why he takes these beliefs to their logical limits. We are able to chart his gradual enslavement to Gil-Martin, the elusive figure who is either a devil or a figment of Robert's fevered imagination, and even to sympathize with him as he resorts to murder in the name of his religious cause. Robert's descent into internal torment leads in the end to his suicide.

Hogg's purpose, however, is not simply to tell the story of Robert's demise, and the novel offers a much less clear account of itself than the above summary suggests. The 'editor' is an especially complex and self-contradictory character, claiming to be an objective man of science, while revealing many flaws and weaknesses. By the end, he too has descended in a 'chaos of confusion' as deep as the religious despair of Robert, the nar-

2.   Anon. Rev., *Westminster Review*, October 1824, pp. 560-62.

rator he mirrors. In the closing pages of the novel, abandoning any pretence of objectivity, the 'editor' resumes his narrative and embarks on a journey to the Ettrick Forest to search for Robert's grave. The character 'Hogg' himself appears in the narrative and declines to help the 'editor' in his quest, suggesting that Hogg does not wish to be identified with the 'editor' and his perspective. Both the 'editor's' rationalism and Robert's religious theories are shown to be inadequate ways to live in the world.

Modern critics continue to debate the real meaning and purpose of the text, and the level of indeterminacy within it which resists any explanation. The purpose of this chapter is to consider Hogg's use of the Bible in the *Confessions* and elsewhere. How influenced was he by the preaching he heard in church, the teaching he received at home and his own devotional reading?

2. *The Reading of the Word*

If there is a single thread running through the whole story of the Reformation, it is the explosive and renovating and often disintegrating effect of the Bible.[3]

The Bible had a central role in the Reformation church in Scotland. Indeed, Wright comments that 'the "scriptural principle" was applied more rigorously to the purification of Church life in Scotland than in most areas of Reformation Europe'.[4] Each of the foundation documents of the Church—the Scots Confession and *The First Book of Discipline* of 1560, and the *Book of Common Order* first authorized in 1562—all stressed the importance of Bible reading and teaching in the vernacular tongue, although, paradoxically, it was the Bible in English rather than in Scots that was available at the time and soon widely accepted. 'Gods plaine Scriptures' were understood as 'the expressed commandment of Gods word', and this entailed that 'all honouring of God, not conteined in his holy word'[5] was to be considered idolatry. The people were to meet regularly to hear the Bible read and expounded, and the best way for its plain meaning to be gleaned was for it to be followed one book at a time. The previous prac-

---

3. G.R. Elton, *Reformation Europe, 1517–1559* (London: Collins, 1963), p. 52.

4. D.F. Wright, ' "The Commoun Buke of the Kirke": The Bible in the Scottish Reformation', in D.F. Wright (ed.), *The Bible in Scottish Life and Literature*, (Edinburgh: St. Andrew Press 1988), pp. (155). This essay offers an excellent place to begin any consideration of the role of the Bible in Scotland.

5. J.K. Cameron (ed.), *The First Book of Discipline* (Edinburgh, 1972), pp. 86, 88, 208.

tice had been the following of a lectionary, which skipped from one passage to another.

In addition to hearing the Word preached in church, believers were exhorted by no less than the great reformer John Knox to 'let no daye slyppe or want some comfort receyved from the mouth of God'. The man of the house should understand that 'your wyfe, chyldren, servauntes, and familye are youre bishopryke and charge…ye must make them partakers in readyng, exhorting, and in makying common prayers, which I would in every house wer used once a day at least'.[6] Common understanding of the mind and message of the Bible, rather than liturgical recitation, was rediscovered as the goal of Bible reading in Reformation Scotland. The conviction of the Scottish Reformers that the meaning of Scripture was clear, obvious and simple informed all their attempts to promote its reading and exposition in church and in the home. The result was remarkable: 'the Bible seems to have attained almost at once, in a dramatic resurgence, a quite unique hold on the Scots imagination and mind'.[7]

The first reformers' emphasis on Scripture is continued in the influential Westminster Confession of Faith of 1640. The Confession affirms that because natural knowledge of God and his nature is inadequate, God made a supernatural revelation of himself that was committed to writing in the form of the Scriptures. In their original languages, the Old and New Testaments were directly inspired by God and are kept pure by his providence. Because they are divine, they are authoritative for individuals and the Church. It is their author, the Holy Spirit, who brings their meaning to their hearers, and who guides between different interpretations.[8]

This belief in the Bible as the holy, infallible Word of God seems to have been held by the majority of Scottish Protestants well into the nineteenth century, and certainly during Hogg's formative years. Cheyne comments that the Bible at this time was regarded as 'the supreme rule of faith and life, both personal and national, whose divine authority very few were disposed to question'.[9] The Age of Enlightenment had brought with

---

6.   J. Knox, *A Letter of Wholesome Counsel*, in *The Works of John Knox* (6 vols.; Edinburgh, 1846–64), IV, pp. 129-40.

7.   G. Johnston, 'Scripture in the Scottish Reformation', *Canadian Journal of Theology* 8 (1962), p. 250, quoted in Wright (ed.), *Scottish Life and Literature* (1988), p. 176.

8.   *Westminster Confession of Faith*, ch. 1, paras. 8 and 10, summarized in A. Cheyne, *The Transforming of the Kirk: Victorian Scotland's Religious Revolution* (Edinburgh: St. Andrew Press, 1983), p. 5.

9.   A. Cheyne, 'The Bible and Change in the Nineteenth Century', in D.F. Wright (ed.), *The Bible in Scottish Life and Literature* (Edinburgh: St Andrews, 1988), p. 192.

it scepticism towards the Bible, and 'Higher Criticism' was beginning to be developed elsewhere, but there is little evidence that ministers or their congregations were interested in such views.

The late eighteenth and early nineteenth centuries were a time when a high proportion of the population of Scotland attended church. The reading and preaching of the Bible was central to each act of worship, and this was reinforced by the common practice of morning and evening devotions in the home. The principal object of parish school education was to help children to read Scripture for themselves. The history and literature of ancient Israel was as much part of common knowledge as the history of Scotland, and ordinary speech seems to have been peppered with biblical references and allusions.

It is well documented and much commented upon that Hogg's exposure to the Bible from an early age was typical of his time and situation.[10] Along with the Catechism and the Biblical Paraphrases, the King James Bible was the text from which he began to read. His enthusiasm for the biblical text seems to have gone beyond the usual, however, if his brother is to be believed:

> When he [James] learned to read he read much on the Bible; this was a book which our mother was well acquainted with, and was in it better qualified to detect him when he went wrong, than if he had been reading any other book. And I can assure you, that in all my circle of acquaintances, either among old or young people, I was never conversant with anyone who had as much of the Bible by heart, especially of the Psalms, or could have told more readily where any passage was recorded than my brother James could have done. And, in my opinion, the beautiful descriptions of the nature and excellencies of the Divine Being, the sublime addresses of His grace and goodness that are interspersed through that invaluable work, more disposed his mind to utter his feelings in harmonies and poetic effusions than any native energy derived from either father or mother.[11]

Much later in life Hogg was to enter a heated debate with James Tennant and others in the *Edinburgh Literary Journal* about the status of the Scottish metrical version of the Psalms.[12] Tennant argued that Scots was inadequate to express the beauty and subtlety of the original Hebrew, while the

10. For example, I. Campbell discusses the issue of Hogg's childhood experience of the Bible in 'James Hogg and the Bible', in D.F. Wright (ed.), *The Bible in Scottish Life and Literature* (Edinburgh: St Andrews, 1988), pp. 94-109.

11. Part of a letter from Hogg's brother, William, sent in 1818, and quoted in A. Strout, *The Life and Letters of James Hogg, the Ettrick Shepherd*, I (Lubbock, TX: Texas Technical Press, 1946), pp. 8-9.

12. More details about the debate are to be found in J. Watson's article, 'William

King James version was a more than suitable translation. Such infelicitous Scotticisms as 'Froward thou kyth'st / Unto the froward wight' (Ps. 18.26) are for Tennant the result of

> the uncivilised state of our Scottish literature as compared with that of England, and to a want of familiarity with the models of good taste and elegant style which had already become acknowledged as standards in the capital, but which were little read, or not at all known, in that provincial degradation to which Scotland was then reduced.[13]

To correct this, Tennant advocates a 'purification' (p. 36) of the Scottish Psalmody by clergymen and not poets, which would combine English 'taste and correctness with…Scottish fire and originality'. His argument clearly demonstrates that Scots had lost its status and appropriateness as the language for all classes and levels of formality. Scots no longer communicated the Word of God successfully to certain influential groups of people.

Hogg's response is vehemently conservative. He declares that '[t]hese Psalms have an old watchman guarding over them here, who has had them all by heart since he was ten years of age; and what he want in education and ability, he has in zeal, to keep every innovation in due subordination'.[14] The Psalms in Scots share the 'simplicity and energy' (p. 26) of the worship for which they were written. In an even bolder claim, Hogg suggests that the Scots translation enjoys a relationship with the original text that other versions lack, and he asks, 'Is it not a glorious idea that we should be worshipping the same God in the very same strains that were hymned to him by the chosen servants in the tabernacle 3000 years ago?' (p. 29).

Hogg's love of tradition and concern for his rural, working-class roots seem to have combined with a belief in the appropriateness of the Scots language for worship. Whereas Tennant is keen to allow good taste and fashion to dictate the language of the Psalms, indicating a fluid understanding of Scripture, Hogg's concern is to retain the text he has known and loved all his life. Other aspects of Hogg's work, however, reveal a

Tennant, the Ettrick Shepherd and the Psalms of David: A Linguistic Controversy', *Scottish Language* 3 (1984), pp. 60-70.

13. W. Tennant, 'Remarks on the Scottish Version of the Psalms, with a View to its Amelioration', in J. Tennant *et al.*, *Critical Remarks on the Psalms of David and their Various English and Latin Versions; Particularly on the Version Now Used in our Scottish Church* (Edinburgh, 1830), p. 13.

14. J. Hogg, 'A Letter from Yarrow—The Scottish Psalmody defended', in J. Tennant *et al.*, *Critical Remarks on the Psalms of David*, p. 27.

much less conservative attitude towards the Scriptures, and we shall return to some of these more ex-centric views later in the chapter.

3. *The Preaching of the Word*

Eighteenth-century Scots read the Bible for themselves, but they also looked to preachers of the Word for guidance and inspiration. One such preacher with a local connection to Hogg, although born nearly a century before him, was Thomas Boston. By 1880 there had been 20 reprints of his *Human Nature, in its Fourfold State*, based on sermons preached at Ettrick and originally published in 1720. Hogg mentions Boston in several of his works, and even credits him with the differences between the shepherds of Yarrow ('devout and decent, but [with] no desire for reading') and those of Ettrick, who are 'intelligent and dogmatic, great readers, and fond of research in history and polemical divinity'.[15] According to Hogg, Boston's memory lives on in his parishioners, and his *Fourfold State* is written with 'fervour and strength' and an 'originality of thought' which is 'quite delightful and refreshing' (p. 304).

Boston was involved in the rediscovery, publication and defence of Edward Fisher's *Marrow of Modern Divinity* (originally published in 1646), and this brought him into conflict with the Church of Scotland's General Assemblies of the 1720s, which judged the book to have clear antinomian tendencies. However, it is in Boston's approach to Scripture that we are interested here. For Boston, the Bible is like no other book. It is directly inspired, to be revered in its entirety, and has salvific power to impart to its reader:

> It is the book of the Lord, dictated by unerring, infinite wisdom. There is no dross here with the gold, no chaff with the corn. Every word of God is pure. There is nothing for our salvation to be had in other books, but what is learned from this… And it has a blessing annexed to it, a glory and a majesty in it, an efficacy within it, that no other book has the like.[16]

Because of its particular nature, Boston concludes that 'the sense of the scripture must be but one, and not manifold, that is, quite different and no wise subordinate to another, because of the unity of truth, and because of the perspicuity of the scripture' (p. 7). Multiple interpretations of the text are simply not allowed.

15. James Hogg, 'Statistics of Selkirkshire', in *Prize-Essays and Transactions of the Highland Society of Scotland*, IX (Edinburgh: Blackwood, 1832), p. 303.

16. S. M'Millan (ed.), *The Beauties of Boston: A Selection of his Writings* (Inverness: Christian Focus Publications, 1979 [1831]), pp. 22-23.

More contemporary preachers might not have expressed their hermeneutical practices with quite such dogmatism, but most were equally resis-
tant to any notion of indeterminacy in the text. Thomas Chalmers was
minister of the Tron Parish Church in Glasgow from 1815 to 1823, and
Andrew Thomson was minister of St George's in Edinburgh from 1814
to 1831. Both were well-known and widely published preachers.

Chalmers believed that the preacher should ensure that 'the things which
are written pass without change or injury from the Bible to the pulpit'.[17] In
his preaching, the doctrine of atonement featured prominently, and the
desire to awaken a need for salvation in the consciences of his hearers was
a guiding motivation. Chalmers was also very selective in his use of the
Bible, preferring Pauline to gospel texts. This selectivity, coupled with an
emphasis on the role of the Bible in elucidating doctrine, are dominant
features of his approach to Scripture.

Andrew Thomson was less preoccupied with doctrine or with such narrow readings. He was aware of the potential within the Bible for multiple
interpretations, and sought to guide his listeners and readers into a proper
understanding of the text by following these precepts:

> The Gospel consists of a variety of parts, but these parts are all in com-
> plete harmony; they are necessary to the beauty and perfection of the
> whole, and none of them are intended for separate exhibition, or capable
> of being detached from the rest, and yet answering their destined purpose,
> in forming the faith and the character of the Christian, and preparing him
> for heaven.[18]

Thomson, unlike either Boston or Chalmers, preaches from a wide variety of texts, and is more aware of the dangers of reading an isolated text in
such a way that it colours the meaning of Scripture as a whole. Nevertheless, Thomson is as convinced as the others that his readings are the true
ones and argues as forcefully that his interpretation reflects the intended
meaning of the Bible, as a unit and in part.

4. *The Writing of the Word*

The picture of the role of the Bible in late eighteenth- and early nineteenth-
century Scotland has so far been varied and yet with a common tone. The
Bible is generally viewed as a univocal text with clear links to the Word
of the creator God. Its meaning is accessible to lay readers, while depth of

17. T. Chalmers, *Institutes of Theology*, I (Edinburgh, 1849), p. 263.
18. A. Thompson, *Sermons on Hearing the Word Preached* (Edinburgh, 1825),
p. 69.

meaning is to be gained from the preaching of those in authority in the Church. Any difficulties or contradictions in the text, if they exist at all, may be explained with reference to other parts of Scripture. In this way, the Bible is regarded as a self-glossing, internally coherent text.

Before considering the writing of James Hogg, a brief account of the Bible in the writing of two of his great Scottish contemporaries, Robert Burns and Walter Scott, might be useful. Burns grew up in rural Ayrshire in the 1760s and 1770s, and, like Hogg, received only limited formal schooling. His reading and learning as a young man was therefore largely self-directed, but certainly included the Bible ('a glorious book', as he wrote to Margaret Chalmers in 1787)[19] and other religious works. His familiarity with the Bible and the doctrines of the Church are clearly to be seen in his famous Kirk satires, such as *Holy Willie's Prayer* (1785), which demolishes the popular concept of predestination, and *The Kirk's Alarm* (1786), written to defend the progressive minister William McGill of Ayr.

Also like Hogg, Burns was well-versed in the metrical Psalms, and could quote (and misquote) them with ease. Burns went further than Hogg by producing two paraphrases of Psalms: the whole of the first psalm and the first six verses of the ninetieth (written between 1774 and 1784 and published in the Edinburgh edition of 1787). Despite his well-known and complicated moral life, Burns was a deeply religious man. Although, as Roy points out in his essay, 'The Bible in Burns and Scott',[20] poetry does not lend itself to the inclusion of biblical quotations, there is plenty of evidence in Burns's correspondence that he took the Bible and his faith seriously. As he wrote to his friend Mrs Dunlop in 1788, 'A mathematician without Religion, is a probable character; an irreligious Poet, is a Monster'.[21] In another letter to Mrs Dunlop, Burns responded to her comment that her son had had a 'great disappointment' with a slight misquotation from Prov. 14.10: 'The heart knoweth its own sorrows, and a Stranger intermeddleth not therewith.'[22] Perhaps his most moving defence of the faith comes in his poem 'To the Rev. John M'Math, Inclosing a copy of *Holy Willie's Prayer*':

---

19. G. Ross Roy (ed.), *The Letters of Robert Burns* (2 vols.; Oxford: Clarendon Press, 2nd edn, 1985), I, p. 183.

20. In Wright (ed.), *Scottish Life and Literature*, p. 84.

21. Ross Roy (ed.), *Letters*, I, p. 230.

22. Ross Roy (ed.), *Letters*, I, p. 301.

> All hail, Religion! Maid divine!
>
> Tho' botch't an' foul wi' mony a stain,
> An' far unworthy of thy train,
> With trembling voice I tune my strain
> To join with those,
> Who boldly dare thy cause maintain
> In spite of foes.

If Burns and Hogg share many similarities in terms of their upbringing and education, Walter Scott comes from a very different background. Scott was the son of a Writer to the Signet, comfortably brought up and university trained, an advocate by training and a man at ease with the more liberal wing of the Church. However, like both Burns and Hogg, Scott's familiarity with the Bible is clearly visible in his work and letters.

Whether the struggle described is between Covenanters and redcoats under Claverhouse in *Old Mortality* (1816) or between Catholics and Presbyterians in *Rob Roy* (1817), Scott makes frequent reference to the Old Testament in particular. When in *Old Mortality*, Balfour, one of those who had murdered Archbishop James Sharp, is overheard speaking of the event in his sleep, even the dream is expressed in biblical terms: 'Thou art taken, Judas. A priest? Ay, a priest of Baal, to be bound and slain, even at the brook of Kishon' (ch. 6). And in ch. 31 of his novel *The Heart of Midlothian* (1818), set in Scotland at the time of the Secession, Scott takes the biblical story from 2 Kgs 5 and places a reference to it into the thoughts of Jeanie, as she debates with herself about the propriety of entering a church in England:

> The prophet, she thought, permitted Naaman the Syrian to bow even in the house of Rimmon. Surely if I, in this streight, worship the God of my fathers in my own language. Although the manner thereof be strange to me, the Lord will pardon me in this thing.

Just as Burns frequently quoted from the Bible in letters, so too did Scott, although he was more likely than Burns simply to work a short biblical passage into the text of his letter without using quotation marks. Roy has noted that certain quotations were favourites, including Ps. 37.35 ('I have seen the wicked in great power, and spreading himself like a green bay tree'), which appears at least eight times in the correspondence now available, and which works well in both political and business spheres.[23] Scott

---

23. G. Ross Roy, 'The Bible in Burns and Scott', in D.F. Wright (ed.), *The Bible in Scottish Life and Literature* (Edinburgh: St Andrews Press, 1988), p. 90.

was also, like Hogg, passionate in his support of the metrical Psalms. In 1818 he had been invited by the Principal of the University of Edinburgh, Rev. George Husband Baird, to collaborate in a new metrical version. In the end, the project came to nothing, but Scott was moved to defend the well-known version in response:

> I am not sure whether the old fashioned version of the psalms does not suit the purpose of public worship better than smoother versification and greater terseness of expression... The expression of the old metrical translation though homely is plain forcible & intelligible and very often possesses a rude sort of majesty which perhaps would be ill exchanged for more elegance.[24]

Scott and Burns, like Hogg as we shall see, knew and used the biblical text. All reflected the naturalness of biblical speech in all levels of Scottish society, and could use biblical language in the mouths of their characters either sympathetically or satirically. As Roy concludes, Burns and Scott,

> [l]ike Hogg, like Galt, like all their literate contemporaries in Scotland... would have found the common use of the Bible quite natural; its place in their writing is equally natural and illuminating.[25]

Turning now to James Hogg himself, we find that, although he apparently fitted well into the pattern of belief in and use of the Bible already sketched, on closer inspection his use of the Bible in his work could be much more subversive. A good example of what I call Hogg's biblical excentricity[26] is the 'Chaldee Manuscript'.[27] This text appeared in *Blackwood's Magazine*, vol. 7, no. 2 (1817). Claiming to be a translation from 'an Ancient Chaldee Manuscript' held in the Library of Paris, it was published anonymously. Clearly a parody of the book of Revelation, the Manuscript is written in the same apocalyptic tones and charts a similar clash between the forces of good and evil. The narrative begins with a description of the visionary experience of the observer-narrator:

---

24. H.J.C. Grierson (ed.), *The Letters of Sir Walter Scott* (12 vols.; London: Constable, 1932–37), V, p. 166.

25. G. Ross Roy, 'Burns and Scott', p. 92.

26. See A. Jack, *Texts Reading Texts, Sacred and Secular* (Sheffield: Sheffield Academic Press, 1999), Chapter 2 for a much fuller account of Hogg's use and 'misuse' of the Bible.

27. J. Hogg, 'An Ancient Chaldee Manuscript', *Blackwood's Magazine* 72 (1817), pp. 89-96.

> And I saw in my dream, and behold one like the messenger of a King came toward me from the East, and he took me up and carried me into the midst of the great city that looketh toward the north and toward the east, and ruleth over every people, and kindred, and tongue, that handle the pen of the writer (1.1-2).

From the opening verses, comparisons with Revelation are clearly invited, and here the strong echo is of Rev. 1.10-11. In the Manuscript, two factions, the 'man clothed in plain apparel', who has both a name and a number (1.3), and the 'crafty man', who has a 'notable horn wherewith he ruled the nations' (1.17), vie for the ownership of a book. Their efforts to gather supporters and to prepare for the final battle 'in the place of princes' (1.47) forms the basis for the plot of the text. The function and control of a book is also a key theme in Revelation. Heaven and earth are searched in vain for someone worthy to open the sealed book (ch. 5), but only the Lamb who was slain is able to open the seals and thus set in motion the apocalyptic events of the rest of the book. Later, in ch. 20, judgment is carried out depending on 'those things which were written in the books, according to their works', and whoever's name is not found written in the opened book of life is 'cast into the lake of fire' (20.15).

Whereas the function of Revelation is deadly serious, the Chaldee Manuscript is of course a joke. Anyone with a knowledge of the literary characters and disputes in nineteenth-century Edinburgh would recognise that the man in plain apparel was the publisher Blackwood and his opponent was the publisher of the rival magazines the *Scots Magazine* and the *Edinburgh Review*. The book at issue was none other than *Blackwood's Magazine*. The identity of the author of the Manuscript has caused some debate,[28] although it is now generally agreed that Hogg wrote the text, which was then revised by others at Blackwood's. On its publication, the article caused great offence and outcry. The magazine was sued in the Court of Session for its 'indecent, irreverent, and blasphemous application of Scriptural language',[29] and in the following issue an apology appeared and the offending article removed from the second edition. Royle sums up the piece as 'literary dynamite',[30] and later Hogg himself was to compare the effect of its publication with that of allegations that a group of shepherds

28. See T. Royle, *Precipitous City: The Story of Literary Edinburgh* (Edinburgh: Mainstream Publishing, 1980), pp. 132-33.

29. M. Oliphant, *Annals of a Publishing House: William Blackwood and his Sons, their Magazine and Friends*, I (Edinburgh, 2nd edn, 1897), p. 131.

30. Royle, *Precipitous City*, p. 132.

had raised up the devil.[31] In the minds of many of its readers, the parody
of the Bible that was the Chaldee Manuscript was devilish, shocking and
dangerous. By claiming the status of a sacred text, however satirically, it
deprivileged Scripture in the eyes of those who believed that God had
taken responsibility for every syllable contained in the Bible. The Manuscript thus deliberately parodied both individuals and an over-reverent
view of Scripture.

The Chaldee Manuscript is a slight work compared with Hogg's later
masterpiece, *The Confessions of a Justified Sinner*. Here more than in any
other text, the extent of Hogg's ex-centricity towards the Bible is revealed.
In the *Confessions*, it is the polyvalence of Scripture and the dangers of a
fixed interpretation of the text that Hogg explores. The purpose of the exploration is to warn his readers against accepting the preaching of the
Word that allows the Bible only one, fixed meaning. The devil-figure Gil-
Martin and Robert's 'father' follow the hermeneutical principles of Boston,
Chalmers and Thomson, and their dangerous readings of the Bible are
shown to be as plausible as any other reading. Hogg seeks to show that far
from being the stable, illuminating text of churchmen, the Bible is in fact
so ambiguous and contradictory as to be inadequate as a basis for life.

The teaching of Robert's 'father' is clearly mirrored in the doctrinal
positions of both Chalmers and Thomson. The theology of atonement is
pushed to the forefront with no mention of other theological ideas. It is on
the writing of Paul, rather than the Gospels, that Wringhim concentrates,
and the hermeneutical lens through which he focuses his preaching and
teaching is the doctrine of the eternal predestination of the elect. Because
Robert can assure Wringhim that Gil-Martin adheres to the tenets of this
doctrine, Wringhim is convinced that 'he [Gil-Martin] was no agent of
the wicked one…for that is the doctrine that was made to overturn the
principalities and powers, the might and dominion of the kingdom of darkness'.[32] Wringhim's words are an echo of Eph. 6.11-12, in which the metaphor of armour is related not to a belief in the doctrine of predestination,
but to such qualities as 'truth', 'righteousness' and the 'gospel of peace'.
For these qualities, Wringhim has little time. Furthermore, the doctrine on
which he depends, far from offering protection from the 'rulers of the darkness of this world', seems to encourage their attack. The tragic conclusion
of the *Confessions* points to the dangerous inflexibility of Wringhim's

31. J. Hogg, 'Storms', in D. Mack (ed.), *Selected Stories and Sketches* (Edinburgh:
Scottish Academic Press, 1982), p. 17.

32. J. Hogg, *Confessions* (Edinburgh, 1824), p. 98. All quotations are taken from
the Canongate edition of 1991.

doctrinal approach, but it is the text of the Bible itself that has offered him the vocabulary he needs.

The Bible as it was preached also mirrors the way in which Gil-Martin persuades Robert to act in increasingly outrageous ways in the name of his religion. One example from many comes at the point after which Blanchard, the liberal preacher, has been murdered by Robert. Robert is having second thoughts about his actions, and is in conversation with Gil-Martin, who is trying to persuade him to murder his own half-brother, George:

> It was not easy to answer his [Gil-Martin's] arguments, and yet I was afraid that he soon perceived a leaning to his will on my part. 'If the acts of Jehu, in rooting out the house of his master, were ordered and approved of by the Lord,' said he, 'would it not have been more praiseworthy if one of Ahab's own son's had stood up for the cause of the God of Israel, and rooted out the sinners and their idols out of the land?'
>
> 'It would certainly,' said I. 'To our duty to God all other duties must yield.'
>
> 'Go thou then and do likewise,' said he. 'Thou art called to a high vocation; to cleanse the sanctuary of thy God in this thy native land by the shedding of blood; go thou forth like a ruling energy, a master spirit of desolation in the dwellings of the wicked, and high shall be your reward both here and hereafter' (pp. 120-21).

Gil-Martin appeals to the story of Jehu killing Ahab in 2 Kgs 9–10 as scriptural warrant for the murder of George, and urges Robert to 'Go then and do likewise'. These words come of course from Jesus' exhortation at the end of the parable of the good Samaritan, urging his followers to care for their neighbour (Lk. 10.37). Robert, so intoxicated by the twisted gospel of Gil-Martin, hears only an exhortation to kill his brother. Here and in many other places, biblical phrases and words have been wrenched from their contexts and applied in ludicrous but dangerous ways. The reader is presumably expected to recognize their inappropriateness in Gil-Martin's speech; the fact that Robert never does is an indictment of a biblical hermeneutic, which looks for only one meaning in the text and reads the words as the literal word of God.

Gil-Martin adds weight to his arguments in much the same way as such preachers as Boston, Chalmers and Thomson did in their sermons. In the above example, Gil-Martin uses the words 'cleanse', 'land' and 'shedding of blood' in a way that seems plausibly biblical, although they are found together in completely different contexts in the Bible. The conditions of God's covenant are set out in Gen. 9, and one of that is that fratricide will require the penalty of the murderer's blood. The land is polluted by the shedding of blood in Num. 35.33 and cannot be cleansed except by the blood of the murderer. Robert, despite his religious upbringing, hears only Gil-Martin's interpretation of the text. In fact, these examples point forward to signal Robert's eventual fate, his death. They tell the truth about the consequences of his actions, but he is not able to discern their implication because he is so enthralled by Gil-Martin's rhetoric. Hogg's point is that when responsibility for the interpretation of the Bible is given to others, its hearers may lose their ability to distinguish alternative meanings for themselves and may lay themselves open to being manipulated or deceived.

Throughout the novel, Robert fails to read Gil-Martin correctly because he reads his Bible in the way in which contemporary preachers urged. Following Boston, he accepts that everything in the Bible is trustworthy and inspired, with only one clear and discoverable meaning that is supported by selected readings from other passages in Scripture. Once that meaning has been discovered, the truth has been revealed for all situations and all time. Robert's narrow exposure to the Bible has left him no strategy to deal with the devil's use of the Bible, as the devil, in the guise of Gil-Martin, uses the very hermeneutical principles he has been taught.

Gil-Martin acts as a warning to all of Hogg's readers about the dangers of the prevailing attitude towards the Bible. Dependence on a text that has been granted sacred status and is interpreted by a small but very influential group of people is shown to carry real risks. As the liberal preacher Blanchard comments, under the influence of Gil-Martin, Robert has carried his faith to 'an extent that overthrows all religions and revelation together; or, at least, jumbles them into a chaos out of which human capacity can never select what is good' (p. 107). More strikingly, Hogg fails to offer any positive or helpful readings or readers of the Bible to counteract Gil-Martin's approach. Blanchard may recognize the dangers of the extremity, but he has only a very limited and weak preaching role in the text. As he himself comments, 'There is not an error into which a man can fall, which he may not press Scripture into his service as proof of the probity of' (p. 107). In the *Confessions*, it is not just the events of the novel that remain ambiguous and open: the Bible is an equally dangerously ambiguous book.

Although Hogg's background is thoroughly orthodox in its exposure to the Bible and the preaching of the Church, I have sought to show that his use of the Bible in his work is much more subversive. Hogg's attitude towards the Bible, particularly in his *Confessions*, is decidedly ex-centric, criticizing the hermeneutical principles of influential preachers from a marginalized position that recognises the difficulty of interpreting the Bible definitively. Hogg seems to argue that it is only when the Bible is stripped of its sacred status and escapes the control of powerful religious interpreters that its instability and ambiguity may be recognized. This was a very different approach from that of most of his contemporaries.

BIBLIOGRAPHY

Campbell, I., *Nineteenth Century Scottish Fiction* (Manchester: Carcanet New Press, 1979).

Gifford, D., *James Hogg* (Edinburgh: Ramsay Head Press, 1976).

Gifford, D. (ed.), *The History of Scottish Literature*, III (Aberdeen: Aberdeen University Press, 1988).

Groves, D., *James Hogg: The Growth of a Writer* (Edinburgh: Scottish Academic Press, 1988).

Jack, A., *Texts Reading Texts* (Sheffield: Sheffield Academic Press, 1999).

Miller, Karl, *The Electric Shepherd: A Likeness of James Hogg* (London: Faber & Faber, 2003).

Wright, D.F. (ed.), *The Bible in Scottish Life and Literature* (Edinburgh: St Andrews Press, 1988).

THE RISE OF PREMILLENNIAL DISPENSATIONALISM AS THE CORNERSTONE OF AMERICAN FUNDAMENTALISM

Jennifer Martin

Editor's Introduction

This paper was written by an American student on a one-year exchange at the University of Kent. The title suggests that it addresses a specific and limited topic, but such are the issues involved that it is actually well-placed to illuminate (in prospect and retrospect) some of the main movements of modern thought about the Bible.

James Barr's classic study Fundamentalism *(1977) advises the reader not to start with a definition of something not yet understood, but rather to work towards a definition of this topic, assembling the various components that have contributed towards, and which characterise, the attitudes of Fundamentalism. Such a process of investigation may also take the form of a history of development. In the case of Fundamentalism there are two main types of development: in association with basic philosophical ideas, a development of the doctrine of biblical inerrancy; and in relation to such religious movements as Revivalism, a development of beliefs such as Dispensationalism, linked to Millenarian expectations. In Fundamentalism the predominantly, but not exclusively, literalist reading of the Bible is founded on an anti-liberal, anti-intellectualist view of the inerrancy of the text (e.g. the work of B.B. Warfield); the principal philosophical ingredient is Scottish Common Sense Philosophy from the eighteenth century, but also using Francis Bacon's theory of Induction from the seventeenth century. Historians differ in the importance they accord to either Revivalism or Millennialism. George Marsden's study* Fundamentalism and American Culture *(1980), which is used substantially in this paper, generally takes a broad view of the Fundamentalist phenomenon, but concludes by seeing Revivalism as the key. In contrast Ernest R. Sandeen's* The Roots of Fundamentalism *(1970) is rather narrowly focused on Millennialism. Revivalism stresses the need for personal conversion and spiritual experience; Millennialism stimulates a sense of urgency in converting the world before Christ's return. Both movements are fed by the belief in the inerrancy of Scripture and, in turn, strengthen the conviction about the direct relevance and application of the Bible.*

Underlying American Christian Fundamentalism is a unique system of biblical analysis that surfaced at the end of the nineteenth century. Some dismiss it as a fantastic and complex web of mythology; others, particularly the thousands of Americans raised on the Scofield Bible, have grown up believing it, unaware that there are any alternatives.[1] Indeed, an informal survey of popular Christian authors and speakers in the United States likely would show that premillennial dispensationalism is still the prevailing belief among Evangelicals and Fundamentalists. It is a philosophy that echoes its severe Calvinist forefathers, holding that the world is a sinking (or sunk and rotting) vessel from which only Christ will save humankind (or rather, the world's believers) upon his second coming.

Yet the most prominent Evangelicals of the day did not, throughout American history, cling to such gloomy beliefs. To understand why premillennial dispensationalism has pervaded fundamentalist thought, it is necessary to examine its birth as a theological and a social reaction among certain nineteenth-century events in the world of biblical criticism and in secular society.

John Nelson Darby (1800–82) is credited with bringing dispensationalism's precursor, simple premillennialism, to America from his separatist Plymouth Brethren group in Ireland. Welcomed by Calvinist Presbyterians and Baptists, his views took root and grew alongside the revivalist movement of the nineteenth century, which placed an especially heavy emphasis on personal piety, supernatural conversion and emotional (rather than intellectual) faith.[2] On the surface, the two movements complemented each other—with premillennialism, firmly espousing absolute humility before the sovereign God and the need to keep evil at bay, serving as an intellectual defence of revivalism.

Yet more than revivalistic fervor was at work in premillennialism's rise and evolution into the more complex scenario of dispensationalism. Revivalism, in fact, was not an offshoot of premillennial dispensationalism. Throughout the nineteenth century, revivalism had been backed by premillennialism's antithesis: postmillennialism, essentially a belief in the spiritual evolution of man. Underlying both was a belief in the cosmic struggle between the forces of good and evil, and a belief that biblical prophecies were in the process of being fulfilled; however, premillennialism was relatively obscure at first, while postmillennialism was the prevailing

---

1. James Barr, *Fundamentalism* (London: SCM Press, 1977), pp. 191, 6.
2. George M. Marsden, *Fundamentalism and American Culture* (New York: Oxford University Press, 1980), pp. 46-47.

Evangelical view, between the American Revolution and the Civil War.[3] Devoted to such practical issues as the conversion of souls, such revivalists as Charles Finney, Reuben A.Torrey and D.L.Moody (who once maintained that no-one could be 'argued' into the kingdom) nevertheless benefited from the optimistic strains of thought among postmillennialists like Jonathan Edwards, who believed that the spirit of God would be 'poured out' worldwide in the millennium before Christ's return to Earth (the thousand years referred to in Rev. 20).[4] It seemed that the 'golden age' of global Christianization had arrived, America was the epicenter, and revivalism was the evidence. Why, then, toward the end of the century, was premillennialism not only espoused by Calvinists, but embraced by the rising Evangelical theologians of the time, and absorbed quickly by the 'everyday' Evangelicals in the revivalist movement?

One certain blow against postmillennialism was struck by the changing strains in intellectual thought at the end of the nineteenth century. Postmillennialism, it could be said, was born of Old Scottish 'Common Sense' Realism, a pervading philosophy that harmonized with the intellectual ethos during the birth of America proper, in the seventeenth-century Age of Enlightenment.[5] 'Common Sense' held that the mind was 'fashioned' to know God and morality as certainly as it was created to understand the world around it. Evangelicals, along with the liberal philosophers of the time, assumed that scientific inquiry was ultimately a path to God, because all natural laws revealed their Creator. God's truth was unified, and Scripture was known intuitively.[6] Francis Wayland said, 'An order of sequence discovered in morals is just as invariable as an order of sequence in physics.'[7] 'Common Sense' philosophy naturally gave way to postmillennialism's optimistic beliefs concerning a 'golden age' coming upon us. Not only morally, but also culturally and scientifically, the West (and America in particular) was leading the way to the 'New Jerusalem'. To quote George Marsden: 'The old order of American Protestantism was based on the interrelationship of faith, science, the Bible, morality and civilization. It was about to crumble.'[8]

---

3.   Marsden, *Fundamentalism*, p. 49.
4.   Marsden, *Fundamentalism*, pp. 47-49.
5.   Marsden, *Fundamentalism*, p. 14.
6.   Marsden, *Fundamentalism*.
7.   Francis Wayland, *The Elements of Moral Science* (London: Joseph Angus, n.d.), p. 4.
8.   Marsden, *Fundamentalism*, p. 17.

The order was doomed to collapse, as Transcendentalist Oliver Wendell Holmes, Sr predicted in 1869.[9] With the rise of Darwinism and naturalistic beliefs, it no longer seemed inevitable that science would confirm Scripture. To the contrary: the Bible could no longer pass scientific muster and come out as an unerring, infallible document. 'The truth is staring the Christian world in the face, that the stories of the old Hebrew books cannot be taken as literal statements of fact,' said Holmes.[10] There were attempts to reconcile Christianity with Darwinism; however, in the minds of most educated Evangelicals, the two were incompatible. Presbyterian minister Charles Hodge, of Princeton Theological Seminary, put the question bluntly: 'Is development an intellectual process guided by God, or is it a blind process of unintelligible, unconscious force, which knows no end and adopts no means?'[11]

Faced with this dilemma, some Evangelicals followed the path of Kant and German Idealism, the teachings of Friedrich Schleiermacher and Albrecht Ritschl, and the ideals of romanticism, thereby extricating religion from the realm of scientific inquiry. Firmly placing spiritual questions back into their ambiguous and untouchable realm, these Evangelicals indirectly helped fuel the emotional revivalism ('Great Awakenings') of the century, whose leaders, as mentioned earlier, considered their doctrine virtually divorced from intellectualism.[12] Some of these, such as Henry Ward Beecher, the most popular American preacher of his day, 'a popularizer who gloried in ambiguity and sentiment',[13] limited themselves to innocuous sermons that pacified their Victorian culture.

Yet underlying much of Beecher's theology was a liberal belief in scientific progress as God's blessing, and here is where the rift that produced Fundamentalism occurred. To liberal New England theologians like Beecher, theological truth was no longer as static as a sequence of numbers, but was an evolving concept in harmony with the evolution of humankind. This 'New Theology' eventually spread throughout the United States, marking a shift away from 'Common Sense' philosophy. The shift was largely regarded as prompted by the import of European intellectual-

---

9.   Marsden, *Fundamentalism*.

10.   In a letter to Frederic Hedge, quoted in Francis P. Weisenburger's *Ordeal of Faith: The Crisis of Church-Going America, 1865–1900,* (New York, 1959).

11.   Charles Hodge, *What Is Darwinism?* (1869) quoted in Marsden, *Fundamentalism*, p. 19. Cf. Charles Hodge, *Systematic Theology*, I (New York, 1874).

12.   Marsden, *Fundamentalism*, pp. 20-21.

13.   Marsden, *Fundamentalism*, p. 25.

ism, comprising evolutionary naturalism, biblical criticism and the newer idealistic philosophy and theology.[14]

To conservatives who clung to 'Common Sense' philosophy, however, it seemed that the world was ending before their eyes. Their formerly christocentric society had taken a strong turn away from its omniscient Creator, in siding with the concepts of speculative science, cultural relativity and biblical inaccuracy. While many diehard postmillennialists floated in response towards liberal theology (most notably at the influential Andover Theological Seminary[15]), the Old Calvinism maintained its momentum and created a new breed of followers. Alliances shifted. Postmillennialist Jonathan Blanchard, founder of Wheaton College, Chicago, had always identified more strongly with revivalists than with intellectuals. However he found himself irreconcilably divided in theory from his former close friend, Henry Ward Beecher. Blanchard said,[16] 'If Mr. Beecher's teachings are the gospel of Christ, what need had Christ to be crucified?' The strong Puritan influences in Blanchard's thought were obvious in his criticism of the New England Congregationalists and the New Theology, which was too generous toward human nature, even in his own optimistic eyes. Blanchard said that Beecher was 'dealing out the love of Christ to sinners with the indiscriminate fondness of a successful prostitute', and he admonished the minister and his sister Harriet Beecher to remember the biblical verse (Jas 4.4) that would capture the spirit of Fundamentalism: 'Ye adulterers and adulteresses, know ye not that friendship of the world is enmity with God?'[17] Blanchard's postmillennialist views gradually slipped away. It was his son, Charles Blanchard, Wheaton College's second president (from 1882), who helped solidify premillennialism among conservative Evangelicals toward the end of the nineteenth century.[18]

Especially troubling to premillennialists was the new biblical scholarship that suggested, among other things, that Old Testament prophecies did not pertain to the Christian Church; that Jesus had expected the coming of God's kingdom to occur very quickly (an expectation that was disappointed); and that many of Jesus' teachings conflicted with Pauline theology. The response among conservatives was to insist on biblical inerrancy and simply to create an elaborate scheme that supported obscure

14. Marsden, *Fundamentalism*, p. 26.

15. Marsden, *Fundamentalism*, p. 25, shown by the publication in 1886 by the renewed faculty of a volume entitled *Progressive Orthodoxy*.

16. Marsden, *Fundamentalism*, p. 30.

17. Marsden, *Fundamentalism*, p. 30.

18. Marsden, *Fundamentalism*, p. 31.

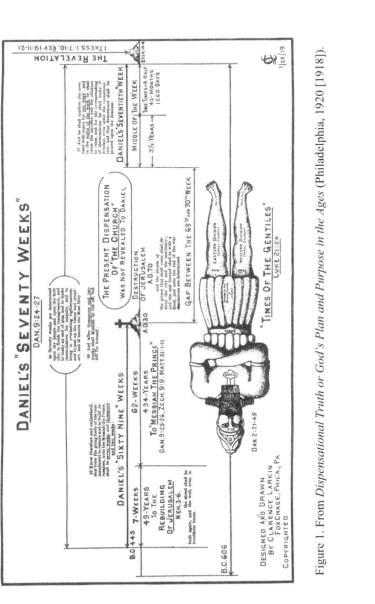

Figure 1. From *Dispensational Truth or God's Plan and Purpose in the Ages* (Philadelphia, 1920 [1918]).

prophecy in Daniel and Revelation, and explained away in the same process the differences between the teachings of Jesus and Paul.[19] Specifically
dispensationalism divides world history into seven 'dispensations' (the
equivalent of apocalyptic ages) which are defined by the character of the
relationship between God and humankind. These comprise Innocency,
Conscience, Human Government, Promise, Law, Grace (the current age,
marked by the existence of a secret army of the faithful—God's 'true
church') and the Kingdom, or Millennium (God's final utopia).[20] At a
time known only by God, Christ will return and save believers from the
world's catastrophic end. Known as the 'rapture', this scenario was
based on 1 Thess. 4.17: 'Then we which are alive and remain shall be
caught up together with them in the clouds, to meet the Lord in the air:
and so shall we ever be with the Lord' (KJV).

The events of the final weeks, according to this scheme, involve the
conversion of the Jews in the Holy Land to Christianity. Thus Old Testament prophecy (particularly Dan. 9.24-7) pertains to the future of Israel
—the regrafting of Jews into God's family, following the age of the
Gentiles (see Lk. 21.24; Rom. 11.15-18). The current age of the Church
is a parenthetical gift of grace, with the purpose of calling more and more
Gentiles to salvation. This scheme explains, for dispensationalists, the
differences between the teachings of Jesus and of Paul. The age, or 'dispensation' of Grace began with the resurrection of Christ, and therefore
the *doctrine* of Grace is to be found in the Epistles. Jesus, during his lifetime, was addressing his sermons to Jews in a legalistic context. Thus the
Scofield Bible editor and premillennialist A.C. Gaebelein writes:

> Under the Law of the kingdom, for example, no-one may hope for forgive-
> ness who has not first forgiven. Under Grace the Christian is exhorted to
> forgive because he is already forgiven... It is the Gospel of the kingdom
> which he preaches (in the Sermon on the Mount). The Gospel of Grace is
> something different.[21]

Premillennialists took very literally Christ's statement, 'Upon this rock
will I build my church' (Mt. 16.18, emphasis added). The new kingdom
was to be a future event that could only be preceded by Christ's coming.
Postmillennialist doctrine of the capacity of humankind to bring about
God's kingdom was anathema to premillennialists; on the contrary for the

19. Marsden, *Fundamentalism*, pp. 48-54. See the accompanying chart to interpret
the prophecy of Dan. 9.24-27.
20. Barr, *Fundamentalism*, p. 192.
21. Barr, *Fundamentalism*, p. 193.

premillennialist the decline of civilization (and even of the church) was inevitable.

Premillennialists were to encounter much social ostracism, particularly during the coming years of World War I. (Some, however, distinguished themselves from their fellow-believers in their patriotism. Perhaps most notable among them was Billy Sunday, famous for concluding his sermons by jumping on the pulpit and waving the flag; he once said, 'If you turn hell upside-down, you will find "Made in Germany" stamped on the bottom.')[22] Premillennialist pessimism had no room for hope of social progress, and placed no trust in political leaders or governments. Ironically premillennialists benefited from an increase in the general interest in prophetic teaching during the war: 'We are living in a time of prophetic fulfilment, though just now how far that fulfilment may reach no man knows.'[23] However, it remained primarily a backlash against humanistic teaching, and as such became the firm base on which Fundamentalism grew.

BIBLIOGRAPHY

Barr, James, *Fundamentalism* (London: SCM Press, 1977).

Court, John M., 'Millenarianism', in R.J. Coggins and J.L. Houlden (eds.), *A Dictionary of Biblical Interpretation* (London: SCM Press, 1990), pp. 459-61.

Handy, Robert T., *A Christian America: Protestant Hopes and Historical Reality* (New York, 1971).

Marsden, George M., *Fundamentalism and American Culture: The Shaping of Twentieth-Century Evangelicalism, 1870–1925* (New York: Oxford University Press, 1980).

Niebuhr, Richard H., 'Fundamentalism', *Encyclopedia of Social Sciences*, VI (New York, 1937), pp. 526-27.

Russell, Allyn C., *Voices of American Fundamentalism: Seven Biographical Studies* (Philadelphia, 1976).

Sandeen, Ernest R., *The Roots of Fundamentalism: British and American Millenarianism 1800–1930* (Chicago, 1970).

22. Marsden, *Fundamentalism*, p. 142.

23. Marsden, *Fundamentalism*, p. 145. The quotation is from the Editor of the *Christian Herald*, George Sandison, writing in January 1917.

VICTORIAN PREACHERS AND THE NEW BIBLICAL CRITICISM

T. Mervyn Willshaw

Editor's Introduction

An underlying tension between what may be termed the 'intellectual' and the 'spiritual' approaches to the Bible has probably existed from the very earliest stages in the production of the documents themselves, if not pre-dating this in the oral phase of audience response and interaction with the first preachers. But this tension is easier to define and evaluate if one concentrates on a much later stage in the history of human thought, granted the pervasive influences of the Enlightenment.

In the latter half of the nineteenth century a great wave of criticism (direct and indirect, intentional and unintended, within the Church and outside it) broke upon the Bible and demanded a new approach to basic questions on its nature, authority, inspiration and interpretation. Recent developments in science had an impact, if only indirect. Moral objections to traditional Christian teaching had a more direct impact. But most significant of all was the rise of higher (or literary) and historical criticism, which was concerned with questions of the dating, authorship, composition, purpose, meaning and religious and historical value of the various books of the Bible. The work of German historians and biblical scholars gradually became known in England through the work of such men as Coleridge, Arnold, Thilwall and Stanley. George Eliot's translation of the work of David Strauss was a major event in 1846.

Preachers who were aware of what was happening could not ignore it. Integrity demanded a response, but the responses varied. Dr Willshaw shows how three prominent preachers of the period did respond. The selection of Henry P.Liddon, Robert Dale and Benjamin Jowett is made because they were almost exact contemporaries, subject to the same influences and forced to ask the same questions, but even more because they represented different styles of theology and churchmanship and did their preaching in different contexts.

1. *Introduction*

During the Victorian Age, a great wave of new criticism, direct and indirect, intended and unintended, from within and without the Church, broke upon the Bible and demanded a new approach to questions about its nature, authority, inspiration and interpretation. Developments in science had an indirect impact. Moral objections to traditional Christian teaching had a more direct one. But most important was the rise of higher (or literary) and historical criticism concerned with questions of the date, authorship, composition, purpose, meaning and religious and historical value of the various books of the Bible.

The beginnings of a historical-critical approach to the Bible go back to at least the sixteenth century. The Reformers gave it impetus with their insistence that Scripture can only be explained by itself. Luther, recognizing that meaning cannot properly be imposed upon it from outside, abandoned allegorical interpretation and stressed the single, literal sense of the text. The variety of literature within the Bible was acknowledged, as was some unevenness in religious and theological quality. But it was the development of historical study during the latter half of the eighteenth century, in Germany, that led to a great surge in critical biblical study in the nineteenth. By 1850 the need for a thoroughly historical approach to both Old and New Testaments had gained wide acceptance among German biblical scholars. Each document, it was now held, must be interpreted by giving it its special place within the course of Jewish and primitive Christian history.

As a result, traditional understanding of the nature and authority of the Bible was gradually undermined. More seriously, the historical basis of the Christian faith came into question. F.C. Baur, for example, thought that the New Testament must be read against the background of a conflict between Pauline and Petrine Christians, which did not begin to be resolved until the middle of the century. The dates and authenticity of the New Testament writings could be determined, he argued, in the light of that conflict. So the only genuine Pauline epistles are Romans, 1 and 2 Corinthians and Galatians. Acts exhibits a conscious tendency to set aside the differences between Peter and Paul and has altered the historical facts in the interests of this concern. John is later than the other writings and comes from a time when reconciliation has at last been effected. Each book must be placed within the total historical perspective, and he recognized that there is theological development within the New Testament itself.

Baur's pupil, David F. Strauss, broke away from all previous methods of interpretation. In his *Life of Jesus Critically Examined,* published in 1835, he argued for the recognition of a mythical element within the New Testament as well as the Old. Early Christians surrounded the historical figure of Jesus with a 'myth' compounded of supernatural elements from the Old Testament and their own conviction that he was the Messiah of Jewish expectation. It is difficult, therefore, to separate the historical kernel from the engulfing crust of legend. Strauss's scepticism was too much even for his German colleagues and he suffered professionally for his views. But he represents a watershed in the critical study of the Gospels because of his destruction of earlier conservative and rationalist methods of interpretation, his understanding of the cultural and temporal conditioning of the writers, his introduction of the mythical criterion and his daring to raise an uncertainty about the Jesus of history that has exercised scholars ever since.

In the early decades of the nineteenth century few English churchmen were aware of developments in German scholarship. Henry Hart Milman was an exception. His Bampton Lectures in 1827 aroused little comment, but his *History of the Jews*, written a couple of years later, brought about what his biographer calls a 'tempest of disapprobation'.[1] Dean Stanley said it

> was the first decisive inroad of German theology into England: the first palpable indication that the Bible could be studied like another book; that the characters and events of the sacred history could be treated at once critically and reverently. Those who were but children at the time can remember the horror created in remote rural districts by the rumour that a book had appeared in which Abraham was described as a 'sheikh'[2]

The book was bitterly attacked from many pulpits. It was denounced as rationalistic, 'German' and likely to undermine biblical authority. The publication of George Eliot's translation of Strauss's book in 1846 had a similarly disturbing effect.

In 1860, Benjamin Jowett, in his essay 'On the Interpretation of Scripture', wrote: 'As the time has come when it is no longer possible to ignore the results of criticism, it is of importance that Christianity should be seen to be in harmony with them.'[3] But Jowett's conviction was not shared by

---

1. Arthur Milman, *Henry Hart Milman: A Biographical Sketch,* (London, 1900), p. 83.
2. Milman, *Henry Hart Milman*, p. 86.
3. B. Jowett, *Essays and Reviews* (London, 1860), p. 408.

all and *Essays and Reviews,* like the other works mentioned, was received with a cry of dismay and officially condemned by both Houses of Convocation in June 1864 'as containing teaching contrary to the doctrine received by the United Church of England and Ireland, in common with the whole Catholic Church of Christ'.

Nevertheless the tide was turning. During the next 40 years British scholars did much to calm the situation and bring about a greater, though by no means universal, acceptance of critical thought. Notable amongst Old Testament scholars were S.R. Driver, H.B. Swete and the more radical T.K. Cheyne. The Cambridge trio of B.F. Westcott, J.B. Lightfoot and F.J.A. Hort led the way in New Testament studies. Bernard Reardon writes:

> The initial reaction of public opinion in this country to critical bible study —the 'higher criticism', as it came to be called—was thus far from favourable. The upshot had been controversy, denunciation by authority and legal prosecution. But the progress of scholarship could not be halted indefinitely. When indignation and fear at last subsided reason resumed its sway. By 1884 Mandell Creighton, in his inaugural address as Dixie professor of ecclesiastical history at Cambridge, could state it virtually as a truism that the traditions of theological learning had been thoroughly leavened by the historical spirit.[4]

For those preachers who were aware of what was happening and whose integrity forbade them to ignore it, the implications were enormous. Preaching had traditionally rested on the Bible. Here was the authority that guaranteed the truth of the preacher's claims. But if the Old Testament story could not be taken at face value, if the Jesus of history was obscure, if the epistles were not all they seemed to be, if inspiration did not imply infallibility, if the Bible was, after all, human, flawed and incomplete, what was the preacher to do?

No doubt the vast majority of preachers, lay and ordained, continued as though nothing had happened. It takes a great deal of effort to keep up with the scholars and a busy, pastoral ministry hardly allows it. Even the more informed preachers would generally be wary of disturbing the (assumed) simpler faith of their congregations. The new criticism would be largely ignored. But there were some whose prominence, knowledge, theological seriousness and personal integrity precluded such negligence. The issues had to be faced however distasteful or attractive they may be.

The aim of this essay is to examine how three such preachers responded to the challenge. They are chosen because they were almost exact contem-

---

4. B. Reardon, *Religious Thought in the Victorian Age* (London: Longmans, 1980), p. 346.

poraries and thus were subject to the same influences and forced to ask the same questions, but also because they represented different styles of theology and churchmanship and did their preaching in different contexts. They are Henry Parry Liddon (1829–90), Robert William Dale (1829–95) and Benjamin Jowett (1817–93).

2. *Henry Parry Liddon*

Henry Liddon was one of the second generation of Tractarians in Oxford, the devoted disciple and biographer of Pusey. From 1870 he held simultaneously the positions of Professor of Exegesis in Oxford and Canon of St Paul's Cathedral in London. About a third of the year was spent in London and the rest in Oxford. His preaching generally had an apologetic emphasis, especially in the university, but he was highly popular and drew great crowds to St Paul's. A poll organized by the *Contemporary Pulpit* magazine in 1885 revealed that he was regarded as the greatest preacher of the day.

Even his strongest critics had to concede that Liddon did his homework well. He was thoroughly familiar with both German and British scholarship however much he disliked it. A note in his diary for 14 November 1865, reads, 'Read some of Strauss's new "Life of Jesus" and felt wretched. His cold infidelity chill's one soul to the core.'[5]

Again, in a letter to C.T. Redington in December 1888, he writes:

> I have read Wellhausen and have a robust confidence that he will go the way of other Rationalists before him. In September I spent four days with Dr. Dollinger at Tegernsee, and among other things we talked over Wellhausen's 'Prolegomena'. 'I could not get on with it at all,' D. said; 'it is full of unproved assumptions.' Anyone who takes the trouble to read it carefully will, I think, share his opinion.[6]

References to German scholars are frequent in his sermons and the published volumes are extended with numerous footnotes referring to their works. His Bampton Lectures[7] of 1866 contained his refutation of much that he had read in people like Strauss, Baur, Renan and Colenso.

Despite this clear awareness of and keen interest in contemporary scholarship, he could still preach as though nothing had happened. As late as

---

5.   J.O. Johnston, *Life and Letters of Henry Parry Liddon* (London: Longmans, Green & Co., 1904), p. 82.

6.   Johnston, *Liddon*, p. 361.

7.   H.P. Liddon, *The Divinity of our Lord Jesus Christ* (London, 1867).

Advent 1881, in a sermon on a text from 2 Timothy, he takes the epistle at face value, accepting Pauline authorship and setting it in the context of Paul's life and ministry, despite the fact that the Pauline authenticity of the epistle had been questioned as early as 1812 by Eichhorn and again in 1835 by Baur.[8]

Liddon takes all the Gospel stories at face value. Where he thinks they can be harmonized, he is happy to do so. Putting together the accounts of the anointing of Jesus with ointment by a woman in Matthew, Mark and John, he pictures Jesus

> reclined between the two trophies of His power: on this side was Lazarus, silent, reserved, self-involved, as became one who had passed the portals of the grave, and had seen sights at which the living can only guess; and on that side was Simon, who, by his special grace and mercy, had escaped from the terrible scourge of leprosy.[9]

Where the differences appear too great for this treatment, he accepts that the incident, however unlikely it may be, must have occurred more than once. None of this is due to ignorance of what critical scholars may have said about the historicity of the Gospels. He is quite prepared to defend his method, as he does with reference to the Cleansing of the Temple:

> During the course of His short earthly ministry our Lord Jesus Christ twice cleansed the temple of the traffic that took place within its courts. St. John describes the first occasion; he places it just after the wedding of Cana in Galilee, when our Lord went up to Jerusalem to keep the first Passover after entering on His ministry. The second occasion…took place immediately after the public entry into Jerusalem, and, as St. Mark's account would seem to imply, on the following morning. The close of the ministry of the Son of Man was to be marked by a solemn act corresponding to that at its commencement. And here, observe in passing, that it is impossible to treat the narrative in St. John as referring to the same event as that described by the first three Gospels, without supposing that the fourth Evangelist had, for purposes of his own, torn away this episode from its true place at the close of our Lord's life, and placed it at the commencement. Those who have gone so far as to maintain this, contend that it is very improbable that an event of such marked character should have occurred twice within a short lifetime. But, not to insist on the unwisdom of settling beforehand what is or is not likely in such a life as our Lord's, let us observe that the action itself, and the language used by our Lord, are reported to have varied significantly on the two occasions, while the recurrence of the circumstances

8.   H.P. Liddon, *Advent Sermons*, II (London, 1888), p. 82.
9.   H.P. Liddon, *Passiontide Sermons* (London, 1891), pp. 227-28.

which provoked our Lord's act on the first occasion would have led Him to repeat it on the second.[10]

The Old Testament is similarly taken at face value. In his sermon on 'God and the Soul', based on Ps. 63, he says:

> Ewald, indeed, would exclude this Psalm from that small number of sixteen in which his arbitrary criticism still consents to recognise the thought and style of the son of Jesse. But scholars, like Delitzsch, deem this estimate nothing short of literary vandalism, which would sacrifice even the certainties of Biblical science to its own morbid dread of a traditional position. The title 'A Psalm of David when he was in the wilderness of Judah' is in the strictest harmony with the contents of the Psalm itself.[11]

His treatment of the book of Isaiah shows the same insistence on taking Scripture at face value and on clinging to traditional interpretations, with the oddest results. He is entirely familiar with the arguments against the authenticity of the book and sees their strength, yet still he rejects them:

> The last twenty-seven chapters of Isaiah are so unlike those which precede them that they might seem to form a separate book. The Prophet appears to live in the days of the Babylonish Captivity; he is carried by the Spirit away from the days of Hezekiah, and from his own home in Palestine; and prophesies as if he were dwelling among the exiles under a heathen king.[12]

He acknowledges that the purpose of the words, which he uses as his text, from ch. 40, is to reassure the Jews of the Exile. Nevertheless he refuses to date the writing during the Exile, insists upon the integrity of the book, and explains it all by the predictive nature of prophecy. Any suggestion to the contrary is seen as an attempt to limit God.

Again, when he takes as his text the words 'Behold a Virgin shall be with child' he is fully aware that Matthew is quoting a passage from Isa. 7 that scholars interpret as being concerned with the immediate situation confronting Judah and in which the familiar translation 'virgin' would be more accurately rendered 'a young woman'. But he refuses to be restricted to a purely historical interpretation, and though the alternative rendering may have great antiquity, he rejects it because of what it might suggest about the evangelist:

> If the Prophet whom St. Matthew quotes said nothing about a 'Virgin', but was only predicting a marriageable maiden, and a natural birth, St. Matthew's quotation is not only irrelevant; it is an attempt, by means of a false

10. H.P. Liddon, *Sermons on Some Words of Christ* (London, 1892), pp. 284-85.
11. H.P. Liddon, *University Sermons* (London, 1866), pp. 1-3.
12. H.P. Liddon, *Christmastide in St. Paul's* (London, 1889), pp. 224-25.

translation, to claim for his narrative the sanction of prophecy, if we are not prepared to say that the ignorance or the bad faith of the Evangelist is fatal to his authority as a religious teacher, we must continue to read the Prophet as our forefathers read him; we must believe him to have foretold that Emmanuel would be born of a Virgin-Mother.[13]

There are at least two occasions, both when he is addressing a university congregation, on which he claims to take a positive view of biblical criticism, when it is not too extreme. He asks:

Have we never banned the Nazareth of criticism; too readily supposing that because some teachers of Heidelberg or Tubingen have mistaken wild imagination for history in their treatment of the Holy Gospels, no good thing can be expected to come from any critical school? The loyalty to Revelation which animates our prejudice does not justify it.

We must welcome the critical and scientific spirit 'assured that, whatever its exaggerations, we have much to learn from it, and that in the long run it must do the work of Him Whom we adore'.[14]

Again, he says:

Criticism may have done us an ill turn in unkindly or unskilful hands; but it has more weapons to place at the disposal of the Faith than opportunities for wounding it.[15]

Even so, it is difficult to find passages in any sermons in which he makes positive use of the results of criticism or shows any signs of having been influenced by it. Liddon is too aware of what is happening, and too troubled by it to ignore it. References to the work of the critics are frequent but always his purpose is to refute it and to defend the traditional interpretation.

The reasons for his stance are clearly revealed in his sermons. For example, he believes in the intrinsic power and inspiration of the Bible. He asks:

What is the Bible? To sight, it is a book that may be read like any other book; it is a vast, a beautiful but a human literature; it is human in its sympathy, human also in its imperfections. To faith, it is throughout inspired and unerring; it is the very voice of God speaking in human language to His listening children.[16]

13. Liddon, *Christmastide*, pp. 89ff.
14. *University Sermons* (2nd series; London, 1879), p. 11.
15. *University Sermons* (1879), p. 181.
16. *University Sermons,* previously published as *Some Words for God* (London, 1869), p. 204.

Closely related to his view of inspiration is his understanding of revelation. He claims to see it as 'a perpetual progress'[17] but the implications of
this in the way books of the Old Testament are used and regarded pass
him by. In any case, if as he says, progression were allowed as far as Cal-
vary, it came to an abrupt stop there. The truth of God was revealed in
Christ once and for all and no advance is possible:

> [Jesus] brought from heaven a Body of Truth, containing whatever we now
> know in respect of questions which must always possess the deepest inter-
> est for the human soul. He told us all that is to be apprehended here
> concerning life and death and God and eternity. Thus the essential faith is
> fixed. No advance is possible in the way of distilling its spirit from its
> dogma with a view to rejecting the dogma while we retain the spirit. The
> spirit of Christianity is in fact inseparable from the Christian faith. No
> advance is possible in the way of enlarging the dogmatic area of the Creed
> by a process of accretive development.[18]

This very significant passage reveals Liddon's anxieties clearly. On the
one hand, he is worried about the liberal wing of the Church, represented
by people like Benjamin Jowett, who, in coming to terms with biblical
criticism, are cutting Christian faith loose from reliance upon the Bible
and are content to talk in a vaguer way about the spirit or 'idea' of Christianity in Platonic fashion. On the other, he fears Rome with its tendency
in the later nineteenth century to create new dogmas for which Liddon
could find no biblical warrant. For Liddon, to undermine biblical authority
is to destroy the Christian faith. In another sermon, he says:

> If the Church be forgetful of the supreme claims of Scripture, she soon
> becomes a prey to superstition and follies which fatally discredit her mes-
> sage to mankind; if Scripture be not interpreted by the original and general
> sense of the Church, it comes in time to be treated as the plaything of
> individual fancy, as a purely human literature, as so much material to be
> torn to shreds by some negative and anti-religious criticism, for the amuse-
> ment, if not exactly for the improvement or edification, of the world.[19]

But Liddon's primary objection to biblical criticism was dogmatic. He
saw clearly that it had serious implications for the catholic faith to which
he held so firmly. The doctrine of the person of Jesus and the veracity of
the Holy Spirit were at stake. The publication of *Lux Mundi*, a volume of
essays written by a group of Oxford high churchmen and published in

17. *University Sermons* (1869), p. 31.
18. *University Sermons* (1869), p. 32.
19. Liddon, *Advent Sermons*, II, p. 219.

1889, drew from Liddon two sermons in which he made it clear that where dogma and critical scholarship were in conflict, he was firmly on the side of dogma. The essayists would have claimed to be as zealous for the catholic faith as Liddon himself but they also knew that they were living in a period of intellectual and social transformation. New points of view, new questions, were arising that must be faced and were certain to involve 'great changes in the outlying departments of theology'.[20] Liddon knew that that was a superficial comment and that the challenge was much more profound. On 8 December 1889, in St Paul's, he preached a sermon on 'The Worth of the Old Testament'. His first point was concerned with the trustworthiness of the Old Testament. Paul, he was sure, would have had nothing to do with any estimate of the books of the Old Testament, which was fatal to belief in their trustworthiness. 'Inspiration' has never been closely defined, he acknowledged, but untrustworthiness is incompatible with any claim to be inspired by the Author of all truth. For example, the idea that Deuteronomy was written, not by Moses, but by some later Jew 'is irreconcilable with the veracity of the book, which by its use of the name of Moses claims an authority that, according to the critics in question, does not belong to it'.

Unless there exists such a commodity as 'the inspiration of inveracity',

> we must choose between the authority of some of our modern critics and the retention of any belief in the inspiration of the books which they handle after this fashion—even of the belief in the permanent value of these books as sources of Christian or of human instruction.

Not every trustworthy book is inspired. But a book claiming inspiration must at least be trustworthy.[21]

An even more sensitive issue is that of the person of Jesus. Jesus 'set the seal of His infallible sanction on the whole of the Old Testament'.[22] He went out of his way to sanction not a few portions of it which modern scepticism rejects, such as Lot's wife (Lk. 17.32), Noah and the Flood (Lk. 17.27), Jonah (Mt. 12.40). Was he talking down to a popular ignorance that he did not share? That would have been inconsistent with his character as a perfectly sincere religious teacher. Did he then share a popular belief that our higher knowledge has shown to be popular ignorance? Some so-called Christians dare to say so. But if he could be mistaken about this, why not about other things too? The trustworthiness of the Old Testament

---

20. H.P. Liddon, *Lux Mundi* (London: John Murray, 1889), p. viii.
21. H.P. Liddon, *The Worth of the Old Testament* (London, 1890), pp. 20ff.
22. Liddon, *Worth*, pp. 23ff.

is, in fact, inseparable from the trustworthiness of our Lord Jesus Christ. In a clear reference to *Lux Mundi,* now just a few weeks old, he concluded: 'If we believe that He is the true Light of the World, we shall close our ears against suggestions impairing the credit of those Jewish Scriptures which have received the stamp of His divine authority.'

The second sermon, 'The Inspiration of Selection', was preached before the University of Oxford on Whit Sunday, 1890. In the second section he dealt with the inspiration of Scripture by the Holy Spirit. The Holy Spirit is true and therefore he cannot contradict himself. He cannot 'take into his service literary fictions which trifle with the law and the sense of truth'. If it could be shown that the addresses of Moses in Deuteronomy were by a later writer, or the speeches of David in Chronicles, or that passages in Daniel that claim to be predictions of future events are really a history of events that the writer had himself witnessed, or that words of Jesus reported in John were not verbatim reports of what he said, or the sermons of Peter and Paul in Acts were not theirs, or that the Pastoral epistles were not Pauline, it would surely have been shown at the same time that the Holy Spirit could not have inspired the writings in question:

> If the Holy Spirit is in any degree concerned in the production of its (the Bible's) contents, we may at least be sure that language is not used in it to create a false impression and that that which claims to be history is not really fiction in an historical guise.[23]

Liddon is prevented from making a more positive response to biblical criticism by the presuppositions he brings to it. His understanding of inspiration, like his theology of Jesus, is imposed upon Scripture from outside. Consequently, he cannot be open to new scholarship and he is led to question the motives of those who are not so inhibited. At best some scholars have tended to treat the study of the Bible as an end in itself:

> They have sometimes seemed to regard the Christian Revelation as mainly interesting on account of the consideration it secures for philological studies. To adapt a famous saying—they encourage the suspicion that God had become Incarnate in order to aid the sale of their grammars and dictionaries.[24]

If this half-humorous comment on scholars is allowed, some of his other comments, like the suggestion that critics are sometimes motivated by a self-advertising intellect that delights to shock or disturb the faithful[25] or

---

23. H.P. Liddon, *The Inspiration of Scripture* (London, 1890), pp. 10-17.
24. H.P. Liddon, *Clerical Life and Work* (London, 1894), pp. 359-60.
25. Liddon, *University Sermons*, 1865, pp. 170-71.

the assertion that the critic who refuses to take Jonah at face value is really unwilling to believe in a living God[26] are more regrettable.

Liddon's response to biblical criticism is nothing less than serious. He paid his opponents the compliment of taking the trouble to read what they wrote and he recognized that it was about more than determining dates and authorship. It had serious theological implications, so serious that it had to be resisted at all costs.

3. *Robert William Dale*

On 8 October 1889, R.W. Dale preached at the Hundredth Anniversary Service of the Argyle Chapel in Bath. In his sermon, he noted the changes that had taken place, during his lifetime, in the style and ethos of Evangelicalism. Nearly 50 years earlier the ideas of younger men had caused consternation amongst Congregationalist elders and authorities:

> The younger men began to care for truth for its own sake—not merely as an instrument for converting the world. What may be called the scientific spirit, the disinterested love of truth…began to take possession. They were interested in Biblical criticism. They wanted to make sure of the authorship and the dates of the books of the Old Testament and the New. They discussed the nature of Inspiration. They distinguished between verbal inspiration and plenary. The Bible was authoritative; but they wanted to construct a theory of its authority.

Later in the sermon, he said they

> insisted that they were under the most solemn obligations to be scrupulous; that since the Bible contained the record of Divine revelations, they were bound to discover exactly what it meant; that to put a meaning of their own into a Bible sentence and to claim Divine authority for it, was just as bad as to put a sentence of their own into the Bible and to claim Divine authority for it.[27]

The old evangelical passion for souls was not lost but it was combined with a new passion for truth expressed chiefly through meticulous exegesis.

Dale expressed full approval of this development. In fact, he was talking about his own student days, or perhaps the period immediately before he entered Spring Hill College and identified himself with those 'younger men'. Yet, curiously, he speaks of them in the third person plural rather than the first. He casts himself in the role of spectator rather than partici-

---

26. H.P. Liddon, *Sermons on Special Occasions* (London, 1897), pp. 164-65.
27. R.W. Dale, *The Old Evangelicalism and the New* (London, 1889), pp. 23-25.

pant and so perhaps hints at the somewhat ambivalent approach to biblical criticism that can be detected in his preaching. Generally he expresses total openness to the new criticism and yet, in practice, his words sometimes betray an instinctive drawing back, born of fear about what the new scholarship might do to faith.

There is no doubt that Dale was familiar with most of the scholars of his day. He had read Strauss, Baur, Renan, Seeley and Jowett.[28] Quotations from such scholars as Driver, Westcott and Lightfoot pepper his sermons. Westcott and G.G. Findlay both sent him copies of their biblical commentaries when they were first published.

Three of his letters indicate Dale's general approach to criticism. The first was to Sir E.R. Russell on 27th November 1880, in which he wrote:

> As I want Science to be absolutely free from any control of faith, so I want Criticism to be free from any entanglement with questions concerning the contents of the Christian Revelation. If I publish anything it will be an attempt to vindicate the autonomy of Science, Criticism, Faith.[29]

It is a very clear statement of his ideal.

But the second indicates a measure of qualification. It is addressed to Miss Phipson on 24 December 1880. She had evidently raised queries about his sermon on the previous Sunday. He replied:

> That God in divers manners spoke in times past by the prophets, that Judaism was from Him—these are not open questions to any who have got beyond the elements of Christian Faith; but whether the Book of Jonah is literal history—whether early chapters of the Book of Genesis were meant to be literal history, whether the Books of Chronicles were written under a sacerdotal bias—are questions which may be determined in a sense contrary to that of tradition without touching the Divine and supernatural character of the ancient revelation; it is to this latter that Christ and Christianity are pledged.[30]

So there are, after all, limits to the critic's freedom, which do not trouble Dale too much because he is convinced that historical and literary criticism is concerned with matters that lie on the periphery of Christian concern.

The correspondence went on for some considerable time. In a later letter Miss Phipson accused him of 'remarks of a depreciating character' on 'the inspired record' made for the 'conciliation of unbelievers'. In a third

---

28. A.W. Dale, *The Life of R.W. Dale of Birmingham* (London, 1902), pp. 163-64, 199-200, 231, 350.

29. Dale, *Life*, p. 350.

30. Dale, *Life*, p. 534.

letter, dated 12 April 1882, Dale protested that nothing could be further from the truth. On the contrary:

> I am afraid that if I were charged with desiring to conciliate believers, most impartial judges would say that there was ground for the charge. But my desire, however far I fall short of it, is to bear witness to the truth.[31]

Here is Dale's problem in a nutshell. His intellectual commitment to the disinterested pursuit of truth is compromised by a refusal to allow that any of the central tenets of Christian doctrine are negotiable and a fear lest anything he might say should disturb the faith of his congregation. He was minister of Carr's Lane Church in Birmingham for over 40 years. He had a congregation of around a thousand to sustain. They seem to have been people of remarkable theological awareness and enthusiasm. It is not surprising that he felt a need to be cautious and reassuring. He was especially keen to persuade his hearers that the results of criticism would be positive. So, in 1890, he said:

> As far as the books of the New Testament are concerned, I think that we are within sight of the practical close of the controversy. After a century of struggle the historical trustworthiness of the Four Gospels and the genuineness of, at least, all the important epistles are secure. But with regard to the earlier books of the Old Testament, their sources and the times at which they received their present form, the battle is at its height… I cannot doubt that the issue of the controversy will, in any case, be to enlarge and exalt our conceptions of the methods of Divine revelation.[32]

A second quotation reinforces the point:

> We need regard with no anxiety or alarm the investigations of criticism, nor suppose that the fortunes of the Christian faith depend upon the dates and authorship of sacred books: there are limits to the ultimate modifications of the traditional opinion on these questions; and no possible results of Biblical criticism can shake the foundations of that Eternal City, of which we may say with greater confidence in our time than in any preceding age, that its Builder and Maker is God.[33]

How then does Dale's appreciation of contemporary scholarship affect the style and content of his preaching? It does not prevent him from accepting the substantial historicity of the Bible. In 'The Cloud of Witnesses', a sermon based on ch. 11 of Hebrews, for example, there is no hint that Adam, Cain, Abel, Seth, Enoch, Noah and Abraham are anything less than

---

31. Dale, *Life*, p. 535.
32. R.W. Dale, *Fellowship with Christ* (London, 1891), pp. 266-67.
33. Dale, *Fellowship with Christ*, pp. 76-77.

solid historical figures. The book of Acts is a reliable account of the early years of the Church.[34] He recognizes differences in the Gospels and sees them as evidence for varieties of theology in the New Testament.[35] His use of the Bible is invariably marked by soberness and a strict adherence to the literal sense. There are no flights of fancy, no violations of the literal meaning, no texts torn from their context. Allegorical or mystical meanings do not interest him. He frequently tries to enter imaginatively into the situation of the writer and to let his sermon arise out of that context.

Perhaps his response to criticism is best indicated by summarising his sermon on 'The Son and the Prophets'.[36] This is important both for the use it makes of Scripture and for the explicit references to current scholarship it contains. The text is from Heb. 1.1-3: 'God, who at sundry times and in divers manners spoke in time past unto the fathers by the prophets, hath in these last days spoken to us by His Son.'

He begins by pointing out the difference between the Jewish convert to Christianity and the Gentile convert. The Gentile would be unlikely to revert to the worship of idols and the ways of the old paganism. For the Jew it was different. Racial solidarity and patriotism were closely related to love for the institutions of the Jewish religion and he would continue to feel the pull. The purpose of the Epistle is to warn those who are so tempted.

Both Jew and Gentile acknowledged the voice of God in the prophets. But their revelation of God was fragmentary, partial and incomplete. Only in Christ could God speak fully. What human language was inadequate to express has been said in his divine person. By him God created. Through him he cleansed the world from sin and now Christ is made 'heir of all things' and seated at the right hand of God. This passage, he says, has important bearings on controversial questions agitating many Christians: 'Does the Old Testament contain the record of a Divine revelation, or is it a badly edited, ill-digested collection of the untrustworthy traditions of an illiterate and superstitious people?' Dale offers three thoughts by way of answer.

It is a logical mistake to abandon faith in Christ because of difficulties, insoluble perhaps to us, that occur in the books of the Old Testament.

---

34. R.W. Dale, *Christian Doctrine* (London, 1894), pp. 283-84.
35. Dale, *Fellowship with Christ*, p. 99.
36. R.W. Dale, *The Jewish Temple and the Christian Church* (London, 1865), pp. 11-22.

There are two great divisions of divine revelation, fragmentary through the prophets, complete through the Son.

Some of the Old Testament material looks very uninspired to us. But, he says:

> The clearest, fullest and most direct evidence of prophetic inspiration would be given to those to whom the prophets spoke; and it is very possible that people living in remote lands and remote ages, may be unable either to recover the external evidence of their divine commission, or to solve many questions which the contents of their books suggest.

The New Testament recognizes the authority of the Jewish prophets and the divine sanction attaching to Jewish institutions. But it does not thereby guarantee that the Old Testament is free from all error. If it could be proved, which he doubts, that mistakes existed in the Pentateuch from the beginning, the authority of the Lord Jesus Christ and of his apostles would not be overthrown. 'They are directly responsible only for the Divine authority of the Jewish system, and the Divine commission of the men by whom it was founded and maintained.'

He makes it clear in a footnote that he is not thinking here of what may now be regarded as unscientific references to the physical universe in the Pentateuch. Revelation can only be given in the thought forms of the people to whom it is given. Had the creation stories been 'in perfect harmony with modern science, the Pentateuch would have been not more Divine but less natural; it would have been a prodigy to be wondered at, but not a whit more precious as the record of divine revelation'. Further, a distinction has to be drawn between Divine revelation and the human record of it. What God said to Moses is one thing. Moses' account of it is quite another.

Clearly Dale is aware of some the problems thrown up by Biblical criticism and he has the courage to face them with his Carr's Lane congregation. He allows for a human element in producing the Bible and recognizes the distinction between revelation and record. He even takes account of the cultural determination of the books of the Old Testament. At the same time, there is still the easy optimism born of concern to reassure his hearers. He does not, for example, deal with the problem of Jesus' apparent sanction of some of the most debated parts of the Old Testament, which, as we saw, so troubled Liddon. He gives way to feeble sentiments, such as 'I can trust to the simple and irrepressible instincts of the human heart, the wide world over, for a recognition of the divine origin of Jewish Books'.

For all his keenness to be as open as possible to new scholarship he has hesitations about it. Quite properly, he argues that the tyranny of an infallible Bible must not be exchanged for the tyranny of infallible scholars. The so-called 'final results' of criticism must be examined, tested, controverted and sometimes rejected in favour of the new findings of later scholars.

Dale is also inclined to suggest that some of the concerns of biblical criticism are trivial. People should not get too caught up in them lest they are diverted from what is central to Christian faith. Moreover, controversies over dates and authorship create unease and distrust of the Bible in the minds of unlearned Christians, and the critical attitude of mind leads to atrophy of other qualities, such as the passion for souls and openness to the Word of God.[37]

Dale was beginning to feel the impact of historical criticism. He glimpsed the way in which the books of the Bible are conditioned by time and culture and perhaps by the outlook and personality of the writer. The Bible is being humanized and relativized. He was prepared to give more ground than Liddon but that was because he did not see the theological implications of criticism so sharply. Had he done so he would not have been able to maintain his optimistic stance. Critical scholarship may have influenced his treatment of Scripture by increasing his background knowledge and generating, or perhaps strengthening, a concern for its literal, historical and contextual meaning. But, as with Liddon, there are limits to his openness. A final quotation sums up his position:

> It is our duty to keep an open mind to the discoveries of the theologians and scholars; but this does not mean that we should consent to regard all the articles of the Christian faith as open questions. On the great subjects our mind is made up. The facts we know and under God we have to assert and defend them. We are willing, if necessary, to revise definitions; but can accept no definition which obscures the Divine glory of the Lord Jesus Christ, Son of God, Son of Man, Creator, Brother, Lord, Redeemer of the human race.[38]

4. *Benjamin Jowett*

Benjamin Jowett was well aware of what was happening in biblical studies in Germany as well as in England. He spoke German well and sometimes used it in his letters to Dean Stanley. In the mid-forties, he made a trip to Germany with Stanley and his biographers report that 'to converse with Gottfried Hermann, with Lachmann, Immanuel Bekker and Ewald

---

37. Dale, *Christian Doctrine*, p. 285.
38. Dale, *Fellowship with Christ*, p. 111.

made an era in his intellectual life'.[39] He was familiar with Strauss and Baur. Of Baur, he said, 'Baur appears to me the ablest book I have ever read on St. Paul's Epistles: a remarkable combination of Philological and Metaphysical power, without the intrusion of Modern Philosophy'[40]—an odd statement given both Baur's dependence upon and Jowett's interest in Hegel.

With such knowledge of what was happening, it was impossible for Jowett to ignore it. He must take account of all new thinking and knowledge and seek to incorporate it into his understanding of the Christian faith. Fundamental to all his work was the belief that truth mattered above all things and that it must be followed wherever it might lead. After all, he wrote, 'No man of sense can ever imagine that the enquiry into truth can be displeasing to the God of truth, even if carried to the uttermost in a reverent and earnest spirit.'[41] Any truth, in any area of human enquiry, must speak to us of God: 'There is no truth, though distant from religion, which is not the manifestation of his goodness.'[42]

Jowett believed that the Church could only harm itself by standing in the way of new truth. It had done so before and it was in serious danger of repeating the same mistake. In a sermon on Bunyan and Spinoza, he wrote:

> In religion we are always returning to the past, instead of starting from the past; learning nothing, forgetting nothing; trying to force back modern thought into old conditions instead of breathing anew the spirit of Christ into an altered world.[43]

Jowett's most famous and developed statement of his position with regard to Biblical criticism came in his essay 'Interpretation of Scripture', which he contributed to *Essays and Reviews* (1860). He argued that the results of criticism could no longer be disregarded and should not be treated as 'the mischief of atheists'. That would be to divorce Christianity from reason and from the educated classes. The Bible must be interpreted by the same rules of evidence and the same canons of criticism as any other book. Scripture has only one meaning and that is the meaning it had to the mind of the one who first uttered or wrote it and to the hearers or

---

39. E. Abbott and L. Campbell, *Life and Letters of Benjamin Jowett*, I (London, 1897), p. 90.
40. Geoffrey Faber, *Jowett* (London, 1957), p. 212.
41. B. Jowett, *College Sermons* (London, 1896), p. 118.
42. B. Jowett, *Sermons Biographical and Miscellaneous* (London, 1899), p. 231.
43. Jowett, *Sermons Biographical*, pp. 52-53.

readers who first received it. The interpreter's task is to get inside the situation of those earliest people. Differences within Scripture are to be accepted and each writer, each type of literature, taken on their merits. When the Bible is approached in this way both its uniqueness and its continuity, which can be thought of as a progress from childhood to adulthood, can be seen.

Most of Jowett's preaching was done in the Balliol College Chapel after he became Master in 1870. Thus his was not really public preaching. His hearers formed a relatively circumscribed and academic group amidst whom Jowett might be expected to feel a strong degree of intellectual freedom. That he did is illustrated by an incident in 1874. On 24 November the bishop of Oxford refused Bishop Colenso permission to fulfil a preaching engagement in the church at Carfax. Instead, Jowett invited him to preach in the afternoon in the chapel of Balliol, which was outside the bishop's jurisdiction. Nevertheless, even in this setting, Jowett, a sensitive man, was not free from criticism for his liberal theological views and perhaps even had to endure a measure of persecution.[44]

It is much more difficult to assess the degree to which Jowett's appreciation of contemporary criticism affected his preaching than is the case with Liddon and Dale. He was a more complex person and his preaching style is quite different to theirs. He was not a biblical or expository preacher in the same way that they were. His use of texts was often perfunctory and conventional. Often they were no more than pegs on which to hang a sermon. Especially in his earlier sermons, they were rarely expounded at any length and sometimes hardly mentioned after the original announcement. It is not easy to be sure whether this was because his grasp of critical scholarship had lessened the importance of the Bible for him or whether it was due to other factors. A sermon preached at Balliol in 1869 reveals some impatience with critical questions.[45] He wrote:

> The first truths of religion cannot be rocking to and fro with successive schools of criticism... We cannot suppose that anything important in human life is really affected by the date or mode of composition of a book, except in so far as our mistaken opinion has made it so.

Similar sentiments were expressed again in 1876:

44. For ten years, following his appointment as Regius Professor of Greek in Oxford, Jowett received practically no pay. It has sometimes been alleged that this was because of objections made by E.B. Pusey to Jowett's theological views. But Faber, *Jowett*, pp. 222-23, contests this view.

45. Jowett, *Sermons Biographical*, p. 368.

> Whatever uncertainty there may be about the early history of Christianity, there is no uncertainty about the Christian life. Questions of criticism have been raised concerning the Gospels... But that which truly constitutes religion, that in which they chiefly resemble Christ, remains the same.[46]

Jowett was supremely interested in the 'Idea' of the Christian faith as opposed to its outward form or manifestation, and it was this that made it possible for him to regard critical questions as peripheral. It sprang from his Platonism, but whether it was also the result of his Biblical study and a concern to separate Christian truth from a now uncertain historical foundation, it is difficult to be sure.

During the 1870s Jowett's willingness to talk more openly about the historical approach to the Bible and to use its findings developed. In another sermon from 1876 on 'The Hebrew Conception of God', his aim is to consider the revelation of the divine nature given in the Old Testament. In contrast to his doubts about supposing that anything important is really affected by 'the date or mode of composition of a book', mentioned above, he now asserts, 'Unless we can form an idea of chronology we can obtain no adequate conception of the progress of religious ideas among the Jewish people.'[47] We need to see what refinements of faith have taken place and what has been added or discarded at each stage. So he traces the process in the history of the Jews, allowing that there is 'much more of superstition and idolatry than it was once common to acknowledge'. When they knew God simply as 'Elohim', he was scarcely distinguishable from the gods of polytheism all around them. But the Jews had discarded the anthropomorphism of the earliest times by David's time and the prophets were to carry that correction and refinement much further. First among the Old Testament conceptions of God is that 'He is the God of nature'. Then to his physical government of the world is added a moral government. He is Judge as well as Creator. But he is also in a special manner the God of the Jewish people and out of this the prophets developed the tender, human relation of God to all people.

This links the Old Testament with the New: 'When God is said to be represented in the one as the God of justice, in the other as the God of love; when the Old Testament is opposed to the New as the law to the gospel, the thunder of Mount Sinai to the meekness and gentleness of Christ; this is really a very inconsiderate and partial way of viewing the subject. For in the Old and New Testaments alike God is equally repre-

---

46. B. Jowett, *Sermons on Faith and Doctrine* (London, 1901), p. 92.
47. Jowett, *Sermons on Faith*, pp. 57ff.

sented to us as a Father as well as a king, as a God of love and mercy as well as of justice; in both he is the God of individuals as well as of nations, who is not far "from every one of us". The truer distinction is that in the Old Testament he is revealed to Israel as his people and in the New to the world.'

At the close of the sermon he finds it necessary to add some words of justification of the place he has given to biblical criticism in it:

> I have been treating in this sermon of a very solemn subject in the language of criticism. In these days there are many things which we must criticize, although, they are the foundation of our lives, for otherwise they would become mere words, and have no meaning for us. We cannot expect that without any effort of thought we can understand the thoughts of 2,500 years ago. The realities which underlie our criticism, though manifested in different forms, remain the same; though the world grows old they change not; though at times obscured they are again revealed, deriving, as in past so also in future ages, light and meaning from the history and experience of mankind.

A further sermon of the same year also deals with the subject of the relation of the Old Testament to the New. He complains that the New Testament is too often read backwards into the Old. We cannot interpret the Old by the New. But there is a harmony between Old and New that is the harmony of goodness and truth everywhere. The difference between the Old and the New is that what is more outward and visible in the Old becomes inward and spiritual in the New.[48]

Numerous references indicate Jowett's acceptance of the current conclusions of the scholars on matters such as the dating of Psalms and Deuteronomy, the late compilation of the Pentateuch, the division of Isaiah into three parts and Zechariah into two. The prophets are to be treated in their historical context, no longer as fortune-tellers but as the revealers of the will of God to people in particular situations. Jowett recognizes the underlying religious purpose of writers even in the more historical parts of the Old Testament. He rejects the attempt to rationalize the miracle narratives of the Old Testament as Dean Milman had done. Already, he believes, the attempt to explain miracles by natural phenomena is a form of apologetics that has had its day. This is in 1878! It is far better not to worry about historicity but to seek out the religious significance and purpose that the writer discerns.

With the New Testament he is understandably more cautious. The Acts of the Apostles he assumes to be historical. The Gospels likewise seem to

---

48. Jowett, *Sermons on Faith*, pp. 77ff.

be accepted as historical, though they are fragmentary, and he recognizes the impossibility of ever attaining to anything like a biography of Jesus. We should not attempt to harmonize discrepancies in the Gospels:

> ...there is little wisdom is applying to Scripture a mode of reconciliation which we should not apply to an ordinary history. The thought of Christ which has filled the mind of the world has nothing to do with those microscopic enquiries respecting the composition of the Gospels which have so greatly exercised critics for more than a century.[49]

Jowett's appreciation of a progression of thought in the Bible, his conviction that God is at work in every fresh discovery of truth in any field of human enquiry and his belief that the essence of the Christian faith is independent of historical happenings gave him the freedom to go beyond the Bible in his preaching. The Bible could not be God's last word. His use of a text for his sermons, however perfunctory it might sometimes be, showed a concern for continuity with the past but he would not be bound by it. For him the Bible was relativized by the new criticism in a way that neither Liddon nor Dale could countenance. As a consequence, there is in Jowett's preaching the beginning of an attempt at the re-presentation and redaction of the biblical message.

An example is found in a sermon on Ps. 127.1, 'Except the Lord build the house, their labour is but in vain that build it.'[50]

The law of God (by which is meant not the Torah but the highest truth and rule of life which he was capable of conceiving) was to the Jew what the idea of the Good or Beauty was to the Greek. He wanted to rise out of himself to rest in God and in his truth. By the help of God the Israelites seemed able to do anything. Without him they could do nothing.

But language like this belongs to an earlier age than ours. The religious ideas of one age require to be translated into those of another, otherwise error creeps in or, at least, misunderstanding. The Psalmist talks of God as though, like human beings, he has his favourites. He prefers one man or one nation to another. He encourages one undertaking and thwarts another. Thus prophets and psalmists present us with an imperfect and partial conception of the divine nature. Now we know that law, which is impartial, governs the world and so there must be, what Jowett calls, 'a silent correction' of the familiar words of the Psalmist when we use them. But, since a preacher cannot remain silent, Jowett offers his own re-statement of the Psalmist's words 'Except men build the house, the Lord will not build

49. Jowett, *Sermons on Faith*, p. 327.
50. Jowett, *Sermons on Faith*, pp. 41ff.

it', which is paraphrased as 'We know that God helps those who help themselves'.

At first sight that may seem like the very opposite of what the Psalmist is saying. It is not that because what it means is that we can only prosper when we fall into line with the laws by which God orders the world. Nevertheless it is something very different from what the Psalmist is saying. He is trying to persuade people to live by faith in God rather than by anxious self-reliance. He would hardly be content with the platitude that life involves adjustment to reality. Jowett is aware of this and it prompts him to ask the question, How does this higher work differ from the results of ordinary human prudence? The answer, he thinks, is in the different attitude by which religious people are motivated and the unselfish end they have in view.

It may not be the most exciting or satisfying message. The ancient text has lost something in the restatement but at least it represents a serious attempt to bridge the credibility gap between the Bible and contemporary experience. Jowett alone of our three preachers understands the problem, though the loss of continuity in the content of the message may raise more questions than it answers.

Jowett's openness to the new criticism and, indeed, to the new intellectual climate as a whole is impressive. He dares to believe that God is in the change and for him that conviction is not compromised by dogmatic inhibitions. He has no doubt that, in the end, the new criticism will lead not only to a purging but also even to a strengthening of Christian faith.

Here, then, are three distinctive responses to the new criticism from preachers of different theological persuasion. They illustrate the radical questions raised for the Victorian Church by contemporary scholarship. Liddon impresses by his absolute seriousness. He knows that there are serious implications for catholic orthodoxy and he offers a robust, but reactionary, defence. Dale, initially at least, is rather more superficial. He wants to be open. He thinks that criticism only touches peripheral matters and he talks optimistically about criticism strengthening and illuminating faith. When the truth dawns that it may be more serious than that, his own sticking points are exposed. Jowett is more of an Enlightenment man, influenced by Greek culture as well as Christian thought. He has a better grasp of how preachers need to respond and his Platonism releases him from an undue reliance upon the Bible so that he can attempt to make that response. Impressive about all three is their awareness that the new criticism is raising issues that must be dealt with and their determination to deal with them, qualities which, on the whole, twentieth-century preachers have lacked.

'WE ARE TIED TO THESE TEXTS':
SCRIPTURE IN THE WORK OF KARL BARTH

Richard Arrandale

Editor's Introduction

It is probably not too controversial to claim that Karl Barth was the greatest theologian—at least the greatest Protestant theologian—of the twentieth century. In terms of productivity, about 9,600 pages of the uncompleted Church Dogmatics *is a fair indication of scale. English religious thought was much less directly influenced by him, but in European theology he stands as a revolutionary against the liberal processes of nineteenth-century thought. Barth's* Commentary on the Epistle to the Romans, *published in German in 1918 'fell like a bomb on the playground of the theologians'. In Alasdair Heron's words, 'he did not seek so much to* answer *the questions posed from the Enlightenment onwards as to* reverse *them'. The basic issue was one of theological orientation. Sir Edwyn Hoskyns made this explosive commentary accessible in English in 1933; gradually after this Barth's central concerns of divine transcendence, of the sole basis of Christian faith in the self-revelation of God in the Scriptures, and of the consequent authority of the Word of God, had their impact in the English-speaking world. In some quarters they served to reinforce existing absolutism and the rejection of compromise or any alternative foundation for theology.*

Richard Arrandale's piece originated as a seminar at University College, Chichester. He seeks to recapture the original impact and shock effect of Barth's insistence on the priority of Scripture by means of a postmodern retrospective and comparison with Gadamer's 'game theory' and Artaud's 'theatre of cruelty'. The resemblances are stressed within a limited but provocative comparison; surrealist echoes are not intended to detract from the realism of Barth's theology, but rather to demonstrate the revolutionary impact Barth made on early twentieth-century thought. Barth was a theological and philosophical realist, as his studies of St Anselm and John Calvin also make clear.

There are many things claimed on behalf of Barth, one of them being that he was very much a theologian of Scripture. As Paul Avis has recently commented: 'More than anyone else, he [Barth] helped modern theology to rediscover the otherness, the difference of the Bible. He evoked its numinous power and reminded us that to enter the Scriptures is to tread on holy ground.'[1]

In looking at Barth's relationship to Scripture it is important to appreciate, as the work of recent writers like Graham Ward has shown,[2] that the relationship is not a simple one, and that there are possible resonances with those who come under the labels of postmodern or post-structuralist. But it is also important to stress, as Dalferth so powerfully argues, that philosophically and theologically Barth is a realist and that in theology we are most definitely talking about 'a reality which precedes everything we say about it and cannot be exhausted by anything we say about it'.[3] Moreover, for Barth God is not regarded as purely a construct of language in Scripture. As Dalferth observes, even if theological statements are not 'directly descriptive' they are 'reality depicting'.[4] It is important to suggest that we can see Barth as a textual theologian, or perhaps a theologian of textuality, in that he is clear about the centrality of Scripture for theology, because it is through Scripture that the revelation of God is mediated to us. It is in this sense that as Christians and as theologians we are 'tied to these texts'. In what follows, I want to explore a few of the implications of this claim.

1. *Barth and Scripture*

While scripture is of central importance to the theology of Barth, and that he is a theological realist, it is important to note that Barth was not any sort of biblical or hermeneutical literalist, and that he 'consistently rejected the kind of scriptural interpretation which saw no discrepancy between text and referent' as for Barth this relationship was never 'one of perfect coincidence'.[5] Barth is absolutely dependent on Scripture as it is our wit-

1.   Paul Avis, *God and the Creative Imagination: Metaphor, Symbol and Myth in Religion and Theology* (London: Routledge, 1999), p. 49.

2.   See Graham Ward, *Barth, Derrida and the Language of Theology* (Cambridge: Cambridge University Press, 1995).

3.   Ingolf U. Dalferth, 'Karl Barth's Eschatological Realism', in S.W. Sykes (ed.), *Karl Barth: Centenary Essays* (Cambridge: Cambridge University Press, 1989), p. 17.

4.   Dalferth, 'Realism', p. 18. Although I have juxtaposed Ward and Dalferth, it is important to see that the two differ vastly in their approach to the theology of Barth.

5.   George Hunsinger, 'Beyond Literalism and Expressivism: Karl Barth's Hermeneutical Realism', *Modern Theology* 3.3 (1987), pp. 209-23 (209). More recently the 'slippery' nature of Barth's theological language has been explored in great detail by Ward, *Barth, Derrida*.

ness to divine revelation, but he is careful to distinguish the Bible from revelation itself, for a 'witness is not absolutely identical with that to which it witnesses' (*CD*, I.2, p. 463). What the Bible does is set before us that to which it witnesses, and this is connected to Barth's threefold understanding of the Word of God (cf. *CD*, I.1, pp. 88-124).

In this understanding, the primary form of the Word of God is God's revelation of himself, which is Jesus Christ, the Son of God. The Church proclaims the message, or 'good news', of this revelation of God, but does not do so from some vague recollection or feeling but from a particular form, namely, Holy Scripture. For Barth the Bible is 'the concrete means by which the Church recollects God's past revelation, is called to expectation of His future revelation, and is thus summoned and guided to proclamation and empowered for it' (*CD,* I.1, p. 111). In the same way that Barth sees preaching, which is the proclamation of the Word of God, as secondary to God's own message,[6] so it is the case with Holy Scripture.

It is very important for Barth, however, to see that Scripture is qualitatively different to the Word of God preached, in that Scripture must be singled out as 'the written words of the prophets and apostles over the later words of men' (*CD,* I.1, p. 102). In accepting this, Barth also clearly acknowledges that in Holy Scripture 'the writing is obviously not primary, but secondary' (*CD,* I.1, p. 102), because in origin the Bible was the oral proclamation of its human writers. But it is important to see that, as opposed to a 'historical monument', it has becomes an ecclesiastical document that is to be seen as 'written proclamation' (*CD,* I.1, p. 102). Holy Scripture then cannot be identified with revelation itself (because there is only one primary revelation, which is Jesus Christ himself), but as a genuine witness it brings us into contact with that revelation. If the revelation of God is that God (is) with us, then Scripture must be seen as the words of those who, 'yearned, waited and hoped for this Immanuel and who finally saw, heard and handled it in Jesus Christ' (*CD,* I.1, p. 108). It is in Holy Scripture, for Barth, that we have 'the object of authentic recollection', through which we are confronted by the 'magisterial and ultimate word' (*CD,* I.1, p. 108) which cannot and should not be confused with, or seen as equal to, any other human document.

In the sense that for Barth the Bible is a genuine witness of revelation, Bromiley is correct in asserting that for Barth Scripture is 'genuinely and

---

6. Although it is secondary Barth argues that it must be seen as a vehicle which God uses so that human talk about God, in the context of the preaching of the Church, can become that 'in which and through which God speaks about Himself' [*CD*, I.1, p. 94] in the event of real proclamation.

objectively God's Word'.[7] In Barth this must be understood in the context of his ideas regarding 'event', the primacy of God, and apostolic succession. For Barth the Bible cannot be seen as the Word of God purely in its own right, nor does it become God's Word 'because we accord it faith' (*CD*, I.1, p. 110). Rather, it becomes God's Word because it can become an 'event of real proclamation' (*CD*, I.1, p. 109), which means that in this event 'it becomes revelation for us' (*CD*, I.1, p. 110). It is worth quoting Barth at length here as he sums up his position with great clarity:

> The self-imposing Bible in virtue of its own content, and therefore the existence of real apostolic succession, is also an event, and is to be understood only as an event. In this event the Bible is God's Word. That is to say, in this event the human prophetic and apostolic word is a representative of God's Word (*CD*, I.1, p. 109)

What is equally important for Barth to deal with is the fact that this unique witness to the divine revelation has been written in human words. At this point it would be easy for Barth to produce a long rhetoric about the inability of human language, especially in its written form, to convey anything of the divine. Barth does not do this inasmuch as he takes this as his starting point. Of course, for Barth, human language cannot, through our own effort and agency, say anything about God, but the miracle is that this is the vehicle God has chosen to be the unique witness of his self-revelation.

That the Bible becomes an 'event' through which we gain access, and become witnesses ourselves, to that revelation does not come about because of our own faith, or our exegetical skill, but rather, 'the fact that God's own address becomes an event in the human word of the Bible is, however, God's affair and not ours' (*CD*, I.1, p. 109). For Barth it is in the Bible that 'we meet with human words written in human speech, and in these words, and therefore by means of them, we hear of the lordship of the triune God' (*CD*, I.2, p. 463). Though as a witness the Bible is not identical with the revelation, it still has 'something very positive to say' (*CD*, I.1, p. 463).

In taking both the human and the divine elements of Scripture seriously, Barth develops a hermeneutic in line with this entirely Chalcedonian view of the Bible. For Barth Scripture is 'neither divine only nor human only. Nor is it a mixture of the two nor a *tertium quid* between them. But in its own way and degree it is very God and very man' (*CD*, I.2, p. 501). The

---

7.   G.W. Bromiley, *Introduction to the Theology of Karl Barth* (Edinburgh: T. & T. Clark, 1979), p. 43.

Bible is not solely a human document, a text which is nothing more than a record of human religious feelings about the God revealed in Jesus Christ. But neither is it entirely divine, which would in effect make a Eutychian view of Scripture where the humanity of the text is totally swallowed up by the divine component.[8] Thus, we do not have a language devoid of God, and neither do we have a divinized language. We have elements of both. As Barth argues: 'The Bible is not a book of oracles; it is not an instrument of direct impartation. It is genuine witness' (*CD*, I.2, p. 507), which is what marks Scripture out from any other (even classic) text. It is also why McCormack sees the *analogia fidei* as an essentially dialectical phenomenon in that what we have in Barth is a 'dialectic of "veiling and unveiling" in revelation' because for Barth 'God unveils Himself by veiling Himself in human language'.[9] This is the tension in Barth, that God is 'utterly unique objectivity' (*CD*, II.1, p. 14) but gives Himself to be known (in secondary objectivity) 'clothed under the sign and veil of other objects different from Himself' (*CD*, II.1, p. 16). God is 'both a known and yet also an unknown God' (*CD*, IV.4, p. 115) and chooses, in his radical otherness, to make himself known through that which he is normally absent from. To put this another way we have an example of a 'presence sheltered in absence', to borrow a phrase from Heidegger.[10]

There are quite radical consequences for Barth in holding such a position. What I want to suggest is that in doing so, what happens in Barth's work can be seen as a reversal of the normal protocols of reading, in that as Scripture takes primacy, rather than we reading it, we are being read. To develop this a little more I want to go back to Barth's essay, 'The Strange New World within the Bible'.[11] In this essay Barth suggests what I would describe as the first stage of this reversal,[12] namely, that what we

8. As Barth says: 'The human element does not cease to be human, and as such and in itself is certainly not divine' (*CD*, I.2, p. 499).

9. B. McCormack, *Karl Barth's Critically Realistic Dialectical Theology: Its Genesis and Development, 1909–1936* (Oxford: Oxford University Press, 1995), p. 18.

10. M. Heidegger, *Poetry, Language, Thought* (trans. A. Hofstadter; New York: Harper Colophon Editions, 1975), p. 199.

11. In K. Barth, *The Word of God and the Word of Man* (trans. D. Horton; London: Hodder & Stoughton, 1928), pp. 28-50.

12. What I mean by the 'first stage' is that, in this early essay, Barth is in his so-called dialectical period where God is seen as 'Wholly Other', in an extreme sense. It is a first stage because when, in his 'mature' theology, Barth develops his 'analogy of faith', we see a softening of the radical difference, or separation between God and humanity. In his later work Barth still retains the radical difference, and there is still no

find in this 'strange new world' (which for Barth is 'the world of God')
are not 'the right human thoughts about God…but the right divine thoughts
about men. The Bible tells us not how we should talk with God but what
He says to us.'[13] Given that we have already said the witness is not identical to that to which it is a witness, what Barth suggests is that because the
Bible is the witness of how God has spoken to us, it is in this way that we
can understand it as the 'Word of God'. And, as the Word of God it confronts us and dares us to 'reach far beyond ourselves'.[14]

What becomes important for Barth, as these consequences are worked
out in the *Church Dogmatics*, is the priority that Scripture has over us. We
do not have mastery over the text, in that we do not stand over against the
subject-matter of Scripture as some form of isolated, judging subject.
Rather, it is 'a question of our being gripped by the subject matter' (*CD*,
I.2, p. 470). Scripture confronts us in a radical way because as the Word
of God it confronts us with the revelation of God. The Bible is only the
Word of God because it 'grasps at us' and God only causes it to be his
Word 'to the extent that He speaks through it' (*CD*, I.1, p. 109). And in
the end this means for Barth that Jesus Christ 'speaks for Himself whenever he is spoken of and His story told and heard' (*CD*, IV.1, p. 227),
which it is solely in Scripture. Thus reversal begun in the earlier essay can
be seen to have come to full fruition. We now see that in Scripture we are
being supremely confronted by the risen Christ, speaking to us. What
Barth wants to do is make sure that we are 'restrained in our evil domination of the text' (*CD*, IV.1, p. 471), because to dominate this text would be
to dominate (and domesticate) God himself who speaks to us through the
human words of the Bible.

sense in which it is our human religiosity or piety that gives us any knowledge of, or
access to, God. But, as Barth works through to his doctrine of reconciliation, he becomes
very clear that as we look at the redemptive act in Scripture it does not 'put God ab-
stractly at the heart of the message, but man with God' (*CD*, IV.2, p. 10). No discussion of Barth's move from the dialectical phase to the 'analogy of faith' can afford to
ignore Bruce McCormack's magisterial work. This is not the place to develop this
discussion, but I think that what I call a 'softening' McCormack describes as a 'shift of
emphasis', rather than the 'turn' of Von Balthasar's reading, between the so called 'dialectical' and 'analogia fidei' phases in Barth's work. McCormack crucially observes
that in Barth's work the '*analogia fidei* is itself an *inherently dialectical concept*'
(*Theology*, p. 16). Thus, Barth needed to work out the radical otherness of God in
order to give the correct context for the analogy of faith. If an analogy of faith were to
be worked out outside such a context it would easily become another natural theology.
    13. Barth, *Word of God*, p. 43.
    14. Barth, *Word of God*, p. 33.

There are some resonances here with the work of Hans-Georg Gadamer, and especially his development of the concept of 'understanding as play'. In his essay 'On the Problem of Self-Understanding',[15] Gadamer considers what he sees as 'the peculiar relation between myth and logos that we find in the beginning of Greek thought'.[16] Gadamer suggests that to ask what a Greek person believed about their myths would be to ask the wrong question in this situation. This is not that their myths were considered in any superficial way, but that an individual would not consider standing outside of their myths as an isolated judging subject. The ancient Greeks, according to Gadamer, stood in a relationship to their myths 'which is best understood as a game in which the myth is so much part of who he is, so determines his consciousness, that he cannot reduce it to a mere "object" to accept or reject'.[17]

Gadamer does not go as far as Barth, in terms of the idea that we are somehow read by the text, but there is a similarity in that the reading of Scripture cannot be seen as merely a spectator sport. For Gadamer, to stand outside the game (as an individual judging subject) would only disrupt the game and make one a 'spoilsport'.[18] It is only from the perspective of being involved in the game that we can interpret our myths, for it is impossible to abstract ourselves from the very things that determine our consciousness and shape our understanding of ourselves and the world. But he comes closer to Barth in the sense that he sees writing as 'iconic' in some way in that it is 'not a reproduction of something that is past, but the sharing of a present meaning'.[19] Although Barth may have problems with the term iconic, the idea that a text (in this case the specific text of Scripture) is not just a set of historical oracles, but has a present meaning is central to his understanding that Scripture is a witness to the Revelation

15. In Hans-Gerog Gadamer, *Philosophical Hermeneutics* (trans. D.E. Linge; Berkeley: University of California Press, 1977), pp. 44-58.

16. Gadamer, *Philosophical Hermeneutics*, p. 51.

17. William Gray, 'Gadamer on Theology', *Encounter* 46.4 (1985), pp. 327-37 (328). I am deeply indebted to Dr Gray for earlier help in understanding and appreciating the significance of the work of Gadamer. Although I am sure that this has led me in very different directions, it was fundamental to my own later position.

18. Hans-Georg Gadamer, *Truth and Method* (ET; London: Sheed & Ward Stagbooks, 1988), p. 92. For Barth, when he is addressing the issue of having knowledge of God, he writes (in a way which can be seen to have similarities with Gadamer): 'Lead us not into the temptation of wanting to know thee in thy objectivity as if we were spectators, as if we could know, speak and hear about thee in the slightest degree without at once taking part' (*CD*, II.1, p. 26).

19. Gadamer, *Truth and Method*, p. 354.

and places us in a relation as witnesses. If Scripture is thus seen as sharing
a present meaning in terms of a Gadamerian game, then it is in this sense
that Barth does not have a model of Scripture in which it has a dominating
form of mastery over us.

It is equally important, however, to see that neither do we master it
ourselves. In Gadamer it is the game that has primacy over the players. In
Barth it is important to see: 'No longer is the interpreter autonomously
standing over the records of past history, but instead the interpreter is himself being questioned by the living Christ.'[20] Ultimately this is because,
like the Greeks and their myths, Barth does not see Scripture as an object.
And it is here that Barth and Gadamer can be seen (at least hermeneutically)
to coincide, for Gadamer is clear that in terms of the game a player 'cannot behave towards play as if it were an object'.[21] The game in Gadamer,
like Scripture for Barth, always has primacy over the players. For it is
the case that for both of these thinkers, what they ultimately want to do
(though in different ways and for different reasons) is 'to realise afresh the
distinction between text and commentary and to let the text speak again'
(*CD*, I.1, p. 107). For both thinkers this means that interpretation is always
on-going. For Gadamer, fixity in writing means that a text becomes detached from 'the contingency of its origin and its author and made itself
free for new relationships'.[22] Although for Barth any interpretative freedom has to conform to and come under the judgment of Scripture, nonetheless, in a way similar to Gadamer, Barth sees that the Bible is 'constantly
exposed to absorption into the life, thought and utterance of the Church
inasmuch as it continually seeks to be understood afresh and hence exposed
and interpreted' (*CD*, I.1, p. 106).

2. *Artaud and the 'Theatre of Cruelty'*

At this point, and in order to help explain the idea that Barth reverses the
normal protocols of reading in that we have an approach where Scripture
reads us, I want to suggest some striking analogies with a thinker who was
contemporary with Barth. Although they were (historically) contemporary,
there is no suggestion that they influenced each other in any direct way. The
thinker I want to explore is the French dramatist, writer and theoretician,
Antonin Artaud, and most especially his concept of the 'Theatre of Cruelty'.

---

20. D.F. Ford, 'Barth's Interpretation of the Bible', in S.W. Sykes (ed.), *Karl Barth:
Studies of his Theological Method* (Oxford: Clarendon Press, 1979), pp. 55-87 (74).
    21. Gadamer, *Truth and Method*, p. 92.
    22. Gadamer, *Truth and Method*, p. 357.

Artaud lived and worked in the first half of the twentieth century (1896–1948). He was very influenced by the surrealist movement, of which he was an active member from 1923 to 1927, and although he formally left the movement, the influence, at some level, remained. Apart from his influence on the theatre, he has also had a marked influence on a variety of postmodern thinkers. By suggesting a correspondence between Barth and Artaud, I want to make it clear that I am not suggesting such a close association that the differences between them (and they are immense) should be neglected, or that (from their different perspectives) they were saying the same thing. What I do want to suggest is that there are at least some 'family resemblances' which are worth exploring.[23]

Artaud was disillusioned with the theatre of his time. According to him society had 'lost the idea of theatre', and all he saw happening in the contemporary drama of his time was 'probing the intimacy of a few puppets, thereby transforming the audience into Peeping Toms'.[24] Theatre consists of a passive audience, watching actions on a stage, and Artaud 'despised

23.　In this sense I am wanting to avoid some of the problems highlighted by Bruce McCormack in his review of Graham Ward's *Barth, Derrida*. While I do not entirely agree with all of this review, which at times is very brutal, I am trying to take seriously McCormack's warning against any kind of 'illegitimate appropriation of Barth'. See Bruce McCormack's article review, 'Graham Ward's *Barth, Derrida and the Language of Theology*', *Scottish Journal of Theology*, 49.1 (1996), pp. 97-109. See also similar comments made in W.S. Johnson, *The Mystery of God: Karl Barth and the Postmodern Foundations of Theology* (Louisville, KY: Westminster/John Knox Press, 1997), pp. 21, 198 n. 45. With this said, it is important to see that Ward does at least show some new possiblities even if they are not fully worked out. I see Ward's work in relation to David Ford's excellent book, *Barth and God's Story: Biblical Narrative and the Theological Method of Karl Barth in the Church Dogmatics* (Bern: Peter Lang, 1985). Here, Ford reads Barth in a literary critical way in order to suggest that there are parallels between 'what literary critics say about realistic novels and what Barth says about certain biblical narratives' (p. 13). Ward, in line with this approach to Barth, tries to read him in the light of the literary-philosophical work of Derrida. Perhaps where Ward is helpful is in highlighting the textuality and provisionality of Barth, and we should always remember that at the heart of some realistic novels is a level of uncertainty and non-realism (such as Eliot's *Middlemarch* where we would be hard pressed to describe the very place in which the whole novel is set). But Ward takes this too far, and I am arguing that, even accepting provisionality and language not directly referring, Barth is nonetheless a (critical) realist to a greater extent than Ward allows.

24.　A. Artaud, *The Theatre and its Double* (trans. V. Corti; London: John Calder, 1970), p. 64.

the view that the theatre was a mere place of entertainment'.[25] In terms of his approach to writing, Artaud wanted to 'violate the self-protective distance between reader and text',[26] and he wanted to do something similar with that distance, which is also 'self-protective', between audience and stage. Thus, in an attempt to remedy this, Artaud tried to develop a new approach to theatre in which there would be 'no barrier between actors and audience'[27] He wanted a type of theatre that 'wakes us up heart and nerves',[28] and he called his approach the *Theatre of Cruelty.*

One can see many of the later elements of the Theatre of Cruelty in Artaud's earlier work, perhaps especially in his work on the Theatre Alfred Jarry.[29] But there were three key events in 1931 that propel Artaud's thinking towards a 'truly dangerous theatre which would threaten the security both of the word and of the world'.[30] First, in August, Artaud saw a group of Balinese dancers, the experience of which highlighted to him the idea of a type of theatre that consisted of physical signs and violent gestures and was not dependent on a script.[31] Secondly, Artaud came across the fifteenth-century painting by Van Leyden in the Louvre called *The Daughters of Lot*. He saw many parallels with the Balinese dancers and 'began to

25. M. Esslin, *Antonin Artaud: The Man and his Work* (London: Calder Publications, 1976), p. 76.

26. S. Sontag (ed.), *Antonin Artaud: Selected Writings* (trans. H. Weaver; Berkeley: University of California Press, 1988), p. xxiv.

27. Esslin, *Antonin Artaud*, p. 84.

28. Artaud, *Theatre*, p. 64.

29. For a good, brief description of the Alfred Jarry Theatre, see Stephen Barber, *Antonin Artaud: Blows and Bombs* (London: Faber & Faber, 1994), pp. 38-41. See also Esslin, *Antonin Artaud*, esp. pp. 76-95 which gives a good overview of Artaud's theory and practice of theatre as well as making some connections between his earlier Theatre Alfred Jarry work and the Theatre of Cruelty. Esslin argues that 'the programmatic statements for the Theatre Alfred Jarry already contain the essence of Artaud's most radical concepts' (p. 78).

30. Barber, *Antonin Artaud*, p. 45.

31. Artaud writes of the Balinese theatre that it was 'not a revelation of a verbal but a physical idea of theatre where drama is encompassed within the limits of everything that can happen on stage, independently of a written script' (*Theatre*, p. 50). In this essay ('Oriental and Western Theatre'), Artaud develops much which will become pertinent to a Theatre of Cruelty, such as the idea of a pure language of theatre; theatre as religious and metaphysical; and the use of gestures and signs combined with a lessening of the importance of speech (which is part of Artaud's pure language of theatre). This is developed against the literary and psychological theatre of the West. Also of great importance in this regard is Artaud's essay, 'On the Balinese Theatre', in *The Theatre and its Double* (trans. V. Corti; London: John Calder, 1970), pp. 36-49.

consider the painting as the result of a finely elaborated creative direction, like that governing a theatrical spectacle'.[32] Artaud sees in this painting 'what theatre ought to be, if it only knew how to speak its own language'.[33] In the same essay that he discusses this painting, Artaud details what is considered to be the third element important to the development of the Theatre of Cruelty, the films of the Marx Brothers (in particular *Monkey Business*, but he later saw and was influenced by *Animal Crackers*). Artaud used elements of what he saw in these films and translated them in terms of theatre. From these films Artaud recognized the importance of humour, as well as the significance that 'producing the concept of danger on stage' would have in a theatrical production.[34]

Artaud now had all the major components ready to develop his concept of the Theatre of Cruelty. But, before moving on, it is worth outlining what Artaud meant by 'cruelty' as this will become significant for our present context. For Artaud, 'cruelty' was not that cruel and bloody scenes would be enacted on the stage, but that theatre becomes a spectacle of 'sensory violence, rather than sensory enchantment'.[35] Part of the nature of this 'cruelty' is the attempt to 'overwhelm the spectator in such a way that he cannot be left intact'.[36] Or, to put it into Artaud's own words, it is an approach to the theatrical experience that makes the 'theatre a believable reality inflicting [a] kind of…laceration'.[37] Thus, the theatrical experience should have the effect of shocking and transforming us.

This cruelty, for Artaud, should have a positive and liberating outcome. Indeed, he thinks generally that 'art must have a beneficial spiritual effect on its audience',[38] but that theatre in particular 'must embrace a wholly serious, ultimately religious purpose'.[39] He argues that this is exactly what does not happen in the sterile, Peeping Tom, psychological and literary

32. Barber, *Antonin Artaud*, p. 46. See also Artaud's own essay where he comments on this painting: 'Production and Metaphysics', in *The Theatre and its Double* (trans. V. Corti; London: John Calder, 1970), pp. 23-35.

33. Artaud, *Theatre*, p. 26.

34. Artaud, *Theatre*, p. 32. It is important to note that Artaud was already working in the film industry so it is not strange that he would try to make these connections. As with much that Artaud did himself, his film career as both actor and film maker was largely unsuccessful.

35. Sontag, *Antonin Artaud*, p. xxxii.

36. J. Gassner and E. Quinn, *The Reader's Encyclopedia of World Drama* (London: Methuen, 1970), p. 841.

37. Artaud, *Theatre*, p. 65.

38. Sontag, *Antonin Artaud*, p. xxxiii.

39. Sontag, *Antonin Artaud*, p. xxxvii.

theatre of his day. This is where one can still see the surrealist influence on Artaud even though he had formally left the movement, for he is working with what can be seen as one of the principle tenets of surrealism: 'Art is a real experience that goes far beyond human understanding and attempts to reach a metaphysical truth.'[40] For Artaud the theatre was not just an art form that served religion or life, it 'was a manifestation of the religious impulse itself'[41] and the 'double' of life itself.

In order to achieve his aims, Artaud attempts to develop a new language of the theatre, which means for him breaking 'theatre's subjugation to the text', or what Derrida terms, in his writings on Artaud, his trying to break with the 'dictatorship of the text'.[42] In doing this, Artaud claims that he wants to find a 'kind of unique language somewhere in between gesture and thought'.[43] Artaud's new language of the theatre wants to transcend the limits of language imposed by human speech, and wants to develop a language out of 'symbolic gesture, movement, sound, and rhythm'.[44] This new and unique language, which theatre can call its own, will involve gestures and signs taking over from mere speech.

Jacques Derrida, in his reflections on the work of Artaud,[45] sees that in attempting to produce a stage of non-representation, in effect Artaud's 'theater of cruelty expulses God from the stage'.[46] For Derrida this does not mean that Artaud's theatre is a platform for atheism, or is a form of atheistic theatre, but rather that his theatre produces a 'nontheological space'.[47] What Derrida means by this is that he sees the stage as theological because it is tied to a text and an author who has control over the text and its presentation, in much the same way as God stands over against the text of Scripture. In this sense the theological stage is like the concept of the book, which, for Derrida, is an enclosed totality where meaning is determined and controlled by something (i.e. author, god, etc.) outside the text. What I am arguing, then, is that in Barth, especially when seen in the

---

40. Sontag, *Antonin Artaud*, p. 33.

41. Esslin, *Antonin Artaud*, p. 79.

42. J. Derrida, *Writing and Difference* (trans. A. Bass; London: Routledge & Kegan Paul, 1978), p. 190.

43. Artaud, *Theatre*, p. 68.

44. P. Hartnoll (ed.), *The Oxford Companion to the Theatre* (Oxford: Oxford University Press, 4th edn, 1984).

45. See his two essays in *Writing and Difference*; 'La parole soufflée', pp. 169-95, and, 'The Theater of Cruelty and the Closure of Representation', pp. 232-50.

46. Derrida, *Writing and Difference*, p. 235.

47. Derrida, *Writing and Difference*.

Artaudian terms I am suggesting, provides an approach to Scripture that can be seen as being a middle way between the Derridian totality of the book, or a form of textual nihilism.

3. *Barth and Artaud: Some 'Family Resemblances'*

A first point of interest I wish to comment on, is the idea in Artaud, that the theatre of cruelty involves a deconstruction of the audience and the stage. There is a move away from the theatre, outside ourselves, towards the idea that we (as audience) are a 'passive, seated public, a public of spectators, of consumers, of "enjoyers"'.[48] Although there is, of course, always a sense in which we (as audience) go to watch a stage production, Artaud argues that audience and stage, spectator and actor, are part of the same thing. We as audience are involved with and in the production.

The fact that we are somehow involved in the story or 'production' (to use a more 'theatrical' language) of Scripture is important to Barth. For although Scripture has primacy over us, it is not as an evil and dominant master, but rather there is some form of relationship. The divine revelation in the Bible is addressed to all, it 'comes to every man, all men', which for Barth means that it 'in a measure includes them in itself' (*CD*, I.2, p. 486). Because the Bible is the witness of divine revelation, in being confronted by Scripture we too stand in a relationship of witness to that revelation. The Scriptures confront us, not as dead letters, or inert marks on a page, but as 'living documents of that unique event' (*CD*, I.2, p. 486) which is the revelation of God in Jesus Christ. For Barth this means that 'rightly understood, all humanity...does actually stand in the Bible, and is therefore itself posited as a witness of divine revelation' (*CD*, I.2, p. 486). To stand in such a relationship with Scripture, which is partly one of involvement, means that we must let the text speak to us; we must 'let it say all that it has to say in its vocabulary and context, to allow the prophets and apostles to say again here and now to us what they said there and then' (*CD*, I.2, p. 533).

The second point of connection between Barth and Artaud that I want to highlight leads on from this first one. If we stand in a relationship to Scripture understood as involvement, and although it has primacy over us, it does not seek to crush us, then there are radical consequences. Part of the point of the 'Theatre of Cruelty', for Artaud, was that the experience of involvement would 'overwhelm us' so that we would not 'be left intact'.[49]

---

48. Derrida, *Writing and Difference*, p. 235.
49. Gassner and Quinn, *Reader's Encyclopedia*, p. 841.

What this means is a rejection of what Artaud sees as dead and fossilized forms of rationalism in the psychological theatre of his time. For Barth it is something similar, for in giving primacy to Scripture (plus his rejection of natural theology) he too is rejecting what he sees as equally fossilized and dangerous forms of liberal rationalism in theology. Barth raises a challenge to a self-assured form of liberal theology (in a similar way that Artaud does to theatre) that seeks to dominate and domesticate Scripture for its own (sometimes evil) ends.[50] If we see Scripture as a an Artaud-like 'theatre of cruelty', then if we engage with Scripture, or more properly Scripture engages us, we too should not be 'left intact', not least of all due to its radical call to both repentance and to drop everything and follow him to whom Scripture refers.

Before moving on to my conclusion I want to highlight one final similarity between Artaud and Barth that is important to the thrust of this paper. I have already highlighted Artaud's wish to produce a language somewhere between gesture and thought, and his attempt to produce a pure language of theatre that is not dictated to by the text. Artaud sees that there is a 'rupture between things and words, between things and the ideas and signs that are their representation', but this gap is to be overcome in 'a language of living signs'.[51] There are great resonances with Barth here, for he too sees that there is a 'rupture' between the text and that to which it refers, in that it is never one of direct or perfect correspondence.

Artaud's dream of a pure language of theatre involved, as we have seen, escaping from the domination of the text to a very directorial type of theatre. When Derrida reads Artaud he points out that one of the paradoxes of Artaud's 'pure signs' is that they fail to acknowledge that 'signs by their very nature are representations and not the presence of what really is'.[52] It is here that we can see how Barth works with a more subtle view of the language of Scripture and that to which it refers. For Barth there is not a direct correspondence between language and referent, but his approach to Scripture produces a language that has some of the hallmarks

---

50. I am merely agreeing here with those thinkers who argue that we partly need to understand Barth's rejection of natural theology, and the theological liberalism of his time, as a political response.

51. M. Fortier, *Theory/Theatre: An Introduction* (London: Routledge, 1997), p. 42.

52. Fortier, *Theory/Theatre*, p. 43. It be must highlighted here that Artaud saw that all of the elements on the stage, especially that which is normally seen to accompany a production (such as scenery, costume, lighting and suchlike) should not be seen to represent something but are things. The stage does not represent something, as the double of life, it *is* something.

of Artaud's 'pure language' (of the theatre), in that the language of Scripture can become an event (as it read us) that can lacerate, transform and awaken us. Not least of all in the fact that for both Barth and Artaud the idea of 'event' is crucially important. In Artaud's Theatre of Cruelty, he wanted the theatrical experience to 'merge with real life to form a genuine event'[53] that would lacerate and awaken us in order that we 're-establish contact with the true metaphysical basis of human existence'.[54] As I have argued, in Barth the event of real proclamation the Bible becomes an event through which God's own address is heard through the human words of Scripture. And, for Barth, the event of real proclamation should 'call' us to a new and radically changed life, for it is through God's revelation that he gives us the possibility, through his grace, to re-establish the true (metaphysical) basis of our lives. Indeed for Barth this is an 'awakening' from the 'sleep of death' that is the 'sleep of covenant-breaking humanity, of the world in conflict with God' (*CD*, IV.2, p. 555), and the only way that such an awakening is effected is through 'the mystery and miracle of God' (*CD*, IV.2, p. 555).

4. *Some Concluding Remarks*

All I am doing here is tracing the outline of the terrain, and there is much more to do here. What I hope to achieve is to show that this avenue is a fruitful one to explore in trying to understand the way in which Barth views Scripture. In trying to make some concluding remarks, therefore, one needs to bear in mind that I am doing so in a provisional way. By considering Artaud's concept of the 'Theatre of Cruelty' what I hope to have shown is that Artaud can be of use, alongside a such theologian as Barth, in challenging a particular form of liberalism that I have suggested will seek to master, dominate and domesticate Scripture.

To see Scripture, at least for a short moment, in terms of a provisional working hypothesis, as a 'theatre of cruelty' means that Scripture, as it engages us and reads us, will be a constant challenge to any human-constructed certainty we may care to develop. It would be an interesting point of development of what I am suggesting, to liken our domination and domestication of the text of Scripture to other forms of domination of the other. Barth clearly saw that the conversion to a new life in Christ was not to be seen merely in terms of our relationship with God in isolation from considering this in the context of our relationships with our brothers and

53. Esslin, *Antonin Artaud*, p. 93.
54. Esslin, *Antonin Artaud*, p. 81.

sisters. For Barth we are not 'whole' without reference to our fellows, and 'it would not be the conversion of the whole man if it did not commence and work itself out at once in this relationship' (*CD*, IV.2, p. 563).

In Barth's theology, if God is for us and we for him, then this must include the fact that (because God is also for all others) we must be for our brothers and sisters. Barth clearly sees that 'the biblical individual is not selfishly wrapped up in his own concerns', because conversion to God the Lord must mean our 'entry into the service of His cause on earth and His witness in the cosmos'. Thus as a 'convert' we 'cross the threshold of our private existence and move out into the open' (*CD*, IV.2, p. 565).

To return to the main point of this paper, the consequences of viewing Scripture in terms of a type of 'theatre of cruelty' in which we are both involved, but which has primacy over us, thus engaging and reading us, means to acknowledge the disruption that Scripture can—perhaps even must—cause in our Christian life. For if, like the Theatre Of Cruelty, it will not leave us intact, it is because (like Artaud's theatre) Scripture is a 'believable reality' that inflicts a 'kind of…laceration'.[55] And that laceration, in more Christian language, needs to be seen in terms of crucifixion, for if it is in and through Scripture that we are witnesses to the revelation of God in Jesus Christ, then part of that call from him is to take up one's cross and follow. Or if, as Paul describes the Christian life, it is about being 'crucified with Christ' (Gal. 2.20), then part of that crucifixion must be about letting Scripture engage and lacerate us. And such 'laceration', or 'textual crucifixion', as Scripture reads us, must challenge any self-assured certainty we may come up with in our 'evil domination of the text', which often finds its expression in a desperate search for the absolute certainty of objective meaning. This, too, Scripture will 'lacerate'. If Artaud's idea of a language of theatre that exists somewhere 'between gesture and thought' is applied to theology, then I would suggest that it can be seen in the view of Scripture I have begun to highlight, and therefore that the language of theology exists in that space between the gesture of God and the thoughts of humans. That space is Scripture, and it is this space in which and through which we live, move and have our being. This will always be a provisional space, so as Christians and as theologians we must live in this space with an eschatological humility, until the gesture of God comes to its fullest expression at the eschaton, when the space between gesture and thought will be erased.[56]

55. Artaud, *Theatre*, p. 65.

56. I am very grateful to Professor Gareth Jones for his close reading of the text and many helpful suggestions.

BIBLIOGRAPHY

There is obviously a wealth of material on Barth and I would suggest the reader follows up any of the references in this article. In terms of Artaud, the best way is to read his short collection of essays, *The Theatre and its Double*, which contain much of the important material relating to the Theatre of Cruelty. Unfortunately a lot of the good material previously published on Artaud is quite difficult to come by, or very expensive. What follows a selection of good, reasonably priced, and easily accessible material.

Artaud, Antonin, *The Theatre and its Double* (trans. V. Corti; London: John Calder, 1970).
Barber, Stephen, *Antonin Artaud: Blows and Bombs* (London: Faber & Faber, 1994).
Barth, Karl, *Church Dogmatics* (ET; Edinburgh: T. & T. Clark, 1936–1969).
Esslin, Martin, *Antonin Artaud: The Man and his Work* (London: Calder Publications, 1976).
Sontag, Susan (ed.), *Antonin Artaud: Selected Writings* (trans. H. Weaver; Berkley: University of California Press, 1988). This collection contains Sontag's brilliant essay on Artaud, 'Approaching Artaud'.

BIBLICAL STRUCTURALISM AND THE COMPUTER

Ian Mitchell Lambert

Editor's Introduction

Few areas of human knowledge and endeavour have developed—and continue to develop—as rapidly as Information Technology. Little purpose would therefore be served by a chapter that surveyed the 'state of the art' in the interaction of Bible and Computer; it would be out of date before this year was much older. But in this collection of historical studies there is great significance in a retrospective look at a relationship of theology and technology that was widely regarded as controversial, revolutionary and threatening to traditional methods of biblical interpretation (and in those respects comparable to several other 'revolutions' considered in this volume).

A symposium on the Computer in Literary Research held in Cambridge in March 1970 was very largely concerned with practical problems of programming and the choice of the ideal computer language for literary research. The positive uses of the computer in compiling concordances and dictionaries and in textual criticism were highlighted; despite the energetic work of A.Q. Morton (largely on the Pauline epistles) computer analyses of style and authorship were seen as 'clearly controversial'; the report concluded that the 'interpretation of texts is not an obvious area for the use of the computer'.

Ian Mitchell Lambert's contribution to our collection is based on a paper he delivered in 1988 to the Jerusalem meeting of Association Internationale Bible et Informatique. By the late 1980s his own research work—and of others in that gathering—had given the lie to the last conclusion of the Cambridge symposium. He asked the question whether the process of constructing a structuralist interpretation of text (particularly popular in French-speaking circles since the work of Ferdinand de Saussure) was similar to that of computer programming (computer modelling). His paper gives an outline of structuralist methodologies, then discusses what was then the current state of computer work on literature and language, and finally outlines his own research project, to analyse responses to the structural analyses of selected texts (particularly Numbers 11–12 and the story of the Good Samaritan).

1. *Introduction*

This chapter seeks to capture a moment in history when those researching in biblical studies and theology were becoming aware of the growing use and reliance on computerization in the disciplines around them. My interest in exploring the relationship between structuralist modelling and computer modelling of the biblical text stemmed from two questions that arose on meeting structuralist thinking for the first time: (a) does structuralism provide a new perspective on the biblical text? and (b) is the process of constructing a structuralist interpretation similar to computer programming? I therefore plan to examine structuralism initially, elaborating on the first question; then I shall develop the second question before completing this chapter with some details of my elementary computer programming attempts to tackle the issues raised.

2. *Why Structuralism?*

Biblical scholarship was invariably thought of in terms of form criticism, redaction criticism or phenomenology.[1] Structuralism takes a totally different perspective and excludes a great deal of material on which traditional criticism relies.

For instance, it is fundamental to a pure structuralist approach that the boundary of interest is the text itself. Its composition, its history, its authorship, the influences on the author and similar extraneous considerations in the reader are understood to be outside a structuralist understanding of a text. The immediate problem that raises for a theologian is that authors claim to have written under the guidance of God and/or his Spirit. Indeed, it is that claim that differentiates biblical text from any other text, and the ability to verify that claim that entitles the Church universal, or the Synod of Jamnia to pronounce the New Testament or the תורה *torâh Law* as being more than just text written by men.

However, the stance of the structuralist creates its own problems, with the claim that a deep code lies behind the surface, which communicates itself subliminally to each of us. This is seen particularly in the works of Lévi-Strauss, and those who follow him, as a means through which values and essential structures of society are preserved and subsumed. If that were to be accepted, it seems reasonable to wonder whether religious values are

---

1.   Brevard Childs, *Myth and Reality in the Old Testament* (Studies in Biblical Theology, 27; London: SCM Press, 1960).

contained within that code, since the majority of human beings interact in some form or another with religious values.

3. *Ferdinand De Saussure*

To proceed together, it may be necessary to explain a little more about structuralism itself. It is not a biblical critical tool itself. Structuralism began life as a branch of linguistics and Ferdinand de Saussure is universally regarded as its father.[2] He defined four basic dichotomies that exist in all text, namely

1. the synchronic ‖ the diachronic;
2. what is called *langue* ‖ *parole*;
3. *signifié* ‖ *signifiant*;
4. the syntagmatic ‖ paradigmatic.

Briefly, these dichotomies are known to structuralists as *binary opposites*. This suggests a link with the computer programmer. However, we shall discover that structuralists and computer programmers do not mean the same thing by the same term. The heart of structuralism relies on the concept of the binary opposition and the relationship within that opposition. Theologically, this is of interest, specifically in terms of the overall belief in a divine ‖ human binary opposition, which is mediated, in Christian terms, in the very name Jesus ‖ Christ, that significantly is expressed in a human ‖ divine structure. The Jewish mediation has seemed to be related at times to a desert ‖ civilization opposition mediated by משה *mosêh Moses*, or an אדני ‖ אדן (or אדני ‖ דון) opposition mediated by the anointed משיה. In all these examples, anthropomorphic projections are present. Only in the אדן ‖ אדני opposition is there a יהוה concept outside human experience. If one begins to consider these examples from the viewpoint of someone like Cupitt then the nature of those oppositions takes on new perspectives: 'I continue to speak to God and pray to God… He is needed—but as a myth…God is a myth we have to have.'[3]

Cupitt provides one of the ways in which a believer's world vision can enter the orbit of the pure structuralist.

We return to basic structuralism and the meaning of the four binary oppositions. De Saussure believed you could detect movement sequen-

---

2.   De Saussure's work first appeared after his death in 1916 in *Cours de linguistique générale* (ed. C. Bally and A. Sechehaye; Paris: Payot, 3rd edn, 1949). English translation *Course in General Linguistics* (trans. W. Baskin, C. Bally and A. Sechehaye; New York, 1959).

3.   Don Cupitt, *Taking Leave of God* (London: SCM Press, 1980), p. 166.

tially in a text, and at the same time move deeper into meaning *at any point you chose to stop*—synchrony versus diachrony. He also claimed there was an overall innate structure in a text through which meaning develops. This structure (*langue*) acted in opposition to the most fundamental constituent units of the text (*paroles*)—his *langue* || *parole* concept. To make clear what he meant, he explained that it was like a game of chess. *Langue* was the totality of the game; *parole* equated to each chess piece.

It is in the tension between *signifié* and *signifiant* that de Saussure believed that we innately apprehend meaning. This concept relies on the use we make of signs in communication. The letters *l*, *o*, *v* and *e* in themselves have no value, meaning or significance. When put together they have a meaning, that happens to match that of meaningless signs, such as *a*, *m*, *o*, *u* and *r*, or α, γ, α, π and η or ה,ֹ, בַּ, הַ , and א). That led de Saussure to another important perception—that the sound is arbitrary to actual understanding and meaning. The discovery of the *signifié* || *signifiant* relationship, together with the work of Charles Saunders Peirce, gave birth to semiotics, which is seen by many structuralists as contained, or partly contained within their discipline.

It is, though, the syntagmatic || paradigmatic opposition to which de Saussure claims all linguistic systems are ultimately reducible. Paradigmatically, various levels (sounds, words, sentences, texts and a complete linguistic system) coexist within a text. Working at one level has implications for all other levels of the text. Syntagmatically, a linear progression through the text, places, for example, words in a position of opposites. 'Jesus' is in opposition to 'died' in the sentence 'Jesus died' and through that opposition, each word acquires greater meaning in relationship to each other, the significance of which will vary according to who is reading the sentence.

De Saussure's work led to many branches of structuralism, and, consequently, it is not easy to talk of one structuralist position. For our purposes, the gurus are Vladimir Propp of the Russian Formalist school, Claude Lévi-Strauss of the French school and Algirdas Julien Greimas, who sought to fuse together the perceived fundamental differences of several schools.

4. *Vladimir Propp*

It is through Propp that structuralists receive the proposition that all folktales contain variable and constant factors. He drew up a table of 31 functions that he maintained reflected the constant factors in any folktale—not necessarily present in every tale, but at whatever point a tale starts, it must progress through to its conclusion in the order of the 31 functions.[4] These 31 functions can be grouped in pairs, or opposites (e.g. prohibition ‖ violation; struggle ‖ victory; persecution ‖ deliverance) and others can be seen as a sequence (e.g. villainy → dispatch → decision for counter action → departure from home). The example enables us to see how biblical scholars look at structuralism and ponder its application. What of the Christian theological perspective on the Λογος? or Jonah and Nineveh?

The computer programmer can see similarities when Propp goes on to codify his 31 functions and produce a formula that, while lacking overt statements of relationship, described each folktale uniquely, as, for example

$$\alpha^1 \ \delta^1 \ A^3 \ B^1 \ C\!\uparrow \ H^1 - I^1 \ K\!\downarrow \ W^\circ$$

which can be read

α^1	A king/father of three daughters
δ^1	the daughters go walking
A^3	stay late in the garden
B^1	a dragon kidnaps them
$C\!\uparrow$	call for help
H^1	quest of three heroes
–	battles with the dragon
I^1	victory
$K\!\downarrow$	rescue of the maidens
W°	rewarding

An obvious question of interest to a theologian is whether such models, when applied to biblical myth, result in similar patterns, formulae, or types of models, a search in which the computer would play a valuable role.

5. *Claude Lévi-Strauss*

With this development we should link Lévi-Strauss, who, in the 1940s, through meeting the outstanding work of Roman Jakobson's linguistic structuralism, perceived that structuralist principles were equally applicable to social anthropology. In parenthesis, it ought to be said that this is a feature of structuralism. It no longer is the domain of linguistics. Piaget and Lacan in psychology, Althusser in history, Foucault, Derrida and

---

4.   V. Propp, *Morfologia skaski* (Leningrad: Academia, 1928) was translated into English as *Morphology of the Folktale* (ed. S. Pirkova-Jakobson; trans. L. Scott; Bloomington, IN: Indiana University Research Centre in Anthropology, Folklore and Linguistics, 1958). The English publication has opened renewed interest in Propp, a detailed contribution being Pamela Milne's *Vladimir Propp and the Study of Structure in Hebrew Biblical Narrative* (Sheffield: Sheffield Academic Press, 1988).

Bremond in philosophy and Schiwy, Greimas and Marin in theology are a small sample of the wide application across subject disciplines of structuralism. Indeed modern architecture, fine art and drama and biology also employ similar concepts.

Lévi-Strauss saw that binary opposition was at the heart of culture and society, and saw kinship as the ultimate language of cultural communication, through which the values of a society were expressed and communicated. And it is Lévi-Strauss who made the major breakthrough, after studying Propp, on structuralist understanding of myth in which he claimed atemporal binary oppositions represent universal truths. Lévi-Strauss established that structural patterns of the mind found expression in totemism, kinship and myth, and that all three are ultimately forms of communication.[5]

Myth brings us directly into some modern biblical criticism and anthropology. Although Lévi-Strauss studied primitive societies, he always maintained that the biblical record was worked over too greatly to enable any meaningful original myth to be retrieved.[6] Ricoeur has challenged him[7] for restricting his work to 'the geographical areas of totemism and never from Semitic, pre-Hellenic, or Indo-European areas'. Despite Lévi-Strauss's reticence over the application of structuralism to the Bible, Leach led the way,[8] widening the scope of structuralist interpretation in the process. It is through Leach that we find ourselves comparing Miriam, sister of Moses with Mary, mother of Jesus, Mary of Magdala and Isis.[9]

That is clearly a much wider and different level from linguistic structuralists who study phonemes and morphemes and their relationships.

6. *Algirdas Julien Greimas*

Greimas was heavily influenced by the work of Hjelmslev, a Danish structuralist whose work is among the most objective applications of structuralism. Greimas also sought to integrate the work of Propp and Lévi-Strauss,

5.   The literature is wide, but Claude Lévi-Strauss's major works are *The Raw and the Cooked: Introduction to a Science of Mythology* (London: Harper & Row, 1969); *The Savage Mind* (London: Weidenfeld & Nicolson, 1966); *Totemism* (Harmondsworth: Penguin Books, 1969); *Structural Anthropology* (2 vols.; Thetford, Norfolk: Lowe & Brydone, 1973).

6.   Quoted in 'Interview', *Diacritics* 1 (1971), p. 47.

7.   Paul Riceour, 'Structure et hermeneutique'[in *Esprit* NS xi 1963], p. 607.

8.   Edmund Leach, *Genesis and Other Essays* (London: Cape, 1971).

9.   Edmund Leach and D. Alan Aycock, *Structuralist Interpretations of Biblical Myth* (Cambridge: Cambridge University Press, 1985), pp. 33-66.

and over a lifetime of research he has developed his thinking dramatically. His explanatory diagrams are similar to the way computer programmers explain their thinking.

Greimas's first structure concerns the area Propp handled. Greimas reduced Propp's 31 functions to 20, and identified three basic relationships of opposition—which interacted in a way that enabled myths and folktales to be expressed in the form of his *actantial* model:[10]

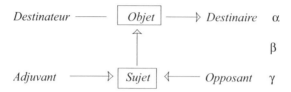

In the actantial model there exists three relationships—α (above) knowledge, β desire and γ power. This is not the place to explore these, but their mention draws attention to the distinction between the meaning of binary opposition to a structuralist and a programmer—a distinction that itself could be a binary opposition! Binarity for computer purposes is concerned with truth ‖ falsity, either ‖ or. No other option is ultimately available. It can be expressed in other ways using a combination of either ‖ or – such as both ‖ and, or if ‖ then ‖ else. For a structuralist, the point of studying binary polarity is to examine and define the relationship that exists, or is in tension, between the elements. For the computer programmer, binarity is absolute and irreducible. For the structuralist, binarity is relative and thus negotiable or open to influence, as post-structuralists and deconstructionists proved later.

Looking at Greimas's thinking, though, the computer similarity is not exhausted, for in his second structure, relationships *are* either ‖ or, or both ‖ and—binarity is contrary, contradictory or complementary. Here we are looking at the semiotic square, which bridges the disciplines of structuralism and semiotics. An analytical tool, the semiotic square expresses *one level* of binary oppositions and their relationships, which leads on to at least two other levels, each expressed in a new related but semiotic square.

10. Algirdas Julien Greimas, *Sémantique structurale* (Paris: Larousse, 1966), p. 180. Greimas's use of the term *actant* is his own, but is widely used by structuralists and semioticians. It seeks to take the reader away from seeing only human *actors* as the source of activity in narratives. *Actants* can be any quality, person, thought or stimulation that causes an action to happen.

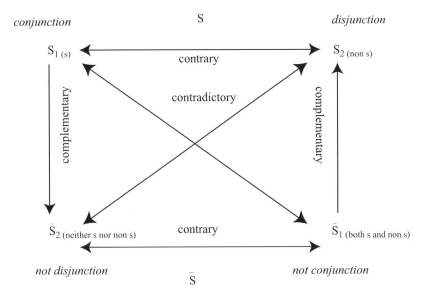

Greimas addresses the question of theological involvement in structuralism in a much more direct way than his predecessors. For him the relationship divine ‖ human is part of a wider binary opposition of knowing ‖ believing.[11] Such proposition marks a development in his thinking that caused him eventually to reject the power dimension (γ above).

7. Surveying Existing Studies of Structuralism and the Computer

Existing work relating structuralism to the computer appears to be surprisingly limited. From a bibliography of 400 plus books and articles, and almost 300 contacts worldwide, one would be forgiven for believing that those who work in this area mirror their subject matter and are hidden below the surface somewhere!

a. *1974 Wisconsin*
Work was carried out at Wisconsin[12] the purpose of which was to construct and execute an automated model of Propp's *Morphology of the*

---

11. Algirdas Julien Greimas, *On Meaning* (Minneapolis: University of Minnesota Press, 1987), p. 176.

12. Sheldon Klein *et al.*, *Modelling Propp and Lévi-Strauss in a Meta-symbolic Simulation System* (Technical Report 226; Computer Sciences Department, University of Wisconsin, October 1974).

Folktale, and a simpler automated model for generating myths from Lévi-Strauss's *The Raw and the Cooked.* The researchers created a special behavioural simulation system that they named a *meta-symbolic simulation system.* Their models integrated a variety of behavioural and semantic/grammatical models which had three main components, namely:

1. a behavioural simulation;
2. a semantic network;
3. a semantics-to-surface structure generation mechanism.

The method they employed converted the Propp and Lévi-Strauss folktales and myths into databases. A test model was used, one that Klein and his associates had already created, for generating murder mystery stories. Because of Propp's assertion that folktale functions followed a predetermined sequence, the meta-symbolic simulation system sought to test the potential to predict. Through that work, the authors claimed to have created a system that had the ability to present simulation language in the same notation as natural language. Such a breakthrough enabled them to test and inspect non-verbal rules of behaviour, presuppositional analysis and ultimately to produce automated structural analysis. With the passage of time, this achievement has proved difficult to transfer to other contexts.

It would be of interest to apply their methods to biblical myths. First, such a test would serve the overall interest of this paper concerning the status of biblical myth as religious text in the context of structuralist limitations. Secondly, the claim to have created an automated structural analysis in itself deserves testing, bearing in mind the high degree of subjective judgment involved in structuralist analysis. While it remains true that a structuralist analysis delimits interpretation within strict bands of movement, the whole analysis depends on the initial identification, for instance, of the fundamental binary oppositions. That appears to be primarily a subjective operation.

However, I have applied the principles involved manually to Phil. 2.6-11, using Propp's model for folktales, and discovered that a reasonable outcome can be achieved. Of significance is that it was much quicker and more efficient to produce the outcome manually. The outcome, of course, inherently carries my subjective interpretation. There is no reason why the entire biblical corpus could not be encoded in this fashion and fed into a computer database. From such a database comparisons between texts for similar formulae could well produce worthwhile results. The question that would arise about computerising the database, is, To what purpose? Such a database would be my subjective perception of the biblical text, and the results would be revealing my personal brain patterning. While this may attract researchers in other disciplines, it is difficult to see such a database as a worthwhile theological tool.

Using my interpretation, Phil. 2.6-11 produces this Proppian formula:

$$\alpha\,\beta\,B\uparrow D\,J\,K\downarrow Q\,T$$

that can be read as follows: α Introduction; β family member absents himself; B misfortune or lack is made known; $\uparrow$ the hero leaves home; D the hero is tested or attacked in preparation to receive a magical agent or a helper; J the hero is branded; K the initial misfortune or lack is liquidated; $\downarrow$ the hero returns; Q the hero is publicly recognized; T the hero is given a new appearance.

b. *Forester*

Judson Parker's doctoral thesis[13] in 1976 sought to create a language that would enable morphological analysis of hierarchical systems. His particular reference was to structural exegesis of the synoptic traditions. Although his title implies a wide-ranging field of biblical application, his thesis was only applied to the parable of the prodigal son, as recorded in the Synoptic Gospels.

Forester is an interesting language for the structuralist community, since its declared aim is to distinguish between form and content, a matter of some concern to A.J. Greimas,[14] allowing the user access to the content, and the ability to ignore form in the process. The distinction stems from de Saussure's definition of linguistics as the science of forms,[15] in which the definition of form as not being a substance bears some comparison with Platonic perceptions of the Word. It is the structures of the *content* that exercises the structuralist, not the form of the language. Parker argues powerfully that traditional critical methodologies of the biblical text are preoccupied or give clear preference to form rather than content.

Relying on the structuralist interpretations in the *genre* of Greimas, Roland Barthes and Louis Marin, Parker concentrates on the structures at the various levels of a text, and through *Forester* seeks specific patterns.

---

13. Judson Floyd Parker Forester, 'A language for Morphological Analysis of Hierarchical Systems, with Reference to Structural Exegesis of Synoptic Traditions' (PhD thesis, Vanderbilt University, 1976; Xerox University Microfilms 76-22), p. 360.

14. A.J. Greimas and Joseph Cortés, *Semiotics and Language: An Analytical Dictionary* (trans. Larry Crist *et al.*; Bloomington, IN: Indiana University Press, 1982). Originally published as *Sémiotique dictionnaire raisonné de la théorie du langage* (Paris: Libraire Hachette, 1979).

15. De Saussure, *Course in General Linguistics*, p. 113.

By this method he allows the possibility of creating a story in hierarchical terms that are not dependent on narrative sequence. His further aim, to discover the relationships among the *contents* of each level of the hierarchy, reveals his hope that the thought categories of the author can be revealed. This aim probably comes close to crossing the line for a structuralist. Certainly, in later developments from structuralism, such as reader response criticism, the thought categories of an author holds little importance.

Through *Forester* Parker believes form and content can be separated and evaluated separately. Such an achievement places structuralism in the context of the full battery of biblical critical methods, of course. In email conversation with Parker in October 1988, I learned that he did not take this work further because of a fundamental misconception:

> Almost immediately after the research was published, it became clear that the appropriate structural model for all but the simplest texts is not hierarchical... Intuitively, each of the actants in the domain of the text is pursuing a distinct agenda, and these interact at multiple points with plural semantic investments... There was no direct way to extend either the distance metric or the *Forester* language to meet this more general problem...

With *Forester*, I believe we reach the same position as above when I discussed creating computerized databases for Proppian formulae. At the end of all the effort, the results would have been achieved more efficiently and perhaps with even greater validity had the operation been done by hand.

c. *Computer Assisted Learning*

Parker's supervisor, Daniel Patte, is one of the foremost scholars in both structuralism and its application by computer. Apart from two substantial books[16] that Patte added to his lengthy list of published contributions, he developed a computer-assisted learning package with his students at Vanderbilt University.

This package combines a computer program developed by Patte with wider studies and worksheets entitled *A Critical Study of the Religious Teaching of the New Testament*. The purposes of this paper are well served by this work of Patte, since he takes the question of the text on into the context of the *faith* that it aims to convey. Specifically, Patte raises not

---

16.   Daniel Patte, *Paul's Faith and the Power of the Gospel: A Structural Introduction to the Pauline Letters* (Philadelphia: Fortress Press, 1983) and *The Gospel according to Matthew: A Structural Commentary on Matthew's Faith* (Philadelphia: Fortress Press, 1987).

just *what* are texts conveying to their reader, but *how*. This is at the heart of the structuralist's agenda.

An opening exercise based on John 10 is balanced by exercises from the משנה *mišnêh Mishnah* and מכלתא *mêkilta' Mechilta*, the *Gospel of Thomas*, and the *Rule of the Community* and פשר עלחבקוק *pesêr 'alhavaquq pesher Habakkuk* from the Dead Sea Scrolls. By exploring opposites such as blessedness || evil, loving one's neighbour || biting and devouring one another (Gal. 5.14-15) and identifying, for example, the divine, a mediator, believer(s), or leader(s), the student is guided behind the surface narrative to perceive the faith being expressed in the text. By so doing, it enables valid comparisons to take place with the faith expressed and so measured in other religious texts. Patte's course for his students then culminates in the acquired skills to recognize Christian faith in New Testament texts. *Paul's Faith* and *Gospel according to Matthew* are Patte's own application of such insights.

It is worth noting, though, that what students achieve through these exercises is an understanding of *Patte's* structural exegesis, rather than their own. Answers are registered as correct or incorrect as the program proceeds, the correctness dependent, of course, on the perception Patte is guiding the students towards, and that is written into the programming. That is a proper educational method, and one hopes that through such learning, students gain skills that they learn to apply independently. As a former headmaster with close to 30 years' teaching experience, I know that learning to transfer skills outside the environment in which they were learned is the most difficult part of the education process!

This observation, though, has significance in terms of the degree to which subjectivity is a major element of structuralist interpretation. Patte's interpretation is valid because structurally speaking it results from the interaction between him and the text.

In retrospect I find some concern about this level of subjectivity. It can be argued that any educative process is subjective, and I would further argue that total objectivity is unattainable. The structuralist endorses the degree to which the *valeur* and *langue* of our cultural and received knowledge predetermine the way we look at the world.

Patte went on in later years to draw a much closer relationship between his structuralist and semiotic research. Patte relies heavily on a small part of the Greimas theories, namely, the veridictory theory. It is found in Greimas's *On Meaning*[17] and is imbued with greater attention and importance

17. Greimas, *On Meaning*, pp. 125-26, 140.

by Patte.[18] It may well be a natural and proper development, but it seems to me that an embryo discipline, which could be named biblical structuralism, has been forged. It is neither structuralism as known in other arenas, nor do its assumptions match other biblical forms of criticism.

d. *Purity Can(not) Exist*

At the Tübingen conference of Association Internationale Bible et Informatique (AIBI) in September 1991, a great excitement was the launch of the Westminster–CATSS version of the BHS database. Professor Alan Groves presented the culmination of over a decade of work on the BHS text, and specifically on a four year sub-task of lemmatizing and marking the transliterated form of the complete BHS text. It was the first time that the entire Hebrew text of the Bible had been analyzed word for word from beginning to end for the computer. The operation was carried out from scratch.

The feat was enormous. Not only was the whole alphabet and the נקודם *nikkudim* of the text encoded but also every cantellation is coded. Every word is lemmatized by mood, gender, person, and even by root. The corpus is a remarkable contribution on its own to Hebrew and biblical scholarship in its simple printed form without any application of computer programs to the text. During the four years of final entering of the data, Groves and his colleagues, not least at Maredsous,[19] around the world shared notes and encouraged biblical scholars, particularly inside AIBI to submit corrections, scribal errors, variants and comments on early drafts of the Westminster database. The intent and purpose was academically creditable. There is no value in using the computer as a tool without the database on which it is working being accurate. Entire projects are invalidated if the original database is seriously faulted.

At Tübingen, Groves presented a perfect BHS text.

The first question raised in discussion was whether there was such a thing as a perfect text, and thereby whether the database is valid.

A decade of work was apparently undercut with the first question. On the one side, the contention was that this was an invalid database because it actually contained a text of the Bible that no one in history had ever

---

18. Daniel Patte, *The Religious Dimension of Biblical Texts* (SBL; Atlanta: Scholars Press, 1990), §2.212, p. 79.

19. The headquarters of AIBI in Belgium, and the location of Probi Biblique et Informatique, the project that prepared the *Bible de Jerusalem* in computer format and mounted it on to the French Minitel system, as well as the *Texte hébreu/araméen de la BHS.*

seen or used. On the other hand, the counter-proposal was that it was not possible to undertake any examination of the complete text without errors having been eradicated.

By the end of the conference it was freely being accepted in discussion that there were many biblical texts. Computerization had to accept that. The reasons for this position were only peripherally those of the structuralist or the biblical critic who accepts that there is no such thing as *a* biblical text, but rather many. The literary position that there is no original text, no original Bible to which a reader can turn as the definitive version,[20] is not exactly the same as saying that a database is invalid. Both positions are effectively rejecting the concept that there is a perfect version of the Bible, of course, but the argument in terms of database perfection is also revealing that the effective use of a computer is demanding a non-existent precision in the quality of the text.

e. *Tax(i)ing CABS?*

Has Groves wasted his time? Not only is the answer a negative one, but the question misses something rather fundamental. The use of the computer is the planting of a new seed in the groundwork of biblical studies. Computers as a tool in biblical studies have changed the work of the scholar to such an extent that in the AIBI it is freely believed that we are dealing with an embryo discipline whose future is still being uncovered. Just as biblical structuralism is a discipline of its own within the structuralist movement, so there is now a new discipline emerging among those biblical scholars who use the computer as a tool. Computer applications in biblical studies (CABS—an acronym of my own creation!) results in outcomes when studying the biblical text that would never be achieved in traditional forms of critical, exegetical or hermeneutic studies. The reason simply is that it handles the biblical text in a completely new way. As a result a new discipline emerges in which we are learning to see the biblical text in a new light, and with a different perspective.

The fact that we can digitally hear Beethoven's Ninth Symphony with a perfection that his deafness would have prevented him from hearing does not preclude, invalidate nor lessen the experience of its performance and reception. We can also hear the symphony in a more perfect form than any of Beethoven's contemporaries.

As an interjection, the problems of coding and using the computer in non-Latin languages raises much deeper questions for a structuralist about

20. A Catholic, Orthodox or fundamentalist theologian would challenge that, of course.

the mechanisms of power and control in our contemporary world. To use Hebrew, Aramaic, Syriac or Greek, an ability to adapt to different keyboards may seem little, but what in effect is happening is that all non-Latin language users are being forced into the binary thinking of the Western world. Computers are only binary based because we all agree that they should be. They can be, and in some cases have been, based on other numeric bases. The Western world naturally has no problem since its own thought patterns are binary based. At a cultural level there are dangers that the dominating of disciplines like biblical studies and theology with computerization will be an imprisonment and a severe restriction to future understanding of non-Western perceptions of the world and culture.

8. *My Basic(A) Program*

I developed a simple program as part of an overall project, the direction of which is somewhat dependent on the incoming results from this program. The basic aim of the program is to gather individual responses to a structural analysis of one or more predetermined biblical texts.

a. *Initial Subjectivity*

Bearing in mind the problems already mentioned about the subjectivity in structuralist decision-making, I sought to address this problem at the outset. It has been designed to record every idea entered on the keyboard, even if that idea is later rejected. My interest is in learning what thought processes the user went through before reaching a conclusion that satisfied them. It will be apparent that this is an attempt to test and codify the initial subjectivity from which a subsequent structural interpretation is made.

b. *Sample Group*

The program was freely available to anyone. In particular selected users were invited whose experience ranges from biblical scholarship to those who have never approached the subject, and similar human binary opposites in computer studies, the academic world, linguistics scholars, Christian believers, in business and in the professions. In that way, a wide range of experience was drawn upon, and the program encouraged the users to record that experience, both professionally and in terms of leisure interest. It does not seem unreasonable to test the hypothesis that an interpretation by one user will be strongly influenced by the current and former experiences s/he has had.

Individuals were given the opportunity to remain anonymous if they wished. It was a matter of little relevance to the analysis.

c. *Cross-Cultural*

My plan to translate the program into a number of languages and invite responses in order to test the question of cross-cultural interpretation has not yet been achieved. My thinking was that if, for example, the structural anthropologist is right in claiming that myth speaks with universal truths to all humankind, then one should be able to test that from cross-cultural returns.

d. *Hard and Software*

The program was constructed in the days before regular use of email and the popular use of the Internet. UNIX and FORTRAN were the most advanced computer languages available, and so to assist easy access to contemporary hardware for such a diverse group, the program was written in BASICA on an IBM PC with a CGA board, or a Hercules board adapted by software to simulate CGA. The program fitted comfortably on to a 5.25-inch disk, thus easing the problem of returning the results.

e. *Selected Texts*

Numbers 11–12, and the Good Samaritan texts were selected for the analysis. I encouraged users to tackle both. One text is far more well known than the other in Christianity, and it would be interesting to see whether that would lead to a greater uniformity of interpretations in the Good Samaritan story.

Deliberately choosing a story from the Hebrew Bible and one from the New Testament allowed for believers in both traditions to tackle texts that have special meaning for them. Existing scholarship of both texts already exists in traditional and structural exegesis.

The program reflected my teaching experience in that it attempted to emulate directed learning methods. The user determined the outcome, and this meant allowing for an infinite number of variables at every stage. Every input was designed to have significance—an important structuralist principle among some adherents. Later in the program, early choices were re-presented, so that early 'readings' were not lost. The data saved recorded all responses, accepted or rejected. Both were important.

After initially collecting the user's age, gender, employment, education level and faith commitment for later analysis against the user's choices, the program asked the user to narrate the story in their own words from *either* Num. 11–12 or the Good Samaritan account in Lk. 10. This would allow any movement in understanding the story to be measurable when asked to narrate the story again at the closure of the exercise.

The program then required the user to identify any actants that came to mind in the text they had selected. These were collected in a database and offered back, asking the user to select any oppositions in the story that emanated from their choices of actants, or any other oppositions that came to mind at that stage.

Users then were invited to collect their oppositions into the categories of contrast, contrariety or complementarity. That stage enabled the construction of a semiotic square. Following the rules of the semiotic square, the user then moved on to two other levels of reading the text, the details of which do not need explanation here.

At the final stage, users were invited to look at the three levels of narrative that they had produced, and asked to retell the story.

There were many discoveries from the 112 users who returned responses. Only 44 felt able to take the program beyond the first invitation to narrate the story in their own words; 29 of those were men and 15 were women.

The responders were in large measure graduate (18.2 per cent) or post-graduate/professionals (47.7 per cent) with 10 per cent either with no qualification or none expressed. Of this group only 12 per cent were restricted to English, the remainder having working knowledge at least of 15 modern or ancient languages.

Of all 112 responses Christians dominated the declared commitment answers (43.8 per cent), with Jews (1.8 per cent) and Muslims (6.8 per cent) forming too small a group for sensible comparisons between the faiths; 2.6 per cent defined themselves as agnostic or non-believers, while the largest group (44.6 per cent) elected not to answer this question.

Returning to the 44 who tackled the texts, the program was confusing for many (12 per cent). With retrospective eyes, this seems to reflect the limitation of either the contemporary software that users had experienced (providing the program with major detail at every stage was not widespread then), or the lack of experience of using a computer, which was widespread in biblical studies and theology departments.

A total of 34 per cent of respondents also reported a difficulty in differentiating contrary, contradictory and complementary oppositions in English. Two thought it impossible to make such distinction. Four had sufficient understanding of biblical Hebrew to recognise oppositions not immediately apparent in the English text.

In the Good Samaritan story, 220 oppositions were identified, of which 204 were different. Of these, 27 were not technically oppositions, leaving

177 actual binary oppositions.[21] Further analysis revealed at least 31 different readings of the text in Lk. 10.

The strongest correlation undermined the structuralist claim of a deep universal reading of the same narratives. This was revealed when searching for the common factors among the 107 oppositions. The strongest factor by far, out of age, gender, employment, educational level and faith commitment, was employment.

Later work in reader response criticism would confirm the impression that people regularly do not read the same meaning in a narrative. Employment is one of the major ways in which people today are categorized and valued in society, and the respondents to this program appear to see the world and the reading of these biblical texts from that perspective.

In today's computerised world, the program and its structure look almost risible. Structuralist thinking has moved on to allow semiotics a much louder voice. Deconstruction and other poststructuralist methods of interpreting text have created more evanescent problems for computer programmers.

Two scholars, though, have made dramatic contributions. Andersen[22] worked with the theories of his countryman Hjelmslev (who was also a great influence on Greimas) in the Cambridge Series on Human–Computer Interaction. He demonstrates admirably that any structuralist or poststructuralist computerization will benefit if it is centred on the concept of the sign.

Talstra[23] has uncovered another fruitful area in his analysis of synchrony and diachrony in 1 Kgs 8.14-61 in the Hebrew Bible. Instead of reading the narrative through a synchronic ‖ diachronic opposition, he performs a synchronic analysis, followed by a diachronic analysis, independently of each other, and sees them complementing each other.

There is fruit to be picked in CABs and biblical structuralism, but we have only seen the first petals of the blossom.

---

21. 80 binary oppositions were identified in the Num. 11–12 narrative.

22. P.B. Andersen, *A Theory of Computer Semiotics* (Cambridge: Cambridge University Press, 1990).

23. Eep Talstra, *Solomon's Prayer* (Kampen: Kok, 1993).

Rainbow Hermeneutics and St Paul's Letter to the Galatians

G. Daan Cloete

Editor's Introduction

The rainbow is a powerful symbol for the reality of a cosmopolitan nation, weathering the political storms. It must be a symbol of hope and trust in God's future, after the biblical pattern of the covenant with Noah. The new South Africa rejoices in the title of 'the rainbow nation' and the latest phase of biblical interpretation in that country, post-liberation theology, is known as African or Rainbow Hermeneutics.

South Africa reflects a dominant modern Western culture in tension with a nascent African cultural and religious experience. It seeks to liberate itself from the grip of the histories of colonialism and apartheid, and at the same time it struggles to develop its own new identity. Integral to this dynamic process is the manner in which the Bible has been read in the past and the impact on future readings. In past biblical scholarship the focus was on historical criticism and the meaning behind the text; for the present and the future there is a shift of emphasis to meaning in front of the text. This is a reading in dialogue with the text, a reading at the crossroads of modernity and postmodernity, a reading that seeks to reclaim the African past, and a reading with the Rainbow Nation in the momentum of Thabo Mbeki's African Renaissance. African society is still very religious, compared with other nations, but in many socio-economic and cultural respects it can be regarded as a microcosm of the world.

In the context of Rainbow Hermeneutics Daan Cloete suggests a way of reading Paul's letter to the Galatian church as a document of transformation. The traditional arguments of the Pauline text, between Jew, Gentile and Christian, are transposed into the debates of the new South Africa, so that Paul speaks afresh about 'intercultural communication, recognising plurality, but, by integration, offering the vision of an ultimate unity'.

Reading the Bible in the African context, in the aftermath of decolonialization and with the expectation of an African renaissance, is becoming an exciting venture. Identifying the real issues, finding the appropriate

methodologies, eventually defining the particularity of the African contribution to the universal theological discourse—these are some of the challenges. In a dynamic process of transition, some contours (such as the
following) are emerging that help to define the African context and enable
Africa to become the agent for its own transformation.[1] So reading takes
place within the bounds of these contours.

1. *Reading with Africa*

a. *Reading for Freedom*

While in colonial times, reading the Bible happened in a way that was
adversative to the indigenous culture, and even justified oppression, racism,
slavery and patriarchalism, but in the present process of awakening, it has
become an indispensable tool and a considerable force in the search for
socio-economic justice and liberation. The transcendental schemes, universal constructions and absolute truth claims of the traditional readings are
now being challenged by more contextual and praxis-orientated readings,
prescribed by an agenda of fundamental issues, such as survival and transformation. Reading to transform is now the fullest expression of those
incidental attempts at reading to resist that which already took place in
colonial times. It now voices the latent desire for freedom fully.

b. *Reading to Affirm Plurality*

Africa has also been the victim of Western cultural imposition through
the projects of modernity and now globalization.[2] Western culture became
the universal norm, absorbing, ploughing under, or pushing to the periphery, other cultures. However, postmodernism has assisted by dispatching
the myth of a homogeneous culture for all Africa. There is an upsurge
in the appreciation of cultural diversity and equality without fear of
fragmentation.

---

1.   T.S. Maluleke, 'The Discovery of the Agency of Africans', *Journal of Theology
for Southern Africa* 108 (November 2000), pp. 19-37. On 32 he sees this as 'the one
factor that cuts across all (other) factors…the discovery of the agency of Africans'.

2.   H.J. van Rinsum, *Slaves of Definition* (Maastrict: Shaker Publishing BV, 2001),
pp. 14-15 describes globalization as the 'historical process by which the West…spread
out its tentacles, economically, politically…religiously and epistemologically…to bring
other parts of the world within its sphere of influence'. It also ' implies a continuous
reduction of local traditions…'

c. *Reading, Conscious of Innate Religiosity*

Africa's inherent religiosity has long been acknowledged.[3] This religious experience that permeates almost all spheres of life[4] was first treated as inferior 'heathenism' which had to be replaced by the ultimate religion, Western Christianity. Now that Africa's cultures, primal religions and philosophies are in the process of being retrieved, Christianity is becoming part of Africa's religious plurality. Interesting discourses have emerged about how to utilize the receptiveness of traditional religions for Christianity. These include, regarding African traditional religions[5] as the 'Old Testament' of African Christianity[6]; phenomenalising the African Independent Churches as an authentic expression of African Christianity;[7] and contextuality and the issue of religious syncretism. Mercy Oduyoye, one of Africa's most well-known feminist African theologians of our time, is very determined that African Christianity does not become an addendum to or an alien variant of Western theology. She says:

3.   J.S. Mbiti, *African Religions and Philosophy* (London: Heinemann, 1969), p. 262.

4.   Okot p'Bitek, *African Religion in an African University: Africa's Cultural Revolution* (Nairobi: Macmillan, 1973), p. 86, puts it well: 'The knowledge of the religions of our people is the key to the knowledge of our culture. The aim of the study of African religions in an African university is to know our people…so that we can serve them better.'

5.   Van Rinsum, *Slaves*, p. 3, describes African Traditional Religion (singular), as a Western construct that originated with missionaries, like G. Parrinder and E.W. Smith, who were from a liberal theological background. It suggests a single, pan-African belief system with a pyramid structure (God, spirit world, human). African scholars like J. Olupona, F. Mbon and U. Danfulani (p. 46), reject the 'homogeneous concept'.

6.   J.S. Mbiti, 'African Theology', in S. Maimela and König (eds.), *Initiation into Theology* (Pretoria: J.L. van Schaik, 1998), p. 142, comments: ' For traditional Africa, the world of the Bible is not a past world of two to three thousand years ago, but a real world of yesterday, today and tomorrow.' Also, on p. 277: 'I consider traditional religions, and…other religious systems to be preparatory and even essential ground in the search for the Ultimate. But only Christianity has the terrible responsibility of pointing the way to that ultimate Identity, Foundation and Source of security.'

7.   C.B. Thetele, 'Women in South Africa: The WAAIC', in K. Appiah-Kubi and S. Torres, *African Theology en Route* (Maryknoll, NY: Orbis Books, 1979), p. 151, makes the point: 'The Independent Churches in South Africa in many ways are both pre-revolutionary and actively revolutionary at the same time…they do not operate according to a set plan or strategy but they are creating a change that provides the dispossessed people with a sense of hope and a vision for the future…and begin to sense their role as creators of their own histories…'

African theology is nothing less than the theological insights that Christians in Africa are bringing to Christian theology. The challenges to theology in Africa may be specific to Africa in the details of the confrontation, but they are part of the challenges of our human realities as a whole. To treat them as exotic additions would be sin against the Holy Spirit, and *that* would be heresy.[8]

d. *Reading to Restore Humanity*

Western cultural imperialism has been in many respects a destructive and dehumanizing experience for Africans. Therefore, central to the rehabilitation of Africa's cultural identity is the restoration of its people's human dignity. This means reviving the spirit of *ubuntu*, by which the individual lives for the welfare of the community through virtues of sharing and compassion. Against this background, the primary aim of theologizing is not simply to theorize, abstract and speculate, but to bring renewal and to restore human dignity to the benefit of humankind.

e. *Reading as the Community*

African lifestyle is characterized by communalism, the extended family and harmony with nature. Religious experience entails the communion with God and fellow humans including the ancestors. Therefore, communication favours inclusiveness and consensus. The individualizing and rationalizing tendencies of modernity are having devastating effects on this communal lifestyle.

To summarize, in its search to develop an African spirituality, that is, an African expression of its Christian faith experience, Africa favours reading the Bible for freedom, healing and wholeness. It is further informed by the consciousness of its cultural plurality, the desire to communalize, and with compassion for all humanity. Mercy Oduyoye sees the challenge as follows:

> As we Africans re-read the bible and books on Western missionary theology, we unmask their ideological components, but we draw toward the ecumenical truth they embody and are thereby freed to move to re-interpretation and re-statement and to uncover aspects of the truth that may have remained concealed to the Western mind.[9]

8. M.A. Oduyoye, *Hearing and Knowing* (Maryknoll, NY: Orbis Books, 1986), p. 76.

9. Oduyoye, *Hearing*, p. 148.

2. Reading with the South African Rainbow Nation in Renaissance

The encounters between Western cultural imperialism and the African cultural renaissance are perhaps experienced most rigorously in South Africa.
Here, through apartheid, colonialism was able to sustain itself longer than
anywhere else in Africa. The dramatic political reversal of the past decade
has now presented a very interesting situation. It has become a site for the
fusion of horizons, the interaction of cultures and the dialogue of histories.
A number of factors impact on this dynamic process:

1. The potential to become economically and technologically very
    strong is undermined by the endemics of poverty, racism, sex-
    ism, crime, AIDS, child abuse, etc.
2. The gains of the 'church-struggle' to liberate the Bible from the
    hands of its colonial interpreters[10] through black, contextual,
    African, liberation theologies, etc., are now being threatened, by
    such factors as the coercion of the former exponents into the
    public and private sectors, a dearth of second generation theo-
    logians, fundamentalism, secularism, globalization, etc. Also, the
    institutions particularly known for contextual theology have
    become economically very vulnerable. It seems that the public
    forums of the church and the society[11] are now becoming the
    sites for intercultural reading of the Bible.
3. Africa's dream was articulated most eloquently in President
    Mbeki's 'I-am-an-African' speech and South Africa has now
    taken the initiative in the transformation of the continent. It con-
    tains all the ingredients that would constitute an authentic iden-
    tity, namely, the call to embrace all cultures, to respect all races,
    to share in all suffering, to seek everybody's wellbeing, to cherish
    all traditions, to celebrate everybody's contribution. It visualizes
    Desmond Tutu's dream of an all inclusive rainbow nation.[12]

10. G.O. West, *Biblical Hermeneutics of Liberation* (Pietermaritzburg: Cluster Publications, 1991), p. 31, says that the challenge to the Church in South Africa 'impels us
to return to the Bible and to search the Word of God for a message that is relevant to
what we are experiencing in South Africa today'.

11. West, *Biblical Hermeneutics*, p. 61 puts it as follows: 'The challenge from the
South African context of struggle is, first, to affirm that one does and should have commitments in reading the Bible and, second, to argue that these commitments should be
shaped by the poor and the oppressed.'

12. Tutu's dream of 'rainbow-nation' for the new South Africa, may sound too
idealistic for some given the socio-economic powers that still dominate but it is a

In this climate of an awakening Africa, creative methodologies that will help 'decolonize the mind'[13] have to be developed. Of course, biblical criticism itself has gone through various phases through the centuries. Past approaches have this in common, that they 'emerged out of a Eurocentric setting, and, as such remained thoroughly Eurocentric at every level'.[14] Calls from the Third World, and pressure from groups within the West itself, for more relevant readings gave birth to more contextual approaches, such as cultural studies.

It is within this broader cultural studies framework that a dialogical-narratological method is now attempted. Dialogue involves the reader directly, and is characteristic of both the African literary tradition and the New Testament, not least in Paul's Letters.[15] Similarly, the narrative is typical of both Africa[16] and the world of the Bible. It is agreed that New Testament writings in general do not simply convey doctrinal treatises or ethical imperatives, but are carried by a basic narrative structure. They contain

biblical vision, the eschatological sign of Gen. 9.13 that God will remember the everlasting covenant between him and all flesh that is on the earth. W. Brueggemann, *The Bible and Postmodern Imagination* (London: SCM Press, 1993), p. 51, puts it as follows: 'The rainbow marks the world of true evangelical discernment'.

13. Van Rinsum, *Slaves*, pp. 141-52. This conceptualizes a recent movement at African universities to become free from (mental) dependency, to counter cultural alienation and to Africanize. A.A. Mazrui, 'Towards Diagnosing and Treating Cultural Dependency: The Case of the African University', *IJED* 12 (1992), pp. 95-111, identifies three stages in this process: firstly, the domestication and appropiation of modernity; secondly, allowing an inflow of cultural diversification: thirdly, reversing the process by exporting African cultural richness to the West.

14. F.F. Segovia, 'And They Began to Speak in Other Tongues', in F.F. Segovia and M.A. Tolbert (eds.), *Reading from This Place*, I (Philadelphia: Fortress Press, 1995), p. 31. He discusses the development of biblical criticism from historical criticism to literary criticism to cultural social-scientific criticisms. He sees cultural studies as the fourth paradigm or umbrella model of interpretation that interrelates the other approaches and posits the real flesh-and-blood reader. As such, it is a development that carries the ongoing process of liberation and decolonialization in the discipline further. 'Such a reading is the inevitable result and mode of a postcolonial Christian world and a postcolonial biblical criticism.'

15. J.D.G. Dunn, *The Theology of Paul the Apostle* (Grand Rapids: Eerdmans, 1998), p. 13, describes Paul's theology as 'a dialogue…and not merely a description of what he believed'. It 'embraced Christian living as well as Christian thinking', 'a sequence of occasional conversations'. Also on 713, 'Of the methods mentioned for the task of writing a theology of Paul, the one which most commended itself was that of a dialogue'.

16. West, *Biblical Hermeneutics*, p. 44, indicates the significance of the rediscovery of narrative and story in recent times.

the bigger stories of God, his plans of creation, salvation for Israel and the nations; through Jesus and the Church (naturally including Paul)[17] decorated by the smaller stories of persons and events. All of these stories convey moments of transformation and development. Mindful of these, we now involve ourselves in a dialogue with Paul through his letter to the Galatians as a document of transformation.[18]

3. *Reading in Dialogue with Paul and the Galatians.*

A dialogue between a first-century Palestinian Christian and a second to third millennium South African Christian obviously has its limitations. These include the distance in time and space, differences in culture and worldview, in being an author and being a reader. It also happens that both participants are involved in multiple other dialogues that invariably impact on this one. Also we are fully aware that all of this is based on the one-sided, Pauline version about the issue in Galatians. Therefore, to reconstruct the Galatian situation requires some mirror-reading of Paul's response to it, as contained in this letter.[19]

Galatians reflects a deep crisis in early Christianity, namely, the struggle to integrate into one Christian faith community both Jewish–Christianity, which is primarily homogeneous and monotheistic, and Hellenistic Christianity, which is more heterogeneous and cosmological. Although Paul's response focuses on the religious aspect, it clearly has social, cultural and gender implications. To facilitate the dialogue, texts that seem to express particularly themes of transformation in the story of Galatians are now highlighted.

a. *In Dialogue on Location*

> Paul, an apostle—sent not from men nor by man, but by Jesus Christ and God the Father who raised him from the dead—and all the brothers with me, to the churches in Galatia (1.1-2):

17. R.B. Hays, *The Faith of Jesus Christ* (Chico, CA: Scholars Press, 1983), pp. 5-6, says: '[T]he framework of Paul's thought is constituted neither by a system of doctrines nor by his personal experience but by a "sacred story", a narrative structure'; '[T]he story provides the foundational substructure on which Paul's arguments are constructed.'

18. J.D.G. Dunn, *The Theology of Paul's Letter to the Galatians* (Cambridge: Cambridge University Press), p. 118, notes: 'A term which catches the essence of this motif in Galatians is "transformation"...for him [Paul] the template and goal of Christian transformation is Christ.'

19. B. Lategan, 'The Argumentative Situation of Galatians', *Neot* 26.2 (1992), pp. 259-61, for the different audiences and fronts involved in Galatians.

> But when God, who set me apart from birth and called me by his grace, was pleased to reveal his Son in me so that I might preach him among the Gentiles, I did not consult any man (1.15-16).

My location as a reader is that I am a South African, from a Western, Oriental and autocthonous ethnic and cultural background. Of my triple consciousness,[20] the Western has been by far the dominant one, but because of my creolization, I was officially segregated from this dominant culture. As a result, I became a victim of racial discrimination, economic deprivation and political disenfranchisement. I was born into the Christian religious tradition. Initially, as an ordinary reader, I understood the Bible rather literally. Through my studies to become a minister of the church and later as a theologian, I became a scientific professional and consequently a more critical reader. However, I remain committed to read with the eyes of the oppressed.

Paul gives his location in the biographical section of the letter. From this, and through other sources, we may conclude that he was a Pharisaic Jew who kept orthodox views that he zealously tried to protect during his early life, especially by persecuting the people of the Way, as the first followers of Jesus were called. It is also known that he was born in the Diaspora and was quite familiar with the Graeco-Roman culture. Then he underwent a personal transformation (conversion experience). The manner in which he introduces himself in the letter was probably necessitated by the suspicion sown about him by his adversaries. He had to convince his audiences, first, that, although he was a circumcised Jew, he became a Christian and did that on the basis of his faith (in the expiatory, sacrificial and saving work of Jesus Christ and his resurrection from the dead by the Father alone); secondly, that he belongs to that special group of people who were personally authorized by Jesus Christ to be his apostles and that he was commissioned to go to the Gentiles. Both his 'conversion' and his 'call' happened in a single act, in the road-to-Damascus experience, where he had an encounter with Jesus Christ himself. From his location as a Christian and an apostle, he could now dialogue on equal footing with the other apostles, but also with Judaistic and Gentile Christians, the broader society

---

20. W.E.B. du Bois, *The Souls of Black Folks* (New York: Knopf, 1986 [1903]), p. 2, used the term, 'double consciousness', which 'is a peculiar sensation, this double consciousness, this sense of always looking at one's self through the eyes of others, of measuring one's soul by the tape of a world that looks on in amused contempt and pity. One ever feels his two-ness...two souls, two thoughts, two unreconciled strivings; two warring ideals in one dark body.'

of his time and with the universal audiences. His authority is recognized by a group who are his co-workers and co-authors who form the Pauline collective in his dialogue with these different fronts.

My dialogue with the Pauline collective would centre around the significance of a personal transformative experience and covenantal faith. For me the tension is that, although I was not 'converted' into Christianity from another religion by an analogous Damascus experience, but was born into Christianity in the covenantal faith manner, yet I am being treated by the dominant Western Christianity in my country as an object of missionary ministry. This could only mean that, although my Christianity is of a second or third generation from a non-Western perspective, it is evidently regarded as of an inferior kind because of my partial non-Western ancestry.

b. *In Dialogue on Religio-Cultural Equality*

> We who are Jews by birth, and not 'Gentile sinners' know that a man is not justified by observing the law, but by faith in Jesus Christ. So we, too have put our faith in Christ Jesus that we may be justified by faith in Christ and not by observing the law; because for by observing the law no one will be justified (2.15-16).

I can claim at least three distinct cultural roots: European colonist, Oriental slave and Khoisan indigenous. However, I grew up primarily according to European cultural values to the extent that it has become almost impossible to retrieve any particular pre-Christian religious and cultural relic from my Eastern or African past. My creolistic background resulted in me being excluded from the mainstream Western Christianity even though I was born into Christianity. Ethnic dissimilarities with the dominant Western culture were the cause for racially segregated churches, which were then biblically justified, and in turn served as a blueprint for the political policy of apartheid. From the position of a separate Church, the Western 'civilized' Christianity could Christianize my non-Western 'primitive' Christianity. So an impression is created of a superior and an inferior Christianity.

Paul seems to be dealing with similar tensions in the relationship between Jewish and Gentile Christians in the so-called doctrinal section of the letter, which starts at Gal. 2.15. His Jewish-Christian opponents apparently demanded from Gentile Christians that they uphold the full law, including circumcision. This demand reflects an attitude of religious superiority, probably on the basis of being God's chosen people. Because the law and circumcision had come to be so closely identified with Jewish ethnic and cultural identity, this demand could also imply the substitution of Galatian culture with Jewish culture, and therefore a case of Jewish proselytizing via Christianity.[21] Paul seems to articulate Jewish sentiments that regarded Gentiles as ipso facto sinners, while those born Jews could only become sinners through disobedience to the law.[22] Challenging his fellow-apostles in Antioch, Jewish and Gentile Christians of his time, but also challenging his universal audience, Paul now refutes this Jewish position and, in doing so, reminds them of an important truth, namely, that Jews, Gentiles and all humankind are equal in their sinfulness and, as a consequence, in their need of faith in Jesus Christ, in order to be declared righteous before God. By this statement, Paul levels the religio-cultural playing fields among Jews, Gentiles and all religions and cultures.[23] All humankind belong to the present evil and enslaving age. The emphasis on universality seems to suggest that this equality has always been a basic point of departure even though God's message of salvation was carried through history by the Jewish religious culture. Using a paradigmatic 'I',[24] Paul argues very strongly that, in terms of obtaining righteousness before God, works of the law and faith in Jesus Christ are mutually exclusive. Noting Jesus' work of salvation, he expresses an absolute bias towards faith in him, otherwise Jesus' death would have been futile.

My dialogue with Paul would be on the relationship between the gospel and culture. The gospel has always been carried in and through culture, and cannot be extracted from culture. It passed through his history clothed in the cultures of Judaism and Graeco-Romanism, became intimately associated with Western culture and has since been passed on to other cultures. This gives some cultures a historical advantage over others, which also leads to a perception of cultural superiority. Being 'civilized' was often equated with being 'Christian'.

c. *On Reinterpreting History and Traditions*

Consider Abraham: He believed God, and it was credited to him as righteousness'. Understand, then, that those who believe are children of Abraham. The Scripture foresaw that God would justify the Gentiles through faith, and announced the gospel in advance to Abraham: 'All nations will be

21. The use of the concept 'brethren' for his co-workers who were of different cultural backgrounds indicates their equality as Christians through faith in Jesus Christ.
22. H.D. Betz, *Galatians* (Hermeneia; Philadelphia: Fortress Press, 1979), p. 115.
23. The use of the words 'man' and 'no flesh' indicate the universal significance.
24. B. Lategan, 'Argumentative Situation', p. 259, notes that Paul 'uses the first person, not in a personal autobiographical sense, but as an "uberindividuelles ich", which transcends the confines of a specific historical setting and which assumes a certain timeless quality'.

blessed through you'. So those who have faith are blessed along with Abraham, the man of faith (3.6-9).

A situation of transformation invariably demands a reinterpretation of
history. In our context the dominant Western culture of the past four centuries inevitably justified its position by interpreting specific past events
mostly as heroic moments of conquest and in this way presented its history as the authentic history of the country. It is clear that both the South
African and African histories have to be reinterpreted in a manner that
will do justice to the contributions of all its peoples.

Paul's adversaries probably impressed upon the Galatians that it was
important to be a true son of Abraham. The traditional Jewish interpretation linked kinship to Abraham with the law and circumcision. The
implication was that only those who are keepers of the law, and are circumcised, could claim this kinship as heirs of what had been promised to
him. Therefore it became incumbent upon Paul to reinterpret the history of
Abraham in the light of the Christ event.

He focuses primarily on the understanding of God's promise to Abraham. To him the most significant aspect of God's dialogue with Abraham
was his faith-acceptance of the promise. Some time afterwards the instruction to circumcise himself as a sign of the covenant between them was
given. Paul interprets this initial acceptance in faith, without circumcision,
to mean that for all practical reasons Abraham was a 'Gentile' when he
trusted God, accepted the promise and was justified (Gen. 15.6). Paul
downplays the significance of the sign of circumcision. Abraham demonstrated himself to be a person of faith previously by going out from his
land and his family at God's call. It endorses the fact that he is reckoned
justified because of this faith.[25] Therefore, anyone who follows faithful
Abraham's example in accepting God's promise also receives the blessing
of Abraham, that is, justification, and is therefore a legitimate child of
Abraham.

The Jews claimed the promise for themselves by emphasizing the sign
of the covenant, namely, circumcision. To them, this received affirmation
centuries later in the law when circumcision became their ethnic identity
marker. This meant that any person who wants to claim kinship to Abraham has to embrace the law, including circumcision. Paul criticizes this

---

25. L. Morris, *Galatians, Paul's Charter of Christian Freedom* (Downers Grove,
IL: InterVarsity Press, 1996), p. 98, believes that 'for the Jews, it seems that it was the
deed that counted... For Paul it was the faith that was the reason for the deed that
mattered...'

position by again noting the timespan of 430 years between the promise to Abraham and the promulgation of the law to Moses.

For Paul, the use of the singular noun 'seed' (of Abraham) points to the fulfilment of the promise in one person and therefore to an indication of the messianic nature of the promise. This means that the promise found its true fulfilment in the Christ-event. By correlating the faith of Abraham with the faith of the believer in Christ, justification does become directly accessible for all. To Paul the promise to Abraham and his response of faith corresponds exactly with the gospel. Therefore, those who believe in Christ are also the heirs[26] of the promise to Abraham. In this understanding of salvation history the focus is on the pre-circumcision period, the faith character of the covenant whereby the works of law are excluded, and the inclusive nature of its content. This proves to Paul that faith is a truly scriptural (Old Testament) concept.

I can concur with Paul that the heritage of Abraham is the heritage of faith, and also that the concept of faith levels the playing fields for all nations to obtain righteousness before God through Christ. It does pose the question of God's particular purpose with Israel and the relationship of Israel with the Church.

d. *The Dialogue on Cultural, Social and Gender Imbalances*

> There is neither Jew nor Greek, slave nor freeman, male nor female; for you are all one in Christ Jesus. If you belong to Christ, then you are Abraham's seed, and heirs according to the promise (3.28-29).

I have experienced racial discrimination as a human being, and, even more surprising, as a Christian by the Christian Church. Racial distinctions were particularly used to inform missionary approaches and practices and the Bible was read to justify these, which in turn informed political policies in a country based on Christian principles. It is clear that similar oppressive structures also existed in the time of Paul.

Paul realized that to argue for the equality of Jew and Gentile on the basis of faith in Christ would inevitably have implications for the society of his time. It is interesting that the three objects of unenviable discrimination in Jewish daily prayers of thanksgiving (namely, to be a Gentile, a slave and a woman) correspond with Paul's statement here. Faith in Christ does not mean that the ethnic, cultural and gender distinctions should dis-

---

26. F.F. Bruce, *The Epistle to the Galatians* (Exeter: Paternoster Press, 1982), p. 155, states: 'Abraham's heritage is the heritage of faith, and those who share this heritage are thereby manifested as sons of Abraham.'

appear, but it does relativize their significance, especially when these dis-tinctions become arguments for discrmination. For his time, Paul's position may have been quite revolutionary, but it initiated a process of awareness for subverting the status quo.[27] In emphasizing equality without minimiz-ing the distinctions, he is also laying the foundation for the principle of plurality on the basis of equality. In the search of one new humanity, these ethnic, social and gender particularities will only be of importance to the extent that they contribute equally towards the unity of humanity. Faith in Christ creates a new eschatological people of God based on diversity within unity.

In my interaction with Paul, I would like to express my appreciation for his view of the equalizing significance of baptism, but also establish that the theological assertion he made has shown insufficient progress on the sociological description, after 2,000 years of Christianity, both in the Church and in society.

e. *The Dialogue on Ethics*

> You, my brothers, were called to be free. But do not use your freedom to indulge the sinful nature; rather, serve one another in love (5.13).

I grew up in a rather legalistic sphere. The oppressive political policy demanded strict law enforcement to suppress any resistance of the dis-enfranchized majority. The religious context collaborated with this politi-cal legalism in that I, being an object of mission, was educated according to many 'musts' and 'must nots'. With the arrival of democracy the situation became relaxed. However this sudden turn-around may have contribuited to the present moral disintegration of the society, to the extent that it threatens the stability of society in general.

Jews in particular probably experienced the Roman rule as very oppres-sive. After his Damascus experience, Paul came to realize the legalistic character of Judaism of which he previously had been a champion. For him religious freedom arrived with the Christ event.[28] Consequently, faith

---

27. Bruce, *Galatians*, p. 169: 'It is not their distinctiveness, but their inequality of religious role, that is abolished "in Christ Jesus".'

28. Betz, *Galatians*, p. 255, sees freedom as 'the central theological concept which sums up the Christian's situation before God as well as in this world'. D. Patte, *Paul's Faith and the Power of the Gospel* (Philadelphia: Fortress Press, 1983), p. 72 says: 'Freedom from Judaism and from Hellenistic religions does not mean their pure and simple rejection, but it does mean freedom from their bondage, that is, freedom from the curse of the Law or freedom from the slavery to the elemental spirits of the universe'.

and freedom are closely correlated, just as the law and the flesh are.[29] The Galatians probably initially experienced a sense of insecurity and confusion after embracing the 'lawless' gospel that Paul brought to them, and for that reason found the legalistic option of the Judaizers more attractive. Paul now realized that freedom can become an unrestrained licence for misconduct and immorality. Therefore, he immediately correlates freedom with walking in the Spirit and keeping the law of Christ, which is love. In this way he apparently hoped to preserve and exercise freedom, and counter its misinterpreation. Characteristic of Paul's imperative to stand firm in freedom, is, first, that it is based on a very sound theological premise of faith in Christ,[30] and, second, that he does not promote a new, distinctively Christian ethic or give precedence to the ethics of a particular culture over another; third, that his ethic is proposed to be inclusive, because it concurs with many of the norms and values in other cultures, in as much as they agree with his theological stance; and, fourth, that he does not substitute for the law a new set of rules, which could eventually degenerate into another rigid legalistic system. All of this points to the conclusion that his intention is rather to create a new ethos through the law of love and the guidance of the Spirit.

My engagement with Paul on issues of morality would be to share his hesitancy on prescriptions and rules. I would also rather focus on shaping attitudes that are aimed at bringing about a culture of responsibility. In our society of plurality in cultures and religions, I would also appreciate his open approach, which could help to develop a culture of human rights.

f. *The Dialogue for a New Vision*

> Neither circumcison, nor uncircumcision means anything; what counts is a new creation. Peace and mercy to all who follow this rule, even to the Israel of God (6.15-16).

The past decade has seen a dramatic change in my country from apartheid to a participatory democracy. The change has been described as miraculous because the transition was almost non-violent. The challenge is now

---

29. F.J. Matera, *Galatians* (Sacra Pagina; Collegeville, MN: Liturgical Press, 1992), p. 192, comments that in the earlier part of Galatians, *sarx* has been employed in a neutral sense, but from 5.13 forward it takes on an ethical tone.

30. Matera, *Galatians*, pp. 194-95, discusses the views on parenetic material within Galatians and agrees: 'Indeed, if Paul cannot establish a relationship between his Torah-free gospel and the moral life, his argument in the first four chapters of this letter loses its force. Galatians 5.13–6.10, however, is the culmination of Paul's argument.'

to transform the society to the vision expressed in the constitution for a non-racist, non-sexist, socio-economically just society. The question is what should be the role of Christianity in this transformation?

Paul is not too explicit about the outcome of the transformation that he envisaged. That he does have a vision of a new age has already become clear when he talks about becoming the children of Abraham, and about the equality of Jew and Greek, slave and freeman, man and woman. The lack of an original visionary framework was probably the cause of the developments in Galatia. So he seems to be advocating the concepts of a 'new creation' and 'the Israel of God' for this purpose. Both imply a process of transformation. A new creation emphasizes the radicality of the change that has to take place, while the Israel of God[31] seeks to indicate the historical-eschatological character of this new creation. While focusing on the final congregation of God's people in the future, it does not sever the relationship with his people from the past.

My dialogue with Paul will be on the role of God's people in upholding the dream of a free, just and inclusive society, through the Church being the vanguard of such a society.

In conclusion, it seems that the way forward for biblical scholarship in South Africa anyway is to continue with our twofold movement of intercultural communication, whereby, on the one hand, we focus on our inclusive dialogue within the plurality of our humanity, and, on the other hand, we continuously commit ourselves to the ideal of the future unity of our humanness and to the overthrow of all that inhibits it. This dialogue of ours must take place on a biblical basis, because this is indeed the hermeneutical process that is happening within the Bible itself, and is central to its message.

BIBLIOGRAPHY

Betz, H.D., *Galatians* (Hermeneia—A Critical and Historical Commentary on the Bible; Philadelphia: Fortress Press, 1979).
Boers, H., *The Justification of the Gentiles* (Peabody: Hendrickson Publishers, 1994).
Bois, W.E.B. du, *The Souls of Black Folks* (New York: Knopf, 1986 [1903]).

31. F. Thielman, *Paul and the Law* (Downers Grove, IL: InterVarsity Press, 1994), pp. 135-38, notes: 'Paul views the Galatian believers as the eschatologically restored people of God about whom the prophets spoke, and he constructs a picture of life in the eschatological era which borrows key features from the Mosaic covenant.' Some of these features are 'The promised Spirit'; 'The new exodus'; 'God's adoption of his people'; 'No longer slaves'; 'The Israel of God'.

Bruce, F.F., *The Epistle to the Galatians* (Exeter: Paternoster Press, 1982).

Brueggemann, W., *The Bible and Postmodern Imagination* (London: SCM Press, 1993).

Dunn, J.D.G., *The Theology of Paul the Apostle* (Grand Rapids: Eerdmans, 1998).

—*The Theology of Paul's Letter to the Galatians* (Cambridge: Cambridge University Press, 1993).

Hays, R.B., *The Faith of Jesus Christ* (Chico, CA: Scholars Press, 1983).

Holy Bible, New International Version.

Lategan, B., 'The Argumentative Situation of Galatians', *Neotestamentica* 26.2 (1992).

Maluleke, T.S., 'The Discovery of the Agency of Africans', *Journal of Theology for Southern Africa* 108 (November 2000), pp. 19-37.

Matera, F.J., *Galatians* (Sacra Pagina; Collegeville, MN: Liturgical Press, 1992).

Mazrui, A.A., 'Towards Diagnosing and Treating Cultural Dependency: The Case of the African University', *IJED* 12 (1992), pp. 95-111.

Mbiti, J., *African Religions and Philosophy* (London: Heinemann, 1969).

—'African Theology', in S. Maimela and A. König (eds.), *Initiation into Theology* (Pretoria: J.L. van Schaik, 1998).

Morris, L., *Galatians, Paul's Charter of Christian Freedom* (Downers Grove, IL: InterVarsity Press, 1996).

Oduyoye, M.A., *Hearing and Knowing* (Maryknoll, NY: Orbis Press, 1986).

Okot p'Bitek, *African Religion in an African University: Africa's Cultural Revolution* (Nairobi: MacMillan, 1973).

Patte, D., *Paul's Faith and the Power of the Gospel* (Philadelphia: Fortress Press, 1983).

Segovia, F.F., 'And They Began to Speak in Other Tongues', in F.F. Segovia and M.A. Tolbert (eds.), *Reading from This Place*, I (Philadelphia: Fortress Press, 1995).

Thetele, C.B., 'Women in South Africa: The WAAIC', in *African Theology en Route* (Maryknoll, NY: Orbis Books, 1979).

Thielman, F., *Paul and the Law* (Downers Grove: InterVarsity Press, 1994).

Van Rinsum, H.J., *Slaves of Definition* (Maastricht: Shaker Publishing BV, 2001).

West, G.O., *Biblical Hermeneutics of Liberation* (Pietermaritzburg: Cluster Publications, 1991).

The Epiphany of the Dove: Healing and Prophecy in Mark's Gospel (New Approaches in Women's Studies)

Julie Hopkins

Editor's Introduction

The Coptic text of the Gospel of Thomas *contains two sayings (22, 114) to confront a masculine prejudice against women, which seems to have become prevalent fairly early in Christianity and to have been powerfully influential through much of Church history until quite recent times. 'Jesus said to them, "When you make...male and female into a single one, so that the male will not be male nor the female be female...then you will enter the kingdom" ' (22) Such a prophetic transcendence in the Spirit of male–female gender categories can be paralleled elsewhere in early Christianity; it is a focus of this chapter to pursue related ideas within the mainstream tradition of the Gospel of Mark. In this way a modern reading from the field of Women's Studies can be linked precisely to ancient text examples.*

To judge from its results, Feminist Theology has been a remarkably pluralist endeavour. While some readers dismiss the Bible as a totally prejudiced text, others have established in open discussion firm evidence for diversity on gender issues within this collection of books. Julie Hopkins's contributions, while strongly argued and formulated on the deeply-felt principles of Women's Studies, offer a creatively positive response to historical questions. As the author of Towards a Feminist Christology *(Kampen: Kok, 1994; London: SPCK, 1995) she has subsequently developed her interests in a wide-ranging exploration of religious experience, ecstatic prophecy and Coptic spirituality. It is good to have in our collection of essays an example of a text reading of Mark's Gospel that has both a strong undergirding of theory and a demonstration of the possibilities for deeper understanding by such an association of ideas. The reading illustrates very well how such a concentration on the themes of prophecy and suffering can develop the significance of the female paradigm of discipleship, which is a recurrent theme in theologically orientated Women's Studies. The role models of discipleship supplied in John's Gospel by the mother of Jesus, the woman of Samaria, Mary of Bethany and Mary Magdalene offer an interesting comparison to this Marcan reading.*

1. *Introduction*

> Jesus saw the heavens opened and the Spirit descending upon him like
> dove; and a voice came from heaven, 'Thou art my beloved Son...' (Mk
> 1.10b-11a).

This rereading of Mark's Gospel is influenced by the new methodological
and hermeneutical tools and research developed in Women's Studies over
the past 20 years. However, the interpretative framework I employ here is
the often overlooked *religious experience focus* of the Gospel itself. For
Mark opens with a communal vision, the epiphany of the Holy Spirit, and
the in-breaking of her inspirational power into Israel through her beloved
One, Jesus of Nazareth. This phenomenon of the long-awaited return of
the *Ruach Ha-kodesj,* was the context and content of the spirituality of the
Markan church. As the 'community of the New Age' (Howard Kee), the
manifestations and dynamics of the Spirit constituted the matrix for its
sense of identity, mission and relationships.

To begin to explore the far-reaching implications of this emphasis upon
the spirituality of the Markan community, I shall demonstrate how two
feminist theologians, Isabel Carter Heyward and Rita Nakashima Brock
are able to offer radically new and inspiring readings of the stories of the
healing of Jairus's daughter and the woman with the haemorrhage in Mark
5. Neither of these writers usually speak of 'the Spirit', preferring their
own vocabulary, nevertheless their rereading of Mark's Gospel is based
upon a reworking of pneumatology in terms of the therapeutic dynamics
of interpersonal power.

Carter Heyward makes a basic contrast between what she calls *exousia*
(socially licensed [patriarchal] authority) and *dunamis* (raw, spontaneous,
transpersonal power). In her opinion, Jesus realized that his own self-
authenticating *dunamis* was divine and he could not possess or control
this power. The very nature of *dunamis* is relational, 'a dynamic exchange
between and among persons'.[1] She continues:

> Jesus is not a peculiarity, someone who 'possesses' God, someone who
> 'has' the power-in-relation as his own. Jesus willingly facilitates the revela-
> tion, or making-known, of God as the creative *dunamis* in intimate relation
> between and among human beings. God is no 'one', but rather is the spirit
> which drives Jesus both into the wilderness (Mark 1.12) and into human
> community in order to reveal to human beings the possibility of their own
> godding.

1.   I. Carter Heyward, *The Redemption of God: A Theology of Mutual Relation*
(Lanham, MD: University Press of America, 1980), p. 47.

In her book, *Journeys by Heart: A Christology of Erotic Power*, the Japanese-American writer Rita Nakashima Brock develops Heyward's approach to Mark's Gospel in her reflection upon the nature of the power evident in the exorcism and healing miracles. She too analyses personal interaction in term of the exercise of two sorts of power, which she calls 'vertical/hierarchical' power (based on domination and control) and 'horizontal/erotic' power (based on the fundamental power of existence as a relational process). By choosing the term *erotic* Brock allies with those feminist poets and writers who wish to reclaim a forgotten knowledge through the desire and feeling for 'connectedness'. In metaphysical terms Brock claims, 'Connection is the basic power of all existence, the root of life. The power of being/becoming is erotic power. Erotic power leads us, through the human heart, toward life-giving cocreating.'[2]

Brock's term 'erotic power' may seem an unnecessarily provocative innovation to Mark's Gospel, but, as I shall try to show, this stress upon the interpersonal bonds that create and sustain life-giving wholeness helps to throw light upon the therapeutic dynamics of the Spirit in the Jesus Movement. That 'erotic power' correlates with the activity of the *Ruach-Sophia* is hinted at in a note in which Brock cites the New Testament exegete, Elisabeth Schüssler Fiorenza:

> The gospel is not a matter of the individual soul; it is the communal procla-mation of the life-giving power of Spirit-Sophia and of God's vision of an alternative community and world... The focal point of early Christian self-understanding was not a holy book or a cultic rite, not mystic experience and magic invocation, but a set of relationships: the experience of God's presence among one another and through one another.[3]

In the following Markan account, this interpersonal dimension of divine healing power becomes clear.

2. *Two Therapeutic Encounters*

And when Jesus had crossed again in the boat to the other side, a great crowd gathered about him; and he was beside the sea. Then came one of the rulers of the synagogue, Jairus by name; and seeing him, he fell at his feet, and besought him, saying, 'My little daughter is at the point of death. Come and lay your hands on her, so that she may be made well, and live.' And he went

---

2.   Rita Nakashima Brock, *Journeys by Heart: A Christology of Erotic Power* (New York: Crossroad, 1988), p. 41.
3.   Elisabeth Schüssler Fiorenza, *In Memory of Her* (London: SCM Press, 1983), p. 345.

with him. And a great crowd followed him and thronged about him. And there was a woman who had a flow of blood for twelve years, and who had suffered much under many physicians, and had spent all that she had, and was no better but worse. But she had heard the reports about Jesus, and came up behind him in the crowd and touched his garments. For she said, 'If I touch even his garments, I shall be made well'. And immediately her haemorrhage ceased; and she felt in her body that she was healed of her disease. And Jesus, perceiving in himself that power [*dunamis*] had gone forth from him, immediately turned about in the crowd, and said, 'Who touched my garment?' (Mk 5.21-30).

The Markan story of the healing of the woman with the haemorrhage is highly unusual not only because of its narrative structure, but also because the feelings and thoughts of the principal characters are described. We are given a window into the hearts of the healer and the healed that makes it possible to gain an insight into the interpersonal dynamics of communication, power and shared experience of the *Ruach* that bonded the early Christians into a religious community. Because Mark graphically described Jesus as feeling a loss of power, preachers often use this miracle to 'prove' that Jesus was the font of divine power, the incarnate Son of God. However, Heyward and Brock claim that the story is better understood as an image of the nature of relationships both between healer and healed and between women and men in the force-field of *dunamis*.

If we look at the context it becomes clear that the story of the woman with the flow of blood, and the story of the healing of the daughter of Jairus that precedes and follows it form together a commentary upon the social and religious situation of women inside and outside the Markan community. Elisabeth Schüssler Fiorenza first pointed out that these two stories are purposely juxtaposed by Mark. It cannot be a coincidence that the daughter of Jairus was *twelve* years old and the woman had been losing blood for *twelve years*.[4] Further, both women are called 'daughter', both women are ritually unclean and both women have a malaise that connects with their fertility (Jewish girls on reaching puberty at twelve became marriageable). If we follow the clues in the text and read these healing stories as a commentary upon therapeutic relationships in the Jesus Movement, the dynamics of the *Ruach* as relational power become evident.

Rita Brock writes, 'The woman's haemorrhage is the affliction of adult women in magnified form; she bleeds endlessly and is perpetually polluting.'[5] According to the cultic Holiness Code in Lev. 15.19-31 a menustrat-

4.   E. Schüssler Fiorenza (1983), p. 124.
5.   Brock, *Journeys*, p. 83.

ing woman polluted everyone and everything she came into contact with. As such we can assume that this woman was barred from the congregation of Israel. Further, she could not perform her social and religious duty to bear children and therefore she was bereft of her role as a Jewish woman. Weakened and sick, she was also destitute, having spent all her money on the search for a cure (this implies her husband had divorced her on the grounds of her infertility and that she had to fend for herself).

During the years of this woman's physical deterioration, social isolation and financial impoverishment, a girl had been growing up in a wealthy and prestigious household. But the daughter of Jairus, the president of the synagogue, was now 'at death's door' (Mk 5.23). Jesus and her father were on the way to see her when the woman with the haemorrhage touched his cloak from behind. And 'immediately' both the woman and Jesus *felt* changed. Heyward understands this touch as an intimate physical expression of the woman's faith in the transpersonal *dunamis* that flowed between Jesus and others. She writes, 'To touch is to signify a relation that exists already. It is an expression of confidence in *dunamis*, the power in relation.'[6] Brock rightly stresses the courage and desperate need of this 'unclean' woman who violates every social and religious taboo by touching a male rabbi in public.[7] It is the woman who takes the initiative, breaking through the structures of hierarchical power in order to enter into a new relationship of erotic power. Brock comments:

> We are not called to place our faith in benignly paternalistic powers who will rescue us or protect us from suffering. We are to have faith in our own worth, which empowers us to be healed by each other. Despite fear of the consequences, we are summoned to take heart, refuse despair, and to act for ourselves and each other.[8]

Jesus turns around. He has felt power leave him. Brock suggests that this power should be interpreted as 'patriarchal' privilege, what Heyward would call *exousia*. Brock comments, 'She breaks through the barrier of male privilege and status that separated them. Again, an old hierarchical power in Mark is replaced with a new vision, this time by the woman's actions.'[9] I do agree that the *touch* of this woman did change the perception and actions of Jesus' ministry. That Jesus reached out and touched the dead daughter of Jairus immediately after this healing cannot be a coincidence. His encounter

---

6.   Heyward, *Redemption*, p. 45.
7.   Brock, *Journeys*, p. 84.
8.   Brock, *Journeys*, p. 86.
9.   Brock, *Journeys*, p. 84.

with this woman gave him the courage to touch women who were 'unclean' (according to Num. 19.11-13 dead bodies are polluting). However, the *power* that Jesus felt flowing from him was surely healing power, *dunamis*. Heyward comments, 'The healing was enabled not by Jesus "in himself", but by Jesus in relation. Healing and the intimacy that grounds it in relation, is a reciprocal process in which the healer is affected by the healed.'[10]

> And his disciples said to him, 'You see the crowd pressing around you, and yet you say, "Who touched me?" ' And he looked around to see who had done it. But the woman, knowing what had been done to her, came in fear and trembling and fell down before him, and told him the whole truth. And he said to her, 'Daughter, your faith has made you well; go in peace [*shalom*], and be healed of your disease.'
>
> While he was still speaking, there came from the ruler's house some who said, 'Your daughter is dead. Why trouble the Teacher any further?' But ignoring what they said, Jesus said to the ruler of the synagogue, 'Do not fear, only believe.' (Mk 5.31-36; continued below).

One of the most interesting aspects of the Markan story of the healing of the woman with the haemorrhage is what might be called 'the follow up'. The woman knows that she is healed, she has it were 'stolen' intimacy with Jesus through her secret desire and touch but he seeks a more reciprocal relationship based upon a face-to-face encounter. Despite the ridicule of the disciples, Jesus actively seeks the toucher in the thronging crowd. Finally she makes herself publicly visible by directly approaching him and 'fell down before him' (or 'embraced him'). Now that they can see each other the relationship becomes mutually empowering. She can tell him her life-story; of her pain, humiliation and loneliness. The very telling heals years of psychological and spiritual damage. Jesus listens with respect, learning as her disciple about the invisible suffering and oppression of women from a daughter of *Hokmah*. With this new Wisdom he will be empowered to break through the most terrifying barrier that can block the flow of relational power. For while they are still speaking, a messenger announces that the daughter of Jairus is dead (Mk 5.35).

Immediately before and after the arrival of the messenger, Jesus speaks of faith. After listening to the woman's story Jesus says, 'Daughter, your faith has made you well; go in *shalom*, and be healed of your disease.' With these words he acknowledges the role that her belief in *dunamis* and her own initiative played in her healing. These are therefore words of respect; the woman has the right to be a daughter of Israel and a disciple,

---

10. Heyward, *Redemption*, p. 46.

she is blessed with *shalom*, which Schüssler Fiorenza describes as 'the eschatological well-being and happiness of God'.[11]

The delay has fatal consequences for the 'little daughter' of Jairus. But Jesus tells the distraught father, 'Do not fear, only believe.' Fear of death, of the absence of relation and erotic power undermines faith in *dunamis*. It is interesting to note that Mark continually stresses the pivotal role of faith in the healing miracles. In the next chapter we are told that Jesus could not heal in his home town of Nazareth because of their unbelief (Mk 6.1-6). This supports the view of Brock and Heyward that Jesus did not control the therapeutic power that he mediated, he could not direct it at will; rather it flowed between him and others when both parties had open hearts and mutual respect. In the case of Jairus's daughter, the parents acted as inter-mediaries for their dead child, but, as we shall see, Jesus insisted that she was not dead but asleep and sought to contact her directly by taking her hand and calling her back from her coma.

> And he allowed no one to follow him except Peter and James and John the brother of James. When they came to the house of the ruler of the synagogue, he saw a tumult, and people weeping and wailing loudly. And when he had entered he said to them, 'Why do you make a tumult and weep? The child is not dead but sleeping.' And they laughed at him. But he put them all outside, and took the child's father and mother and those who were with him, and went in where the child was. Taking her by the hand he said to her, '*Talitha cumi*'; which means, 'Little girl, I say to you, arise.' And immediately the girl got up and walked (she was twelve years of age), and they were immediately overcome with amazement. And he strictly charged them that no one should know this, and he told them to give her something to eat (Mk 5.37-43).

The gentle words of Jesus, '*Talitha cumi*' ('Little girl, I say to you, arise'), express the intimacy that, according to Heyward, is the deepest quality of relation. She writes, 'Re-image the ministry of Jesus as a ministry of intimacy, of persons knowing and being known by Jesus—intuitively? insightfully? spontaneously?—at such depth that they and he were affected'.[12] Brock suggests that Jesus learnt to empathize through wrestling with his demons after receiving the *Ruach* at the River Jordan. She writes

> The temptation stories point to the image of a wounded healer, to an image of one who by his own experience understands vulnerability and internal-ised oppression. In having recovered their own hearts, healers have some understanding of the suffering of others.[13]

---

11. E. Schüssler Fiorenza (1983), p. 124.
12. Heyward, *Redemption*, p. 45.
13. Brock, *Journeys*, pp. 80-81.

In Heyward's rereading of the Gospel of Mark, Jesus as the facilitator of *dunamis* plays the central role. Later in her theological reflection however, Heyward emphasizes *our* contemporary struggles for passionate justice-making as the locus for power-in-relation. Building bridges of understanding, reconciliation and liberation between lovers, friends, communities, nations and all planetary life is both a human project and a manifestation of *dunamis*, God embodied in human creative loving.[14] Brock too envisions divine power as a contemporary interpersonal dynamic. She claims that:

> Erotic power is not brought about by faith in a past salvation, but in the healing deeds of the church as the community of heart, of courage, and of hope as the incarnate presence of Spirit-Sophia. In Jesus' death and resurrection the church focuses its ability to heal life through erotic power.[15]

For Brock the communal dimension of erotic power rather than individual 'hero' Christology is central to her reading of Mark's Gospel. She claims that Mark purposely wrote his gospel of Jesus in order to focus the faith of his *own* community upon their experience of *being* church. The healings and exorcisms and even the suffering of the passion narrative witness to the new understanding of divine power *within* the Markan community. The ever-widening therapeutic circle of wounded healers who shared the Way of Jesus needed a theological reflection upon his ministry in order to test and strengthen their lifestyle in the face of persecution and doubt. Their gospel of the eschatological presence of *Ruach-Sophia* with Jesus portrayed their experience of the 'force-field' that sustained and empowered them even in the midst of brokenheartedness.

3. *Mark's Gospel as Prophetic Literature*

In recent years, New Testament scholarship has begun to reappraise the gospels as prophetic literature. In other words, there is a new appreciation of the fact that the writers of the gospels were attempting to write prophecy under the inspiration of the Holy Spirit by 'relating the *past* of Jesus to the *present* of the Church with an openness to the *future*'.[16] Prophecy in this sense involved both interpretation of the tradition, critical awareness of the contemporary situation and predictions of the future. What made it

14. Heyward, *Redemption*, pp. 149-78.
15. Brock, *Journeys*, p. 103.
16. J.M. Court, 'The Gospels as Prophecy', in *EPI TO AYTO: Studies in honour of Petr Pokorný on his sixty-fifth birthday* (Prague: Mlýn, 1998), pp. 55-66 (55).

prophecy and not simply biography, commentary and speculation was the belief that the Risen One spoke through the Spirit to the Christian churches. Divine inspiration was authoritative, revelatory and enthusiastic. The gospel writers had at their disposal collections of sayings of Jesus, healings and longer (passion) narratives, but they also had the living oracles of prophets within their own congregations and their own overall prophetic interpretation of events. According to Court, it is possible to distinguish three distinct prophetic viewpoints in the New Testament. These he calls 'apocalyptic threat' (focused upon the nearness of the end of the world, second coming and last judgement), 'realised eschatology' (the opposite belief that salvation and eternal life are already present) and 'the social gospel' (living between the ages and imitating Jesus).[17]

If the Gospel of John is the most obvious example of realized eschatology, and the Lukan writings of the social gospel, how do we characterize Mark? On the one hand, in Mark 13, the so-called 'Little Apocalypse', we have the most graphic oracles of imminent destruction and judgment to be found in the New Testament gospels. It begins with Jesus predicting the destruction of the Temple in Jerusalem (Mk 13.1-2), then goes on to describe a period of war, famine, earthquake, persecution and betrayal. Jesus foretells the desecration of the Holy of Holies by the pagans and warns:

> …then let those who are in Judea flee to the mountains; let him who is on the housetop not go down, nor enter his house, to take anything away; and let him who is in the field not turn back to take his mantle. And alas for those who are with child and for those who give suck in those days! Pray that it may not happen in winter (Mk 13.14b-18).

False prophets and messiahs arise and then there will be a cosmic cataclysm. Finally the 'Son of man' will appear in the clouds. He will send his angels to gather the elect from every part of the world. The disciples are warned to be alert and watch, for no one knows when these imminent events will take place, not even Jesus.

This Little Apocalypse, which was probably circulating in Palestine from the beginnings of the Jesus Movement, is a classic example of Jewish-Christian prophecy. The language and imagery reflect popular apocalyptic speculation drawn from the books of Daniel, Zechariah, Malachi, *Baruch* and *4 Ezra*. While some of the details suggest that it was embellished after the Jewish Revolt of 66–70 CE, the eschatological oracles may well have gone back to prophecies of Jesus himself. Mark

17. J.M. Court (1998), pp. 60-65.

portrays Jesus as having insight into the future. In particular, Jesus three times predicts his own suffering, death and resurrection (Mk 8.31; 9.31; 10.33-34). The *resistance of the disciples* to these prophecies is one of the most dramatic and tragic elements of the Markan narrative.

One of the most interesting aspects of the Little Apocalypse for our understanding of the nature of prophecy in the Markan community is the *apparent contradictions* between prophetic oracles. In 13.30, Jesus promises that the second coming of the 'Son of man' as Messiah will take place within the lifetime of his disciples: 'Truly, I say to you, this generation will not pass away before these things take place.' However, two verses later he says: 'But of that day or that hour no one knows, not even the angels in heaven, nor the Son, but only the Father.' For the first Christians who experienced the traumatic destruction of Jerusalem and the savagery and persecution that followed, there must have been a longing for their vindication. And yet Jesus did not return as their conquering messiah and there was no apparent end of the old age. Verse 30 is therefore an unfulfilled prophecy! As an authentic dominical oracle it could not be omitted but a second prophecy emerged *within the community* that helped them to cope with the disappointment. In the extraordinary story of the transfiguration, this process is taken one step further, when an ecstatic visionary trance of the Markan prophets is projected back into the pre-Easter narrative. The community's anticipation for the future is relocated in the past, a process that Court calls 'cognitive dissonance'.[18]

The Gospel of Mark therefore witnesses to a *transition in early Christian spirituality*. Through the inspiration of Spirit-Sophia, the faith community was gradually abandoning its obsession with apocalyptic threat and moving towards a new realized kind of prophetic mentality, of living creatively between the *now* and *not yet* of the Kingdom of God. In spite of its social alienation as a persecuted sect, the Markan community found its fulfilment in its new identity as those baptized into the Spirit of Jesus. Her presence was interpreted as a foretaste of the messianic age. As the Revealer and Wisdom of God, she interpreted the teaching, death and resurrection of Jesus and empowered them for ethical courage and liberative praxis. Through her they began to experience the new creation of a spiritually transformed subjectivity. Paul described this in terms of the eschatological harvest: 'But the fruit of the Spirit is love, joy, peace, patience, kindness, goodness, faithfulness, self-control; against such there is no law' (Gal. 5.22-24).

18. J.M. Court (1998), p. 61.

However, Paul's letters, which were written before the Gospel of Mark, also demonstrate that this new life in the Spirit created tension and confusion in the early Christian communities. The question as to who might publicly prophesy during worship and how to discriminate between true and false prophecies dominates much of his first letter to the church at Corinth. The ethical implications of freedom in the Spirit from the Jewish Law (*Torah*) is a recurring theme in all his correspondence. Later in this essay I shall return to these issues in the light of new research concerning the role of women prophets. However, the point I wish to emphasize here is that there was obviously a growing need in the early Church to *ground prophecy in ethical behaviour and community life*. The danger that anything and everything might be said in the name of the Risen One needed to be checked. Eugene Boring has claimed that Mark wrote his gospel in order to stem the proliferation of vague revelations by presenting the *historical life of Jesus* as the measure and guide for genuine prophecy.[19]

Boring's interesting thesis is substantiated by some convincing arguments. First, that Mark wrote in the historical present tense so that Jesus seems to speak *now*. There are 143 instances of this direct discourse by Jesus in Mark's gospel (which both Matthew and Luke drastically reduced). Further, Jesus sometimes directly addresses the hearer/reader (e.g. 8.27-9.1). Also Jesus is portrayed as himself the one who proclaims 'the word' (*ton logon*), which is Mark's technical term for the Christian message (see 1.45; 2.2; 4.14-20, 33). A similar observation first made by Willi Marxsen is that Mark's use of the word *evangelion* (good news/gospel) in 1.1, 8.35 and 10.29, implies 'that it is (the risen) Jesus himself who preaches the gospel contained in Mark's writing'.[20] Mark's literary creation was the first attempt to mediate the Spirit of the Risen One to the Church through the channel of writing. Language, interpretation and the hermeneutical circle of dialogue between reader and text had become prophetic mediums.

4. *Prophecy and Suffering*

And when they bring you to trial and deliver you up, do not be anxious beforehand what you are to say; but say whatever is given to you in that hour, for it is not you who speak but the Holy Spirit (Mk 13.11).

---

19. M. Eugene Boring, *Sayings of the Risen Jesus: Christian Prophecy in the Synoptic Tradition* (Cambridge: Cambridge University Press, 1982), pp. 199-202.

20. Willi Marxsen, *Mark the Evangelist* (Nashville: Abingdon Press, 1969), pp. 126-38.

In the Gospel of Mark, Jesus does not claim to be a prophet. Rather he refers to himself by the enigmatic title 'Son of man'. However, whenever he uses the term instead of the normal 'I' it is always connected with a prophetic oracle. As we have seen, these oracles have two themes. Either they reinterpret traditional Jewish expectations for the Messiah in terms of a suffering servant identity drawn from prophecies in Isa. 53, or they refer to a future apocalyptic judgement in which a 'Son of man' descends in glory and power from heaven. These two 'Son of man' figures are so different, the one a persecuted wandering teacher (*sophos*), the other an angelic cosmic conqueror, that it is impossible to know whether they refer to the same person. What is clear is that in Mark's teaching on the secrets of the Kingdom, *the Jesus of history had a suffering destiny* and that *the true disciple in this age* is the one who follows his example even to the point of execution.

But why, according to Mark, did Jesus suffer? Jesus is portrayed in the Gospel as identified with and serving the needs of prostitutes, outcasts and sinners. His table-fellowship with the ritually impure, his healings on the Sabbath and his rejection of scribal authority brought him directly into conflict with the established religious and social institutions of his day. Fiorenza comments: 'Suffering is not an end in itself, but is the outcome of Jesus' life-praxis of solidarity with the social and religious outcasts of his society.'[21] Through words and symbolic actions Jesus sought to restore to his people a vision of the Kingdom of God as an all-encompassing community where the first shall be last and leadership was based on the innocence and vulnerability of children. This ethical appeal related his mission directly with the Old Testament prophets who championed the widows, orphans and strangers. And that the true prophet must suffer like a lamb led to the slaughter was part of the eschatological message of the prophets from the time of Jeremiah (see esp. Jer. 11.18-19; Isa. 53.7). Even Second Isaiah, the most eloquent and successful prophet of the Golden Age of Prophecy, was popularly believed to have been martyred (see the *Asc. Isa.* 5.1-14).

Prophets were (and are) unpopular. As a cognitive minority they felt compelled to resist the generally accepted norms and values, 'in the name of *Adonai*'. However, in first-century Palestine it was inevitable that they would be persecuted by the Roman occupying power. Their ability to enthuse crowds and undermine political authority made them a dangerous threat to the *Pax Romana*. The Jewish historian Josephus, writing propa-

---

21. E. Schüssler Fiorenza (1983), p. 317.

ganda for his patron the Emperor Vespasian, offers a graphic account of
the 'imposter' prophets who fermented the nationalistic dissent which
finally led to the Jewish revolt of 66 CE. Even during the destruction of
their city and temple these prophets continued to interpret the signs as the
apocalyptic birth pangs of the new messianic Age (see Josephus, *War*
2.259-60, 261-64).

In the religious ferment surrounding the Jewish revolt, the Markan community also faced hostility from Jewish purists. This was directly related
to its belief in the outpouring of the Spirit of Prophecy 'in the name of
Jesus'. Rabbinical Judaism in the first century CE regarded the *Ruach Ha-
kodesh* to have been 'quenched' since the time of the Latter Prophets five
hundred years before. Although there was a popular belief that the Spirit
would return before the Messiah, she was always connected with the coming of a last eschatological prophet, such as Elijah or Moses. It is clear that
the Markan Christians believed that John the Baptist was Elijah *redivivus*
(see Mk 9.13), but the scribes and Pharisees regarded him as a deceiver
(Mk 11.27-33). If John the Baptizer was considered a false prophet it was
inevitable that his successor, who 'will baptise you with the Holy Spirit'
(Mk 1.8) would be considered both a false prophet and false messiah. In
the Markan account of the trial of Jesus before the Jewish Sanhedrin (the
Council of Seventy Elders) this conflict over the nature of messianic prophecy reached a dramatic climax:

> And the high priest asked him, 'Are you the Messiah, the Son of the
> Blessed?' And Jesus said, 'I am; and you will see the Son of man seated at
> the right hand of Power and coming with the clouds of heaven.' And the
> high priest tore his garments, and said, 'Why do we still need witnesses?
> You have heard his blasphemy. What is your decision?' And they all
> condemned him as deserving death. And some began to spit on him, and to
> cover his face, and to strike him, saying to him, 'Prophesy!' And the guards
> received him with blows (Mk 14.61-65).

This is the only time in Mark's Gospel that Jesus publicly reveals his
messianic identity. But Jesus immediately draws a distinction between his
present situation as a suffering messiah and the coming of the 'Son of
man'. This figure is described in the visionary apocalyptic formula that we
have already seen in 13.26. Was it the oracle of a Markan prophet or the
very words of Jesus? What is clear is that in this account of the trial Jesus
is treated by his accusers as a *false prophet*. David Hill comments:

> This ugly little scene…strongly suggests that Jesus was accused before the
> supreme council of being a false prophet: and as a false prophet he had to
> die (Deut.18.20) and the sentence had to be carried out at the feast 'when

all the people shall hear it', in order that others might be deterred from the crime (Deut. 16.16 and 17.10-13).[22]

If Jesus was rejected and condemned as a false prophet and messianic rabble rouser, his followers, who shared his gift of prophetic inspiration and spoke in his name, would have experienced persecution. The second half of Mark's Gospel graphically focuses on the suffering and death of Jesus and his teaching on the nature of suffering discipleship. Rita Naka-shima Brock comments:

> The earlier joy of erotic power appears to have gone underground. Images of suffering—picking up one's cross, of losing one's self to gain self, and of coming persecution—seep up through the angry cracks of the cleansing of the temple, the cursing of the fig tree, the parable of the tenants, and the arguments with Scribes and Sadducees. The images of suffering and anger culminate in the apocalyptic visions of Mark 13 which immediately pre-cede the passion narrative.[23]

Brock claims that far from undermining the divine milieu of good news, healing and empowerment in the Spirit that characterizes the first half of the Gospel, the second half deepens the reader's understanding by empha-sising faith, commitment and community.

There is a wisdom that can emerge from patient and heartfelt endurance in the face of suffering for truth or justice. The wisdom that Mark reveals in his tragic narrative is portrayed by the women disciples, who, having followed Jesus from Galilee, refuse to abandon him in his need but wait and grieve, risking their own security under the cross, and dare the terror of his tomb. These women play a pivotal role in the Markan description of the true disciple. In particular Mary of Magdala; Mary the daughter or the wife of James the younger; the mother of Joses; and Salome are contrasted with Peter, Andrew, James and John, who, having consistently rejected the suffering messiahship of Jesus, deny him and abandon him to his fate. In the opinion of Fiorenza, the negative portrayal of the leading male dis-ciples by Mark is not simply a criticism of their failure to understand the identity and mission of Jesus but also a rejection of their desire for power and control:[24]

> And James and John, the sons of Zebedee, came forward to him, and said to him, 'Teacher, we want you to do for us whatever we ask of you.' And

22. David Hill, *New Testament Prophecy* (London: Marshall, Morgan & Scott, 1979), p. 52.

23. Brock, *Journeys*, p. 89.

24. E. Schüssler Fiorenza (1983), p. 319.

he said to them, 'What do you want me to do for you?' And they said to him, 'Grant us to sit, one at your right hand and one at your left, in your glory.' But Jesus said to them, 'You do not know what you are asking. Are you able to drink the cup that I drink?' (Mk 10.35-38a).

For Mark, the women who emerge as the true disciples during the time of trial represent the empowering nature of spiritual leadership within the Kingdom of God. This leadership is based on pastoral service and being prepared to undergo suffering for love of others within the community of the New Age. This form of leadership, which rejected the pattern of dominance and submission that characterized the Graeco-Roman culture, was based upon the prophetic imitation of Jesus who, according to Markan Christology, gave up his life to buy back those sold into slavery to the evil powers of the age:

> 'You know that those who are supposed to rule over the Gentiles lord it over them, and their great men exercise authority over them. But it shall not be so among you; but whosoever would be great among you must be your servant, and whoever would be first among you must be the slave of all. For the Son of man came also not to be served but to serve and to give his life as a ransom for many' (Mk 10.42-45).

5. *The Prophetess of Bethany*

When reading scholarly books about New Testament prophecy, one is struck by the absence of discussion about women prophetesses. Sometimes Elizabeth the mother of John the Baptist or the four daughters of Philip are mentioned in passing, usually within a description of Luke's overall scheme of salvation history, but the presence and influence of prophetesses within the life of early Christian communities is simply not assumed. For example, in his detailed analysis of the oracles of the prophets whose 'sayings of the risen Jesus' play such an important role in the Synoptic Gospels, Eugene Boring consistently refers to the masculine gender. In a description of the prophet's sense of call, authority and mission, he claims, 'The prophet speaks with a sense of immediate authority resulting from his conviction that he has been personally commissioned by the deity to deliver a message to the people.'[25] In the following pages I shall attempt to demonstrate that women in fact played a central role in early Christian prophecy. I shall be using new insights and discoveries developed by women scholars and theologians. However, my starting point for this reconstruction is rather different than the discussion in Women's Studies

25. E.M. Boring, *Sayings*, p. 88.

to date. I begin with an intuition that since Spirit-Wisdom was feminine in the language and spirituality of the Jesus Movement, it was natural that women should be her mediums once the new gospel of 'freedom in the Spirit' came to be understood as freedom from proscribed gender roles in worship and spirituality.

The Markan community knew and honoured a prophetess who had the extraordinary insight and courage to break into a private male dinner party two nights before the arrest of Jesus and anoint him as the suffering Messiah. Let us examine this dramatic prophetic symbolic action with the help of commentary from Fiorenza and Brock.

> And while Jesus was at Bethany in the house of Simon the leper, as he sat at table, a woman came with an alabaster flask of ointment of pure nard, very costly, and she broke the flask and poured it over his head. But there were some who said to themselves indignantly, 'Why was the ointment thus wasted? For this ointment might have been sold for more than three hundred denarii, and given to the poor.' And they reproached her. But Jesus said, 'Let her alone; why do you trouble her? She has done a beautiful thing to me. For you always have the poor with you, and whenever you will, you can do good to them; but you will not always have me. She has done what she could; she has anointed my body for beforehand for burying. And *amen*, I say to you, wherever the gospel is preached in the whole world, what she has done will be told in memory of her' (Mk 14.3-9).

Both Fiorenza and Brock interpret the anointing of the head of Jesus with the costly oil of nard as the prophetic action which holds the key to the interpretation of this story. For Fiorenza the messianic implications are clear. She writes: 'Since the prophet in the Old Testament anointed the Jewish king, the anointing of Jesus' head must have been understood immediately as the prophetic recognition of Jesus, the Anointed, the Messiah, the Christ.'[26] The unnamed woman took on the role of a Samuel or Elijah, an extraordinarily daring, unorthodox and politically provocative act. Fiorenza's claim seems plausible for several reasons. First, because the Lukan and later Johannine versions of a similar story deliberately played down the Markan messianic implications by describing the woman as anointing the feet of Jesus and wiping them with her hair (see Lk. 7.36-38; Jn 12.1-8). Further, both the Lukan and Johannine accounts dramatically undermine the spiritually authoritative status of the women. In Luke she becomes a repentant 'sinner'. The thoughts of the host clearly imply that she was a prostitute: 'If this man (Jesus) was a prophet, he would have known what sort of woman this is who is touching him' (Lk. 7.39). John

---

26. E. Schüssler Fiorenza (1983), p. xiv.

identifies her with Mary, the sister of Martha and Lazarus. His story is sympathetic to her, but the important prediction of Jesus that she would be remembered for her deed wherever the gospel is preached is omitted. Mary of Bethany is a dear friend of Jesus but the fragrant perfume with which she, according to John, fills the house, is a scent of adoration and love not political or religious revolution.

For the Markan community, as we have seen, the secret of the identity of Jesus as the historical 'Son of man' is that he was their suffering Messiah. The male disciples had resisted this vocation and are replaced in the passion narrative of Mark by women as paradigms of true discipleship. It is this context of gender role reversals that the woman prophetess appears in Bethany to fulfil a classic male prophetic function, the anointing of the Messiah. But her symbolic action takes on a very female dimension for she uses nard, an oil with burial connotations, and it was the task of Jewish women to wash and anoint dead bodies for burial. For Jesus this was 'a beautiful thing' because her work anticipated his imminent torture and crucifixion. But also, for the post-Easter Markan community, her anointing for burial anticipated the resurrection. Because according to Mk 16.1-8, when Mary Magdalene, Mary the mother of James, and Salome went early in the morning to the tomb in order to anoint the body of Jesus, he was not there.

There is therefore a double motif in the messianic dimension of this prophetic action. The prophetess anticipated that Jesus would be tried, convicted and executed as a false messiah and yet she foresaw this apparent disgrace as the consummation of Jesus' messianic vocation. Her actions encouraged and authorized this difficult path for Jesus at a time when his own circle of disciples offered no support. She is criticized and rejected by the male disciples, but Jesus defends her action as the key to his ministry, life and forthcoming death. Immediately after these words of praise, Judas Iscariot went to the chief priests in order to arrange the betrayal of Jesus. Later in the same chapter, Peter denied knowing Jesus three times. The loving symbolic action of the prophetess was only understood by Jesus and the Markan readers. She was the link between the *Ruach* in Jesus and the Spirit-filled community who shared the difficult path of taking up their cross daily and following their suffering Messiah.

Brock, while agreeing with Fiorenza's messianic interpretation, adds a new perspective from her interest in the therapeutic dynamics of 'erotic power'. She points out that nard was an unguent, a salve with healing properties. As such, this oil, worth we are told three hundred *denarii* (the wages of a labourer for a whole year), represents divine healing power. The laying on of hands by the prophetess therefore had also a healing aspect. Brock comments:

> While Jesus is not physically sick, he is about to enter the realm of death, but he has been prepared for death by the woman. By her labour, she moves him into another realm from which he will emerge reborn.[27]

In Brock's interpretation, the role of healer and healed is by this action reversed, allowing the flow of divine power to pass between Jesus and the woman, creating a connection and community that would both encompass suffering and finally overcome it.

6. *In Memory of Early Christian Prophetesses*

> 'And *amen*, I say to you, wherever the gospel is preached in the whole world, what she has done will be told in memory of her' (Mk 14.9).

Fiorenza's first book on the feminist theological reconstruction of Christian origins was called *In Memory of Her*. She saw the task of the new generation of women exegetes as reclaiming the memory of such women such as the Markan prophetess in order to fulfil this prophecy. Fiorenza laments:

> the woman's prophetic sign-action did not become a part of the gospel knowledge of Christians. Even her name is lost to us. Wherever the gospel is proclaimed and the Eucharist celebrated another story is told: the story of the apostle who betrayed Jesus. The name of the betrayer is remembered, but the name of the faithful disciple is forgotten because she was a woman.[28]

Fiorenza suggests that name should be Mary of Bethany.[29]

But was it the case that the Markan Christians did not know the name of this prophetess? I think not. The oracle put into the mouth of Jesus in Mk 14.9 clearly reflects the Markan world of Christian missionary expansion rather than the milieu of the Jesus Movement, which was one of inner Jewish renewal. In other words, this oracle of divine approval was spoken by a prophet or prophetess in the Markan community in the name of the Risen One. It is logical to assume, therefore, that for the Markan Christians, the prophetess from Bethany was well known and her story proclaimed as an integral part of the passion narrative and the *kerygma* (that is the core of the gospel message). She was for the Markan community, a

---

27. Brock, *Journeys*, p. 97.
28. E. Schüssler Fiorenza (1983), p. xiii.
29. E. Schüssler Fiorenza (1983), p. 330.

cherished and authoritative link between the Jesus of history and their communal life in the same *Ruach*. Perhaps her name was kept intention-ally secret to protect her from persecution. She is at the very least part of the hidden spiritual life of this community, which is only partially revealed in their gospel. Like the secret meaning of the parables, the enigmatic title 'Son of man', the messianic secret of a suffering Messiah and the preg-nant emptiness of the tomb, she is a veiled figure and yet her actions point to the deepest meaning of Mark's Gospel. She is not only the 'paradigm for the true disciple' (Fiorenza), she is also a prophet of Spirit-Wisdom, combining the roles of revealer, empowerer and healer.

In Western Christendom, the authority of the Markan prophetess of Bethany was slowly undermined by a process of episcopal interpretation. First she was equated with the repentant sinner in the Lukan version and later this prostitute was identified with Mary of Magdala. The new com-posite Magdalene was proclaimed with papal authority in 591 CE in a ser-mon given by Gregory the Great in the basilica of San Clemente in Rome: 'We believe that this woman [Mary Magdalene] whom Luke calls a female sinner, whom John calls Mary, is that Mary from whom Mark says seven demons were cast out.' The historian Katherine Ludwig Jansen comments: 'In other words, Gregory the Great cobbled together a Magdalene from three separate scriptural figures'.[30] This is a classic example of how the memory of early Christian prophetesses was suppressed or sublimated into hagiography during the struggle for spiritual authority that characterizes Christianity from the end of the second century. The question women historians have asked is, assuming prophetesses existed, with what meth-odological tools are we to reconstruct their presence and message?

There are three main sources for this research. The first is literary ac-counts from the second and early third century CE that purport to describe the actual words and spiritual experiences of women prophets. The most important examples of these are the prison diary of the visionary martyr Perpetua and the rediscovered *Gospel of Mary*. Both of these sources have reached their final form through a process of redaction, but, at the very least, they give us some direct insight into the kind of prophetic oracles and behaviour that early Christian women manifested under the guidance and inspiration of the Spirit. Both these women, for example, had direct communication with God or Jesus in *visionary dreams*. Both spoke with

---

30. K.L. Jansen, 'Maria Magdalena: *Apostolorum Apostola*', in B.M. Kienzle and P.J. Walker (eds.), *Women Preachers and Prophets through Two Millennia of Christi-anity* (Berkeley: University of California Press, 1998), p. 60.

extraordinary self-confidence and spiritual authority. And perhaps inevitably, both suffered from hostility from would-be male superiors.

Vibia Perpetua of Carthage was leader of a Christian group and daughter of a wealthy pagan provincial. She refused to accept the demand of both the Roman governor Hilarion and her father that she should recant and was therefore condemned to die with her slave and friends in the arena. She had several visions in prison that she wrote down. Her first-hand account is a rare example and therefore of historical importance, particularly because, according to Rosemary Rader, 'it is one of the earliest portrayals of Christian martyrdom as a powerful symbol of human liberation and self-fulfilment'.[31] The visions demonstrate that Perpetua believed her martyrdom to be a second baptism, assuring salvation without priestly mediation, and that through non-violence she would not only attain ultimate victory but also defeat her evil persecutors. These beliefs took a graphic form in the vision which she received on the night before the public games:

> Coming towards me was some type of Egyptian, horrible to look at, accompanied by fighters who were to help defeat me. Some handsome young men came forward to help and encourage me. I was stripped of my clothing, and suddenly I was a man… I felt myself being lifted up into the air and began to strike [at my opponent] as one who was no longer earth-bound… As he fell on his face I stepped on his head. Then the people began to shout and my assistants started singing victory songs. I walked up to the trainer and accepted the branch. He kissed me and said, 'Peace be with you, my daughter.' And I triumphantly headed towards the Sanavivarian Gate (*Passio Perpetuae*).

Rosemary Rader comments:

> Perpetua's depiction in the role of both male and female intimates the early Christians' conviction that when the prophetic spirit breathes where it will there is no sexual preference. She is called bride, mother, sister, daughter, and lady; but also leader, warrior, victor and fighter.[32]

Freed from a socially constructed gender identity, she was both a spiritual gladiator in the arena of evil and also a caring mother to her infant son in prison.

In the second-century *Gospel of Mary*, Mary Magdalene is described as having a post-resurrection dialogue with Jesus in a dream-vision. Karen

---

31. *Passio Perpetuae*, translation and commentary by Rosemary Rader in P. Wilson-Kastner, G.R. Kastner, A. Millin, R. Rader and J. Reedy, *A Lost Tradition: Women Writers of the Early Church* (Lanham, MD: University Press of America, 1982), p. 2.

32. Rader, *A Lost Tradition*, p. 10.

King, a leading authority on this controversial text, observes that Mary Magdalene is clearly depicted as a prophet:

> She receives a vision of the Lord and assumes the roles of comforter and teacher to the other disciples, admonishing them to be resolute. She turns their hearts toward the 'Good' so that they begin to discuss the words of the Saviour.[33]

But her prophetic insights are rejected by Peter:

> 'Did he really speak with a woman without our knowledge (and) not openly? Are we to turn about and all listen to her? Did he prefer her to us?'
>   Then Mary wept and said to Peter, 'My brother Peter, what do you think? Do you think that I thought this up myself in my heart or that I am lying about the Saviour?' (*The Gospel of Mary* BG 7.17.18–18.1).

King observes:

> The confrontation of Mary with Peter, a scenario also found in *The Gospel of Thomas*, *Pistis Sophia*, and *The Gospel of the Egyptians*, reflects some of the tensions in second-century Christianity. Peter and Andrew represent orthodox positions that deny the validity of esoteric revelation and reject the authority of women to teach.[34]

This controversy between ecclesiastical and charismatic spiritual power is also reflected in a second major source of information, namely, the writings both canonical and episcopal that refer to women prophets. These tend to be ambivalent, praising women prophets for their contribution to the uplifting of the community, on the one hand, but insisting on all sorts of restrictions, on the other. For example, in *The Statutes of the Apostles*, a church order of the early third century, women who prophesy must be ordained into the office of 'widows' and be under the authority of a presbyter:

> Let them ordain three widows, two to continue together in prayer for all who are in trials and to ask for revelation concerning what they require, while the other is to be appointed to wait upon the women who are tried in sickness, ministering well, being sober, telling the presbyters of the things that happen (*Did. Apost.* 21).

---

33. Karen L. King, 'Prophetic Power and Women's Authority: The Case of the *Gospel of Mary* (Magdalene)', in B.M. Kienzle and P.J. Walker (eds.), *Women Preachers and Prophets* (1998), p. 23.

34. *The Gospel of Mary* (BG 8502, *1*) translated by G.W. MacRae and R. McL. Wilson, with a commentary by Karen L. King, in James M. Robinson (ed.), *The Nag Hammadi Library* (Leiden: E.J. Brill, 1988), pp. 523-27 (524).

The Alexandrian theologian Origen further argued that women's prophecy should be restricted to the home: 'It was not in the assembly that the daughters of Philip spoke... Nor did Debra address the people in the form of a public speech as did Isaiah and Jeremiah.' Torjesen comments: 'By equating liturgical prophecy with public speaking, Origen invokes the image of a woman infringing on the masculine privilege of the podium... because the Greco-Roman gender system did not authorize women's public speech, neither did God.'[35] Origen's polemics, however, went further than attempting to silence women prophets, he also claimed that John the Baptist was *the last prophet*. The Holy Spirit had been quenched and 'the grace of prophecy was taken away from the people' as a divine judgment upon the Jews, which was sealed with the destruction of Jerusalem![36]

Origen's claim of the end of the dispensation of prophecy was part of a wider apologetic conflict between the centralized episcopal leadership in the larger cities and the smaller independent Christian communities who sought to hold on to the tradition of charismatic teachers and prophets that characterized the early Church. This struggle for spiritual authority led to the emergence of Montanism, or the New Prophecy movement. Montanist prophetesses, including Maximilla, Priscilla (Prisca) and Quintilla, claimed spiritual descent from a prophetic genealogy going back to the four daughters of Philip the evangelist (see Acts 20.8-9). According to the early Christian historian Papias, these virgin prophetesses had brought apostolic Christianity to the provinces of Asia. But for a gymnasium-schooled theologian philosopher such as Origen, that was a bygone age. The oracles of Montanist women prophets must have seemed to his sophisticated intellect like the ravings of the Delphic Pythia. Maximilla lamented: 'I am pursued like a wolf out of the sheepfold; I am no wolf: I am word and spirit and power.'[37]

Under sustained assault from powerful bishop theologians, Montanism was a short-lived phenomenon. It was declared heretical, and since its writings were ordered burned by an imperial edict in 398 CE, we can only reconstruct its teaching from the slander of its adversaries. Even given the bias of these accounts it does not appear that Montanism was doctrinally unorthodox, rather the clash between Church order and the uncontrollable

---

35. Karen Jo Torjesen, 'The Early Christian *Orans*: An Artistic Representation of Women's Liturgical Prayer and Prophecy', in B.M. Kienzle and P.J. Walker (eds.), *Women Preachers and Prophets*, p.52. The quotation is from Origen, *Fragments on I Corinthians* 74.

36. See Origen, *Commentary on Matthew* 11.1; 10.22 and 14.9.

37. See Eusebius, *Eccl. Hist.* V.16.17.

revelations of the Spirit lay at the heart of this controversy. According to James Ash, while most Church Fathers in their polemic against the Montanists claimed to believe in the *theoretical* continuence of prophecy until the awaited second coming of Christ, they rejected its manifestation *in practice* as 'irrational and psychotic'.[38] The simple fact was that prophecy was antithetical to episcopal and doctrinal control, and women prophets with their enthusiasm, creativity, emotional involvement and spontaneity epitomized the crossing of rational and patriarchal boundaries. In particular, we see from the secondary literature a fear of female sexuality and a rhetorical strategy of linking female prophecy with sexual behaviour. Karen Jo Torjesen comments: 'When women's prophetic status is positively valued, their sexual purity is emphasized, often by pointing out that they were virgins, chaste widows, or even occasionally devoted wives. But when a writer opposes a woman, her sexual status becomes an explicit basis for condemnation.'[39]

7. *The Voice of Spirit-Wisdom*

In the controversy surrounding the New Prophecy movement, both sides appealed to Scripture, particularly to Paul's first letter to the church at Corinth. Here, in chs. 11–14, Paul discussed the role of the *charismata* and in particular ecstatic prophecy in Christian worship. His ambivalence towards prophetesses is clear. On the one hand, women should prophesy in the assembly with a head covering (see 1 Cor. 11.3-16), but later in the same discussion women are forbidden to speak in public (1 Cor. 14.33b-35). The rhetorical and convoluted arguments used by Paul in these chapters suggest that he was faced with the reality of a congregation used to women prophets and that he had to struggle to assert his masculine (apostolic) authority:

> For a man ought not to cover his head, since he is the image and glory of God; but woman is the glory of man. (For man was not made from woman, but woman from man. Neither was man created for woman, but woman for man.) That is why a woman ought to have a veil on her head, because of the angels. (Nevertheless, in the Lord, woman is not independent of man nor man of woman; for as woman was made from man, so man is now born of woman. And all things are from God.)... If any one is disposed to be contentious, we recognize no other practice, nor do the churches of God (1 Cor. 11.7–12.16).

38.   James L. Ash, 'The Decline of Ecstatic Prophecy in the Early Church', *JTS* 37 (1976), pp. 237-43.
39.   K.J. Torjesen, 'The Early Christian *Orans*', p. 28.

Paul's attempt here to ground his authority on the primacy of Adam was supplemented by the claim that he knew a 'secret and hidden wisdom of God' revealed to him by the Spirit (see 1 Cor. 2.6-10) It is almost as if Paul felt obliged to surpass the women prophets of Corinth in order to stamp his doctrines and particularly his theory of liturgy upon this Spirit-led community. In her detailed study of the Corinthian women prophets, Antoinette Clark Wire suggests that Paul himself could not square his rational theory of the ordering of the spiritual gifts during worship with the fluid reality of the Christian assembly inspired by the Spirit. In particular, Paul's appeal for the organization of liturgy to be separated into teaching, preaching, prayer, prophecy and interpretation was in tension with the community's experience of prophecy (speaking for God) and prayer (speaking to God). Wire concludes, 'The spiritual mediate God's insight to each other in wisdom, revelation, knowledge, prophecy, and teaching and in turn respond to God in hymns, blessings and tongues.'[40]

Torjesen calls this integration of prayer and prophecy, 'liturgical prophecy'. She comments:

> Using the adjective *liturgical* calls attention to the fact that it was a constituent element of early Christian worship. The many dimensions of liturgical prophecy—exhortation, revelation, and counsel—invested prophetic speech with considerable authority and gave the prophets a teaching role. Because it took place in the assembly setting, liturgical prophecy was both a 'public' action and an exercise of authority.[41]

Torjesen has developed a new line of research using an alternative source for reconstruction, namely the artistic. She claims to have found a clue in the iconography of early Christian *orans* (meaning literally 'a person praying'). The typical *orans* is the figure of a woman praying in the classical posture of outstretched arms and upturned face. This enigmatic motif is found in catacomb frescos, as relief on sarcophagi, cast in rings and sealed in gold glass. According to Torjesen, 'Whether as a solitary figure or in a setting with other figures, the anonymous *orans* is universally female, and that gendered female figure endured for six centuries.'[42]

In scholarly debate the *orans* has been interpreted as a symbol for the Church or the soul, but Torjesen asks, 'Why should the power, work, service, ministry and authority of prayer be portrayed by a female figure?'[43]

40. A.C. Wire, *The Corinthian Women Prophets: A Reconstruction through Paul's Rhetoric* (Minneapolis: Fortress Press, 1990), p. 142.

41. K.J. Torjesen, 'The Early Christian *Orans*', p. 47.

42. K.J. Torjesen, p. 44.

43. K.J. Torjesen, p. 45.

Her conclusion is that it was normal practice for women to pray and prophesy in the house-churches of the first two centuries and that this practice was only replaced by clerical preaching on the scriptural readings during institutionalization in the third. Later the order of virgins and deaconesses continued some of these functions particularly during funerary rites and all-night vigils at the shrines of martyrs. Only when boy's choirs were introduced in the sixth century did the *orantes* motif finally disappear...

The question remains, what did prophetesses say through the Spirit? The prophetess of Bethany is only described in terms of her symbolic action. Was she silent or were her words considered part of the Markan messianic secret?

King has analyzed the few primary sources for the teaching and theology of women prophets together with the reconstruction of the Corinthian women prophets researched by Wire to produce a list of elements that may have been common to their teaching and practice. Here we come closest to the authentic voice of Spirit-Wisdom in the feminine voice. According to King, their theological emphasis centred on the experience of the risen Christ. The historical Jesus was understood primarily as a teacher and mediator of wisdom rather than a ruler and a judge. These prophets understood the Spirit as available to everyone in the Christian community in the present. As such, women and men have a new identity constructed apart from gender roles, sex and childbearing. She comments: 'An ethic of freedom and spiritual development is emphasized over an ethics of order and control.'[44]

Sadly, the emancipatory good news of early charismatic prophecy was extinguished with the institutionalization of canonical Christianity. The Latin masculinization of the Holy Spirit, which reached dogmatic status with the doctrine of the three male Persons of the Trinity at the Council of Chalcedon in 451 CE can be seen as the ecclesiastical aspect of a wider co-option of the feminine into the masculine in Christendom. If we return to the time of early Christian prophecy before these sociological and theological shifts, we can reclaim a spiritual heritage where women identified with and spoke in the voice of *Ruach-Sophia*. Their symbolic gender affinity with her would help to explain why, in spite of episcopal resistance, the prophetess was popularly considered the paradigm of discipleship and the exemplar of prayer, revelation and wisdom. Further, in this fluid period of theological experiment and ecstatic religious experience, the identification of Jesus the wisdom teacher with Sophia inspired two-way gender transgression. For while, on the one hand, such male theologi-

44. K.L. King, 'Prophetic Power', p. 33.

ans as Paul, John the Evangelist and the Alexandrians, Clement and Origen, developed Wisdom Chistologies, on the other hand women prophets sometimes spoke of the Risen One as a woman. The Montanist prophetess Prisca saw Christ as a female figure in a dream vision. Because of the clash between patriarchal and pneumatic anthropologies and lifestyles, the question of sex-gender, whether in the liberated human or in the nature of God, could not be avoided.

> 'In the form of a woman dressed in shining armour, Christ came towards me and put wisdom in me and revealed to me that this place is holy...' Prisca quoted by Epiphanius (*Panarion* 49.1.2-3).

BIBLIOGRAPHY

Ash, James L., 'The Decline of Ecstatic Prophecy in the Early Church', *JTS* 37 (1976), pp. 237-43.

Boring, Eugene M., *Sayings of the Risen Jesus: Christian Prophecy in the Synoptic Tradition* (Cambridge: Cambridge University Press, 1982).

Brock, Rita Nakashima, *Journeys by Heart: A Christology of Erotic Power* (New York: Crossroad, 1988).

Court, John M., 'The Gospels as Prophecy', in *EPI TO AYTO: Studies in Honour of Petr Pokorný on his Sixty-fifth Birthday* (Prague: Mlýn, 1998), pp. 55-66.

Fiorenza, Elisabeth Schüssler, *In Memory of Her: A Feminist Theological Reconstruction of Christian Origins* (London: SCM Press, 1983).

Heyward, Isabel Carter, *The Redemption of God: A Theology of Mutual Relation* (Lanham, MD: University Press of America, 1980).

Hill, David, *New Testament Prophecy* (London: Marshall, Morgan & Scott, 1979).

Jansen, Katherine Ludwig, 'Maria Magdalena: *Apostolorum Apostola*', in Beverly Mayne Kienzle and Pamela J. Walker (eds.), *Women Preachers and Prophets through Two Millennia of Christianity* (Berkeley, University of California Press, 1998).

— *Passio Perpetuae*, translation and commentary by Rosemary Rader in P. Wilson-Kastner, G.R. Kastner, A. Millin, R. Rader and J. Reedy, *A Lost Tradition: Women Writers of the Early Church* (Lanham, MD: University Press of America, 1982).

—*The Gospel of Mary* (BG 8502,*1*), trans. G.W. MacRae and R. McL.Wilson with a commentary by Karen L. King in James M. Robinson (ed.), *The Nag Hammadi Library* (Leiden: E.J. Brill, 1988), pp. 523-27.

Kee, Howard C., *Community of the New Age: Studies in Mark's Gospel* (London: SCM Press, 1977).

King, Karen L., 'Prophetic Power and Women's Authority: The Case of the *Gospel of Mary* (Magdalene)', in B.M. Kienzle and P.J. Walker, *Women Preachers and Prophets through Two Millennia of Christianity* (Berkeley: University of California Press, 1998).

Torjesen, Karen Jo, 'The Early Christian *Orans*: An Artistic Representation of Women's Liturgical Prayer and Prophecy', in B.M. Kienzle and P.J. Walker, *Women Preachers and Prophets through Two Millennia of Christianity* (Berkeley: University of California Press, 1998).

Wire, Antoinette Clark, *The Corinthian Women Prophets: A Reconstruction through Paul's Rhetoric* (Philadelphia: Fortress Press, 1990).

PRAGMATISM, POSTMODERNISM AND THE BIBLE AS A MEANINGFUL PUBLIC RESOURCE IN A PLURALISTIC AGE

Philip Knight

Editor's Introduction

The humorist Miles Kington once parodied the confident claim, 'The Bible tells us…' in a letter about stubble-burning supposedly written by the Rev. Jack Flannel:

> Why is it that any new rural custom is always greeted with hostility? There must always have been the same resistance to hedge-laying, ditch-draining and the Black Death. Personally there is nothing I like better on a late summer evening than to watch half of England ablaze. The Bible tells us that man is born to stubble as the sparks fly upwards. Let us at least enjoy the sparks, I say.

Today by contrast the public use of the phrase 'the Bible says' may only succeed in stopping public conversation.

One of the problems with postmodernism is to assign adequate meaning to the term, unless one should dismiss it as a 'worthless portmanteau word'. Dr Knight uses the pragmatist Richard Rorty both as a guide and as a partner in debate in his investigation of these contemporary issues for biblical interpretation. 'Postmodern' is a popular word for two reasons: a philosophical pluralism (that is irresistible), and an historical pessimism (that can actually be contested). Pluralism prepared the way for a ready acceptance of Darwinism, which in turn made the legacy of Plato and orthodox Christian theology increasingly implausible. If the interpretations of biblical texts depend upon pre-Darwinian ideas, then they will be accredited with private rather than public meaning. One may contest the attitude of historical pessimism, and suggest that biblical texts may after all be interpreted in the light of public concerns about human moral and social progress; the resourcefulness of biblical meaning may be extended to include contemporary concerns. But if this is to evoke a traditional biblical authority, then it is argued that such interpretations will remain a private affair. In conclusion Knight discusses two examples of such constructive possibilities, in the work of the American Delwin Brown and the Italian Gianni Vattimo. Postmodernism weakens rather than destroys the public use of the Bible.

1. *Introduction*

In our contemporary pluralistic age any reading of the Bible can be privately inspiring and good for just that reason. However, the institutions and ideologies through which we shape our common public life no longer defer to and hardly ever refer to the Bible as a source of public meaning. Consequently, there is a danger that the future of biblical studies may reduce to little more than the private edification of a dwindling number of 'biblical professionals'. This observation is not meant to impugn the important scholarly task of understanding the conversations which the writers of Genesis or the Gospels might have had with their contemporaries. Nor is it meant to devalue the hermeneutical skill of reading into biblical texts the enduring concerns of our own culture so as to be able to hold conversations about these concerns with biblical writers. It is, however, meant to acknowledge the difficulty that biblical critics face getting heard in a secular pluralistic culture that no longer derives normative public meaning from biblical texts.

The American moral philosopher, Jeffrey Stout, recognizes this difficulty. 'Academic theology', Stout writes, 'seems to have lost its…ability to command attention as a distinctive contributor to public discourse in our culture.'[1] Secularizing movements, such as philosophical pluralism and political liberalism, allow people to go about their daily lives without recourse to the Bible or to traditional religious modes of thought. This situation creates what Stout calls the 'theologian's dilemma': the more theologians adhere to meaningful patterns of public discourse the less distinctive is the theological contribution they make to public life and thus the less able they are to voice the traditional concerns of the religious communities they are meant to serve. But the more they are seen to be voicing these concerns the less public relevance is accredited to their utterances. Church leaders and academic theologians who contribute to public debate will have a public audience only if the utterances they make could just as well have been uttered by humanists who need never have read the Bible.

Theological pragmatism dissolves rather than resolves this dilemma by refusing to depict the theologian's task as primarily one of 'voicing the traditional concerns of religious communities'. Instead, it conceives that task as one of bringing those communities and their traditional canonical resources into constructive conversation with dialogue partners in fields of

---

1. Jeffrey Stout, *Ethics after Babel* (Cambridge: James Clark & Co., 1988), p. 163.

human endeavour that, taken together, form the fabric of our common public life. Accordingly, the religious pragmatist, Sheila Greeve Davaney, suggests that the Bible can still inspire worthy public visions even though it cannot be considered their sole or primary justification.[2]

In the next section of this chapter I will show how philosophical pluralism, as presented by the neo-pragmatist Richard Rorty, helps to explain why the Bible often fails to get a hearing in contemporary public debate. Like Stout, Rorty doubts the public relevance of religious sources of meaning, but I shall claim that his pragmatic distinction between public and private discourse actually helps facilitate, if not establish, the reconstruction of theology suggested by Davaney and like-minded publicly orientated pragmatic theologians.[3] In section 3 I will summarize the views of the pragmatic historicist Delwin Brown, and the postmodernist Gianni Vattimo. Dispensing with out-moded notions of biblical authority, both writers argue that the Bible remains a source of reference informing various strands within the fabric of our shared public life.

2. *Philosophical Pluralism and the Public/Private Divide*

Although Richard Rorty has no great liking for the term 'postmodern' its popularity, he argues, can be explained by (1) contemporary culture's 'inability to resist the claims of philosophical pluralism combined with [(2)] a quite reasonable fear that history is about to turn against us'.[4] In this section we will summarize Rorty's account of philosophical pluralism and his contestation of historical pessimism. The former shows why it has become difficult to infuse public debate with a biblical word or two while the latter provides publicly orientated theologians with the means to attempt such an infusion.

(1) According to Rorty, philosophical pluralism recognizes 'a potential infinity of equally valuable ways to lead a human life'.[5] Indebted to the emergence of romanticism, democracy, industrialization and utilitarianism, philosophical pluralism has become irresistible, Rorty argues, because these social and philosophical movements led to the quick acceptance of

---

2.   Sheila Greeve Davaney, *Pragmatic Historicism* (Albany: SUNY, 2000), p. 152.

3.   See, for example, Victor Anderson, *Pragmatic Theology* (Albany: SUNY, 1998); Linell E. Cady, *Religion, Theology, and American Public Life* (Albany: SUNY 1993); William Dean, *The Religious Critic in American Culture* (Albany: SUNY, 1994).

4.   Richard Rorty, *Philosophy and Social Hope* (London: Penguin Books, 1999), p. 276.

5.   Rorty, *Philosophy and Social Hope*, p. 268.

what Daniel Dennett has called 'Darwin's dangerous idea': the idea that human life is the result of '*a mindless, mechanical—algorithmic—process ...called "natural selection"* '.[6] Darwinism makes philosophical pluralism irresistible because it undermines our confidence in the philosophical heritage of Platonism and orthodox Christian theology—a heritage Rorty calls 'theologicometaphysics'.

This heritage posits an ingredient special to humans (variously termed 'spirit', 'soul' or 'mind') that connects us to a realm of reality beyond the surrounds of our immediate material environment. The existence of such a realm makes the notion of a non-human authority—such as a divine voice in Scripture—seem plausible. However, given a Darwinian story of human origins, it has become as difficult to think with the Cartesian–Kantian tradition that humans possess a special representational mental faculty that connects us to the way things 'really' are beyond human needs and interests as it has to think with Genesis and Plato that there is a special quality in human beings that connects us with a perfect, divine realm. By showing us our ancestry with the beasts, Darwin's story repudiates both modern representational epistemology and premodern supernaturalism. In doing so it revolutionizes our understanding of what constitutes knowledge and erodes traditional notions of biblical authority.

Knowledge, Rorty argues, is not a series of mental representations but a skilfully woven linguistic web of beliefs. Rorty defines beliefs as 'sentential attitudes': linguistic 'rule[s] for action rather than...picture[s] made out of mind stuff'.[7] Having beliefs (sentential attitudes) goes with the evolutionary territory of linguistic beings in the same way as croaking goes with the evolutionary territory of frogs. Beliefs, like croaks, are non-representational. They are not externalizations of that which is intrinsically mental but 'tools for co-ordinating...behaviour'.[8] Understood as tools, beliefs are as direct as any contact with reality gets. As a maker of more complex tools than frogs' croaks, human language allows us to fulfil an endless variety of purposes. 'Religious tools', Rorty writes, 'are needed to make possible certain kinds of human life, but not others. Scientific

6.   Daniel C. Dennett, *Darwin's Dangerous Idea* (London: Penguin Books, 1995), p. 60.

7.   Richard Rorty, *Objectivity, Relativism and Truth* (Cambridge: Cambridge University Press, 1991), p. 118.

8.   Rorty, *Philosophy and Social Hope*, p. xxiv. 'This is not to say', Rorty adds, 'that one can "reduce" mental states such as beliefs and desires to physiological or behavioural states. It is merely to say that there is no point in asking whether a belief represents reality, either mental reality or physical reality, accurately.'

tools are of no use for many human projects, and of great use for many others.'[9] Religion, good for getting a person's ultimate concerns out from under the daily round of their other mundane concerns, is not much use for determining a community's public transport needs or predicting the environmental effects of genetically modified crops.

The existence of creatures with the ability to use language to fulfil a variety of purposes means that Darwinian naturalism promotes a non-reductive pluralism. Consequently, Rorty sees no reason to doubt that notions like 'created in the image of God' or 'human rationality' are able to survive in a post-Darwinian world. For Rorty, these notions are none the worse for being human inventions.[10] They help us *cope* with reality in different ways by serving different human needs. Thus, Rorty notes:

> [W]e are free to describe the universe in many different ways. Describing it as the drifting of cosmic atoms is useful for the social project of working together to control our environment and improve man's estate. But that description leaves us entirely free to say, for example, that the Heavens proclaim the glory of God.[11]

The difference between these two freedoms—the difference between atom-talk and God-talk or between Darwin-talk and Bible-talk—will be the difference between public and private discourses.

Beliefs that allow us to predict and control the environment or that allow us to create greater social and economic security have become embedded within the fabric of our common public life, while beliefs about the ultimate purpose of life, including beliefs about God or biblical authority, have not. This is not because the former set of beliefs stand in a privileged relationship to the intrinsic nature of things—both public and private beliefs are historically contingent—but because the former set of beliefs can be justified in term of other beliefs that have clearly articulated practical consequences for mundane human social cooperation, while the latter set of beliefs cannot be justified this way. Another way of putting this difference, Rorty writes, is to treat 'Scripture as useful for purposes for which Aristotle, Newton and Darwin were useless, and as useless for purposes of prediction and control of the environment'.[12]

Darwinism, then, does more than pull the rug out from under a literal

---

9.   Rorty, *Philosophy and Social Hope*, p. 268.

10.   Richard Rorty, *Contingency, Irony and Solidarity* (Cambridge: Cambridge University Press, 1989), pp. 195-96.

11.   Richard Rorty, 'Pragmatism as Romantic Polytheism', in Morris Dickstein (ed.), *The Revival of Pragmatism* (Durham: Duke University Press, 1998), pp. 29-30.

12.   Rorty, 'Pragmatism as Romantic Polytheism', p. 26.

account of the Genesis creation story. It also undermines theologicometaphysics. What we learn from Darwin, Rorty argues, is that there is no way
the world is going to be described antecedent to the plurality of human
needs and interests, all of which are served by particular human projects.
Projects that promote social cooperation, such as learning to control genes
in order to prevent cancer or assessing the best way to educate our five-
year-olds, will be freighted with public meaning; while projects that don't,
won't. Interpretations of the Bible, like interpretations of poetry, will be a
meaningful but private affair.

However, the practical task of creating happier and just forms of human
social relationships is regarded by Rorty as a public enterprise. It is here,
according to theological pragmatists, that the Bible can carry public meaning. They argue that only a misplaced loyalty to past interpretations of
biblical authority would warrant the parcelling out into private categories
alone all contemporary uses of Scripture. On occasions, most notably in
Contingency, Irony and Solidarity, Rorty, like Stout, gives the impression
that this loyalty is the only position open to contemporary theologians. In
some of his recent essays, however, Rorty sometimes seems to accept that
this loyalty *is* misplaced. When interpretations of Scripture are used to
contest historical pessimism and to support a pragmatic faith in human
moral progress, he can be more charitable toward the Bible's public utility.

(2) Among some writers who describe themselves as 'postmodern' there
is, Rorty claims, a pervasive sense of historical pessimism that rejects the
possibility of human happiness and moral progress. Having unmasked the
myth of progress and fallen victim to relativism, postmodern culture no
longer has any confidence in our ability to agree on ideas or develop the
technologies necessary to solve the many problems we face.

Rorty does not share this postmodern historical pessimism. Like his
pragmatic forebear, John Dewey, he believes that social hope and faith in
human moral progress is still worth defending even after the demise of
theologicometaphysics. Faith in human ingenuity to create incremental
improvements in justice and human happiness is sustainable, Rorty believes, even if the various socio-political and moral perspectives human
beings propose are supported by nothing stronger than culturally contingent values. In this context, Rorty affirms Dewey's claim that 'imagination
is the chief instrument of the good' and that 'the moral prophets of humanity have always been poets even though they spoke in free verse or by
parable'.[13] But, Rorty argues, while for some parable tellers private beati-

---

13. Rorty, *Contingency, Irony and Solidarity*, p. 69.

tude and social cooperation coincide, for others they don't. Consequently, in a culture that values pluralism *and* hopes for morally responsible social cooperation, privatization is the price to pay for philosophical, poetic, prophetic and religious liberty.

Here, Rorty's widely criticized distinction between public and private discourse places the Bible outside the folds in the fabric of public debate. However, his distinction might better be understood not as a non-traversable ontological divide, but as a practical suggestion about just how a pluralistic society *can combine* moral progress and social cooperation with the private projects of its citizens. Separating the vocabularies of philosophers, poets and prophets from public moral responsibility does not necessarily preclude the obvious possibility that some aspects of the philosophical-poetic-prophetic complex can easily be justified by reference to public moral responsibility, moral progress and social cooperation. Public faith in the ability of democratic institutions to secure incremental improvements in justice and human happiness is not too distant from the private projects of philosophers, poets and prophets like Derrida, Dickens and Orwell, nor from the rather different faith expressed in the Judaeo-Christian tradition.

Religious pragmatists who share a Deweyan faith in moral and social progress will welcome Rorty's recent willingness to write a paper in which he sees his 'main task [as that of]…defending Dewey's tolerance for religious belief against those who think that pragmatism and religion do not mix'.[14] They will share Rorty's view that rejecting Christianity understood in the terms of theologicometaphysical assurance 'does not, and should not, prevent us from finding inspiration and encouragement in the New Testament'.[15] They will also appreciate Rorty's affirmation that, taken as hope rather than knowledge, the Christian gospel is an inspiring document that 'still names a powerful force working for human decency and human equality'.[16] A Rortyan pragmatic perspective, then, need not deny that biblical texts can inspire a public concern for social cooperation and human solidarity even if Rorty himself insists that in the interests of social cooperation, these texts (like the texts of philosophers, poets and prophets) remain in the background and are read only in private among the members of the particular religious communities that find them useful.

In his book *Pragmatic Theology*, Victor Anderson accepts:

14. Rorty, 'Pragmatism as Romantic Polytheism', p. 25.
15. Rorty, *Philosophy and Social Hope*, p. 202.
16. Rorty, *Philosophy and Social Hope*, p. 205.

> [W]hether theological interpretations of public life get heard in the public arena may depend more on their compatibility with widely shared public interests in health and safety, education, labor, and public administration than on their distinctive languages. For pragmatic theology, the test of relevance is whether theological interpretations…genuinely reflect publicly shared meanings about the goods necessary for a democratic life and the moral ends appropriate for its fulfilment.[17]

Linell Cady agrees. In her book on theology and public life she argues that biblical scholars should be willing to 'extend' the meaning of biblical texts to include the type of contemporary public concerns Anderson mentions and should do so by interpreting the Bible in the most favourable light. She cites feminist theology as an example of 'extensionalist reading' prepared to swap biblical authority for biblical resourcefulness in order to render the Bible more relevant to contemporary public life. Theology, she argues, has always been a creative enterprise, and so biblical scholars should not be unduly troubled by publicly orientated extensionalist readings of Scripture. Cady believes that 'because the story the theologian seeks to tell is one "worth telling now", he or she may legitimately sacrifice the strictest continuity in order to articulate a more adequate story'.[18] According to William Dean, another writer in the tradition of American public theology, theological vitality depends upon the theologian's ability to communicate the public relevance of biblical texts. Dean utilizes James Douglas's notion of 'third sector' voluntary organizations to identify public spaces where private projects of citizens might coincide with public needs. This sector lays beyond governmental (first sector) and commercial (second sector) interests and is constituted by voluntary institutions like churches, campaign movements, charitable foundations, arts groups and, occasionally, universities. In this third sector, Dean notes, 'ideas of the religious critic can become public conventions'.[19]

Nevertheless, important as notions like 'the third sector' and 'extensionalist readings' are, pragmatic theologians accept that they are unlikely in themselves to render the biblical drama of creation, incarnation and redemption any more publicly meaningful than before. Anderson writes, 'In a pluralistic culture…theologians cannot count on such [religious language] as having widespread public meanings beyond the confines of

---

17. Anderson, *Pragmatic Theology*, p. 132.
18. Cady, *Religion, Theology, and American Public Life*, p. 51.
19. Dean, *The Religious Critic in American Culture*, p. 172.

local churches and seminaries.'[20] As Rorty notes, to announce in public debate 'the Bible says…' only succeeds in stopping public conversation.[21] Biblical texts can inspire public action but this does not of itself make the Bible a normative source of public reference. For religious pragmatists this is largely because the authority that is claimed on behalf of the Bible is still too often surrounded by the aura of theologicometaphysics. Dean, for example, accepts that even 'third sector' public spaces will fail to translate religious ideas into public conventions if they rely upon a traditional understanding of biblical authority. Identifying what is required, Cady calls for 'a form of theological argumentation that locates itself within a recognisable tradition of interpretation, but which eschews the authoritarian or confessional tendencies of much theology'.[22] In the next section I will suggest that such a theological argumentation can be found in Delwin Brown's pragmatic 'constructive historicism' and that Gianni Vattimo's weak hermeneutic ontology can be read as a good example of this pragmatic constructive historicism at work. Both writers slough off the theologicometaphysical residue attaching itself to notions of biblical authority but continue to situate the Bible among the canonical resources that inform the secular pluralistic culture in which we now transact our shared public life.

3. *Constructive Historicism,* Kenosis, *and the Bible's Public Meaning*

In his book *Boundaries of our Habitation*, Delwin Brown describes the complex relationship of continuity and change through which a tradition's future is reconstructed from its inherited canonical resources. Change, Brown suggests, occurs in variegated and incremental ways as the custodians of a tradition interact with the socio-political environment that surrounds them. Lasting change is often facilitated by hidden elements within a tradition itself and involves the affective as well as the reflective responses of its custodians. Although sometimes unintended, the requirement to effect change, Brown argues, is nearly always the result of a pragmatic desire by a tradition's custodians to create and sustain viable communal and personal identities in relation to a tradition's canonical resources. Negotiating identities *in* a canonical space also often produces

---

20. Anderson, *Pragmatic Theology*, p. 132.
21. Rorty, *Philosophy and Social Hope*, pp. 168-74.
22. Cady, *Religion, Theology, and American Public Life*, p. 27.

a need to renegotiate *with* a tradition's canon, thereby establishing a dia-lectical relationship between tradition and canon in which 'tradition creates canon as much as canon creates tradition'.[23]

A canon, Brown suggests, is a collection of historical human resources with a sufficient internal 'gravitational pull' to constitute 'a galaxy of meanings'.[24] A traditions canon must be resourceful enough to challenge the *status quo* and stable enough to allow the custodians of a tradition to negotiate and renegotiate their identities. A canon, he argues, is not a monolith but a multilith. Its boundaries are determined not by its unity but by the identities that a tradition's custodians can negotiate with/in it. As such, he notes, 'the normative character of a canon is the depth of its fecun-dity',[25] and its fecundity is exemplified by the various ways different cus-todians have made it their contemporary.

To equate the authority of a canon like the Bible with a particular inter-pretative approach rather than with the diverse identities custodians of various Judaeo-Christian traditions can negotiate with/in it is to obscure the dynamic potentialities of the Bible's own gravitational field and to deny the Bible's normative plurivocal character. Like any canon, the Bible is a field of play with a multiplicity of diverse players. Yet, also like any canon, the Bible is itself a player. To interpret a canon like the Bible, Brown writes, 'can mean only to play with/in it and to be played by it'.[26] To be played in this way is to inherit the Bible as a gift but also as a chal-lenge; as an ally but also as an adversary. To respond to the Bible today as gift and as challenge; to move within its 'gravitational field' with integrity, Brown argues, is both to come under its 'gravitational pull' *and* to accept that 'the adequacy of the identities a canon creates and sustains is tested in the unprotected space of contemporary public discourse'.[27] As Brown sees it, the theologian's continuous creative task is to negotiate and renegotiate Christian identities in the light of contemporary public challenges both to the meaningfulness of its tradition and to the integrity of the canonical space with/in which any such negotiations/renegotiations take place. Con-temporary philosophical pluralism requires the custodians of traditions who negotiate their identities with/in the Bible to depict its authority in ways that emphazise not its unity but its diversity.

23. Delwin Brown, *Boundaries of our Habitation* (Albany: SUNY, 1994), p. 29.
24. Brown, *Boundaries of our Habitation*, p. 77.
25. Brown, *Boundaries of our Habitation*, p. 80.
26. Brown, *Boundaries of our Habitation*, p. 144.
27. Brown, *Boundaries of our Habitation*, p. 90.

Drawing the Bible into public discourse is a function of what Brown calls the theologian's task as 'tradition's caregiver'. Brown divides this task into a threefold diachronic activity and one synchronic activity. The first diachronic activity reshuffles the elements of a tradition's historical resources in order to reform its doctrines and beliefs. Here, Brown refers to the reconstruction of Christology and ecclesiology wrought by liberation theologians as they sought to understand the relevance of biblical teaching on sin and salvation in contexts of communal solidarity. The second diachronic activity not only reshuffles a tradition's existing resources, but it also attempts to remould them in the light of religious demands within contemporary life. Here, Brown cites feminist and process theology as good examples of this second activity by which a tradition's caregiver brings something new into the gravitational pull of an existing canon. The third diachronic activity opens a tradition's canonical resources to wide public scrutiny. '[T]he evaluative claims of theologians', Brown writes, 'must be open to public debate and vulnerable to criticism from all of the communities of contemporary discourse that collectively constitute the public sphere.'[28] As an example of this activity Brown refers to religious pragmatists like Cady.

However, these diachronic activities by themselves are unlikely to bring about a more general recognition of the Bible as a public source of reference without a connection to the synchronic activity. This synchronic activity negotiates with/in a tradition's canon the requisite continuity and change demanded by a contemporary historical context. In the past, Brown notes, Christian theology has tended to emphasize continuity rather than change, thereby giving priority to the repetition of its canon. If Christians want their canon to have public meaning, Brown suggests they should acknowledge that repetition is neither desirable nor possible. They must understand their inherited texts in term 'delineated by other humanistic fields of scholarship', and must accept that these texts are 'answerable to canons of critical inquiry defensible within the various arenas of our common discourse and not merely those that are Christian'.[29] This approach to the Bible remains within its 'gravitational pull' and so maintains some degree of continuity with the past, but it also understands the Bible's authority in terms of the multiplicity of diverse identities it can 'author' and sustain rather than just those identities it has sustained in the past.

As long as theologians take the role of 'tradition's caregiver' seriously

---

28. Brown, *Boundaries of our Habitation*, p. 139.
29. Brown, *Boundaries of our Habitation*, pp. 4-5. (both quotations).

and refuse to depict biblical authority as residing beyond the various historically contingent identities it helps to sustain, there can be no *a priori* reason why traditions that negotiate communal and individual identities with/in a canon containing religious texts should be considered any less the treasury of public meaning than traditions that look to secular canons for such meaning. The theologicometaphysical aura of biblical authority that has given credence to a contemporary suspicion about the Bible's role in public discourse evaporates when theologians and their secular dialogue partners in the public square recognize that the Bible has no more authority than is given it by the custodians of the traditions in which it functions as a normative canonical resource.

Like Brown, Gianni Vattimo argues that any reconstruction of a tradition's future cannot entirely evade the influence of the past. For Vattimo, this means:

> [A]ll the principle traits of western civilization…are structured by their relation to Judaeo-Christian Scripture, the text upon which this civilization is based. While, our civilization no longer explicitly professes itself Christian…it is nevertheless profoundly shaped by that heritage at its source.[30]

Indeed, Vattimo believes that philosophical pluralism can be neither fully understood nor argued for persuasively without a recognition of its provenance in biblical revelation.

Vattimo is most well known for his notion of 'weak thought'—the thought, for example, that attaches itself to questions about truth when the truth of an interpretation is recognized as being itself only an interpretation. Like much post-metaphysical thinking, Vattimo's 'weak thought' is indebted to Nietzschean nihilism and Heideggerean reflection on the historicity of Being (understood as event rather than substance), but it does not share the mistrust that Nietzsche and Heidegger often displayed toward democracy and social hope. Vattimo agrees with Rorty that philosophical pluralism marks the end a period of thought dominated by theologicometaphysics during which 'Being' was understood as the objective foundation of reality and truth. However, Vattimo argues that theologicometaphysics cannot be directly rejected. It can be overcome only insofar as we continue to recollect the history of Being as a history of decline, 'as the story of a "long good-bye", of an interminable weakening of Being'.[31]

---

30. Gianni Vattimo, *Belief* (ET; trans. Luca D'Isanto and David Webb; Cambridge: Polity Press, 1999), p. 43.

31. Gianni Vattimo, *Beyond Interpretation* (ET; trans. David Webb; Cambridge: Polity Press, 1997), p. 13.

Vattimo sees no need to refute Rorty's claim that the 'history of Being' unfolds within a contingent human canon of Western productivity, but he does refute Rorty's insouciance about the need to understand philosophical pluralism in the light of this canon's heritage. Only in this light, Vattimo argues, can philosophical pluralism hope to be read as an effective critique of metaphysics in the forms of humanism, technology and the will to power that it takes today. It is in recollecting the weakening of Being and thus remembering the ontological difference between Being and beings that post-metaphysical thought can maintain a critical attitude toward the metaphysical pretensions of humanism. If it is *true*, as both Vattimo and Rorty claim, that 'truth' has no meaning in philosophical pluralism independent of human interpretative interests—if it is *true*, that is, that hermeneutics replaces metaphysics—then this 'weakened' *truth* will remain unpersuasive, Vattimo argues, if the shift from metaphysics to hermeneutics is merely a shift from the object's mastery to mastery by the subject. To treat the shift from metaphysics to hermeneutics as Rorty does, as of little philosophical interest, not only misses its vital connection with the past—the biblical and Christian past—but also leaves hermeneutics and pluralism bereft of an argumentation able to negate the self-reflexive tendency of metaphysics to turn against those who reject it. As Vattimo sees it, the problem of postmodernity is how to express the *truth* of the end of metaphysics without speaking of this *truth* in metaphysical terms. Vattimo believes that without a connection to a history—the history of the weakening of Being originating in the biblical drama of divine *kenosis* through creation and incarnation—we will never fully succeed in questioning the mastery of metaphysics in the form of humanism.

However, to think beyond metaphysics is *not*, Vattimo argues, to think of humanism and the will to power as further examples in a sequence of human errors that might be overcome by at last getting reality right. Such overcoming would itself be just another example of the will to power. Rather, to think beyond metaphysics, Vattimo argues, is to accept Being's nihilistic vocation of weakening and withdrawal read in the light of Nietzsche's proclamation of the death of God and his claim that there are no truths only interpretations expressed now in current processes of secularization. It is here that Vattimo reinvents Christianity as biblical revelation. He notes:

> [T]he liberation of the plurality of myths, and thus the re-legitimation of religion in the wake of hermeneutics, are wholly dependent on a process of secularization set in train by the story of the *kenosis* of God in the incarnation.

He continues:

> Hermeneutics can be what it is—a non-metaphysical philosophy with an essentially interpretative attitude toward truth, and thus a nihilistic ontology —only as heir to the Christian myth of the incarnation of God.[32]

If we are to overcome Being understood in terms of theologicometaphysical foundations we must, Vattimo urges, think of Being in terms of its historicity as a process of weakening and withdrawal symbolised in the biblical idea that God is friend rather than master, self-emptyingly creative and incarnate throughout the world, and continuing today in the processes secularization.[33] For Vattimo, secularization is the destiny of Christianity understood as the *kenosis* of God. According to Vattimo:

> ...modern hermeneutic philosophy is born in Europe not only because here there is a religion of the book that focuses attention on the phenomenon of interpretation, but also because this religion has at its base the idea of the incarnation of God, which it conceives as *kenosis*, as abasement and, in our translation, as weakening.[34]

This is not a return to what Christianity was in the past. Rather, Vattimo is 'rethinking revelation in secularized terms in order to "live in accord with one's age"'.[35] To use Brown's description of 'care giving', Vattimo is offering 'a creative reconstruction of inherited symbols, [to construct] a tradition's future from the resources of its past'.[36] Vattimo believes that reconstructing Christianity as a *kenotic*, non-metaphysical and therefore salvific faith provides a persuasive interpretative matrix for understanding our own times that does not succumb to humanistic metaphysics.

For Vattimo, our public projects belong to the history of Being just as much as our various private projects do. Recollecting this history as a history of the weakening of Being extends the limits of public discourse beyond the boundaries of scientific and socio-political cooperation to include not only 'the Christian precept of charity and its rejection of violence',[37] but also the whole biblical drama of creation, incarnation and redemption, because without this biblical provenance public discourse will itself remain captive to the authorizing traits of theologicometaphysics. *Pace* Rorty, Vattimo notes: '[A]n ethics of respect and solidarity can

---

32. Vattimo, *Beyond Interpretation*, p. 54 (both quotes).
33. Vattimo, *Belief*, pp. 44, 47.
34. Vattimo, *Beyond Interpretation*, p. 48.
35. Vattimo, *Belief*, p. 75.
36. Brown, *Boundaries of our Habitation*, p. 148.
37. Vattimo, *Belief*, p. 44.

become reasonable, precise in what it says and capable of holding its own in conversation with others precisely by relating itself explicitly to it provenance.'[38]

Vattimo's weak hermeneutic ontology suggests that philosophical pluralism can be persuasively articulated only insofar as it acknowledges its own provenance in biblical revelation. Social cooperation resulting from persuasion rather than force and an ethics based on respect and human solidarity—both marks of Rortyan public discourse—are possible in a Western post-theologicometaphysical pluralistic culture precisely because this culture stands in relation to a heritage of biblical revelation. Our pluralistic culture, Vattimo argues, can neither understand itself nor recognize its emergence from a period of history dominated by theologicometaphysics unless it acknowledges its indebtedness to a biblical heritage. This heritage can no longer be received in orthodox, non-hermeneutical or anti-pluralistic forms but while it remains mute in the public square post-metaphysical discourse is itself denied a plausible public voice.

4. *Conclusion*

Following Rorty, we have suggested that philosophical pluralism has become irresistible because a Darwinian story of our origins has made theologicometaphysics increasingly implausible. To the extent that interpretations of biblical texts lean upon pre-Darwinian ideas about biblical authority they will be accredited with private rather than public meaning, The contestability of a post-theologicometaphysical historical pessimism has suggested the possibility of interpreting biblical texts in the light of public concerns about human moral and social progress. But, insofar as these interpretations do not sufficiently slough off the aura of theologicometaphysical that surrounds the concept of biblical authority, they too will remain a private affair. However, by developing hermeneutic perspectives that dispel this aura, both Delwin Brown and Gianni Vattimo continue to situate the Bible among the canonical resources informing secular pluralistic culture. Consequently, they remain convinced about the Bible's continuing public utility. They suggest that the public meanings that the Bible is able to engender are not exhausted, as Stout and Rorty claim, but are still to be fully articulated at the end of modernity.

38. Vattimo, *Belief*, p. 45.

BIBLIOGRAPHY

Postmodernism and the Bible

Carroll, Robert P., 'Poststructualist Approaches New Historicism and Postmodernism', in John Barton (ed.), *The Cambridge Companion to Biblical Interpretation* (Cambridge: Cambridge University Press, 1998).

Castelli, Elizabeth A. *et al.* (eds.), *The Postmodern Bible* (New Haven: Yale University Press, 1995).

Frascati-Lochhead, Marta, *Kenosis and Feminist Theology: The Challenge of Gianni Vattimo* (Albany: SUNY 1998).

Jobling, David *et al.* (eds.), *The Post Modern Bible Reader* (Oxford: Basil Blackwell, 2001).

Vattimo, Gianni, *The End of Modernity: Nihilism and Hermeneutics in Postmodern Culture*, (ET; Jon R. Snyder; Cambridge: Polity Press, 1988).

—*Beyond Interpretation: The Meaning of Hermeneutics for Philosophy* (ET; David Webb; Cambridge: Polity Press, 1997).

—*Belief* (ET; Luca D'Isanto and David Webb; Cambridge: Polity Press, 1999).

—'The Trace of the Trace'. (ET David Webb), in Jacques Derrida and Gianni Vattimo *Religion* (Cambridge: Polity Press, 1998).

Philosophical Pragmatism and Pragmatic Theology

Anderson, Victor, *Pragmatic Theology: Negotiating the Intersections of an American Philosophy of Religion and Public Theology* (Albany: SUNY, 1998).

Brown, Delwin, *Boundaries of our Habitation: Tradition and Theological Construction* (Albany: SUNY, 1994).

Cady, Linell E., *Religion, Theology, and American Public Life* (Albany: SUNY, 1993).

Davaney, Sheila Greeve, *Pragmatic Historicism: A Theology for the Twenty-First Century* (Albany: SUNY, 2000).

Dean, William, *The Religious Critic in American Culture* (Albany: SUNY, 1994).

Dennett, Daniel C., *Darwin's Dangerous Idea: Evolution and the Meaning of Life* (London: Penguin Books, 1995).

Rorty, Richard, *Contingency, Irony and Solidarity* (Cambridge: Cambridge University Press, 1989).

—*Objectivity, Relativism and Truth* (Cambridge: Cambridge University Press, 1991).

—*Essays on Heidegger and Others* (Cambridge: Cambridge University Press, 1991).

—*Truth and Progress* (Cambridge: Cambridge University Press, 1998).

—*Philosophy and Social Hope* (London: Penguin Books, 1999).

—'Pragmatism as Romantic Polytheism', in Morris Dickstein (ed.), *The Revival of Pragmatism: Essays in Social Thought, Law, and Culture* (Durham: Duke University Press, 1998).

Stout, Jeffrey, *Ethics after Babel: The Languages of Morals and their Discontents* (Cambridge: James Clark & Co., 1988).

INDEX

INDEX OF REFERENCES

OLD TESTAMENT

Genesis

1.3	176
1.6	176
1.9	176
1.16	176
1.20	176
1.24	176
3	95
6	173
6.6	176
9	199
9.13	273
15.6	278
16.7	176
22	95
43	96

Exodus

3.10	79
15.20	177
15.27	84
20.25	113

Leviticus

15.19-31	287
20.1	176

Numbers

11–12	250, 265
11.29	170
19.11-13	289
21.27	15
23.24	16

24.5	16
35.33	199

Deuteronomy

16.16	297
17.10-13	297
18.20	296

Judges

2.18	163
5	95
20	164

1 Samuel

2.6	176
2.7	176
8.18	159
10.24	162
11.15	163
15.26	161
16.1	161
16.12	163
24.6	160
26.9	160

2 Samuel

2.4	163
15–18	160
18	99
20	96

1 Kings

1	162

1.39-40	162
2.9	179
6	101
7	101
8.14-61	267
9–10	199
10	97
11.11	162
19	96
21	50, 165
22	161

2 Kings

5	195

1 Chronicles

29.28	166

2 Chronicles

3	101
4	101
21	97
25.25	160
32.33	166

Job

1.1	176
1.5	176
1.6-8	176
1.7	176
1.12	176
1.14-15	176
1.15-16	176

1.16	176	42.8	176	*Ecclesiastes*	
1.18-19	176	42.9	176	5.13	80
1.21	176	42.10	176	10.16	165
2.2	176	42.11	176		
2.6	176	42.12	176	*Isaiah*	
2.7	176	42.15	176	1.2	165
2.10	176	42.16	176	5.1-7	48
2.12	176	42.17	176	7	216
2.13	176	46	176	10.1	172
3.3	176			40	216
3.7	176	*Psalms*		40.3	85
4.15	176	8.3-4	176	45.1-4	172
4.17-18	176	17.15	176	50	114
7.14	175, 176	22.7	176	53	295
11.7-8	176	25.9	80	53.7	295
12.4	176	34.2	75	61.1	79
13.15	176	37.35	195	63	114
14.1-3	176	38.15	118	64.8	176
19.21	176	46	48		
19.22-27	176	51.16	176	*Jeremiah*	
19.26	176	51.17	113	11.18-19	295
20.5	176	63	216	20.9	171
23.10	176	66.7	163	23.29	114
26.6	176	75.7-8	161		
29.5	176	89.26	176	*Lamentations*	
30.17	176	90	43	1.12	108
30.25	176	103.1	114		
30.30	176	104.3	176	*Ezekiel*	
32.6	176	104.4	176	1	173
33.14-17	176	118.23	161	36.26	114
33.23	176	118.26	162		
33.29-30	176	119.103	106	*Daniel*	
34.21	176	127.1	231	7.9	176
35.5-7	176	132.17-18	161	9.24-27	208
36.17	176	136.23	176		
36.29	176	139.8	176	*Habakkuk*	
37.11-12	176	139.17	176	9.16-28	114
38.1-2	176			10	114
38.7	176	*Proverbs*			
38.28	176	12.25	80	*Zechariah*	
38.31	176	14.10	194	3.3	81
38.41	176	22.20	19	9.9	83
40.15	176	24.21	159	12.11	160
40.19	176	25.2	158		
41.34	176	29.2	164		
42.5	176				

NEW TESTAMENT

Matthew		10.29	294	6.63	49
4.5-7	107	10.33-34	293	6.69	77
5.44-45	176	10.35-38	298	10	261
5.48	176	10.42-45	298	10.30	176
6	94	11.27-33	296	11.47	108
6.9	176	13	292, 297	11.53	108
7	100	13.1-2	292	12.1-8	299
7.12	159	13.11	294	12.31	176
8.20	81	13.14-18	292	14	100
11.29	80	13.26	296	14.7	176
12	92	13.30	293	14.8	176
12.1-7	107	14	114	14.9	176
12.40	219	14.3-9	299	14.11	176
13.10-11	134	14.9	301	14.16	176
14.13	18	14.61-65	296	14.17	176
16.18	162, 208	15.1-39	114	14.20	176
18	180	16.1-8	300	14.21	176
19	180			14.23	176
19.12	11	Luke		14.28	176
19.27	84	1.26	81		
22.21	164	2	99	Acts	
24.39	108	2.1-4	164	2.47	162
		2.8	82	4.12	82
Mark		2.12	83	5.29	159
1.1	294	2.24	83	11.26	42
1.8	296	4.18	79	20.8-9	305
1.10-11	285	7.36-38	299	23.5	165
1.12	285	7.39	299	27	97
1.45	294	8.10	134		
2.2	294	9	98	Romans	
4.11	134	10	265, 267	7	177
4.14-20	294	10.1-2	84	7.16	177
4.33	294	10.2	85	11.15-18	208
5	285	10.17-18	176	11.25	134
5.21-30	287	10.37	199	13	156
5.23	288	11	92	13.1-7	158
5.31-36	289	15.25	177	13.1-2	158
5.35	289	17.27	219	13.1	159
5.37-43	290	17.32	219	13.4	164
6.1-6	290	19.40	114	16.25-26	133
8.27–9.1	294	21.24	208		
8.31	293	23.10	117	1 Corinthians	
8.35	294			1.26-27	176
9.13	296	John		2.6-10	307
9.31	293	2.6	19	2.7	133
10.14	115	6.41	82	2.14	176

4.1	133, 173
6.20	45
7.12	13
11–14	306
11.3-16	306
11.7–12.16	306
13.2	134
14.2	134
14.22	120
14.33-35	306
15.51-52	134

2 Corinthians
3.6	1, 176, 179
3.16	179
8.9	82
11.14	176

Galatians
1.1-2	274
1.15-16	275
2.15-16	276
2.15	276
2.20	248
3.6-9	278
3.28-29	279
4	48
4.21-31	17
4.24	47, 48
5.13–6.10	281
5.13	280, 281
5.14-15	261
5.22-24	293
6.15-16	281

Ephesians
1.9-10	134
3.1-6	134
3.9	134
3.14-19	77

5.31-32	134
6.9	133
6.10	172
6.11-12	198

Philippians
2.5-11	44
2.6-11	258, 259
3.13	16

Colossians
1.25-27	134
2.2	133
4.3-4	133

1 Thessalonians
| 2.7-8 | 80 |
| 4.17 | 208 |

2 Thessalonians
| 2.3-8 | 134 |
| 2.4 | 176 |

1 Timothy
2.1-3	158
2.1-2	159, 164
3.8-9	133
3.16	133
6.8	81

2 Timothy
| 2.24 | 80 |
| 4 | 97 |

Titus
| 3.1 | 158, 159 |

Hebrews
1.1-3	224
9.26	108
10.6	176

| 10.10 | 108 |
| 11 | 223 |

James
1.21	80
3.16	164
4.4	108, 206
5.11	176

1 Peter
2.13-14	158
2.16	165
2.17	158

2 Peter
| 2.9-10 | 158 |
| 2.14-15 | 84 |

1 John
| 3.2 | 176 |

Revelation
1.10-11	197
5	171, 173, 197
6	97
12.10	176
14.13	159
14.14-19	172
14.14	172
15.3	176
20	197, 204
20.15	197

Pseudipigrapha
1 Enoch
6–18	173
12.1	173
14	173
14.8-20	173

OTHER ANCIENT REFERENCES

Alcibiades
128e-129a	65
130c-e	65
133b-c	65

Ascension of Isaiah
| 5.1-14 | 295 |

Augustine
Civitas Dei
| 22.8 | 35 |

Epiphanius
Panarion
49.1.2-3

Eusebius
Ecclesiastical History
6.16   13
6.17   305

Gospel of Mary
7.17.18-18.1   304

Gospel of Thomas
22   284
114   284

John Chrysostom
De sacerdotio
(On The Priesthood)
3.4.177   46
4   46
4.1.357   48
5   46

Homily de Lazaro
48

Homily in Matthew
1.1   49

Homily in Psalms
109.5   50

Isaiah interpreted
5.3   48

Josephus
War
2.259-260   296
2.261-264   296

Origen
Commentary on John
1.10   14
1.26   15
4.22   18
10.18   18
12   16

Commentary on Matthew
10.22   305
10.23   18
11.1   305
14.9   305
15.14   12

De Principiis
4.2.4   19

*Fragments on
1 Corinthians*
74   305

Homily on Numbers
11   18
12   16
13   15
17   16

Statutes of the Apostles
21   304

Abbott, E. 227
Ackroyd, P. 168
Allchin, A.M. 122
Andersen, P.B. 267
Anderson, V. 312, 316, 318
Artaud, A. 240-48
Ascherson, N. 52
Ash, J.L. 306
Avis, P. 233, 234
Aycock, D.A. 255

Backus, I. 50
Barber, S. 242, 243
Barker, M. 173
Barr, J. 202, 203, 208
Barth, K. 233-41, 245-48
Baur, F.C. 211
Beck, L.W. 144
Beer, J. 172
Bentley, G.E. 170
Bériou, N. 83
Berman, D. 138
Betz, H.D. 277, 280
Biddle, J.C. 128
Bihl, M. 79, 80
Blake, W. 168-83
Bloch, C. 105, 107-109, 119
Bois, W.E.B. du 275
Bonaventure 72-86
Booty, J.E. 118
Boring, E.M. 294, 298
Bougerol, J.G. 72, 81
Brady, I. 72
Brock, R.N. 285-88, 290, 291, 297, 299-301
Bromiley, G.W. 235, 236
Brown, D. 312, 318-21, 323, 324
Brown, P. 55
Browne, P. 136

Bruce, F.F. 279, 280
Brueggemann, W. 273
Burdon, C. 171, 172
Butlin, M. 177
Butterworth, C.C. 90
Byrne, P. 137

Cady, L.E. 312, 317, 318, 320
Cameron, J.K. 188
Campbell, I. 190
Campbell, L. 227
Carabelli, G. 138
Cenci, C. 79
Chadwick, H. 11
Chalmers, T. 193
Champion, J.A.I. 137
Chenu, M.D. 73
Chester, A.G. 90
Cheyne, A. 189
Cheyne, T.K. 213
Childs, B.S. 251
Clark, J.C.D. 164
Coleridge, S.T. 169
Cooke, J. 159
Cortés, J. 259
Countryman, L.W. 121
Court, J.M. 3, 17, 291-93
Cupitt, D. 252
Curzon, R. 51

Dale, A.W. 222, 223
Dale, R.W. 214, 221, 223-26, 228, 232
Dalferth, I.U. 234
Daniell, D. 90, 93, 102
Davaney, S.G. 312
Dean, W. 312, 317, 318
Delorme, F.M. 72
De Lubac, H. 55, 60, 62
Dennett, D.C. 313

Derrida, J. 244-46
De Saussure, F. 252, 253, 259
Di Cesare, M.A. 104, 114, 117
Dörrbecker, D.W. 180
Doughty, C.M. 3, 4
Driver, S.R. 213
Dryden, J. 160
Dunn, J.D.G. 273, 274

Eliot, G. 7, 241
Elton, G.R. 188
Erdman, D.V. 181
Esser, C. 79
Esslin, M. 242, 244, 247

Faber, G. 227, 228
Fenn, R.K. 1
Figgis, N.J. 157
Filmer, R. 159
Fiorenza, E.S. 286, 287, 290, 295, 297,
    299-302
Forbes, W. 116
Ford, D.F. 240, 241
Fortier, M. 246
Frye, N. 179

Gadamer, H.-G. 239, 240
Gassner, J. 243, 245
Gay, P. 137
Glen, H. 181
Goldsmith, S. 181
Goslee, N. 171
Gouhier, H. 144
Gray, W. 239
Greimas, A.J. 253, 255-57, 259, 261
Grierson, H.J.C. 196

Hamilton, A. 173
Hanson, R.P.C. 17
Hartnoll, P. 244
Hays, R.B. 182, 274
Hazard, P. 137
Heidegger, M. 237
Heyward, I.C. 285, 286, 288-91
Hill, C. 175
Hill, D. 296, 297
Hodge, C. 205
Hodgkins, C. 120
Hogg, J. 6, 185-88, 190-92, 194-98, 200

Hole, R. 163, 166
Hort, F.J.A. 213
Hugh of St Victor 58-69
Hunsinger, G. 234
Hutchinson, F.E. 110
Huxley, A. 29

Illich, I. 60
Ippel, H.P. 165

Jack, A. 196
Jansen, K.L. 302
Jardine, G.W. 117
Jauss, H.-R. 3
Johnson, W.S. 241
Johnston, G. 189
Johnston, J.O. 214
Jones, D. 86
Jowett, B. 212, 214, 218, 226, 228-32

Karris, R.J. 72
Kee, H.C. 285
Kelly, J.N.D. 46, 48
King, K.L. 304, 308
Klein, S. 257, 258
Knights, L.C. 105
Knox, J. 189

Lategan, B. 274, 277
Latre, G. 90
Lawlor, T.M.C. 92
Le Goff, J. 57
Leach, E. 255
Leclercq, J. 56-58
Lévi-Strauss, C. 251, 254, 255, 258
Lewalski, B.K. 109
Liddon, H.P. 214-21, 226, 228, 232
Lightfoot, J.B. 213
Lindberg, B. 177
Locke, J. 128, 129, 135-37
Luther, M. 92

M'Millan, S. 192
Maluleke, T.S. 269
Marc'hadour, G. 92
Marenbon, J. 73
Marius, R.C. 92
Marsden, G.M. 202-206, 208, 209
Marxsen, W. 294

Matera, F.J. 281
Mayor, J.E.B. 89
Mazrui, A.A. 273
Mbiti, J.S. 270
McCormack, B. 237, 238, 241
McGregor, J.F. 175
Mee, J. 175, 181
Menestò, E. 79
Milman, A. 212
Milman, H.H. 212
Milne, P. 254
More, T. 141
Morinis, A. 31
Morris, L. 278
Moyise, S.P. 182

Nautin, P. 13
Neville, G. 46
Nicholl, D. 17
Nielson, J. 93

Oduyoye, M.A. 270, 271
Okot p'Bitek 270
Oliphant, M. 197
Orrick, J.S. 106

Parker Forester, J.F. 259, 260
Patrides, C.A. 106, 115, 116, 118, 119
Patte, D. 260-62, 280
Price, J.V. 126, 136, 137
Propp, V. 253-58

Quinn, E. 243, 245

Rader, R. 303
Raine, J. 86
Raine, K. 177
Reardon, B. 213
Reay, B. 175
Reist, T. 79
Riches, J.K. 2, 3
Ricoeur, P. 57, 255
Roest, B. 85
Rorty, R. 312-16, 318, 321-24
Ross Roy, G. 194-96
Rousseau, J.-J. 140-49
Rowland, C. 180, 182, 183
Royle, T. 197
Russell, C. 159

Sandeen, E.R. 202
Scalia, G. 78
Segovia, F.F. 273
Shakespeare, W. 101, 102
Sidney, P. 98
Skousen, R. 93
Smalley. B. 57, 58, 62, 69, 72, 79, 86
Smith, W.R. 32
Sontag, S. 242-44
Speed Hill, W. 115
Stephen, Sir L. 127, 128, 136
Storme, A. 27
Stout, J. 311, 312, 315, 324
Strauss, D.F. 212
Strout, A. 190
Sullivan, R.E. 126, 128, 136
Summers, J.H. 104, 105, 118
Swanston, H.F.G. 127
Swete, H.B. 213
Swinburne, A. 180

Taft, R. 51
Talstra, E. 267
Tannenbaum, L. 171, 178
Taylor, A. 4
Tennant, W. 191
Thetele, C.B. 270
Thielman, F. 282
Thompson, A. 193
Thompson, E.P. 175
Timm, H. 1
Tindal, M. 135
Toland, J. 6, 125-36, 138
Tolley, M.J. 171
Torjesen, K.J. 19, 305-307
Tuve, R. 114, 115
Tyndale, W. 88-102

Underhill, E. 122
Urlich, E. 13

Van Den Borne, C. 72
Van Rinsum, H.J. 269, 270, 273
Vattimo, G. 312, 318, 321-24

Wachtel, A. 83
Waley, D. 82
Wall, J.N. Jr 107, 110, 112, 116, 119, 120
Walton, I. 109

Ward, G. 234, 241
Watson, F. 58
Watson, J. 190
Wayland, F. 204
Weisenburger, F.P. 205
Wengen-Shute, R. van 109, 111, 113-15
West, G.O. 272, 273
Westcott, B.F. 213
Whiting, B.J. 101

Whiting, H.W. 101
Wiles, M. 12, 18
Willey, B. 137
Wire, A.C. 307, 308
Wright, A. 177
Wright, D.F. 188

Young, F.M. 15